Have fun reading

Love

D. D. V.

Captain James Cook
and the Search for
Antarctica

Dedicated to
My wife,
Paula Mary Stadtler Hamilton,
in memory of my mother,
Celia Currier Cook Hamilton,
and of my grandmother
Helen Noyes Currier Cook

Captain James Cook and the Search for Antarctica

James C. Hamilton

PEN & SWORD
HISTORY

AN IMPRINT OF PEN & SWORD BOOKS LTD.
YORKSHIRE - PHILADELPHIA

First published in Great Britain in 2020 by
PEN & SWORD HISTORY
An imprint of Pen & Sword Books Ltd
Yorkshire – Philadelphia

ISBN 978-1-52675-357-1

Typeset by Concept, Huddersfield, West Yorkshire HD4 5JL
Printed and bound by TJ International Ltd, Padstow, Cornwall

Pen & Sword Books Ltd incorporates the Imprints of Aviation, Atlas, Family History, Fiction, Maritime, Military, Discovery, Politics, History, Archaeology, Select, Wharncliffe Local History, Wharncliffe True Crime, Military Classics, Wharncliffe Transport, Leo Cooper, The Praetorian Press, Remember When, White Owl, Seaforth Publishing and Frontline Publishing.

For a complete list of Pen & Sword titles please contact
PEN & SWORD BOOKS LTD
47 Church Street, Barnsley, South Yorkshire, S70 2AS, England
E-mail: enquiries@pen-and-sword.co.uk
Website: www.pen-and-sword.co.uk
or
PEN & SWORD BOOKS
1950 Lawrence Rd, Havertown, PA 19083, USA
E-mail: uspen-and-sword@casematepublishers.com
Website: www.penandswordbooks.com

Contents

List of Plates

List of Figures

Acknowledgements

In preparation of this book, the author acknowledges, with thanks, permission to cite material from the sources listed below, as well as suggestions and encouragement from colleagues and friends in my 'search for Captain James Cook':

- The Hakluyt Society, London, for permission to cite material from J.C. Beaglehole, editor, *The Journals of Captain James Cook*, Parts I, II and III (Cambridge: Cambridge University Press, for the Hakluyt Society, 1961, 1967, 1968).
- The Syndics of Cambridge University Library, for permission to cite material from the Royal Greenwich Observatory, specifically the Board of Longitude log books by astronomers William Wales (RGO 14/58) and William Bayly (RGO 14/57).
- The National Archives Image Library, Kew, Surrey, for permission to cite material from Admiralty log books, ADM55 series, for Tobias Furneaux (*Adventure*), Lieutenant Charles Clerke, Lieutenant Robert Cooper, Master's Mates Isaac Smith and John Duvall Barr, Master Joseph Gilbert (all in *Resolution*), Master of *Discovery* Thomas Edgar, Lieutenant James King and Lieutenant John Gore (*Resolution*), the handwritten journals of Captain James Cook (*Endeavour* and *Resolution*), and log books from *Erebus* and *Terror* (1841).
- The Hakluyt Society, London, for permission to cite material from Michael Hoare, editor, *The Resolution Journals of Johann Reinhold Forster, 1772–1775*, four volumes (Cambridge: Cambridge University Press, for the Hakluyt Society, 1982).
- The Navy Records Society, London, for permission to cite *Admiralty Instructions to Captain Cook for his Three Voyages*, edited by W.G. Perrin (1929).
- The University of Hawai'i Press, for permission to cite material from J.R. Forster, *Observations Made on a Voyage Round the World*, edited by Nicholas Thomas, Harriet Guest and Michael Dettelbach (Honolulu: University of Hawai'i Press, 1996).
- The University of Hawai'i Press, for permission to cite material from George Forster, *Journal of a Voyage Round the World*, two volumes, edited by Nicholas Thomas and Oliver Berghof (Honolulu: University of Hawai'i Press, 2000).
- I thank Ian Boreham, editor, *Cook's Log*, the quarterly journal of the Captain Cook Society, for permission to use material from articles previously printed in *Cook's Log* and to cite information related to Cook's ships and officers who sailed with Cook (www.captaincooksociety.com). I also acknowledge, with

appreciation, Ian's review, suggestions and editing of my original articles over the past decade, which have been revised for this book.

- Cliff Thornton, past president of the Captain Cook Society, provided much appreciated advice, suggestions and ruminations about a variety of Cook-related questions and research issues. In particular, during a visit to the 2011 Cook Society annual meeting in Marton, Yorkshire, Cliff suggested I investigate the Colonial Registers and Royal Navy Log Book (CORRAL) project, which placed copies of log books on line, and encouraged me to access these in my research. The site is sponsored by the Centre for Environmental Data Analysis (CEDA).

- I acknowledge and thank Alwyn Peel, Secretary of the Captain Cook Society, for his research and advice regarding my questions about Captain Cook stamps and Cook philately.

- I thank Jerry Yucht, United States' Representative for the Captain Cook Society, for providing copies of some of my articles previously published in *Cook's Log*, after files of these articles disappeared in my computer system's faulty auxiliary hard drive.

- I appreciate and thank Rupert Harding, Commissioning Editor for Pen & Sword Books, Barnsley, South Yorkshire, for his editorial expertise, advice and encouragement in bringing this project to completion. I especially thank copyeditor Sarah Cook for her cheerful, helpful advice and her work to prepare my manuscript for publication. I also thank typesetter Noel Sadler for his advice in preparation of the maps and tables for this book.

- The Inter-Library Loan Department of the Sioux City, Iowa Public Library helpfully and promptly obtained references used in various stages of my research over the past twelve years.

- I thank graphic artist Kari Nelson, who prepared the final design of the twelve maps which accompany the text.

- Special thanks go to my wife Paula, who read the original drafts of articles published in *Cook's Log*, as well as the new chapters in this book, pointing out curious sentence structure, repetitive phrasing or other errors. I also acknowledge her long-standing patience while I conducted research and prepared the final manuscript for this book. Paula and I also travelled together during most of my 'search for Captain Cook' on four continents. Her memories of what we saw and where we saw it, and her extensive collection of travel literature, proved a valuable resource.

- I offer great appreciation to Janet Flanagan, a colleague and friend for forty years, who has consistently expressed encouragement and interest in my research as well as articles published about James Cook and other topics, and her suggestions about writing, layout and design for publication.

- Melissa Goeden, Greg Pirozzi and Michael Lamothe are additional colleagues and friends to be thanked for their interest in, support for and challenging questions about my 'Cook Book'. I also thank Greg for suggesting I investigate historic Antarctica maps located in the online David Rumsey Collection, referenced in the bibliography.

The historian's task is, I believe, best stated by J.H. Hexter as 'an attempt to render a coherent, intelligible, and true account' (*The History Primer*, London: Basic Books, 1971, p. 47). It is my intention that this book contributes to that goal, with the result that the book's readers receive an understanding of James Cook's remarkable voyages which narrowed the options in the search for *Terra Australis Incognita*.

Although I appreciate all the suggestions and encouragement given to me for this project, any errors or faults with this book are mine alone.

James C. Hamilton
30 January 2020: the 246th anniversary of *Resolution*
reaching 71° 10′ south latitude, Cook's 'Furthest South'

Captain James Cook's Three Voyages, 1768–1779/1780

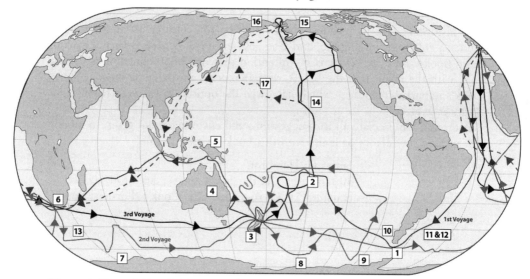

Figure 1. Map of Captain James Cook's three voyages, 1768–1779/1780, edited by the author to show significant locations referenced in this book. Original map attribution: John Platek, Alexius Horatius (2008).

The **route of the first voyage (1768–1771)** is from England (August 1768) around Cape Horn (1) to Tahiti (2), New Zealand (3), the East Coast of Australia (4), to the Dutch East India Company Docks at Batavia (5), then across the Indian Ocean to Table Bay at the Cape of Good Hope (6) and back to England.

The **route of the second voyage (1772–1775)** is from England to the Cape of Good Hope, then south to cross the Antarctic Circle in the summer months and to the South Pacific in other months, crossing the Circle in January (7) and December 1773 (8) and (Cook's furthest south) January 1774 (9), back to New Zealand, and then to Tierra del Fuego (10), South Georgia (11), the South Sandwich Islands (12), to the Cape of Good Hope and back to England.

The **route of the third voyage (1776–1779/1780)** took Cook to the Cape of Good Hope, then south to the Crozet and Kerguelen Islands (13), and then across the Indian Ocean to the Pacific and New Zealand. Cook then made his final sweep of Pacific Islands, headed north to Hawai'i (14) then the coast of North America to Alaska (15) and into the Arctic Ocean (16), returning to Hawai'i for the winter months of 1778/1779. The dotted line (17) traces the route of *Resolution* and *Discovery* after Cook's death in Hawai'i (14 February 1779), back to the Arctic, Siberia (Petropavlovsk, Kamchatka Peninsula, (16)), and then across the coastline of Asia and the Indian Ocean, to the Cape of Good Hope, and back to England (October 1780).

Introduction

There are three reasons to publish this book. Firstly, the primary purpose is to incorporate, into a single volume, a narrative and a detailed analysis of Captain James Cook's Antarctic and sub-Antarctic navigation in the Southern Ocean. The search occurred during portions of his first, second and third voyages. Secondly, Cook's travels to locate the Unknown Southern Continent are less studied than his Pacific travels. Nonetheless, they represent an important 'narrowing of options' to an eighteenth-century understanding of *Terra Australis Incognita*'s location. Thirdly, the timing of this study recognizes the worldwide recognition of the 250th anniversary of Cook's voyages of navigation, geography and science during 2018–2029.

The book is intended for a general audience: for readers interested in Cook, as well as anyone studying exploration and maritime history. Notes identify the sources utilized and offer references for further reading. There is a wealth of secondary material identified in the bibliography which might stir the interest of readers to investigate aspects of Captain Cook's remarkable story.

In reading this book we must understand that, while today we know about Antarctica's location, its physical features and geography, only the 'idea of' or speculation about *Terra Australis Incognita* existed until Captain Cook's voyages. The world's maps changed through Cook's three documented crossings of the Antarctic Circle. He completed his circumnavigation of Antarctica over the course of three summers, and he criss-crossed the vast expanse of oceans to rule out the Southern Continent's location where others suggested it was to be found. Reading Cook's journals, the log books of other officers and journals written by scientists who accompanied Cook on these voyages allows the modern reader to witness how he came to understand and define Antarctica and the Southern Ocean by narrowing the options for the location of a continent at the South Pole.

James Cook (b. 28 October 1728, d. 14 February 1779)[1] was one of history's greatest navigators. His three voyages delineated the Pacific Ocean and reached into the Southern Ocean and the Antarctic Circle as well as into the Arctic Ocean and Arctic Circle. Cook's navigation and exploration occurred in relatively small ships, powered only by wind upon sail, covering 140 degrees of Earth's 180 degrees of latitude and travelling over 200,000 miles – eight times the Earth's circumference and almost the distance from the Earth to the Moon.

In Cook's era, Antarctica was known as *Terra Australis Incognita*, the Unknown Southern Continent. He occasionally speculated whether or not it existed at all, but usually referred to it as the Southern Continent. In 1768, at the beginning of the first voyage, the Admiralty instructed Cook that the discovery of the Southern Continent was 'the object which you are always to have in view'. The voyages in the Southern Ocean include episodes during which Cook's navigational skills, and those of his crew, were on display during often difficult and sometimes dangerous oceanic travels in foul weather and inhospitable, as well as mostly unknown, seas. Although the search for Antarctica was the primary purpose of Cook's second voyage (1772–1775), travels to sub-Antarctic regions also took place during brief periods of the first voyage (1768–1771) and the third voyage (1776–1779/1780).[2]

Captain James Cook's Search for Antarctica

There are four parts to the story of Cook's search for Antarctica and his navigation in the Southern Ocean:

- During the first voyage (1768–1771), sailing in *Endeavour*, Cook rounded the tip of South America by sailing through the Strait of Le Maire, along the coasts of Tierra del Fuego and Staten Island, then rounding Cape Horn in January 1769. He sailed to 60° south latitude and then south-southwest to 110° west longitude in search of the Southern Continent. Later, in August and September 1769, he sailed south-southeast of Tahiti to 40° south latitude searching for Antarctica. He found no Southern Continent (Chapter 4). Cook again visited Tierra del Fuego in December 1774 on his way towards the third 'ice-edge'[3] part of his Antarctic circumnavigation (Chapter 10). This navigation finally ruled out the continent's existence east of New Zealand and west of Tierra del Fuego.
- Cook circumnavigated the Southern Continent in three 'ice-edge cruises' during the second voyage (1772–1775). *Resolution* and *Adventure* first crossed the Antarctic Circle on 17 January 1773. After the two ships separated in early February (off Antarctica) and again in October 1773 (off New Zealand), *Resolution* crossed the Antarctic Circle again in December 1773 and January 1774. In each of the three crossings of the Circle, Captain Cook encountered an impenetrable ice barrier surrounding the continent, along with floating ice and icebergs (Cook's 'ice islands'), as well as penguins, seals, whales and many oceanic birds. Very likely he did not visually 'see' the continent's land, only the ice barrier surrounding it.
- In 1775, on the third leg of his Antarctic circumnavigation, Cook discovered an uninhabited island he eventually named South Georgia (in honour of King George III, 1760–1820). Several weeks later, *Resolution* sailed among a series of volcanic islands he named the South Sandwich Islands, also uninhabited, and named after John Montagu, Earl of Sandwich and First Lord of the Admiralty (Chapter 11). He termed the South Sandwich Islands 'the most inhospitable coast in the world'. On several occasions, Cook also searched for Cape Circumcision, sighted by the French Captain Bouvet in 1739 and rumoured to be a tip of the Southern Continent. During portions of the second and third voyages, Cook never

located the ice-covered sub-Antarctic island, some 19 square miles in size and now a territory of Norway. It may be 'the most remote island in the world', but it is not a tip or a cape of Antarctica. By March 1775 Cook concluded that the Southern Continent existed near the South Pole, was uninhabited, was not accessible by a navigable ocean and was of no significance for exploration or commerce (Chapters 5–11).

• In December 1776, at the beginning of the third voyage (1776–1779), sailing in *Resolution* and accompanied by *Discovery*, Cook confirmed the location of the Crozet Islands. He also sailed to Kerguelen Island, an uninhabited sub-Antarctic archipelago discovered by the French navigator Kerguelen-Trémarec in 1772 (Chapter 13). During the ten-day visit he first anchored at Christmas Harbour and then sailed along part of Kerguelen's coast to assess the territory's value as a harbour and as a source of wood and water for future voyages, also observing its flora and fauna. He termed Kerguelen an 'island of desolation'.

The Contributions of Cook's Voyages to Understanding Antarctica: Navigation, Geography and Natural Science

I use 'Antarctica', 'Southern Continent' and *Terra Australis Incognita* as interchangeable terms. The existence of a continent at the South Pole dates to geographers and philosophers of the ancient world, including Aristotle, and was subject to speculation thereafter. Eighteenth-century geographers and hydrographers suggested Antarctica was populated by millions of people eager to trade with Great Britain. Before Cook's voyages, depictions on maps of the Southern Continent (and unexplored areas of the western hemisphere) were usually exaggerated, imaginative white spaces, perhaps south and east of New Zealand, extending far southwards, or touching the tip of Tierra del Fuego (Chapter 2).

Cook's voyages were not only an exploration of the unknown but are also examples of eighteenth-century navigation as well as scientific inquiry. The Admiralty directed Cook to compile detailed observations of the territories he visited. He was given specific, overall instructions for each of the three voyages, but was allowed the opportunity to use his judgement for on-the-spot situations that could not be anticipated. Cook's remarkable, valuable journals are filled with details and his thoughts about the Southern Continent as his voyages narrowed the available options for the continent's location. Log books of officers who travelled with Cook are further sources of information, not only about the sometimes-dangerous and challenging seamanship required, but also revealing interesting events and offering glimpses into life on the high seas. Several of James Cook's most memorable journal quotations were written during his crossings of the Antarctic Circle: his 'ambition to go further than anyone had done before, but as far as it was possible for a man to go' (30 January 1774); his triumphal conclusion that 'an end has been put' to the search for *Terra Australis Incognita*, a search conducted by maritime powers for 200 years and geographers of all ages (21 February 1775); the description of snow falling on *Resolution* covering sail and rigging (24 December 1774); and his description of the 'romantic views', accompanied by 'admiration and horror' during sailing among ice islands (24 February 1773).

In addition to his own records of the voyages, natural scientists sailed with Cook and their journals are also a source of information, as are the observations of astronomers/mathematicians who accompanied the voyages. Artists also sailed with Cook. Their sketches and paintings provide a record of landscapes, sea-scapes, people and objects in the days before photography. Chapter 3 includes sketches of astronomers, scientists and artists who sailed on Cook's voyages. Science in the eighteenth century meant 'natural science': anything observable, from the Earth to the stars, not made by humans. Observations of travellers to remote or sometimes exotic parts of the world were fascinating to the literate elite of Enlightenment Europe and their colleagues in North America, such as Thomas Jefferson, Benjamin Franklin and others who contributed to the founding of the United States. This trans-Atlantic community corresponded, discussed and argued about the philosophical and scientific phenomena, issues and scholarship of their era. Historian Thomas J. Schlereth points out that the voyages of James Cook and Louis-Antoine de Bougainville (1729–1811) produced the most important travel literature of the age, having a significant impact on the European imagination and bringing about 'a total geographical awareness of the whole earth'.[4] Chapter 14 focuses on natural scientific information from Cook's voyages, in particular testing of the marine chronometer and experimentation concerning how to control scurvy.

During the second voyage, *Resolution* and *Adventure* carried early versions of the marine chronometer, a device to accurately record time and therefore assist calculation of longitude on the high seas. Astronomers/mathematicians (as well as Cook) monitored 'the clock' during Cook's second voyage. Although Cook claimed his confidence with traditional methods of sextant and nautical almanacs was such that he could accurately determine the latitude and longitude of any spot on the oceans, at the conclusion of the second voyage he commented that the marine chronometer was a reliable guide to navigation. This marks an important step in navigation technology. Making determination of longitude less difficult contributed to much safer sailing on the high seas, especially after the Scilly Isles disaster on 22 October 1707 which resulted in the loss of approximately 1,550 lives and four Royal Navy warships because of a failure to accurately calculate position, inadequate charts and faulty equipment in dangerous waters 28 miles (45km) off Cornwall's coast.

Another scientific contribution from the voyages was Cook's various experiments to control scurvy, which plagued long-distance sea travel. He also insisted upon maintaining a clean ship to improve the health of seamen. These experiments occurred during the search for the Southern Continent, as well as on Cook's journeys in the Pacific and Arctic Oceans. Chapters 3 and 14 summarize his methods to combat scurvy and maintain health, which is an aspect of his service for which he was honoured. Although Captain Cook did not 'cure scurvy' by his efforts alone, he contributed to the overall effort, which was one of the reasons why British warships were able to remain on the high seas for extended periods of time during the worldwide eighteenth-century colonial conflicts up to and including the Napoleonic Wars. Other diseases, such as typhus, malaria and dysentery, lurked in ports such as Batavia, visited during the first voyage.

As an officer in the Royal Navy, James Cook was given explicit and secret orders by the Admiralty for each voyage. These orders will be referenced especially in Chapters 2, 4, 5 and 13, and Appendix A contains the complete text of these instructions. It was generally understood and speculated upon that Cook was sailing to the 'South Seas' or 'foreign parts'. The exact purpose of each voyage was divulged by Cook only in stages to those who sailed with him and with Admiralty approval after the conclusion of the voyages. The orders were secret because other competing seafaring nations, especially France, also sent navigators in search of new lands and markets, just as Portugal, Spain and the Netherlands had done in previous centuries.

The Royal Society for Improving Natural Knowledge (founded 1660) contributed funds to promote the first voyage especially. It also suggested scientists to accompany Cook. Naturalist Sir Joseph Banks, who sailed with Cook on the first voyage, was the Society's president (1778–1820). James Cook was elected a Fellow of the Royal Society and was honoured in 1775 with the annual Copley Medal for his letter to the Society's president outlining contributions to improving the health of seamen. Naturalist J.R. Forster (accompanied by his son George) was likewise recommended by the Royal Society to accompany the second voyage. Observations by natural scientists are recorded in Cook's journals as well as in other sources. I will provide examples of scientific information gathered, particularly in Chapters 11, 13 and 14.

Cook's sub-Antarctic and Antarctic exploration might be termed a 'narrowing of options' in efforts to locate the Southern Continent. His navigation in the Southern Ocean occurred during the southern hemisphere's summer months (mostly December, January and February). At other times Admiralty orders directed Cook to more hospitable climates in the Southern Pacific and especially his favourite anchorage at Queen Charlotte Sound on the northern tip of New Zealand's south island.

One of the challenges in writing this book is that it interrupts the broad narrative of Cook's three voyages to focus only upon the sub-Antarctic and Antarctic portions of Cook's travels. His first two voyages included sailing in the South Pacific as well as searching for Antarctica. The third voyage included travel to Kerguelen and also the Pacific, but the over-riding purpose was to search for the Northwest Passage. Whether in the Southern Ocean, the southern Pacific or the Arctic, Cook's three voyages are interconnected. Therefore, attention is paid throughout the study to place navigation in the Southern Ocean within the broader context of the three voyages, both in the introductory chapters and throughout the book. Cook's voyages followed in the wake of much earlier worldwide navigators and he also sailed with contemporary French, Spanish and other navigators. A brief examination of earlier voyages and Cook's contemporaries is found in Chapter 2, beginning with the 'Age of Reconnaissance', from the fifteenth to the early eighteenth century.

Future English navigators also sailed with Cook. William Bligh (1754–1817) served as Master in *Resolution* during the third voyage and as such was responsible for the running of the ship. An able navigator, Bligh is also known for the breadfruit voyage to Tahiti in *Bounty*, during which a portion of his crew mutinied in 1789, and later as Governor of New South Wales. George Vancouver (1757–1798) sailed in *Resolution* during the second voyage and in *Discovery* during the third voyage. Vancouver is best known for the 1791–1795 expedition to the Pacific coast of North America in *Discovery* and *Chatham*. He and a Spanish counterpart prevented the 1790 'Nootka Crisis' from escalating into open warfare in 1792. Vancouver's voyages charted, explored and named many geographical features along the coast, also sailing as far north as the southeast coast of Alaska. Isaac Smith (1752–1831), one of Cook's cousins, at age 13 sailed as an able-bodied seaman (AB) in *Grenville* during one of Cook's surveying missions to Newfoundland. In *Endeavour*, Smith sailed as an AB in 1768, being promoted to midshipman in 1770. In *Resolution*, Smith sailed as a Master's Mate during the second voyage. He later served as captain of Royal Navy ships during conflicts with the American Colonies and the French into the 1790s, and retired as a rear admiral. Cook's widow Elizabeth lived with the Smith family for several years.

Other explorers in addition to Cook pursued the dream of locating the Northwest Passage and/or locating the North Pole. Among these were Captain Constantine Phipps, who sailed towards the Arctic from the Atlantic Ocean in 1773 in *Racehorse*, accompanied by *Carcass*. He reached 80° 48′ north latitude and approximately 15° east longitude on 27 July. There are many similarities between Phipps' and Cook's voyages. Admiralty orders directed Phipps to gather scientific information and make observations on geography, hydrography, navigation, icebergs and impenetrable ice. The ships became temporarily frozen in an ice field north-north-west of Spitsbergen. Horatio Nelson (1758–1805), then a 14-year-old midshipman, sighted a polar bear. Water temperature, ice conditions and migration patterns of birds and herring were also observed and sketched. An astronomer tested 'longitude watches' provided by the Board of Longitude. Phipps' 'bomb vessels' (used to fire mortars in combat) carried added reinforcement to the ships' bows and keels. Heavy clothing was provided for the men.[5] Explorer Alexander Mackenzie (1764–1820) was the first to cross Canada from east to west (1793), with overland expeditions to the Arctic Ocean (1789) and the Pacific Ocean (1792–1793). United States President Thomas Jefferson read James Cook's account of his voyage to the Pacific Northwest. American explorers Meriwether Lewis and William Clark were aware of Cook's exploration of the North American coast as they crossed the Louisiana Purchase to the Pacific (1804–1806). Meriwether Lewis, for example, is described as 'an avid reader of journals of exploration, especially those about the adventures of Captain James Cook'.[6]

Cook narrowed the options concerning the location of the Southern Continent, criss-crossing vast oceanic spaces to prove where it was not located. Others followed Cook to the Southern Ocean and eventually to the South Pole. Chapter 16 considers Antarctica and the sub-Antarctic islands in the 150 years after Captain Cook. It presents a series of vignettes about those with commercial interests (sealers and whalers), as well as navigators, scientists and explorers, who followed up and extended Cook's travels: Fabian Bellingshausen, James Weddell, James Clark Ross, Douglas Mawson, Roald Amundsen, Robert Falcon Scott and Ernest Shackleton, as well as their associates on these often-scientific ventures. Cook paved the way for these later explorers and navigators. Their often hazardous and sometimes dramatic explorations and navigations are in a real sense an extension of Cook's own efforts from 1768 to 1779.

An Historian's Search for Captain James Cook

My interest in Cook is both personal and professional. My full name is James Cook Hamilton. My middle name is from my mother's family, whose origins are in England. My Hamilton great-grandfather emigrated from south-western Scotland in the 1860s, as did James Cook's father from south-eastern Scotland to Yorkshire in the early eighteenth century. Both were farm labourers. There is no doubt the Cook name drew my attention to James Cook, even though I live in the Upper Midwestern state of Iowa, located a thousand or more miles from any ocean. My interest in Cook was also stimulated by study of Cook biographies and journals, philately, research and publication, and travel.

Historian and Philatelist

Although I am an historian and earned BA, MA and PhD degrees in British and European History at the University of Iowa, I did not study James Cook as part of my graduate work, nor during various administrative positions thereafter. It was after my retirement in 2006 that I began reading and researching James Cook, in good part stimulated by my collection of Cook-related postage stamps. As a life-long stamp collector and philatelist, I have amassed a collection of stamps from Great Britain, Canada, Australia and New Zealand, as well as other areas related to Great Britain and the Commonwealth. In pursuing that collection I discovered Captain Cook stamps and postal history. It is anticipated that many more Cook-related stamps will be issued between 2018 and 2029 during the 250th anniversary of the three voyages, just as there were in 1968–1979, during the 200th anniversary.

There are hundreds of postage stamps relating to Cook's voyages and hundreds more related to objects cited in his journals. A Captain Cook Society checklist of Cook stamps is available on the Society's website.[7] A dozen stamps from my collection are included in the colour section. Stamp collecting leads not only to a study of Cook-related events, but also to geography, maps and artefacts. The huge array of stamps issued include various portraits of Cook, his ships and several maps, as well as examples of wildlife or plants and vegetation cited in his journals. Some include paintings by artists who sailed on his voyages, such as Sydney Parkinson, William Hodges, John Webber and Henry Roberts. I exhibited Cook stamps and postal history focused on Cook as a 'millennium traveller', a designation given to him in issues associated with the Year 2000 as one of the most notable persons in the past thousand years.

New South Wales issued the first Captain Cook stamp in 1888, followed by the same design, in varying colours, in 1898 and 1905. Other Cook-related stamps were issued by Australia and the Australian Antarctic Territories, New Zealand and the Ross Dependency, the United Kingdom, Jersey, Ireland, the Cook Islands (Rarotonga, Aitutaki, Penrhyn Island), Norfolk Island, Niue, Tonga, Fiji, New Caledonia, the New Hebrides (Vanuatu), the Falkland Islands Dependencies, South Georgia and the South Sandwich Islands, St Helena, Ascension Island, French Polynesia (Tahiti), French Southern and Antarctic Territories, the British Indian Ocean Territories, British Antarctic Territories, Canada and the United States, many produced during the 200th anniversary of Cook's voyages (1968–1979). If anyone might speculate where Cook's voyages took him, observe the stamps produced since 1888.

Other countries, with no relationship with Captain Cook's voyages, also produced commemorative postage stamps, a diverse, curious list that includes (in part) Mongolia, North Korea, South Korea, Laos, various African nations (Djibouti, Guinea Bissau, the Congo, Central Africa Empire, Gabon, Union des Comoros) or Caribbean and Central American nations (Nicaragua, Grenada, the Grenadines, Dominica), Madagascar, Albania, Hungary, Bulgaria and Umm Al-Quwain (the smallest of the Gulf States). The designs from Albania and Hungary are interesting. It is doubtful whether many of these stamps were ever utilized to move the mail, and are only aimed at attracting collectors.

Some countries issue commemorative series of historical 'famous navigators' or 'famous explorers'. Cook is nearly always included, along with, for example, Leif Ericson, Marco Polo, the half-English Prince Henry the Navigator (who rarely sailed but sponsored significant voyages of exploration), Vasco da Gama, John Cabot (Giovanni Caboto), Ferdinand Magellan, Henry Hudson, Jacques Cartier, Francis Drake, Christopher Columbus, Abel Tasman, Alvarado de Mendaña, Pedro Fernandez de Quiros, Louis-Antoine de Bougainville, Jules Sebastian César Dumont d'Urville and Jean Francois Le Pérouse.

Research and Publication

I am an active participant in the Captain Cook Society, which has a worldwide membership of some five hundred Cook enthusiasts. It publishes a quarterly journal, *Cook's Log*, for which I also serve as editorial assistant. *Cook's Log* has published over a dozen articles I submitted on Cook's navigation in the Southern Ocean, some of which have been revised and extended for this book. I have submitted approximately twenty reviews of 'Cook Books' which are available on the Society's website (www.captaincooksociety.com). The *International Journal of Maritime History* published my review on Cook's 1778 Arctic voyage. I have also contributed Cook-related articles to *American Philatelist* and the *New Carto-Philatelic Journal*.

During a 2011 meeting of the Captain Cook Society in Marton, Yorkshire, I delivered a presentation on Cook as a Natural Scientist of High Southern Latitudes (Chapter 14). The site of the meeting was the Captain Cook Birthplace Museum (Stewart Park, Middlesbrough), where an urn near the entrance marks the site of Cook's first home (likely a two-room rural labourer's hut[8]) where he and his family lived until, at age 16, Cook relocated to Staithes and then to the commercial maritime service in Whitby. I also spent several days in Whitby, visiting exhibits at the excellent Captain Cook Museum. Over a pot of tea, Dr Sophie Forgan, Chairman of the Museum Board of Trustees, showed me documents pertaining to Captain Constantine Phipps' 1773 voyage to the North Pole, from the Atlantic Ocean, four years prior to Cook's exploration of the North American coast. Later, one of the most fascinating experiences of my life was a ninety-minute Esk Valley railway excursion from Whitby through the rolling, brilliant green countryside of North Yorkshire, with sheep grazing in rock-walled pastures, covering much of the distance to Middlesbrough. The trip through the North Yorkshire Moors stopped fifteen times, twice at villages associated with Cook (Marton and Great Ayton), with the next-to-final stop at James Cook University Hospital in Middlesbrough.

Travel

I have enjoyed the opportunity to visit a few of the many locations associated with James Cook. For example, in addition to Marton and Whitby, I observed early versions of the chronometer at the Royal Observatory at Greenwich and the Guildhall Clockmakers Museum. Cook is represented through exhibits at the National Maritime Museum at Greenwich, which also displays his portrait by Nathaniel Dance-Holland.

During a visit to the new British Library we saw one of Cook's handwritten journals and Robert Falcon Scott's diary on display in the 'Hidden Gems' collection. My wife and I have travelled to Cook-associated locations in Australia, New Zealand, Madeira's port of Funchal, Canada (both the St Lawrence River and the north-western coast), South America (Cape Horn, Tierra del Fuego, and the Falkland Islands, where Port Egmont was a potential but unrealized option for Cook's voyages) and Hawai'i (Kealakekua Bay and the Hikiau Heiau temple platform). We also sailed in the Baltic Sea where Cook may have travelled before joining the Royal Navy. In addition to Anchorage, Alaska and the Cook Inlet, my wife, our daughter Celia and I visited Newport Harbour, Rhode Island, where current research is under way to determine the location of Cook's ship *Endeavour*, later named *Lord Sandwich*, which was scuttled in the harbour along with a dozen other vessels in 1778. In September 2018 the Rhode Island Marine Archaeology Project (RIMAP) announced it had narrowed the search to two debris piles, with the likelihood that one of these is the remains of *Endeavour*, with developments summarized in several issues of *Cook's Log*.[9]

Primary Sources and Methods of Citation or Illustration

The main primary sources utilized for this book include Captain Cook's journals edited by J.C. Beaglehole and log books composed by various officers who sailed with Cook. Log books were accessed through the Colonial Registers and Royal Navy Log Books (CORRAL) internet site, now a database for the Centre for Environmental Data Analysis. The log books by astronomers William Wales and William Bayly were accessed online through the Papers of the Board of Longitude records at Cambridge University Library. I also utilized published journals or accounts written by Joseph Banks, J.R. Forster and George Forster, among others. Details about these sources are located in the Acknowledgements, Appendix B and the Bibliography.

In utilizing Cook's journals I make extensive use of direct citations, allowing as far as possible to 'let Cook speak for himself'. I retained the eighteenth-century spelling of words contained in the Beaglehole edition of Cook's journal, providing clarification only where necessary. Rather than footnote every journal entry, which would lead to hundreds of repetitive journal or log book footnotes, I make it clear in the text the source, person and date cited. Since a good deal of the text's narrative flows from day to day, the use of dates in the text helps keep the story in accurate context. The reader will understand the source (a journal or log book) and the date this occurred, which is all I believe to be necessary. Appendix B contains comments about the Beaglehole edition of Cook's journals as well as an explanation of information available in log books.

Description of Native Peoples, Concepts of 'First Discovery' and 'Possession'

Except for Tierra del Fuego, the Antarctic or sub-Antarctic territories visited by Cook were uninhabited. As instructed by the Admiralty, Cook (and naturalists such as Banks, the Forsters and others) recorded observations about the native Fuegians – their appearance, manner of life and livelihood, diet, living quarters, clothing, boats, tools, hunting equipment, jewellery or other art, group authority, and so on. Cook's personal judgement was that their life was the most miserable on Earth, based on the naked (or nearly-naked) appearance of men and women in 40-degree weather (in the sub-Antarctic summer), the women huddled together shivering in sealskins, nursing a few infants, or sometimes scrunched in a small boat/canoe and charged with keeping a fire lit, with few comforts of life in their small huts. According to the visitors, the train oil (from processed blubber) rubbed on their bodies emitted a sour and foul odour. Additional observations were made in Nootka Sound and Alaska. Including these observations in this book is not meant to disparage native peoples but to provide a description of how they appeared to eighteenth-century visitors.

I expect few persons today would enjoy the living conditions pertaining in late eighteenth-century England. Similar socioeconomic observations apply to life onboard Cook's ships. Naval historian N.A.M. Rodger points out that for a son of a gentleman or nobleman, shipboard life as an able-bodied seaman would have appeared 'grim'. However, for a poor boy from a 'cramped and leaky cottage, life on a snug lower deck with hot food daily, clothes and medical attention provided, lifetime employment at a substantial rate of pay, and some prospects of a pension, was probably not unbearable'. Moreover, sailors received 'a more balanced diet' than those who did not go to sea.[10]

Discovery and 'First Discoverer'
Understanding Captain Cook as 'first discoverer' requires some comment. Cook's second voyage marked the first recorded crossings of the Antarctic Circle in 1773–1774, but he never set foot on Antarctica and did not claim possession of it, concluding that there was land near the South Pole, entirely snow- and ice-covered and of little value. Sealers/whalers first landed on Antarctica in the 1820s (Chapter 16).

In January 1775 Cook sighted, charted and claimed possession of an uninhabited island he named South Georgia in honour of King George III, and is credited as its first discoverer. However, merchant Anthony de la Roché likely sheltered *Hamburg* in a South Georgia bay in 1675 after being blown off course and failing to pass through the Strait of Le Maire, which Cook traversed with difficulty in 1769 (Chapter 4). In February 1775 Cook recorded the first discovery of a series of islands he named the South Sandwich Islands in honour of a patron, John Montagu, the First Lord of the Admiralty and the fourth Earl Sandwich (1718–1792). He also gave the Sandwich name to the Hawaiian Islands which were inhabited, with the territory then called 'Owhyee'. He did not claim possession of Tierra del Fuego (1769 and 1774). He displayed British Colours at the Kerguelen Islands (1776), but did not claim possession of the island, acknowledging Captain Kerguelen as discoverer.

Australia, New Zealand and many South Pacific Islands, as well as the coasts of North America, including Alaska, were all inhabited when Cook visited them. In addition, other maritime nations, especially Spain and Russia, had established trading posts or claims in North American locations that were previously populated by indigenous Eskimo and Aleut peoples who migrated to Alaska, across Canada and to Greenland between three and five thousand years ago. The Danish cartographer Vitus Bering (1681–1741) sailed in the service of the Russian Tsar Peter I, the Great (1672–1725). Russia explored Alaska and the Arctic a half-century prior to Cook. Abel Tasman (1603–1599) was the first European to land at Tasmania and then New Zealand (1642). Tasmania is located 150 miles (240km) to the southeast off the Australian continent. The Maori arrived in New Zealand from eastern Polynesia in approximately AD 1250–1300. Australia's aboriginal peoples arrived from Africa approximately fifty to sixty thousand years earlier. That continent was termed 'New Holland' in Cook's day. Tasman also charted the northern coast of New Holland in 1644. It is suggested that Portuguese or Spanish navigators circumnavigated Australia, producing a chart of the continent, perhaps two centuries prior to Cook's first voyage. The English navigator William Dampier (1651–1715) visited the northern tip of Queensland in 1688 and again in 1699.

In addition to being the first European to circumnavigate New Zealand (proving that it comprised two large and some smaller islands separated by a strait, later named the Cook Strait), James Cook was the first to chart the south-eastern and eastern coasts of Australia in 1770, *Endeavour* striking the Great Barrier Reef in June. Louis-Antoine de Bougainville sighted the Reef in 1767 during his circumnavigation (1766–1769). During his Pacific voyages Cook visited many islands, most of them already populated. He eventually realized that strong similarities, including language, existed among peoples of what is now termed 'the Polynesian Triangle', from New Zealand to Rapa Nui (Easter Island) to Hawai'i. Furthermore, Polynesians were also accomplished seafaring peoples, guided by oceanic currents, seasons and the stars, their vessels sailing the same Pacific waters as the ships of Cook and other European navigators.

Polynesian peoples settled in the Hawaiian Islands over varying time-frames beginning as early as AD 300 to as late as the twelfth century. Cook's arrival represented the first European discovery of Hawai'i, but he was not its 'first discoverer', as carved on the marker at Kealakekua Bay. Rather, Cook was the first *European* discoverer of the islands. Cook's arrival at the Hawaiian Islands in 1778 marks the European discovery of islands with an existing Polynesian population. Iron was unknown to the natives but Cook observed a Spanish-style broadsword carried by a Polynesian native.

Spain considered the entire Pacific to be Spanish territory as defined by the Treaties of Tordesillas (1494) and Zaragoza (1529), papal-sanctioned agreements between Spain and Portugal. Other maritime nations, the Dutch Republic, France, England and, later, Russia, were not parties to these agreements and disregarded the pole-to-pole division of the Earth into two hemispheres. Also, in general the Spanish proved very reluctant to voluntarily release information about Pacific territories with which they came into contact, as did other maritime powers. Later eighteenth-century maritime journals (e.g. those of Cook and Bougainville) revealed new geographical perspectives to an interested public, but information released was by approval of the English or French admiralties.

Because Spanish navigators sailed extensively throughout the Pacific, historian Donald Cutter suggests it is possible that some of the Hawaiian Islands were sighted or visited in the later sixteenth century by navigators Juan Gaytan (1555) or less likely Francesco Gali (1582). Other Spanish interest in Hawai'i (and California and the Pacific Northwest coast) is associated with Spanish 'naval pilot' and sometime-resident of Hawai'i Francesco de Paula Marin (from 1792 to the late 1820s), based on fragmentary evidence and conjecture. An alternative explanation is that the broad sword observed by Cook arrived on the wreck of a Spanish ship which floated to a Hawaiian island.

Speculation also exists that Polynesian navigators may have sailed into the Southern Ocean, just as they sailed throughout the vast areas of the Polynesian Triangle. An oral Maori legend recounts the *c.*650 AD war canoe voyage of

Ui-te-Rangiora to an area of bitter cold, snow, rock-like structures (icebergs), monstrous kelp and a frozen ocean. (In 650 AD the Maori were located in eastern Polynesia, not New Zealand.) This area might be the Ross Ice Shelf reached by Cook in January 1774. The Ross Ice Shelf is some 2,800 miles (4,500 kilometres) from New Zealand. Figure 5 (Chapter 2) provides perspective on the possibility of such a voyage. Polynesian artefacts that date to the thirteenth century have been located on the sub-Antarctic Enderby Island (Auckland Islands group), some 290 miles (465 kilometres) south of New Zealand at 50° 29′ 45″ south latitude and 166° 17′ 44″ east longitude. In Cook's era the Antarctic Circle lay at 66° 32′ south.[11]

Possession
The Admiralty directed Cook to take possession in the name of the Crown of those unoccupied territories he discovered. If lands were already populated, he was instructed to seek agreement from the people he encountered to be subject to His Britannic Majesty, although evidence of consent is lacking. A possession ceremony was held, sometimes more than once, in such locations as Tahiti, New Zealand (Mercury Bay), Australia (the east coast which Cook named New South Wales), South Georgia, Hawai'i, portions of the North American Coast (also claimed by Charles III's Spain) and Alaska (claimed by Catherine II's Russia). Although Cook took possession of Tahiti, Captain Samuel Wallis named Tahiti (or Otaheite) King George Island during his 1767 visit, although Bougainville had claimed it for France in 1766. Cook never landed on the South Sandwich Islands to claim possession due to the lack of a safe anchorage, but the territory over time became administratively associated with the Falkland Islands and South Georgia and therefore part of the British Empire. Captain Kerguelen claimed Kerguelen Island for France in 1772 but it may have been sighted earlier by Portuguese mariners. This is only a partial list of those territories claimed for Great Britain by James Cook and documented by accurate coordinates.

The detailed instructions for taking possession are identified in the Admiralty instructions given to Cook at the start of each voyage. It is doubtful whether native peoples who were invited to become part of the British Crown fully understood what was being proposed (if discussions occurred, which is doubtful), or what their acceptance actually meant, so 'possession' meant little at the time. Actual possession and real control were exerted in later years as the 'Second British Empire' (1783–1860) took form, becoming the empire on which the sun never set. In Cook's era Spanish, Portuguese, Dutch and French navigated many of these same waters, also establishing varying degrees of control or influence over Pacific territories.

None of the above reduces the significance of Cook's three voyages. It does point out the need for explanation in claiming 'discovery' or 'possession' of already inhabited territories in the vast areas of the globe which Cook first documented and charted, ranging from the Antarctic to the Arctic, from the Southern Ocean to the Arctic Ocean.

Geography, Navigation and Natural Science

In concluding his *Life of Captain James Cook* (1974), J.C. Beaglehole stated that Cook's memorials are 'geography' and 'navigation'. To these we could add his contributions to natural science, including experimentation on methods to control scurvy, the measures taken to improve the health of men at sea and the successful testing of the marine chronometer, as well as the wealth of information contained both in his journals and in the writings of others such as natural scientists, and the sketches and paintings made by artists during the three voyages. The search for the Southern Continent and exploration of the Southern Ocean are integral parts of all three Cook voyages. How Cook's navigational skills guided him through the Southern Ocean in search of *Terra Australis Incognita*, as well as his visits to various sub-Antarctic islands, is what this book is all about.

PART 1

INTRODUCTION TO CAPTAIN COOK'S VOYAGES

Chapter 1

The Three Voyages of Captain Cook

There is reason to imagine that a continent, or land of great extent, may be found to the southward of the tract lately made by Capt. Wallis in His Majesty's ship the *Dolphin* ... You will also observe with accuracy the situation of such islands as you may discover in the course of your voyage that have not hitherto been discovered by any Europeans, and take possession for His Majesty and make surveys and draughts of such of them as may appear to be of consequence, without suffering yourself however to thereby diverted from **the object which you are always to have in view, the discovery of the Southern Continent so often mentioned**.

Admiralty Secret Instructions to Lieutenant James Cook of His Majesty's Bark the *Endeavour*, 30 July 1768 [Author's emphasis]

James Cook's search for Antarctica occurred within the broader context of his three voyages. During the months when navigation in the Southern Ocean was difficult, Cook's travels included vast areas of the South Pacific and, during the third voyage, the Arctic. The purpose of this chapter is to summarize aspects of the three voyages to place Cook's Antarctic and sub-Antarctic travels within the larger context of his activity from 1768 to his death in 1779.

Yorkshire, Whitby and the Royal Navy, 1728–1768

I will begin with a brief account of Cook's early years in North Yorkshire, his experience sailing colliers from North Sea ports to London, then turning to his 1755 decision to join the Royal Navy, with service to 1768, primarily in Canadian waters.

James Cook was born on 27 October 1728, the son of James and Grace Cook, in Marton-in-Cleveland, Yorkshire. The family lived in a small, likely two-room labourer's hut, the site of which is now adjacent to the entrance of the Captain James Cook Birthplace Museum. In 1736 the family relocated nearby to Great Ayton, where his father was farm manager for Thomas Skottowe of Aireyholme Farm. Skottowe sponsored Cook's education for several years at a charity school in Great Ayton, from about age 8 to 12. Approximately forty years later Skottowe's son John served as Governor of St Helena Island, some 1,200 miles off the southwest African coast. Cook visited John Skottowe at St Helena on 16 May 1775 on his return to England from his second voyage. In 1755 the Cook family built a new home, a two-storey structure known as Cook's Cottage. This was relocated to Fitzroy Gardens, Melbourne, Australia, in 1934 (*see* Plate 4). Cook's mother Grace died in 1765 and his father James died on 1 April 1779, not knowing that his son had died the previous February in Hawai'i.

In 1745, at age 16, Cook began an apprenticeship with a grocer and haberdasher in Staithes, on the North Yorkshire coast, but he was not destined to be a shop-keeper. J.C. Beaglehole writes, 'Nothing can be more reasonably certain than that Cook had his first taste, as well as sight, of the sea at Staithes, and that the experience was convincing.'[1]

Cook's seafaring adventure began in the coastal city of Whitby in 1745 as an apprentice to John Walker, a North Sea coal merchant. Walker's ships conveyed coal from the South Yorkshire mines, with docks on the Tyne, down England's North Sea coast and up the River Thames to London. Located on the River Esk where it empties into the North Sea, Whitby in Cook's time was a well-known city of approximately 5,000 people and it was an important shipbuilding location and whaling vessel centre in the eighteenth and nineteenth centuries. A large whalebone arch stands today in Whitby framing a Cook statue and the North Sea. The shell of a thirteenth-century Benedictine abbey[2] is located on Whitby's East Cliff, an imposing landmark for sailers approaching Whitby from the North Sea. The view from the East Cliff affords the visitor a sweeping panorama of Whitby's port and the North Sea, waters with which Cook became familiar as an young seaman and future navigator.

Cook sailed on Whitby-built vessels later adapted to his Pacific voyages. The 18-year-old Cook began as an apprentice seaman and steadily rose in Walker's confidence. He sailed on four of Walker's ships: *Freelove*, *Three Brothers*, *Mary* and *Friendship*. As an apprentice seaman, James Cook sailed to Norway in *Three Brothers* as well as to Ireland as part of a convoy of ships transporting infantry and cavalry. He also sailed into the Baltic in *Mary*, but its destinations and muster rolls are incomplete or unclear. Voyages to Norway or Baltic ports such as Riga (Latvia) or perhaps St Petersburg (Russia) were likely destinations to obtain timber suitable for Whitby-built ships.[3]

John Walker's house on Grape Lane, on the bank of the River Esk, is today the location of the Captain Cook Memorial Museum (*see* Plate 3), an excellent facility to understand Cook's voyages as well as his era.[4] It has long been suggested that Cook lived in this house while apprenticed to John Walker, with quarters in the attic, now a location for the Museum's special exhibits. Between sailings or in the winter season, Cook and other apprentices may have also lived at Walker's house on Haggersgate Street, as well as Grape Lane, or elsewhere in Whitby.[5]

London's growth in the eighteenth century demanded a ready supply of coal and Whitby served as an important centre for that trade. It took a month to obtain coal from ports on the River Tyne at Newcastle, sail a collier to London, unload the coal and return to Whitby. Colliers sailed along England's North Sea coast on a regular basis except during the winter months. Approximately 400 ships were involved in moving coal south to London.[6]

It was on Walker's ships that Cook learned how to be a sailor. At the conclusion of his apprenticeship, Cook would have been offered command of one of Walker's ships.[7] However, on 17 June 1755, at age 26, leaving behind a secure career in the merchant navy, Cook joined the Royal Navy as a midshipman. John Robson, biographer and historian of Cook's early commercial and Royal Navy years, suggests that the Royal Navy offered new experiences with opportunities for promotion, especially with his acquired skills in commercial service. As a naval midshipman, Cook also obtained protection from press-gangs in major ports. It was a calculated gamble, but, as Robson observes, 'in the long term [it] was a masterstroke'.[8]

Whitby colliers sailed up the River Thames to unload coal at Wapping, an area to the east of the Tower of London. During the week required to unload the coal, Cook may have stayed at the Bell, an alehouse in Wapping run by the Batts family. On 21 December 1762 Cook married Elizabeth Batts, the 21-year-old daughter of the innkeeper, thirteen years junior to Cook. The couple made their home first in Shadwell and then at 7 Assembly Row in Mile End, a district in London's East End in what is now the borough of Tower Hamlets.

Cook's talents as an able Royal Navy seaman and surveyor/cartographer quickly emerged. He passed the Master's examination in June 1757. During five seasons he mapped portions of the St Lawrence River during the Seven Years' War (1756–1763). He was present at the surrender of the French fortress at Louisbourg on Cape Breton Island on 26 July 1758 and during the Siege of Quebec (began September 1759). Cook's chart of the St Lawrence River, and observation of its tides, assisted in landing troops for the assault on Quebec City. He surveyed the islands of St Pierre and Miquelon prior to the islands being ceded to France in 1763 as a part-time port for fish processing by the French at Newfoundland's Grand Banks.[9]

As a ship's master, Cook was responsible for the running of a naval vessel. After the war, over the course of several summers, the Royal Navy put Cook's skills to work charting the mostly unknown coast of Newfoundland. This work raised his reputation with the Royal Navy as a surveyor. Hugh Palliser (1723–1796) served as the Governor of Newfoundland. Cook served under Palliser during the Seven Years' War and he served as a mentor for the young man (as John Walker had done earlier in Cook's life). Palliser also later served as a Member of Parliament and then as Comptroller of the Navy. The map of Newfoundland brought Cook to the attention of the Admiralty as a navigator qualified to lead *Endeavour* on the first voyage. Cook was commissioned as a First Lieutenant in the Royal Navy on 25 May 1768.

The First Voyage, 1768–1771

I will highlight three aspects of Cook's first voyage: (1) the Transit of Venus, (2) the circumnavigation and charting of New Zealand, and (3) the surveying of Australia's East Coast, the Great Barrier Reef and Batavia.

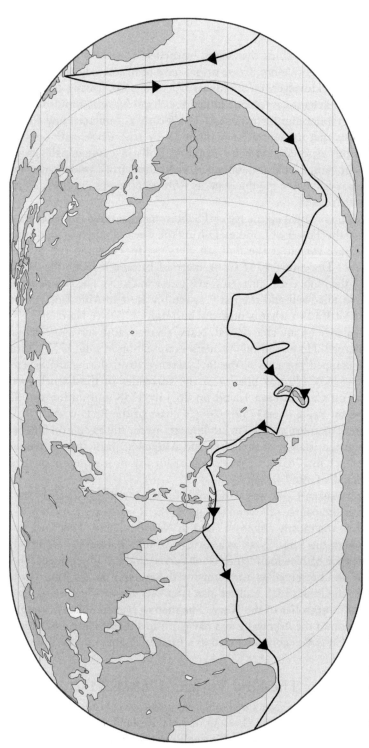

Figure 2. Map of James Cook's first voyage, 1768–1771. The original map is attributed to John Platek, Alexius Horatius (2008).

Transit of Venus

The announced purpose of the first voyage was to observe the Transit of Venus, predicted in 1716 by astronomer Edmund Halley to occur on 3 June 1769. The Transit of Venus occurs when that planet's orbit crosses between the Earth and the Sun, making the planet visible from Earth as a black dot on the Sun's surface. Calculations of the time for this event could be used to determine the distance between the Earth and the Sun. It required knowing the time of the beginning and end of the transit from two locations whose latitude and longitude were known, with calculations then determined by geometry. Observers were also sent to the North Cape of Norway, to Fort Churchill on Hudson's Bay in Canada as well as to Tahiti to observe the Transit. Other observers in other locations also tracked the path of Venus across the Sun. This was a significant scientific mission, explains Andrea Wulf, stating it was

> the most ambitious scientific project that had ever been planned ... It took a great leap of the imagination to propose that astronomers should travel thousands of miles into wildernesses far north and south, laden with instruments weighing more than half a ton ... Calculating exact distances in space was a bold concept too, considering that clocks were still not accurate enough to measure longitude precisely, and there was as yet no standard measurement on Earth.[10]

Generally speaking, Transits of Venus occur in a 243-year cycle, with a pair of transits separated by eight years (e.g. 1761 and 1769) followed by longer intervals. The Royal Society contributed to the cost of the voyage, sending along Joseph Banks and other natural scientists to collect information and artefacts.

Observation of the Transit of Venus was the 'public' purpose of the voyage. However, Cook was also given secret instructions to seek the existence of *Terra Australis Incognita*, an 'unknown southern land', a large landmass thought to 'balance' earth's already known northern continents. In addition, Cook was to determine if New Zealand was part of that fabled southern continent.

The Voyage to Tahiti

The Bark *Endeavour* departed Plymouth on 25 August 1768 with a crew of 83, plus 12 marines and 11 supernumeraries associated with scientific studies. *Endeavour* sailed to Madeira (for wine and other supplies), Rio de Janeiro (supplies) and along the stormy coast of Tierra del Fuego at the Strait of Le Maire. On 25 January 1769 Cook rounded Cape Horn and sailed *Endeavour* 'well to the Southward' to 60° south latitude in search of land (Chapter 4). No new territory was located.

Cook reached Matavai Bay, Tahiti, on 13 April (17° 30′ south latitude and 149° 30′ west longitude) and began preparation of an observatory for the Transit of Venus at Point Venus. On 3 June 1769 Cook and astronomer Charles Green observed the passage of Venus across the Sun, with difficulty noted in timing the exact moment the planet touched the Sun's outer edge, a phenomenon known as the 'black drop effect'. This caused variations in calculations of the distance from Earth to the Sun ranging from approximately 89 million to 109 million miles.[11]

James Cook visited Tahiti at least once on each of his three voyages. *Endeavour* departed Tahiti on 2 August 1769 and, following Admiralty instructions, sailed south in search of the Southern Continent. By 2 September *Endeavour* had reached 40° south latitude without locating a 'land of great extent'. Although the Southern Continent remained undetected, the month's sailing 'narrowed the options' about its location in a region where speculation suggested it was to be found.

Circumnavigating and Charting New Zealand

From 40° south, Cook sailed north and reached New Zealand on 7 October 1769. He was the second European to land in New Zealand, after the Dutch explorer Abel Tasman (1642).

From October 1769 to March 1770 Cook circumnavigated and charted nearly the entire coast of New Zealand. The strait separating the two islands was named after him. His maps clearly demonstrated that New Zealand consisted of two large main and other smaller islands. Moreover, it was not part of the elusive Southern Continent. In New Zealand Cook first encountered the Maori, the Polynesian people he came to most admire among those he encountered in the South Pacific. He also discovered his favourite anchorage off the Cook Strait, named Queen Charlotte Sound,[12] at the north tip of the South Island, a Pacific anchorage he utilized frequently during portions of his three voyages.

As Cook was surveying the New Zealand coastline, Captain Jean-Francois-Marie de Surville (1717–1770) of the French East India Company was proceeding in the opposite direction around New Zealand in *Jean Baptiste*. Michael Lee's account of Surville's voyage suggests the ships passed unseen on 16 December 1769 in clear weather. Visibility from the masthead was approximately 20 miles so at the distance of approximately 30 miles one ship could not see the other.[13] Surville continued to South America, sailing through waters which Cook would navigate in 1774, both men contributing to the understanding that the unknown Southern Continent was not located in the Pacific in 40° to 50° south latitude between New Zealand and South America.

Australia's East Coast, the Great Barrier Reef and Batavia

On 25 March 1770 Cook sailed for Van Dieman's Land (Tasmania), but prevailing winds blew *Endeavour* northward. Land was sighted on 19 April 1770, to be later named New South Wales, Australia. *Endeavour* sailed into Stingray Bay on 29 April 1770, later named Botany Bay because of many naturalist discoveries. The location was also to serve as the First Fleet's destination in 1778 when Great Britain began transporting convicts to the Australian penal colony, and played a role in the subsequent settlement of the continent.[14]

In early June 1770 *Endeavour* began to sail along the southeast coast of Australia. On the 11th, shortly before 11pm, the bark ran aground on a shoal of the Great Barrier Reef, at a location subsequently named Endeavour Reef (16° 6' south latitude and 214° 30' west longitude). In a later letter to the Secretary of the

Admiralty, Cook wrote 'we struck upon a Reef of Rocks, where we lay 23 Hours, and received some very considerable damage'.[15] Endeavour Reef is approximately 7.5 miles (12km) off the Australian coast. This event could have ended in total disaster for the entire voyage.

Immediate efforts began to lighten the ship's weight by tossing overboard cannon and their carriages, casks of stone ballast, supplies and decayed ships' stores, eventually totalling 40 to 50 tons in weight. The three workable pumps were manned continually. The leak into the ship increased with a rising tide at 5pm and again when the ship was righted at 9pm. But at 10.20pm the ship finally floated free of the Reef, with water in the hold almost four feet deep and a gash with a piece of coral in its side.

Endeavour was 'fothered' on 13 June. A sail filled with oakum (tarred rope used for caulking), wool and other packing material, including animal waste, was dragged under the bottom of the ship by ropes and placed over the gash, which stopped the leak to some degree. The ship was partially repaired in a safe harbour at what is now Endeavour River, Queensland (near present-day Cooktown). While the ship was careened on the shore, scientific exploration of the nearby mainland occurred. In early August *Endeavour* cautiously sailed among the Reef's shoals seeking an opening to pass through to reach the safety of open water, and on 17 August safely escaped the Reef. Philip Edwards, editor of an abridged Penguin collection of Cook's journals, comments that saving the *Endeavour* from the Reef, repairing it and navigating a passage through the dangerous coral shoals 'must stand as Cook's greatest feat of seamanship'.[16]

Endeavour then headed north, passing Cape York, the northernmost point in Queensland, and then west through the Torres Strait, which separates Australia and New Guinea. The first voyage headed for Batavia (now Jakarta) for additional repairs at the Dutch East India Company docks. Batavia, a necessary but dangerous port, 'stunk to heaven, [was] corrupt and filthy', its canals 'torpid ordure-choked tanks of disease'.[17] Mosquitoes abounded (malaria) and tainted fresh food proved deadly (dysentery). Batavia was therefore a cesspool and nearly everyone, including Cook, became sick. Even after *Endeavour* limped out of the docks as a virtual hospital ship and anchored at nearby Prince's Island, illnesses and deaths persisted. There were many deaths, among them naturalist Herman Spöring Tupia (or Tupaia) and his servant Taiata (from Raiatea) and several sailors.

On 16 January 1771 *Endeavour* began sailing west across the Indian Ocean. 'The flux' (dysentery) claimed more lives, including both artist Sydney Parkinson and Surgeon Monkhouse. The voyage reached the Cape of Good Hope on 13 March and anchored at Table Bay on the 14th. It reached Jamestown on St Helena on 1 May and sighted Ascension Island on the 10th. *Endeavour* returned to England on 13 July 1771. Cook reported to the Admiralty on the 17th and returned to his home at Mile End, where he began completing reports on the voyage. On 15 August James Cook was promoted to Commander and received by King George III at St James's Palace. In regard to the search for Antarctica, Cook had shown that the elusive continent was not adjacent to New Zealand.

The Second Voyage, 1772–1775

The primary purpose of Cook's second voyage was the search for Antarctica, once again a secret mission to 'foreign parts'. This was to be accomplished during the southern hemisphere's summer months (primarily December, January and February). During the rest of the year, when sailing in the Southern Ocean would be hampered by colder weather, Cook and his ships were to further explore the South Pacific islands, from their anchorage at New Zealand's Queen Charlotte Sound.

The Admiralty sent two ships on the second voyage, to avoid the situation of a single ship sailing in unknown waters with no other vessel available for assistance. Cook's ship was *Resolution*. Captain Tobias Furneaux took charge of *Adventure*. He was to be subordinate to Cook. Joseph Banks and his group of scientists initially planned to accompany Cook's second voyage. Banks demanded extensive renovations to accommodate his entourage and equipment but during sea trials these alterations caused *Resolution* to be unseaworthy. Cook demanded that the Admiralty remove Banks's renovations, at which Banks withdrew from participation. In his place Johann Reinhold Forster and his son George joined *Resolution* as naturalists, as suggested by the Royal Society.

I will organize the second voyage into four parts: (1) the search for Cape Circumcision, the first crossing of the Antarctic Circle and separation in an Antarctic Fog (July 1772–February 1773); (2) Queen Charlotte Sound, the second separation of the ships and the massacre at Grass Cove, May–December 1773; (3) the second and third crossings of the Antarctic Circle and return to Tierra del Fuego, December 1773–December 1774; and (4) South Georgia, the South Sandwich Islands and an end to *Terra Australis Incognita*, January–March 1775. A depiction of Cook's circumnavigation of Antarctica is seen in an Australian Antarctic Territories stamp (*see* Plate 11).

Cape Circumcision, the First Crossing of the Antarctic Circle and Separation in an Antarctic Fog, July 1772–February 1773

Commander Cook sailed on the *Resolution* from Plymouth on 13 July 1772, with a company of 112. Captain Tobias Furneaux in *Adventure* sailed with a crew of 81. On 23 November they departed Table Bay and headed south in search of Cape Circumcision.

The French East India Company's navigator Jean-Baptiste Charles Bouvet de Lozier (1705–1786) sighted 'Cape Circumcision' in 1739. It was thereafter thought to be the tip of the Southern Continent. The Admiralty directed Cook to explore the 'Cape' or sail further south in search of land in high latitudes as near as possible to the South Pole. Once the 'Antarctic summer' passed, Cook was to seek warmer South Pacific territories and then return to the Southern Ocean when weather permitted. Cook did not locate the 'Cape' owing to faulty French coordinates.

On 17 January 1773 *Resolution* and *Adventure* became the first recorded vessels to cross the Antarctic Circle (Chapter 5). The ships encountered a permanent ice

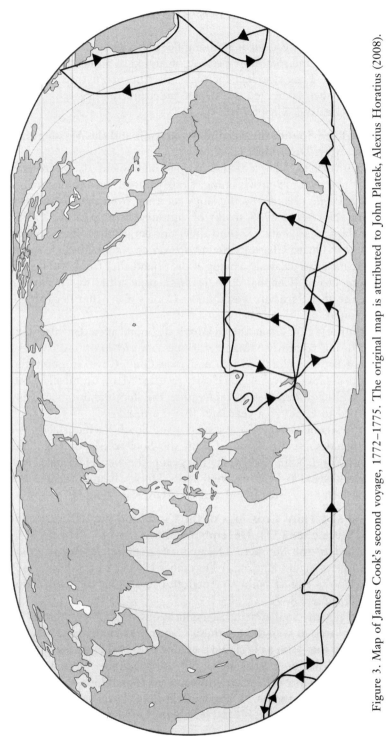

Figure 3. Map of James Cook's second voyage, 1772–1775. The original map is attributed to John Platek, Alexius Horatius (2008).

wall and could not proceed further among floating ice and icebergs (Cook's 'ice islands'). *Resolution* and *Adventure* became separated in a thick Antarctic fog on 8 February 1773. They searched for each other for about three days (by pre-arranged plan), then continued the voyage independently, agreeing to meet up again in New Zealand (Chapter 6).

Queen Charlotte Sound, the Second Separation and the Massacre at Grass Cove, May–December 1773

Resolution returned to New Zealand in May and found *Adventure* at Queen Charlotte Sound. After re-provisioning, Cook planned to continue their 'sweep' of the South Pacific islands. As the ships returned from their island sweep, in October and November 1773 weeks of continual storms in the Cook Strait caused the ships to separate a second time, preventing them from anchoring at the same time in Queen Charlotte Sound. *Resolution* eventually made the anchorage but *Adventure* was delayed, arriving at the Sound after Cook had departed for the Southern Ocean (Chapter 7). A message in a bottle was buried under a marked tree so that Furneaux would know Cook's plans after departing Queen Charlotte Sound.

Captain Furneaux arrived at Queen Charlotte Sound a few days after Cook had departed. During re-provisioning, carelessness by *Adventure*'s crew led to the deaths of ten British sailors and two natives at Grass Cove, an event known as the 'Massacre at Grass Cove', which clearly revealed Maori cannibalism. After the second separation of *Resolution* and *Adventure*, the ships did not meet again until Cook returned to England, a year later than Furneaux.

During the second voyage Cook visited many South Pacific Islands. A partial catalogue includes New Zealand, Tahiti, the Society Islands (e.g., Huahine, Raiatea, Bora Bora), Niue, Tonga, the Fiji group, the New Hebrides, New Caledonia, Norfolk Island and various coral atolls, Hervey Island (Manuae, later one of the Cook Islands), Easter Island and the Marquesas Islands.

The Second and Third Crossings of the Circle and the Return to Tierra del Fuego, December 1773–December 1774

Cook returned to the Southern Ocean in November. *Resolution* crossed the Antarctic Circle a second time on 21 December 1773 and a third time on 26 January 1774. Cook's closest point to Antarctica was at 71° 10′ south latitude on 30 January (Chapters 8–9).

After visiting many South Pacific island locations, on 11 November 1774 Cook began his final trek to seek the Southern Continent, sailing from New Zealand (Chapter 10). At this point he declared that, due to his sailing in the South Pacific, Antarctica could not be located above 60° south latitude. He sailed along the western coast of Tierra del Fuego and rounded Cape Horn on 29 December, anchoring at Staten Island on 31 December, where *Resolution* was reprovisioned with fresh meat – ducks, penguins and seals – and blubber that was to be rendered into oil.

South Georgia, South Sandwich Islands, Cape Circumcision and an End to the Search for *Terra Australis Incognita*, **January–March 1775**

On 3 January 1773 Cook sailed *Resolution* in search of the 'Gulf of San Sebastian', said by hydrographer Alexander Dalrymple to be the coast of the Southern Continent. He saw no signs of land and headed east-northeast.

On 14 January what was initially thought to be a large ice island turned out to be land. Was this, at last, the 'continent of great extent'? Cook took possession of it on 17 January. On 20 January the land turned out to be an island, which was named South Georgia in honour of King George III (to differentiate it from the North American Georgia colony). In early February more islands were located further to the south-southeast, eventually to be known as the South Sandwich Islands. The volcanic islands were shrouded in fog and Cook could not locate a safe anchorage (*see* Chapter 11).

In mid-February Cook searched for 'Cape Circumcision', but did not locate it, concluding that Bouvet had viewed a large ice island in 1739 and not the Southern Continent. British whalers sighted Bouvet's Island in 1808 (*see* Chapter 11).

In late February Cook concluded that *Terra Australis Incognita*, if such a continent existed at all, was near the South Pole and, because of the ice, out of the reach of navigation. He wrote that despite suggestions from ancient geographers and exploration in the past two centuries, his second voyage had put an end to speculation about the Southern Continent. He surmised it was a land of great cold, snow and ice, inaccessible by navigation, uninhabited and of no commercial value.

During the return home, after visiting Table Bay and calling on Thomas Skottowe at St Helena, Cook first saw the printed edition of his first voyage journal. He was quickly enraged at the liberties taken by the editor, John Hawkesworth, who was not interested in the geographical knowledge generated from the voyage of the *Endeavour* and had made things up, attributing it all to a 'mortified' James Cook. He determined to exercise more control over his next journal.

The second voyage ended when *Resolution* arrived at Plymouth on 29 July 1775. At St James's Palace King George III raised James Cook to the rank of Captain on 9 August 1775. The second voyage had disproved the myth of *Terra Australis Incognita* and validated the use of the marine chronometer to determine longitude. Cook's maps of the Central and South Pacific were 'so correct in conception and outline' that French explorer Jean-Francois de la Pérouse complained 'Cook had left nothing for his successors to do but praise him'.[18]

Later in 1775 a protracted dispute arose among the Admiralty, J.R. Forster and Captain Cook regarding the publication of the second voyage journals. Forster and Cook published their accounts of the voyage separately (Chapter 12).

The Royal Society invited Cook to become a Fellow of the Society and awarded him the Copley Medal for his efforts to improve the health of seamen.[19] Cook also sat for a portrait painted by Nathaniel Dance-Holland which today is located at the National Maritime Museum at Greenwich. Although honoured for his experiments by the Royal Society, the Admiralty did not follow up in a timely fashion on Cook's experiments (*see also* Chapter 14).[20]

The Third Voyage, 1776–1779/1780

The secret purpose of Cook's third voyage was the discovery of a navigable Northwest Passage across the top of the northern hemisphere. *Resolution* and a new Royal Navy vessel, *Discovery*, were fitted out for this voyage. The Arctic rather than the Antarctic was the focus of the third voyage, and the ten days spent at Kerguelen Island in late December 1776 was the only sub-Antarctic location visited during the third voyage.

I will organize the third voyage into five sections: (1) the Crozet and Kerguelen Islands, July–December 1776; (2) Hawaii and the North American coast, January–May 1778; (3) Alaska and the Arctic, April–August 1778; (4) return to Hawai'i and the death of Captain Cook, October 1778–February 1779; and (5) the Arctic, Siberia and England, February 1779–October 1780.

The Crozet and Kerguelen Islands, July–December 1776

Upon his return to England, the Admiralty offered Cook an appointment as Captain of the Royal Hospital at Greenwich, with an annual pension of £230, as well as free living quarters and subsidies for other expenses. This gave Cook (then aged 47) a sound and honourable prospect for the future. Cook initially accepted the position but maintained the option to return to the Royal Navy if circumstances arose. The opportunity that Cook excitedly seized upon was the search for a navigable Northwest Passage, not from the Atlantic (like previous attempts by other navigators) but from the Pacific.

The third voyage departed from Plymouth on 12 July 1776, with *Resolution*'s crew of 112. Captain Charles Clerke (1741–1779) commanded *Discovery*, with a crew of 70, but was delayed in departing from England, arriving at Table Bay on 10 November. Clerke had sailed on Cook's previous two voyages. When Cook was killed in Hawai'i, Clerke took over direction of the third voyage, until his death in August 1779, and then Lieutenant John Gore took overall command. After the usual visit to Table Bay, the third voyage sailed into the Southern Indian Ocean to verify the location of the tiny sub-Antarctic Crozet Islands and then the uninhabited Kerguelen Islands (Chapter 13). The latter were named after the French explorer who discovered the group, but did not personally land, in 1772/1773.

Resolution and *Discovery* anchored in a bay Cook named 'Christmas Harbour' at the northern tip of Kerguelen Island and explored the territory, eventually sailing along approximately one-third of the island. He found good harbours, water (but no wood), birds, penguins, seals, the 'Kerguelen Cabbage' (an antiscourbitic) and giant seaweed. He also found frequent fogs and mostly 'naked and barren rocks', describing it as an 'Island of Desolation'. The island's glacier was later named after James Cook and the highest mountain after navigator/explorer James Clark Ross, who conducted magnetism studies at Kerguelen in 1840 (Chapter 16).

During the third voyage Cook also continued his 'sweep' of South Pacific islands, some of which he had contacted previously. A partial list includes Tasmania (Van Diemen's Land), New Zealand, Manuae (or Hervey Island),

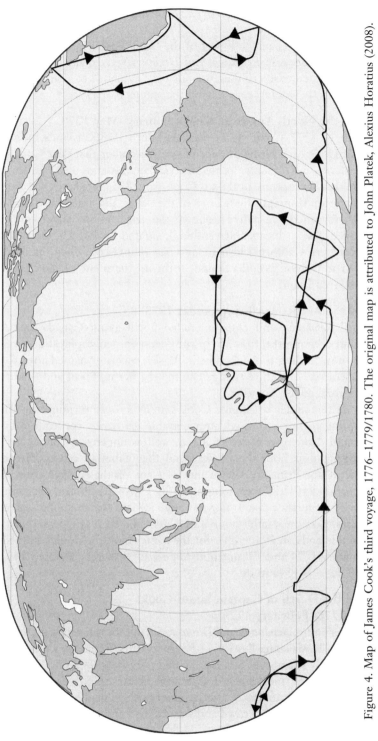

Figure 4. Map of James Cook's third voyage, 1776–1779/1780. The original map is attributed to John Platek, Alexius Horatius (2008).

Aitutaki and Penrhyn Islands (all part of the Cook Islands), Tonga, Tahiti and Christmas Island. Because *Resolution* and *Discovery* arrived in the South Pacific later than anticipated, visits to these islands were extended so that their eventual arrival in the Arctic would occur during the summer of 1778.

Hawai'i and the North American Coast, January–May 1778
During most of 1777 Cook visited various South Pacific islands, periodically anchoring at Queen Charlotte Sound. In late December that year Cook headed east and *Resolution* and *Discovery* located the Hawaiian Islands on 18 January 1778, perhaps the first Europeans to do so. Cook named these islands the Sandwich Islands after John Montagu, First Lord of the Admiralty and Earl of Sandwich, although he recorded the native name of the easternmost island as 'Owyhee'. He then sailed east to locate 'New Albion', sighted by Francis Drake in 1579 (perhaps Northern California near today's San Francisco). Then, on 30 March, Cook landed at Yuquot, Nootka Sound, at the northern end of the channel that forms Vancouver Island.

Alaska and the Arctic, April–September 1778
On 26 April *Resolution* and *Discovery* sailed north along Canada and Alaska, exploring and charting the coast, frequently naming geographical features. The Cook Inlet, now leading to Anchorage in Alaska, was later named after Cook by George Vancouver. The third voyage entered the Bering Strait and then crossed the Arctic Circle on 14 August.

During the remainder of August Cook sought a route through the Chukchi Sea, attempting to break through impenetrable ice packs, confronted by cold, fog, winds and dangerous rocky shoals, as well as uncertainty about his actual location, sailing near both the Alaskan and then Siberian coasts. He reached points named Cape Prince of Wales and Icy Cape on the Alaskan coast (70° 19′ north latitude and 161° 52′ west longitude). By 29 August he had determined he could proceed no further due to impenetrable ice and the changing seasons. He visited locations on the southern coast of Alaska and then sailed south, reaching the Sandwich Islands on 29 October for the winter months. Cook's travels to 70° south in January 1774 and 70° north in August 1778 thereby covered 140 of the Earth's 180 degrees of latitude.

Hawaii and the Death of Captain James Cook,
November 1778–February 1779
After re-provisioning, *Resolution* and *Discovery* set sail for the Arctic on 4 February but returned to Kealakekua Bay on 11 February after *Resolution*'s foremost mast was destroyed in a storm. On Sunday, 14 February Polynesian natives stole one of *Resolution*'s cutters, most likely for its iron fittings. Cook and four marines attempted to recover it and took a native chief hostage pending its return. Cook turned his back on an angry crowd and was stabbed and clubbed to death, along with the four marines.

Cook's body was cannibalized but, at the insistence of Captain Clerke, portions were returned the following day to be buried at sea in a metal container in a deeper part of Kealakekua Bay. Today, memorials commemorate his death on the shoreline and on land. The white marble obelisk monument describes Cook as 'First Discoverer' of Hawaii, but more accurately he was its 'first recorded European discoverer', which is why at the present time the monument is often defaced.

The Return to the Arctic, Siberia and the Return to England, February 1779–October 1780

After Cook's death, *Resolution* and *Discovery* returned to the Arctic, still in search of the Northwest Passage, this time following the Siberian coast. The ships docked at the harbour of St Peter and St Paul and then journeyed to Petropavlovsk on the Kamchatka Peninsula. Throughout the voyage Captain Clerke suffered from tuberculosis. He died on 22 August 1779 and seven days later was buried in Petropavlovsk. There, Cook's journals and a letter to the Admiralty explaining Cook's death in Hawaii were given to Major Magnus von Behm, the Russian governor of Kamchatka.[21] Cook's journals and Clerke's letter then travelled by an astounding overland journey from Siberia to England, arriving in January 1780. It was only then that the Admiralty learned of Cook's death, almost a year after it had occurred. Lieutenant John Gore, born in the Virginia Colony, then took command of the voyage. The second excursion to the Arctic met with little success and the third voyage returned to England on 4 October 1780.

Who Was James Cook?

We know about James Cook's achievements as a navigator. Captain Alan Villiers of the Australian Navy wrote that 'He was [and he still is] the meticulous and infinitely careful explorer by sea, the most consistent and the greatest sailing ship seaman there ever was.'[22] But who was James Cook the man? This is much more difficult to answer because Cook rarely revealed his personal side. A few letters to John Walker, his Whitby mentor, do survive, but not his letters to his wife Elizabeth. Prior to her death, Elizabeth Cook destroyed the letters Cook had sent to her, along with other papers, a loss that prevents historians from gaining deeper insight into Cook's personality.[23] Therefore attempts to attribute human characteristics to James Cook fall to those who offer subjective opinions about him now, at a distance of over 250 years.

James and Elizabeth Cook were married for seventeen years and, as related earlier in this chapter, made their home at Mile End, East London. Cook was often absent, serving in the Royal Navy during the Seven Years' War, then mapping Newfoundland and, after 1768, on his three voyages, with perhaps a year separating the end of one voyage and the beginning of the next. We may assume that Elizabeth knew well that marriage to a Royal Navy navigator meant prolonged periods of absence and danger. Cook always ensured she was provided with funds during his absences and took care to start two of his sons on their Royal Navy careers.

As a mother, Elizabeth had her family around her, but we might today label her as a 'sometime single parent'. Her life was laced with tragedy. Three of James and Elizabeth Cook's six children survived their father but all died before their mother, who lived until 1835, dying at the age of 93.[24] The often-brief lives of James and Elizabeth Cook's children also underscore the demands and dangers of maritime service and eighteenth-century infant mortality rates. James (1763–1794) and Nathaniel (1764–1780) pursued naval careers, but both died at sea, James off Portsmouth and Nathaniel in a West Indies hurricane. News of the deaths of both her husband and son Nathaniel reached Elizabeth in 1780, leading to months of prolonged grief. Hugh (1776–1793) died of scarlet fever while a student at Cambridge. Three children lived only a few months or years: Elizabeth (1767–1771), Joseph (1 month in 1768), and George (4 months in 1772). Elizabeth and five of the Cook children are buried at St Andrew the Great Church in Cambridge, where there is a memorial to the Cook family. Elizabeth Batts Cook is memorialized by a fountain at Sydney's Waterhouse Camellia Garden. There are no direct descendants of James and Elizabeth Cook.

Cook was absent from their London home – either in North America or in the Pacific, Southern or Arctic Oceans –during most of their marriage, between 1762 and 1779. It's estimated they may have spent four years together in total. He was present at the births of his sons Hugh and George, but not at the births of his other four children. He was also absent at the time of their deaths. Sons James, Nathaniel and Hugh died after their father. When Captain Cook was killed in Hawaii at age 50, his widow was 38 years of age. She received a naval pension of £200 per year beginning in 1779, as well as receiving a portion of the income from Cook's journals, and apparently lived comfortably thereafter. For some years she lived with Cook's cousin Isaac Smith, who had sailed with Cook first to Newfoundland, then on the first and second voyages. Smith's Royal Navy career extended into the 1790s. She also lived with other relatives or they lived with her.

New Zealand novelist Graeme Lay recently published three novels about James Cook, creating an imaginary diary as well as occasional letters about his travels to be shared with his wife upon his return. Although a novelist can explore or elaborate upon situations not found in historical documents, Lay's account adheres to the historical context of Cook's voyages and includes journal excerpts. The books provide interesting insights into the relationship between James and Elizabeth Cook for those who want to speculate about personal lives.[25]

What words best describe James Cook? For this writer, he emerges as an extremely competent leader of men, fully in charge, yet also a humane, intuitive, cautious naval commander. Born in the north of England, he brought with him neither birth nor inherited wealth nor a comprehensive education. Instead, he studied, practised and learned to be a sailor, surveyor and navigator, building upon an ever-growing foundation of knowledge and competency, his merit quickly recognized by others. His charts proved consistently reliable. As a navigator he understood astronomical observation. As a sea captain, Cook was determined to complete his missions. He followed Admiralty instructions, balanced with an experienced captain's knowledge of actions required for on-the-spot situations – the condition of the ship, the crew, the oceans, the changeable weather and his acute observations of his surroundings. While he surely learned from Banks, Solander, Spöring and J.R. Forster about botany and the allied sciences of his day, he was also very observant, as is shown in his journal documentation, often citing information commented upon by the naturalists as well as his own observations.

He was often well-received by the native peoples he encountered. There were occasional misunderstandings when people of very different cultures first met, as well as the spread of hitherto unknown disease. Unfortunately, a few Polynesians died as a result of misunderstandings and threats. If Cook and a landing party met resistance, or he discovered that he and his men were in danger, Cook and his crew defended themselves using superior weaponry. Cook sought to establish friendly relationships with native peoples, exchanging gifts and trading for supplies such as wood, water and foodstuffs. His journals contain detailed assessments of the people he met, as well as the territories he visited. Most of the peoples Cook encountered received the ship's company positively and were often very generous in providing supplies to the voyagers.

As a naval leader, Cook earned the respect of his officers and the entire ship's company. Testimony to that is seen in those who served on more than one voyage. Cook did not conduct the voyages by committee or consensus. No twenty-first-century sharing circles or navel-gazing episodes are recorded. He sought information and advice from his officers and issued orders accordingly, following Admiralty instructions. The taciturn James Cook would not tolerate insubordination or neglect of duty. He or his officers ordered punishment by the lash, standard in the Royal Navy for such infractions as not obeying orders, dereliction of duty, disobedience or desertion, but Cook was never known as a captain who frequently resorted to the lash.[26]

Cook's health deteriorated over time. He lay seriously ill for a month in early 1774 on the way from the third crossing of the Antarctic Circle to Easter Island (Chapter 14), but temporarily recovered. Cook occasionally exhibited signs of illness and uncharacteristic behaviour during the third voyage. Upon his return to Queen Charlotte Sound he took no action to avenge the 1773 'Massacre of Grass Cove', asserting that carelessness of British sailors in part contributed to their deaths. His failure to do so angered many who sailed with him and puzzled the Maori. Occasional outbursts later may include his actions leading to the fateful circumstances on 14 February 1779 at Kealakekua Bay. Was his behaviour due to a recurrence of intestinal inflammation? Or was it partially due to his growing despondency about the negative impact of sailors from Britain and other European nations who spread disease and corrupted the Maori and other Polynesian peoples with whom the visitors came into contact? Were his final raised arm gestures at Kealakekua Bay a signal to be rescued – or a selfless humanitarian effort to protect native peoples from harm?

Births, baptisms, marriages and deaths are recorded in parish registers but we know nothing of Cook's religious beliefs. Likewise, we know nothing of his politics or his social opinions. Beaglehole writes, 'Geography provided him with the imaginative, Navigation with morals.' Cook displayed 'a plain heroic magnitude of mind' and he was not a 'simple man'.[27]

In Cook's portrait by Nathaniel Dance (*see* Plate 1), we see a confident-looking man, staring to his left, with brown eyes and hair, and a wig. He is wearing a captain's uniform, and his right hand points to a location on a map, likely the Pacific Ocean, his captain's black cocked hat in the background. However, his right hand does not depict the thumb-to-forefinger scar from an exploded powder magazine off Newfoundland on 6 August 1764 which assisted in identifying his remains after his death in 1779. Other portraits of Cook exist, such as those by artists William Hodges and John Webber from the second and third voyages. They depict a confident, dignified, quiet and serious figure. Similar observations may be made about Cook's statue on the Mall near Admiralty Arch in London (*see* Plate 2), depicting a distinguished, young officer in a captain's uniform, his right hand grasping a telescope.

Not only was Cook competent, he was also a confident navigator and his journals reflect that confidence as well as his ambition. While the second voyage tested the reliability of the marine chronometer, satisfying Cook that it was a reliable guide, he also remained confident that he could determine his location anywhere on the seas, chronometer notwithstanding. Although not given to frequent retrospection, his journals occasionally contain reflective passages, such as his triumphant conclusion towards the end of the second voyage that it, and he, had put to rest the debate of geographers of all ages and exploration of the past 200 years about the Southern Continent, a goal established in Admiralty instructions in 1768. He was an ambitious person. On his third crossing of the Antarctic Circle in January 1774, he recorded in his journal: 'I whose ambition leads me not only further than any other man has been before me, but as far as I think it possible for a man to go,' surely one of the best-known Cook quotations.

So who was James Cook? In the final analysis we have a somewhat incomplete portrait. We still know more about what he did than about the person behind the deeds. He certainly is one of history's greatest navigators. As a leader he was in charge and mission-driven, providing direction and orders, and totally responsible for the success of the three voyages. He was a confident navigator, accurate cartographer, respected and responsible. His portraits show a reflective and dignified figure. His journals and charts stand as documentation of his achievements. Cook displayed the capacity to learn about the wider world in which he travelled, from a farm labourer's hut in North Yorkshire, to the commercial navy in Whitby, to the Royal Navy surveyor, lieutenant, commander and captain of three worldwide voyages. An ambitious and extremely competent navigator, whose voyages increased human knowledge about the planet, and well aware of his achievements, James Cook surely did go as far as a man could go.

Chapter 2

Terra Australis Incognita

Between the middle of the fifteenth century and the late seventeenth, Europeans learned to think of the world as a whole and of all seas as one ... During those two and a half centuries European explorers actually visited most of the habitable regions of the globe; nearly all those, in fact, which were accessible by sea. They found vast territories formerly unknown to them, and drew the rough outlines of the world which we know. [This is] commonly called the Age of Discovery.

J.H. Parry, The Age of Reconnaissance

Captain James Cook was suited to be the world's greatest negative discoverer – by his restless energy, his organizing ability, his vast knowledge of charts and the sea, and his persistence in trying possibilities that others had not the courage or the vigour to pursue.

Daniel Boorstin, The Discoverers

In this chapter, we will first examine ideas about the unknown Southern Continent, especially from the 'Age of Reconnaissance', the European voyages of discovery from the fifteenth to the seventeenth century. These voyages gradually pushed back the ocean's limits to reveal knowledge about the planet's continents familiar to us today. We then turn to contributions in the century prior to Captain Cook's voyages, from Edmund Halley, Jean-Baptiste Bouvet de Lozier, Alexander Dalrymple, George Anson and Samuel Wallis, and the encouragement as well as financial support from the Royal Society for observation of the Transit of Venus.

The Antarctic Circle and the Continent of Antarctica

We know today that the Antarctic Circle encompasses most of Antarctica and it is located at 66° 33′ south latitude. The axial tilt of the Earth and the tidal force of the Moon's orbit lead to fluctuations in the Circle's precise location, causing it to drift minutely on an annual basis. When these comments were written (June 2018), the Circle's precise location was 66° 33′ 47.2″. Some 250 years ago, when Captain Cook recorded the first crossing of the Circle (17 January 1773), its location was 66° 32′. This tilt also affects the location of the South Magnetic Pole (and the North Magnetic Pole). In Cook's era the South Magnetic Pole was located near McMurdo Sound at the end of the Ross Ice Shelf. Today it is located off East Antarctica's George V Land.

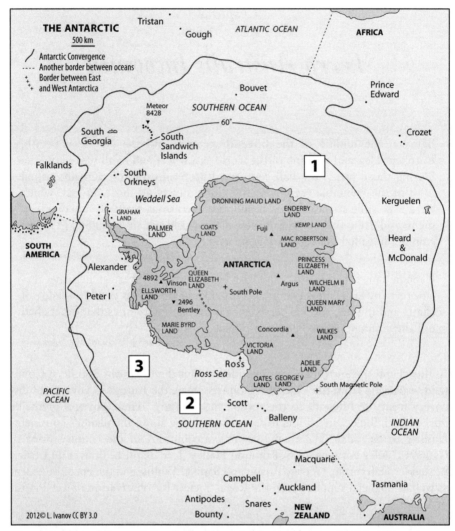

Figure 5. Map of Antarctica and the Antarctic Convergence, edited by the author to identify the approximate locations of Cook's crossings of the Circle on (1) 17 January 1773, (2) 21–25 December 1773, and (3) 26 January to 2 February 1774. The Antarctic Convergence is a wandering line (50° to 60° south) that marks a hydrological change in the Southern Ocean.

Antarctica's territory occupies 5,500,000 square miles (or 14,245,000 square kilometres). In contrast, the European continent covers 3,997,929 square miles (or 10,354,636 square kilometres). Australia's territory is approximately 54 per cent of the size of Antarctica. The Southern Continent is approximately 1.5 times the size of either the United States or Canada. Antarctica is the fifth largest continent, consisting of the largest mass sheet ice, containing 70 per cent of Earth's fresh water and 90 per cent of Earth's fresh water ice. No less than 99 per cent of the continent is covered by ice, which averages a thickness of a mile (1.6 kilometres).

The *Oxford English Dictionary* suggests that the word 'Antarctic' derives from the Greek *Anartkos* and the Latin *Antarticus*, appearing in Old English as *Aentauitk*. One source attributes the use of the word 'Antarctica' in modern English to the Scottish cartographer John George Bartholomew in the 1890s.[1] In James Cook's era the region of the South Pole was termed *Terra Australis Incognita*, the Unknown Southern Land, or often the Southern Continent or the Southern Land. The word 'Antarctica' literally means 'opposite the bear', the bear being the constellation Ursa Major seen in the northern sky over the Arctic Circle. 'Arctic' is from the Greek *Arktos*, meaning bear (or Pole Star). 'Antarctica' is therefore the opposite (antipode) of 'Arctic'.

Speculation about *Terra Australis Incognita*

From Aristotle to the Eighteenth Century

Speculation about Antarctica, the unknown southern continent, dates back at least as far as Aristotle (384–322 BC). He concluded that the Earth was a sphere, with land masses at both the North and South Poles which served to counterbalance each other. Mathematicians, astronomers, geographers and others offered various theories as well as experiments to measure or depict maps of Earth, with occasional reference to Antarctica, or *Terra Australis*. Several centuries after Aristotle, the ancient world's greatest geographer, Claudius Ptolemaeus (or Ptolemy, *c.*90–168 AD), a Roman citizen of Egypt, compiled his *Geographica*. His maps introduced concepts of latitude and longitude as well as a spherical shape for the Earth. Ptolemy's geographical knowledge surpassed medieval cartographers until rediscovery of his work after 1400.[2]

Subsequent maps into the fifteenth century were often additions or elaborations on Ptolemy's maps. For example, the *Map of the Known World* published by Nicholas Germanicus (*c.*1480) shows a vast 'white space' at the bottom of the map, the usual map-maker's depiction of unknown lands that were suspected to exist. Published twelve years before Columbus's first voyage, obviously the western hemisphere is not depicted. This late fifteenth-century map is based on Ptolemy, and his map ended at the Equator, with everything else as *terra incognita*.[3]

The cautious voyages of exploration began to give more specific shape to maps and an accurate understanding of the Earth. These voyages provided additional information to cartographers whose maps depicted continents with accurate detail recognizable today. A half-century ago historian J.H. Parry explained that

> Between the middle of the fifteenth century and the late seventeenth, Europeans learned to think of the world as a whole and of all seas as one ... During those two and a half centuries European explorers actually visited most of the habitable regions of the globe; nearly all those, in fact, which were accessible by sea. They found vast territories formerly unknown to them, and drew the rough outlines of the world which we know. [This is]

commonly called the Age of Discovery ... The seaman, exploring uncharted seas, needed the help of learned men, especially men learned in mathematics, astronomy and physical science; also, though this came later, in medical science ...[4]

These European 'Voyages of Discovery' over several centuries paved the way for Cook's exploration and ultimately his conclusions about *Terra Australis Incognita*. The brief sketch that follows provides only a few examples of exploration as navigators began to sail out of the sight of land and penetrate regions thought by some to be uninhabitable or inhabited by monsters.

Prince Henry the Navigator (1394–1460), from his 'school of navigation' at Sagres, encouraged Portuguese mariners to cautiously explore the Atlantic along the African coast, gradually going further south of Cape Bojador, presumed to be the furthest point south that navigators could safely sail. Early Portuguese mariners began to understand Atlantic Ocean currents and prevailing winds. These navigators sailed vessels called caravels, manoeuvrable ships with broad bows, high sterns and three to four masts. These ships, historian Ian Cameron writes, 'like the Phoenician galleys of old could make headway against an adverse combination of wind and sea [because] ... they have a unique capacity for sailing against the wind'.[5]

Bartholomeu Dias (*c.* 1450–1500) rounded the Cape of Good Hope in 1488. This led to crossing the Indian Ocean and reaching points further east in the fabled Spice Islands. These voyages eventually impacted the old overland Spice Route from Asia to ports in the Levant or at Constantinople and, in the long run, reduced the economic importance of Mediterranean commercial centres such as Venice. In 1500 the Portuguese arrived in Brazil.[6] Ferdinand Magellan (1480–1521), a Portuguese navigator who sailed for Charles V's Spain, completed the first circumnavigation of the globe in 1521. Instead of 'rounding Cape Horn', Magellan sailed through the island waterways of southern Chile, a route known as the 'Strait of Magellan'.

The Portuguese were followed by Spanish, Dutch, French and English navigators in subsequent centuries. These voyages gradually added to Western Europe's navigational knowledge. Some of the sixteenth- and seventeenth-century navigators attempted to discover *Terra Australis* but few of their voyages penetrated the Southern Ocean. Spanish navigators turned the Pacific Ocean into a 'Spanish Lake', creating a vast empire in the western hemisphere. The Spanish 'treasure fleet' transported vast sums of silver and gold to Madrid.

Slowly and cautiously the ocean's boundaries were expanded outwards by navigation and exploration. One example of the evolving image of the continents is shown in the *c.*1570 *Typus Orbis Terrarum*, 'Map of the Entire World,' by Abraham Ortelius. The citation from Cicero could be roughly translated as 'it is a great victory in the affairs of men to be able to view the whole world for all eternity'. As was the case with the Germanicus map, white spaces are used for territory that was unknown and unexplored. It is noteworthy that the map assumes Tierra del Fuego touches the Southern Continent and that Antarctica extends far into the Southern Pacific and Southern Atlantic, nearly reaching the Spice Islands.

The English circumnavigator Francis Drake (*c.* 1540–1596) sought to reach the Pacific via the Strait of Magellan. There is some uncertainty as to the distance his ship, *Golden Hind*, was blown south from the Strait of Magellan in 1578, although later his name was applied to the 'Drake Passage', the body of water connecting the Pacific and Atlantic Oceans and separating Antarctica from Tierra del Fuego. In 1579 Drake also assigned the name 'New Albion' to the coastline of North America, perhaps the northern part of California near Point Reyes in San Francisco Bay. It was to New Albion that Cook sailed after departing from his first visit to Hawai'i in 1778. English navigators explored the Pacific and North Atlantic coasts of America, as did French navigators contemporary with James Cook. Cook's paths crossed the wake of earlier Pacific voyagers. His extensive travels and maps of portions of the Pacific led to the modern understanding of the vast ocean (*see* map of Cook's three voyages, p. xiv).

Spanish navigators also plied the North Pacific waters before Cook, as well as establishing claims to portions of the North American coast also charted and explored by Cook in 1778. Initially the Portuguese and Spanish, and later the Dutch and English, contended for control of the Spice Islands (Moluccas). Russian fur traders penetrated the Alaskan coast, setting up trading posts that Cook encountered. The 1770s to the 1790s were intense years of Spanish exploration of the North American Coast from Northern California to Prince William Sound (at 61° north latitude). Portugal controlled Brazil, while Spain took charge of the remainder of South and Central America and the Pacific Coast of what later became the United States.

Dutch navigators similarly sailed the Pacific, establishing commercial posts in Asia through the Dutch East India Company and also establishing a route around Cape Horn. William Schouten (*c.*1567–1625) and Jacob Le Maire (*c.*1585–1616) sailed from Amsterdam and rounded Cape Horn in 1615, the first Europeans to do so. Le Maire's name is given to the strait separating Staten Island from Tierra del Fuego, which Cook navigated with difficulty in January 1769. Schouten and Le Maire also gave Staten Island its name. Schouten and Le Maire's voyage also proved that the Southern Continent was not attached to Tierra del Fuego. Jacob Roggeveen (1659–1729) passed through the Strait of Le Maire and sailed to 60° south (as did Cook in 1769). He was the first European to land on Easter Island (Rapa Nui), which Cook visited in 1774.

French navigators sailed the Pacific contemporary with James Cook. Among these was Louis Antoine de Bougainville (1729–1811), who sailed in the Pacific and to the sub-Antarctic Falkland Islands, establishing Port Louis on West Falkland in 1764. Commodore John Byron in *Dolphin* established a British settlement, Port Egmont, on East Falkland in 1765. Jean-Francois-Marie Surville (1717–1770) explored the Solomon Islands and New Zealand. Jean-Francois de la Pérouse (1741–1788) explored a huge swathe of ocean around Australia, New

Zealand, the Arctic, the South Pacific, East Asia and Russia before disappearing, perhaps lost at sea between the east coast of Australia and the Solomon Islands. Marc-Joseph Marion du Fresne (1724–1772) and his next-in-command Julien-Marie Crozet (1728–1780) discovered sub-Antarctic islands named after Crozet, who visited Cook at the Cape of Good Hope to discuss his discovery, and which Cook sighted and sailed past in 1776. In 1772 Yves-Joseph Kerguelen-Trémarec (1734–1797) discovered the sub-Antarctic archipelago that bears his name, said to be 'the France of the South', visited by Cook in 1776 to determine its usefulness for supplies of wood and water during extended sea voyages (Chapter 13).

By the eighteenth century knowledge from these earlier voyages defined the Earth as never before. However, the Unknown Southern Continent remained elusive. Up to this point the voyages had piece by piece narrowed the options for where Antarctica might be, but its exact location and geographical features remained unknown. As we will see, Captain Cook penetrated further south into the Southern Ocean than did previous voyagers or his contemporaries (Chapters 5, 8, 9).

Eighteenth-Century Exploration and Ideas about the Unknown Southern Continent

For those who gave serious thought to the existence of *Terra Australis Incognita*, the continent was a mystery in need of resolution. Historian Daniel J. Boorstin terms earlier attempts to locate the Southern Continent, as well as Cook's voyages, as 'negative discovery', writing,

> to prove that some mythical entity really did not exist was far more exacting and more exhausting than to succeed in finding a known objective … So long as the existence and precise location of the Great South Land were legendary, the explorer had to scour all conceivable places, and in fact would have to circumnavigate the globe, before he dared assert that it would never be discovered.
>
> Captain James Cook was suited to be the world's greatest negative discoverer – by his restless energy, his organizing ability, his vast knowledge of charts and the sea, and his persistence in trying possibilities that others had not the courage or the vigour to pursue.[7]

Eighteenth-century voyages of discovery were intertwined with the desire for increased scientific knowledge but were also tied to political, imperial and commercial interests. These voyages greatly expanded geographical knowledge of the planet. For England, at the beginning of the century, the voyages of Edmund Halley (South Atlantic) and William Dampier (circumnavigation, New Holland) spurred interest in seeking Antarctica. At the end of the century, and after Captain Cook's travels, the voyages of Matthew Flinders (1774–1814) and George Bass (1771–1803) proved Australia was an island-continent. By the end of the eighteenth century historian Rob Ilffle comments, 'navigators and naturalists had at their disposal instruments that were undreamed of a hundred years earlier, capable of measuring phenomena of which their forebears were equally un-aware'.[8] It is in this era that James Cook narrowed the options to put Antarctica into accurate geographical context.

Contributions by Edmund Halley and Understanding the Antarctic Convergence

The astronomer, mathematician, cartographer, geographer, inventor and poly-math Edmund Halley (1656–1742) is best known for the comet that bears his name, which can be seen from Earth approximately every seventy-five years, with the next observation in 2061. He also predicted the 1761 and 1769 Transits of Venus. Halley became a sailor and navigator, venturing into the far southern Atlantic. The purpose of his first voyage in 1698–1699 was to evaluate 'variations in the compass' (that is, the magnetic declination of the compass as a ship moves closer to one of the Poles). He reached the coast of Brazil and then returned to England. Halley's second voyage in *Paramore* began in 1699 with the purpose of studying compass variations and searching for land between the Strait of Magellan and the Cape of Good Hope between 50° and 55° south latitude.

Paramore departed from Rio de Janeiro in late December for the Southern Ocean, reaching 50° south. At this point Halley entered the 'Antarctic Conver-gence', a wandering line which encircles Antarctica at 50° to 60° south latitude (Figure 5). The Convergence represents a different nautical environment within the Southern Ocean; it is the point at which 'the near-freezing surface waters sur-rounding the continent slip below the warmer waters of the sub-Antarctic'; as well as being of different temperature, the waters are also of different salinity. It is a harsh and hostile environment of cold, wind, snow, mist, fog and floating ice, as well as icebergs and, sometimes, monster waves. Author and sailor Alan Gurney writes that its emblematic bird is the Wandering Albatross, often sighted during Cook's voyages.[9]

Halley's voyage encountered all of the oceanic conditions enumerated above and reached its furthest south at 52.5° south latitude and 35° west longitude. The voyage also sighted the Tristan da Cunha Islands, the Cape of Good Hope, St Helena, Brazil's west coast, the West Indies, Bermuda and Newfoundland, returning to England in September 1700. Halley's voyage extended from 52° south to 52° north latitude.

Halley's task was to plot longitude according to magnetic variation. His *General Chart of the Variation of the Compass* (1701) included curved lines which joined points of equal magnetic variation, later called Halleyan Lines, today known as isolines. In 1703 Halley developed a chart to cover not only the Atlantic but the entire world. He was appointed Astronomer Royal in 1720 and con-tributed to the development of navigational instruments at Greenwich, such as the transit and quadrant.[10]

Contributions by Jean-Baptise Charles Bouvet de Lozier

Lieutenant Bouvet (1705–1786) was in the service of the French East India Company and led an expedition to the South Atlantic in *Aigle* and *Marie*. On

1 January 1739 he sighted an island which he suggested might be the tip of *Terra Australis Incognita*. The land was ice-capped and shrouded in fog. Bouvet held his ships off the island cape for ten days but was unable to land. Because the date on which it was sighted is traditionally the Christian Feast of Christ's Circumcision, he named the location 'Cape Circumcision'. On his return to France he wrote to the French East India Company's directors, describing sailing 'beyond the Convergence':

> I am sorry to inform you that the *Terres Australes* are much further from the Pole than hitherto believed and completely unsuitable as a staging post for vessels en route to the Indies. We have sailed 1,200–1,500 leagues [3,600–4,500 miles/5,795–7,240km] in unknown waters and for seventy days encountered almost continuous fog. We were forty days among the icebergs and we had hail and snow almost every day. The cold was severe for men accustomed to a warmer climate. They were badly clothed and had no means of drying their bedding. Many suffered from chilblains but they had to keep working. I saw sailors crying with cold as they hauled in the sounding line. To alleviate the men's discomfort I distributed blankets, hats, shoes, old clothes … and I opened two kegs of brandy to issue to the crew. The dangers were as great as the discomforts. For more than two months we had been in uncharted waters. We had very little daylight and there were few times when we weren't encountering some kind of risk … It was not the officers and crew who failed in their mission, but rather the mission that failed them.[11]

Bouvet recorded 54° 00′ south and 11° 20′ east longitude as the Cape's location. Cook searched for Cape Circumcision several times during the second voyage but missed it by about 3° (*see* especially Chapters 5 and 11). Cape Circumcision is now known as Bouvet Island (*Bouvetøya*), and is a possession of Norway. The volcanic, ice-covered island is 19 square miles (49 square kilometres) in total size. A British whaling expedition confirmed its location in 1808. Bouvet's coordinates were not correct (it is actually located at 54° 25.8′ south latitude and 3° 22′ east longitude). One of the most remote of the Earth's islands, it lies approximately 1,100 miles (1,770km) from Antarctica and 1,600 miles (2,575km) from the Cape of Good Hope.

The Contributions of Alexander Dalrymple

For James Cook, Alexander Dalrymple's theories about *Terra Australis Incognita* shaped the goals for the first and second voyages. Dalrymple (1737–1808) began service at Madras with the British East India Company in 1752 and established a career as a geographer and hydrographer. (Hydrography is the study, description, measurement and mapping of the oceans, especially for navigation.) He researched libraries for geographic and other information about the Pacific, based on voyages made by Portuguese, Spanish and Dutch navigators. In 1756 Dalrymple was elected a Fellow of the Royal Society. He published *A Historical Collection of the Several Voyages and Discoveries in the South Pacific Ocean* (two volumes, 1770–1771).[12] Cook's voyages were to serve as a corrective to Dalrymple's theories, much to the hydrographer's distress.

Dalrymple asserted that the Southern Continent had been seen on its west side by Abel Tasman (1642) and on its east side by Juan Fernandes and unnamed others a half century earlier. Therefore, New Zealand was the tip of the Southern Continent. He asserted that the Southern Continent's location was between 40° and 64° south latitude. Its actual discovery remained to be realized. Dalrymple suggested that the many islands in the Southern Pacific were 'swarming with people' and another continent would be located extending from 30° south to the Pole. This supposed territory was beyond the charter of the East India Company. He argued for its exploration in an era when the New England colonies were complaining about taxes and the demands of Parliament, suggesting that the grievances of 2 million North American colonists could be offset by developing commerce with 50 million inhabitants of the South Seas and the Southern Continent. Dalrymple held that the unknown continent covered 100 degrees of longitude in 40° south latitude (4,596 geographic miles). Britain would be rewarded: 'the scraps from this table would be sufficient to maintain the power, dominion and sovereignty of Britain by employing all of its manufacturers and ships'. Dalrymple's analysis concluded with a plea that Britain seize the opportunity to locate and explore the lands to the south, writing, 'it demands the attention of every Englishman, for it may be justly said, that the *being* of the British Empire rests on our insular location and our powerful navy. Were any of our competitors to gain the superiority at sea, the advantages of the first would be lost.' Other nations should not be permitted to seize the advantage by locating and exploring these new lands, or to 'extend their navigation to remote parts, and to gain such an accession of commerce and power as the discovery of a New World would afford … we may then cry, "Time was … but that time is past", and in vain lament the ignorance or worthlessness of ministers who were wanting in pursuing the true interests of their country'.

Prior to Cook's first voyage, Dalrymple expressed interest in leading the expedition to observe the Transit of Venus, but he demanded that he be given control over navigation, even though he was not a Royal Navy officer. The Admiralty refused, causing Dalrymple's subsequent resentment of this decision.[13] Dalrymple argued that exploration demanded action immediately. This is why he vigorously advocated for a voyage to locate *Terra Australis Incognita* and why he was disappointed with the results from Cook's first voyage when it was not located.[14] Cook clearly proved that New Zealand was not part of *Terra Australis*. However, Dalrymple thought that Cook did not persevere in attempting to locate the Southern Continent, returning from the first voyage as ignorant as when he set out. As we will see (Chapters 5–11), Cook addressed Dalrymple's complaints during the second voyage. *Resolution*'s circumnavigation of Antarctica showed there was no land 'swarming with people' to engage in commerce; in Cook's words, it was a land of excessive cold not accessible through a navigable sea.

Cook also pursued Dalrymple's chart and opinions about a 'Gulf of San Sebastian', south of Tierra del Fuego, as a possible path to Antarctica. Cook detected no land in Dalrymple's 'Gulf' and sailed to the east and north, eventually discovering South Georgia and the South Sandwich Islands (Chapter 11). Had he continued southwards, Cook likely would have reached the ice barrier of the Weddell Sea or the Antarctic Peninsula. Dalrymple's theories pointed in the correct general direction, but it was navigators and whalers who charted the path to Antarctica in the early nineteenth century (Chapter 16).

Over the following two decades, Dalrymple continued in service with the East India Company and in 1795 was appointed as the Admiralty's first hydrographer. Citing his contributions to marine cartography and pursuit of economic interests, Dalrymple's entry in the Australian Dictionary of National Biography concludes,

> that [Dalrymple] should be remembered as one who engaged in constant disputes with the East India Co. and the Admiralty, who pursued a foolish and unnecessary vendetta against Cook and who supported erroneous geographical theories is perhaps inevitable; although the latter often reflected skilful deduction, Dalrymple invariably postulated them with a dogmatism unjustified by the evidence. He was over-bearing, opinionated and cantankerous, but also intelligent, enthusiastic and determined.[15]

The Contributions of George Anson, Philip Carteret and Samuel Wallis

In 1740–1744 Commodore George Anson (1697–1762) circumnavigated the globe during a voyage with the intention of disrupting the movement of Spanish silver to the Iberian Peninsula. However, Anson's Pacific travels (accompanied by a horrific loss of life due to scurvy, as well as ships) raised the possibility for future British opportunities in the Pacific, including locating the Northwest Passage.

Contemporaries of James Cook, Philip Carteret (1733–1796) and Samuel Wallis (1728–1795) sailed in a joint 1751 expedition to circumnavigate the globe, Carteret in *Swallow* and Wallis in *Dolphin*. (Charles Clerke, who sailed on Cook's three voyages, sailed with Wallis as a midshipman in 1764–1766). In passing from the South Atlantic to the Pacific, the ships became separated in the Strait of Magellan. Carteret sailed to such Pacific Ocean locations as Pitcairn Island, and a set of islands named after himself, as well as New Ireland and New Britain adjacent to Papua, New Guinea. Schouten and Bougainville also visited these islands. Wallis visited Tahiti (1766/1767), which he named King George Island, the act of possession being conducted by Tobias Furneaux, who sailed as captain in *Adventure* on Cook's second voyage. In addition to Tahiti, other nearby Society Islands received a visit from Wallis and *Dolphin*. The Admiralty provided Cook with Wallis's journal and charts when *Endeavour* sailed to Tahiti in 1768/1769.

The Contributions of the Royal Society

The Royal Society of London for Improving Natural Knowledge was founded on 28 November 1660 and received royal charters from Charles II in 1662/1663. It is the world's oldest learned society. It has a long and storied history, as evidenced by the historical description on its website:

> We published Isaac Newton's *Principia Mathematica* and Benjamin Franklin's kite experiment demonstrating the electrical nature of lightning. We backed James Cook's journey to Tahiti, reaching Australia and New Zealand, to track the Transit of Venus. We published the first report in English of inoculation against disease, approved Charles Babbage's Difference Engine, documented the eruption of Krakatoa and published Chadwick's detection of the neutron that would lead to the unleashing of the atom.
>
> The leading scientific lights of the past four centuries can all be found among the 8,000 Fellows elected to the Society to date. From Newton to Darwin to Einstein, Hawking and beyond, pioneers and paragons in their fields are elected by their peers.[16]

In the eighteenth century 'natural science' covered everything not made by human hands from the Earth to the Heavens. The full Royal Society name, 'for improving natural knowledge', fits an age when science was not compartmentalized or organized into sub-specialities as it is today. The science of 'botany' was just beginning to emerge as a field of scientific endeavour. 'Scientific observations' were often termed 'philosophical observations', the type of commentary J.R. Forster was assigned to prepare from the second voyage.

The Royal Society of London and the Society of Antiquaries (established 1751) are examples of groups, often with interlinked membership, that promoted the investigation, study and speculation about the ever-expanding world, in part stimulated by natural science and the voyages of navigation and discovery. Along with other learned societies that developed in the nineteenth century, historian William C. Lubenow suggests, 'these societies formed an institutional grid or matrix connecting those who would form, organize and dissolve knowledge'. They 'sought to advance critical scholarship and produce reliable information'. Lubenow suggests that one source for investigation was 'corralling knowledge' about 'the exotic world of empire'.[17] Therefore, it is only natural there was an important connection between the Society and James Cook's voyages. Similar societies developed in France, Berlin and other German states, St Petersburg, Stockholm, Italy, Scotland and Ireland. The London Royal Society met weekly. Its members presented accounts of their research, the results of which were often published in its journal, *Philosophical Transactions of the Royal Society*. The Royal Society funded research and, in the case of the Transit of Venus in 1761 and 1769, 'the largest scientific ventures of the eighteenth century',[18] and cooperated with other societies in gathering, sharing and publishing research in periodical journals.

Because the 1769 Transit of Venus would be the last opportunity to view it for the next 150 years, the Royal Society advocated that Britain should actively pursue its observation. The Crown agreed and the Admiralty was charged with providing a ship and a captain. The Royal Society contributed to the cost of

Cook's voyage by providing funds for scientific equipment to observe the Transit of Venus. Joseph Banks paid the expenses for himself and seven others of the 'scientific party' to participate. At the conclusion of the voyage, Banks, who was elected a Fellow of the Royal Society in 1766 and served as its president for forty-two years (1778–1820), arranged artefacts from Cook's voyage for the British Museum, developed the botanical gardens at Kew and served as an informal botanical adviser to King George III. Although Cook's voyages were under the Admiralty's control, the Royal Society could be thought of as a co-sponsor. Banks saw to it that the best scientific instruments and current charts were available for the Transit, as well as antiscourbitics to experiment with in dealing with scurvy. He developed a portable greenhouse in *Endeavour* to protect botanical specimens from harm. The Society's prestige and publications brought knowledge about Cook's voyages and his scientific discoveries to a wide audience.

As a result of navigation and ideas pursued in the century preceding Cook's first voyage, the Admiralty drew upon the contributions of Edmund Halley, Jean-Baptiste le Bouvet, Alexander Dalrymple, George Anson and Samuel Wallis, as well as the encouragement and funding of the Royal Society, to set in motion plans to 'narrow the options' in seeking *Terra Australis Incognita*.

Chapter 3

Ships and the Ships' Companies

Your Lordships could not have made choice of two finer vessels in every respect for such a voyage, more especially the *Resolution* which has every quality I could wish to find in a ship.

Letter from Commander James Cook to the Admiralty, from the Cape of Good Hope, 19 November 1772 (*The Journals of Captain James Cook*)

This chapter is organized into four parts: (1) Captain Cook's ships; (2) what happened to the ships after Captain Cook's voyages; (3) the ship's company (who sailed with Cook); and (4) victualling – food, supplies and equipment.

Captain Cook's Ships

There are four vessels associated with the three voyages of Captain James Cook:

Endeavour, first voyage, 1768–1771
Resolution and *Adventure*, second voyage, 1772–1775
Resolution and *Discovery*, third voyage, 1776–1779/1780

Endeavour

In 1768 the Admiralty purchased a three-year-old east coast collier, *Earl of Pembroke*, at a cost of £2,840.10*s*. Renamed *Endeavour*, technically it was a 'bark', which in Cook's day meant a vessel with a broad, flat bow and a shallow draught enabling it to sail in shallow water – an ideal feature for exploration and coastal sailing. It is sometimes referred to as a 'cat', likely due to its rigging. *Endeavour* was not a 'pretty' ship (*see* Plate 10). Captain Alan Villiers of the Australian Navy writes,

> The outstanding quality in a cat was her ugliness The fat, uncompromising bow, the graceless thrust of the straight cutwater [the forward edge of a ship's prow], the austerity of masts and the rigging, the stubby workhouse of a hull combined (in a harbour containing Indiamen, frigates, swift sloops and rakish brigs) to indicate, at first sight, a lowly vessel, a plough-hauler among the racehorses.[1]

All of Cook's ships were Whitby-built. They may not have been 'swift' or 'rakish', but they were functional for Cook's voyages.

Descriptions of *Endeavour* vary. For example, Alan Villiers uses the phrase 'cat-built bark' to describe it, while Karl Heinz Marquardt uses the term 'cat-rigged bark' for the vessel, suggesting that the features of the hull do not classify it as a cat-built bark.² A 'cat-rigged bark' is perhaps the best term. It contained fore, main and mizzen masts with square rigging, and its average speed was 3 knots.

Thomas Fishburn's shipyard at Whitby in Yorkshire had constructed *Earl of Pembroke*, originally for the coal trade from the northern coal fields to London, or other North Sea journeys, and it was the type of commercial vessel in which Cook sailed before he joined the Royal Navy. The ship contained adequate space for men and supplies, as well as the animals transported on Cook's voyages. If necessary, it could be careened on a beach (tipped on its side) and repaired, as happened in June 1770 after striking the Great Barrier Reef. It was a safe ship for exploring unknown waters.

Endeavour was taken to Deptford Dockyard, located on the River Thames in southeast London to be prepared for the first voyage. She was equipped with three cutters – a longboat, a pinnace and a yawl – and made ready for naval service. These small boats could be used, for example, to survey and sound a bay for potential anchorage, or to take the crew or others to the shore or, in the Antarctic, to collect floating ice to be melted in the 'coppers' for water used on board ship. Two other boats were added to the official complement of three boats: a skiff belonging to Joseph Banks and another small boat (which was lost in a gale on 1 September 1768) belonging to John Gathrey, the boatswain. Banks used his small boat (much like a row boat, and perhaps also equipped with a small sail) for botanizing or shooting birds and wildlife, when the seas allowed.

The standard complement of five anchors included three bower anchors, one stream anchor and one kedge anchor. Several spare anchors were stowed for possible future use. The kedge anchor was lost off Tierra del Fuego in 1768 (Chapter 4). Another anchor, the sheet anchor, was the largest carried on the ship; stowed at the furthest point forward on the starboard side, it was to be used only in cases of emergency (as at the Great Barrier Reef). The bower anchor is fixed at the ship's bow. The light stream anchor is used with a bower anchor to fix a ship's position in a narrow channel so that it is not moved by the tide. 'Kedging' means to move a ship in a particular direction. A kedge anchor, attached to a vessel by a long rope, is dropped in position, and sailors pull on the rope to move the ship to the location desired. The sheet anchor weighed 21cwt, the bower anchor 19cwt, the stream anchor 7.5cwt and the kedge anchor 3.5cwt. The British cwt (hundredweight) is 112lb. The bower anchor, for example, therefore weighed 2,128lb. Anchor cables were stored on the lower deck.

Carpenters installed gun ports. Cannon and weaponry were installed for signalling or protection on the high seas. *Endeavour* carried ten 4-pounder carriage guns. Six of these were mounted on the upper deck and the remainder stored in the ship's hold, to be brought up if required. The ship also carried twelve swivel guns, ten of which were mounted at various locations on the decks. The seams of the ship were caulked to prevent water seeping below from the deck. Four pumps were installed, which were used, for example, when *Endeavour* struck the Great Barrier Reef in June 1770 (Chapter 1).

A single layer of light planking was added to the ship's outside skin to protect it from borer worms, which are found in warm seas. Below the waterline *Endeavour* was painted with a mixture of tar, pitch and sulphur as further protection against worms. Pine varnish was applied to the vessel's sides above the waterline, as well as to the masts, spars and deck furniture. A new deck area was built in the hold for the crew's hammocks, as well as a quarterdeck for ten new cabins, the great cabin, storerooms, pantries, etc. Access to the general crew's quarters was through a fore hatch on the main deck, over which a watertight cover was affixed. The vessel's oven was located forward of the fore hatch staircase, outside the carpenter's and boatswain's cabins. It fitted into a 4×4.25ft space and was made of copper.

The ship was loaded with supplies sufficient for at least eighteen months.[3] During the voyage various foodstuffs, wine, other supplies, wood and water would need to be acquired, for example at the Portuguese island of Madeira, Tahiti or Queen Charlotte Sound, or other locations. A list of foodstuffs and supplies is included later in this chapter.

Resolution

Cook commanded *Resolution*, his favourite ship, on his second and third voyages. He wrote to the Admiralty from the Cape of Good Hope on 19 November 1772, stating: 'Your Lordships could not have made choice of two finer vessels in every respect for such a voyage, more especially the *Resolution*, which has every quality I could wish to find in a ship.'[4] *Resolution* is depicted in Plates 11–13.

For Cook's second voyage the Admiralty purchased two Whitby-built ships, *Marquis of Granby* and *Marquis of Rockingham*. According to Alan Villiers, these ships were not strictly speaking 'either barks or cats but shipped-rigged sloops of war'[5], built in 1770. The Admiralty renamed the two ships *Drake* and *Raleigh*. These names were changed again to *Resolution* and *Adventure* because it was thought *Drake/Raleigh* might unnecessarily offend the Spanish, who had previously sailed extensively in the Pacific and claimed a vast empire in North and South America. The purchase price for *Resolution* was £4,151. At 110ft 8in long and nearly 36ft wide, *Resolution* was about 15ft longer than *Endeavour* and 5ft wider.

It was planned initially that Joseph Banks and his party would join the second voyage. Banks convinced the Admiralty to make additional modifications to *Resolution* which made the ship top-heavy in sea trials. J.C. Beaglehole comments that the additional space to be occupied by Banks and his party represented 'a staggering amount of impedimenta'. These alterations, costing an additional £6,568, were unacceptable to Cook and the Admiralty ordered their removal. This incensed Banks and he refused to sail on the voyage. The cost of the alterations was therefore mostly wasted.[6]

After her return to England in 1775, *Resolution* was to be made ready at Deptford for what was publically described as another 'voyage to remote parts'. Although the third voyage sailed to the South Pacific, its primary (secret) purpose was a search for the Northwest Passage and therefore sailing in Arctic seas. As the third voyage unfolded, however, it was obvious the reconditioning work had been done in poor fashion. J.C. Beaglehole writes that an observer would be indignant that *Resolution*, a ship proudly built in Whitby, 'strong enough to resist the battering of so many Antarctic seas and sub-tropical storms, should begin to leak like a sieve when she was hardly out of the Channel on a new voyage, simply because her caulking had been scamped [careless, inadequate]'. On 16 August 1776 Cook recorded in his journal:

> We had however the Mortification to find the Ship exceeding leaky in all her upper works, the hot and dry weather we had just past through had opened her Seams, which had been badly Caulked at first, so wide that they admitted the rain Water through as it fell and there was hardly a Man that could lie dry in his bed; the officers in the gunroom were all driven out of their cabbins by the Water that came thro' the sides. The sails in the Sail rooms got wet and before we had weather to dry them, many of them were quite ruined and occasioned a great expense of Canvas & time to make them in some degree serviceable. This complaint of our sail room we experienced on my late Voyage and was represented to the yard officers who undertook to remove it, but it did not appear to me that any thing had been done that could answer that end. To repair these defects the Caulkers were set to work as soon as we got into fair settled Weather, to caulk the Decks and inside Weather works of the Ship, for I would not trust them over the side while at sea.

Caulking and other repairs to Cook's vessels continued throughout the voyages, and tasks that were routine requirements were made more difficult by inadequate preparations for the voyages prior to initial sailing.

Adventure
Adventure served as the second ship for Cook's second voyage. The Admiralty decided to send two ships on the second voyage so that if one encountered difficulty, as *Endeavour* had done at the Great Barrier Reef in June 1770, the other ship could render assistance. Although a sound idea in theory, *Resolution* and *Adventure* became separated in a thick Antarctic fog in February 1773 (Chapter 6). By plan, after a three-day search, *Adventure* sailed for New Zealand while *Resolution* continued its circumnavigation of the Southern Continent. The ships joined up in New Zealand but separated again in stormy seas off the Cook Strait in October/November 1773 (Chapter 7). *Adventure* returned to England a year earlier than *Resolution*. Therefore, after the first crossing of the Circle in January 1773, *Resolution* sailed alone during exploration of the Antarctic and sub-Antarctic.

The Admiralty paid £2,103 for *Adventure* and placed the ship under the command of Captain Tobias Furneaux, who had sailed to the South Pacific, including Tahiti, with Captain Wallis in *Dolphin* in 1767, and was one of the first captains to sail a ship around the world from west to east and east to west. Furneaux was

Figure 6. Comparisons of ships on Cook's three voyages, adapted from information in J.C. Beaglehole, introductory material to *The Journals of Captain James Cook*, vols. 1–3. See also 'ships' at the Captain Cook Society website (www.captaincooksociety.com). For *Endeavour* see also K.H. Marquardt, *Anatomy of the Ship, Captain Cook's Endeavour*. Ships' company totals do not include marines or supernumeraries.

	Endeavour	*Resolution*	*Adventure*	*Discovery*
Tons	367	462	340	298
Lower Deck (length)	98'	110' 8"	97' 3"	91' 5"
Beam (width)	29' 3"	35' 5.5"	28' 4.25"	27' 5"
Hold (height)	11' 4"	13' 4.5"	12' 8.75"	11' 5"
Initial Cost	£2,841	£4,151	£2,103	£2,415
Whitby Shipyard	T. Fishburn	T. Fishburn	T. Fishburn	T. Fishburn
Ship's Company	94	112/112	80	69

subordinate to Cook on the second voyage. Later, Furneaux commanded a Royal Navy ship during the American War of Independence. *Adventure* was a smaller ship than *Resolution*, a little over 97ft in length and 28ft wide. The Woolwich naval dock made *Adventure* ready for the second voyage.

Discovery
Resolution sailed on Cook's third voyage, along with a new vessel, *Discovery*. She was another Whitby-built collier constructed by Fishburn, originally named *Diligence*. It cost the Admiralty £1,865 for the hull and another £550 for alterations. *Discovery* was the smallest of Cook's four ships, with a lower deck of just over 91ft long and a width of just over 27ft. An extra layer of planking was applied to *Discovery*'s outer hull as protection against borer worms in warm climates but there was no extra protection for either vessel against the dangers from ice. *Discovery* had three masts and, along with *Resolution*, was classified as a sloop.[7] A John Webber painting of *Resolution* and *Discovery* at Queen Charlotte Sound is shown in Plate 14.

What Happened to the Ships after Captain Cook's Voyages?
Obscure, uncertain or contradictory information surrounds the fate of the ships following their return to England from the first, second and third voyages.

Endeavour
After reaching home, *Endeavour* was renamed *Lord Sandwich*. Used as a store ship, it made the journey to the Falkland Islands three times. It may have returned to the North Sea coastal trade or served as a whaling vessel. It is now believed that she was scuttled in 1778, along with a dozen British naval vessels, at the entrance to the outer harbour and naval base at Newport (Rhode Island) to prevent French ships from entering the naval base during the American War of Independence.

The Rhode Island Marine Archaeology Project (RIMAP) is currently conducting a detailed search for the vessel's final resting place. These harbour sites have been damaged over time by activities such as dredging or bridge construction, while thieves and scavengers removed portions of the ships. After 240-plus years these scuttled ships now consist largely of scattered debris piles. These are being systematically examined by marine archaeologists to determine which debris is associated with *Endeavour*. The lower decks of all these ships are buried in the harbour floor and covered with silt. To some degree, silt and the ship's ballast will protect the ship's remaining wooden timbers from oxygen and disturbance, thereby preventing additional deterioration. Exposure to oxygen will continue the deterioration process so whatever carbon-based items are recovered must be protected. The site is now protected by state law and RIMAP is officially designated to conduct research in the 2 square mile study area.[8] As in the Colonial era, Newport today remains a United States naval base. By late 2018 RIMAP concluded it had narrowed the search for *Endeavour* to one of two remaining possibilities after originally considering other locations in Narragansett Bay.

A replica of *Endeavour* was launched in 1993 with Sydney serving as the home port, adjacent to the Australian National Maritime Museum. It was designed to the specifications of the original *Endeavour* but with modern navigational features. There is an annual schedule of sailings open to public participation.[9] A second *Endeavour* replica was relocated from Stockton to Whitby in England in 2018. It features 'The Endeavour Experience', a series of educational attractions on the main and lower decks.[10] *Endeavour*'s name also lives on in the name for United States Orbiter Vehicle 105 (OV–105), better known as the Space Shuttle *Endeavour* (STS-49). Launched in May 1992, the Space Shuttle *Endeavour* concluded its 25th and final mission to the International Space Station in May 2011 and is now on display at the California Science Centre.[11] The United States Postal Service commemorated *Endeavour* on an Express Mail stamp issued on 4 August 1995. Postage stamps issued by many nations have depicted all of Cook's ships, but none more than *Endeavour*. 'Endeavour' also serves as the first name of Colin Dexter's fictional character in the Oxford-based Inspector Morse detective series, so-named because of his fictional father's life-long fascination with Captain James Cook, a detail revealed in the television series' penultimate episode.

Resolution

After the third voyage, *Resolution* probably served as a transport ship and sailed to the East Indies, where it may have been lost in a hurricane. In any event, it disappears from the records. It may have served as a coal hulk in Rio de Janeiro, but that is unconfirmed, as are more speculative rumours that it may have ended up at Newport, where it was eventually broken up – a somewhat inauspicious end to Cook's favourite sloop.

Adventure

At the conclusion of the voyage, *Adventure* returned to the east coast trade. She also carried goods from England to Canada and was wrecked in dangerous waters on the St Lawrence River in 1811.

Discovery

After her return to England in 1780, *Discovery* was previously thought to have served as a temporary hulk for prisoners awaiting transportation to Botany Bay. It is now believed that in fact it was allowed to 'rot in the mud' at Deptford Dockyard, before being taken to the Chatham Dockyards and broken up in 1797.[12]

The Ship's Company – Who Sailed with Captain Cook?

When *Endeavour* sailed on 30 July 1768 there were 85 men on the ship's muster rolls. In addition, 12 marines were placed on the ship by the Admiralty and 12 supernumeraries (astronomer, natural scientists and servants) also travelled on the first voyage. Replacements were brought in during the voyage to take the place of crew members who died or were lost. Several Polynesians were taken on board at Tahiti to act as guides among the South Pacific islands in 1769. Natural scientist Anders Sparrman joined the second voyage at the Cape of Good Hope in November 1772.

A partial list of officers assigned to various positions during Cook's three voyages is summarized in Figure 7. An explanation of the succession of captains on the third voyage is in order. After Captain Cook died in Hawaii on 14 February 1779, he was first replaced in *Resolution* by Charles Clerke. However, Clerke, suffering from the later stages of tuberculosis, died on the 1779 return to the Arctic and was replaced by John Gore, James King then taking charge of *Discovery*.

Duties on board varied. Classifications of various positions on board one of Cook's vessels is perhaps best observed in the complement of 'Officers & Men' for *Resolution* at the start of the second voyage (Figure 7). Similar personnel classifications are found in varying numbers in *Endeavour*, *Adventure* and *Discovery*.

Responsibilities associated with positions in the above table are generally understood, but a few may require explanation. The master was responsible for a ship's navigation, under the captain's direction, a position similar in my opinion to a chief operations officer in a business organization. Prior to the voyage, the master was to ensure the ship was fitted out for the voyage. This meant, for example, ensuring the quality of stores loaded onboard as well as safely stowing these supplies, ensuring the ship's ballast was loaded properly and maintained in a 'sweet' (fresh) condition, ensuring the rigging was in proper condition and that 'compasses, glasses, log and lead lines be preserved in good order'. Once under way, 'at convenient opportunities' he was to see that cables were 'well coiled' and kept wet with sea water, if necessary. The master was to keep watch on the coastline and record observations for future navigation along with other information about the vessel in a log book. He was to ensure 'a good lookout' was posted. His 'exact and perfect journal' was to be maintained so that stores and provisions were recorded, both those coming into the ship and those leaving the storeroom and he had to ensure that all records were accurate, signing no account unless he had verified its accuracy.[13] This level of detail is provided for the role of master because it was the master's examination that Cook passed on 29 June 1757, leading to his advancement within the Royal Navy. Moreover, during my research

Figure 7. Partial list of ranks of officers on Cook's three voyages, adapted from information on the Captain Cook Society website (www.captaincooksociety.com/the-crew). The information is also located in the appendices to the three volumes of Cook's journals edited by J.C. Beaglehole, in sections titled, 'The Ships' Company'.

	Endeavour	Resolution (1)	Adventure	Resolution (2)	Discovery
Captain	James Cook	James Cook	Tobias Furneaux	James Cook Charles Clerke John Gore	Charles Clerke John Gore James King
Lieutenants	Zachary Hicks John Gore	Robert Cooper Richard Pickersgill Charles Clerke	Arthur Kempe James Burney	James King John Gore John Williamson William Harvey James Burney	James Burney John Rickman
Master	Robert Molyneux	Joseph Gilbert	Peter Fanin	William Bligh	Thomas Edgar
Midshipmen	Charles Clerke William Harvey James Magra Patrick Saunders John Bootie Jonathan Monkhouse	James Colnet William Harvey Isaac Manley Thomas Willis Joseph Price Charles Loggie	Thomas Woodhouse Love Constable Samuel Kemp George Morey Henry Lightfoot James Lambrecht	William Charlton Richard Hergest William Midd James Trevenen William Shuttleworth John Hatley John Watts James Ward	Edward Riou George Vancouver Alexander Mouat John Martin William Harvey
Surgeon	William Monkhouse	James Patton	Thomas Andrews	William Anderson John Law	John Law David Samwell

I found the 'master's log' is often useful for historians in understanding unique or interesting occurrences during a voyage.

If a ship's master was in charge of operations, lieutenants were responsible for order. They rotated watches and were to muster the crew to ensure readiness for duty, maintain order between the decks and ensure that no one departed the ship without their knowledge. When a master was not on duty, a lieutenant ensured smooth operation of the ship, as Lieutenant Clerke did during the 4/5 February 1775 'milkish sea' episode (Chapter 14). Lieutenants identified seamen who misbehaved or failed to maintain discipline, made sure that people were at their posts in time of danger and were also responsible for small arms, and instructing seamen in their use. Lieutenants were required to keep a journal to be given to the Admiralty at the end of the voyage.[14] I have found that lieutenants' log books are often as useful to the historian as those kept by ships' masters.

In the eighteenth century a midshipman was a commissioned junior rank officer. The person in charge of a vessel's crew and equipment was a boatswain, a warranted petty officer, the oldest rank in the Royal Navy. The gunner was responsible for the cannon and weaponry on a ship, with an armourer responsible for the supply of and repairs to weapons, such as muskets. The master-at-arms was responsible for discipline and order, assisted by a corporal-at-arms. The quartermaster was responsible for a vessel's supplies and provisions. The largest group on the voyage was, of course, able-bodied seamen, often listed as 'AB' in journals or logs and collectively referred to as 'The People' in Cook's journals. Young boys made up a small part of any Royal Navy crew, undergoing training in navigation.

Figure 8. Ship's Company in *Resolution*, second voyage, adapted from information in J.C. Beaglehole, editor, *The Journals of Captain James Cook*, vol. 2, pp. 11–12.

Captain	1	Sail Maker's Mates	1
Lieutenants	3	Armourer	1
Master	1	Armourer's Mate	1
Master's Mates	3	Cook	1
Midshipman	6	Cook's Mate	1
Boatswain	1	Captain's Clerk	1
Boatswain's Mates	3	Quarter Masters	6
Gunner	1	Able Seamen and Acting Midshipmen	45
Gunner's Mates	2	*Subtotal*	92
Surgeon	1	Marine – Lieutenant	1
Surgeon's Mates	2	Marine – Serjeant	1
Carpenter	1	Marine – Corporals	2
Carpenter's Mates	3	Marine – Drummer	1
Carpenter's Crew	4	Marine – Private	15
Master at Arms	1	*Subtotal*	20
Corporal at Arms	1		
Sail Maker	1	Total Complement	112

The vessels also carried animals, such as sheep, pigs, goats and chickens, as a source of meat, eggs or milk.[15] One goat, originally a gift from Joseph Banks, is said to have circumnavigated the world twice, once with Captain Samuel Walls in *Dolphin* (1766–1768) and once in *Endeavour* with Cook,[16] before ending its days in Cook's garden. Cattle transported during the third voyage were intended to be given as gifts to native chiefs.

A variety of other persons travelled on Cook's voyages, including astronomers, natural scientists, artists and their servants, under the collective name 'super-numeraries'.

First Voyage Supernumeraries, 1768–1771

Cook's first voyage included a dozen supernumeraries, including servants. Natural scientists included Joseph Banks (1744–1820), the son of a wealthy country squire, knighted in 1781. He studied at Eton and then Christ Church, Oxford, focusing on natural history, especially botany, in an era prior to the emergence of academic departments of botany or zoology and other sub-specialties. Banks sailed to Newfoundland and Labrador in 1766, on Cook's first voyage and, when his renovations to *Resolution* were rejected by Cook and the Admiralty, he sailed to Iceland and western Scotland in 1772. He was elected a Fellow of the Royal Society and served as its president for forty-two years (1778–1820). Family wealth enabled Banks to serve as a patron of natural history and science. He was instrumental in the development of Kew Gardens and in organizing artefacts brought back from Cook's first voyage for the British Museum. His journal is a useful reference for Cook's first voyage. Because of his position in society, the first voyage was seen by the some of the public as 'Mr Banks' Voyage' due to his encouragement of personal publicity after his return to London.

Other naturalists on the first voyage included Daniel Solander (1733–1782). Born in Sweden, he was a pupil of Karl Linnaeus (1707–1778) who developed a classification system for plants and animals. Solander was a close associate of Joseph Banks, a Fellow of the Royal Society and Keeper of the Natural History Department at the British Museum. A third naturalist was Herman Spöring (1733–1771), born in Finland, then part of Sweden. He studied medicine but was an amateur natural scientist who made his way to London, meeting Daniel Solander in approximately 1755 and subsequently serving as his assistant. Spöring was responsible for scientific equipment during the first voyage. He died in Batavia (Jakarta), as did his servant, from dysentery and associated medical problems while *Endeavour* was at that port for repairs after colliding with the Great Barrier Reef in June 1770.

Charles Green (1735–1771) served as the astronomer in *Endeavour*. A son of a Yorkshire farmer (as was Cook), Green served as an assistant to the Astronomer Royal (Nevil Maskelyne) and was assigned by the Royal Society to serve in *Endeavour*. At Tahiti he set up an observatory to observe the Transit of Venus on 3 June 1769 and document the time required for Venus to traverse the Sun (Chapter 1). Green was described by Cook after his death on 29 January 1771 as having led an 'unregulated life' which eventually led to 'the Flux [diarrhoea, dysentery]' and death.

Two artists, Sydney Parkinson (*c.*1745–1771) and Alexander Buchan (?–1769), also sailed in *Endeavour*. Parkinson was a skilled draughtsman and was hired by Joseph Banks for the first voyage. He sketched almost a thousand plants and animals collected by Banks and Solander, producing watercolour paintings for some of the sketches, published over 220 years later as *Banks' Florilegium* (34 parts on a subscription basis, 1980–1990). Parkinson died of dysentery on the way home via Cape Town. Alexander Buchan, a landscape artist, was also brought to the first voyage by Joseph Banks. Buchan suffered from epilepsy and was affected by a seizure at Tierra del Fuego in January 1769. Cook's journal records that he died from a 'disorder in his bowels' which brought on another seizure at Matavai Bay, Tahiti, on 17 April 1769. Parkinson and Buchan were buried at sea.

Other first voyage supernumeraries included Banks' two black servants, George Dorlton and Thomas Richmond. Due to careless behaviour during a trek with Banks and the scientific party in snowy Tierra del Fuego, both got drunk and froze to death on 16/17 January 1769 (Chapter 4). Polynesian supernumeraries included Tupia, who was brought on board in April 1769 to assist in guiding *Endeavour* among the South Pacific islands. He and his servant Taiata both died at Batavia from dysentery in December 1770. Omai (Mai) was a supernumerary in *Adventure* on the second voyage and in *Resolution* on the third voyage. Joseph Banks took Mai to London and he became 'the toast' of society. Mai returned to the South Pacific on Cook's third voyage, where he was discharged at Huahine (Society Islands) on 31 October 1777.

Second Voyage Supernumeraries, 1772–1775
Because Joseph Banks refused to sail with Cook on the second voyage after his modifications to *Resolution* were rejected, Johan Reinhold Forster and George Forster, a father-and-son team of natural scientists, joined *Resolution* at the suggestion of the Royal Society. One servant assisted the Forsters.

J.R. Forster (1729–1798) and his family had relocated to London from Saxony in 1766 and cultivated friendships with members of the Royal Society, the connection which brought the Forsters to the second voyage when Banks declined to participate. Forster was a respected ornithologist. He often displayed an irascible, argumentative and critical personality, which alienated many in *Resolution* during the voyage. He frequently complained about sailing in damp and cold weather, as well as about his draughty, cold and damp cabins in the sloop. George Forster (1754–1794) was mostly educated by his father and was 18 years of age when he sailed on the second voyage, publishing a journal in 1777 during the post-voyage publication controversy (Chapter 12).

During the second voyage the Admiralty planned that both Forster and Cook would compose an account of the voyage, Forster concentrating on 'philosophical' natural scientific findings and Cook on navigation. After their return to England in 1775 a lengthy dispute with the Admiralty ensued concerning how the voyage was to be summarized and who was responsible for which aspects. As a result of this dispute, George Forster published his second voyage journal account in 1777, shortly before Cook's journal was published. J.R. Forster's journals were published much later. In addition to the Forsters, Swedish naturalist Anders Sparrman joined the scientific party as an additional supernumerary at the Cape of Good Hope.

William Wales (1734–1798), a brother-in-law to Charles Green (astronomer on the first voyage), was employed by Nevil Maskelyne at the Royal Observatory and contributed to calculations in *Maskelyne's Almanac* (1767), which, as the first published almanac, was used in working out a ship's longitude at sea. Wales journeyed to Hudson's Bay to observe the 1769 Transit of Venus, just as Maskelyne was sent to St Helena for the same purpose. The Board of Longitude also sent Wales to accompany Cook's second voyage. One of his primary duties was to be in charge of the marine chronometer, discussed below. Historians may access his journal online, as well as that by astronomer William Bayly through the Board of Longitude site at Cambridge University.

London-born artist William Hodges (1744–1797) was sent by the Admiralty to join *Resolution*. He made sketches and paintings during the second voyage, and his engravings were included in Captain Cook's journal. He prepared large-scale landscape paintings based on the voyage, most of which were completed after his return to England, under salary from the Admiralty. Hodges also painted portraits of Captain Cook. Some of his paintings were reproduced on postage stamps and are included in the plate section.

Adventure's supernumeraries included William Bayly (1737–1810), who served as an assistant to Nevil Maskelyne at the Royal Observatory. In 1769 the Royal Society sent Bayly to North Cape, Norway, to observe the Transit of Venus. Bayly also served as astronomer in *Discovery* during the third voyage. After 1785 he was headmaster at the Royal Academy at Portsmouth. Bayly was responsible for the marine chronometers in *Adventure*. He was accompanied by a servant, Robert Mackay.

Third Voyage Supernumeraries, 1776–1779/1780
Supernumeraries in *Resolution* during the third voyage included Omai (Mai), referenced above. In addition, the artist for the third voyage was John Webber (1752–1793), the son of a Swiss sculptor who settled in England. Webber was educated in Berne and Paris, returning to London by 1771. At the conclusion of the third voyage the Admiralty employed Webber to produce drawings for engravings to illustrate the official account of the journey. He also painted a portrait of Captain Cook. Some of Webber's paintings are reproduced on postage stamps, including views of Christmas Harbour at Kerguelen Island (*see* Plate 16).

Midshipman Henry Roberts (*c*.1747–1796) produced sketches during the voyage as well as charts that were later engraved for the 1784 edition of Cook's journal. James Cleveley served as carpenter in *Resolution*. His drawings depicting scenes of the third voyage were turned into paintings by his brother John, among them a portrayal of Cook's death in Hawai'i. Surgeon William Anderson (1750–1778) compiled observations on natural science which are included in Cook's journal. He also sailed in *Resolution* as surgeon's mate during the second voyage. Anderson died at sea on 3 August 1778. William Ellis (?–1785), surgeon second mate in *Discovery* and later surgeon in *Resolution*, also produced sketches during the third voyage.

The third voyage astronomer in *Discovery* was William Bayly (1737–1810), mentioned above. No astronomer served in *Resolution* during the third voyage, Cook himself performing the role. Bayly was assisted by two servants, John Lett and David Nelson. Nelson later sailed with Captain William Bligh in *Bounty*. He was set adrift with Bligh and others after the mutiny and died of fever and exposure at Timor in June 1789.[17]

Victualling, Equipment and Supplies

Victualling is the term used by Captain Cook in his journal description of food-stuffs on board his vessels. An examination of food carried on the long sea voyages provides us with insight into the types of food and the general diet on the voyages. The list of victuals loaded onto the vessels also includes antiscourbitics (foods to combat scurvy), which were used under the direction of the ships' surgeons and led to one of Cook's hallmark contributions to improving the health of sailors.

As examples, I will identify some of the provisions assigned to *Resolution* and *Adventure* during the second voyage, from details incorporated into Cook's journal entry for 13 July 1768. Officers likely brought onboard some personal supplies. Biscuit and flour comprised the largest quantity in the cook's pantry. Meat, packed in casks, included salt beef and salt pork. For *Resolution* this included 7,637lb of beef (in 4lb pieces) and 14,214lb of pork (in 2lb pieces), with approximately half these amounts for *Adventure*. In addition the vessels carried 'salted beef', 1,374lb in *Resolution* and 248 pieces of 4lb each in *Adventure*.

Resolution's beer supply amounted to 19 tons, with *Adventure* receiving 30 puncheons (1 puncheon equalled 80 gallons). *Resolution*'s wine supply totalled 642 gallons, with 400 for *Adventure*. Nearly 1,400 gallons of 'spirit' was assigned to *Resolution* but only 300 to *Adventure*. Other foodstuffs included 'pease' (peas: 358 bushels in *Resolution*, 216 in *Adventure*), wheat, oatmeal, butter, cheese, sugar, olive oil, vinegar, suet, raisins and salt.

Antiscourbitics included malt (80 bushels for *Resolution* and 60 for *Adventure*), nearly 20,000lb of sauerkraut for Cook's ship and nearly 12,000lb for *Adventure*, and nearly 5,000lb of salted cabbage for *Resolution* and just over 4,100lb for *Adventure*. Other antiscourbitics included portable broth (similar to bouillon cubes), saloup (concentrated orange and lemon juice), mustard and marmalade of carrots. The ship's surgeon administered antiscourbitics as required.

Food historian Reay Tannahill suggests that naval officials were as 'unimaginative as they were parsimonious' in provisioning ships. 'Their guiding principle was to ensure a supply of solid, cheap, bulky food which could be expected to remain edible even under unfavourable conditions.' Butter was often rancid, cheese 'tough as old leather', and biscuits (made from weevil-infested flour) were hard and difficult to break open, remaining 'edible, if not palatable, for as much as fifty years'.[18]

Cook's journals also identify the day-to-day allowance for each man. Each person received 1lb of biscuit and as much 'small beer' (low alcohol) as could be drunk. Alternatives were a pint of wine or a half-pint of brandy, rum or arrack (sweet wine, e.g., rum). In *Resolution* the somewhat repetitive routine diet was as follows:

Monday: ½lb butter, 10oz Cheshire Cheese, unlimited boiled oatmeal.
Tuesday: one or two 4lb pieces of beef, 3lb flour and either 1lb raisins or ½lb suet.
Wednesday: ½lb butter, 10oz Cheshire Cheese, unlimited boiled peas (pease).
Thursday: 2lb pieces of pork served with peas.
Friday: ½lb butter, 10oz Cheshire Cheese, unlimited boiled peas (pease).
Saturday: one or two 4lb pieces of beef, 3lb flour and either 1lb raisins or ½lb suet.
Sunday: 2lb pieces of pork served with peas.

Meat was therefore served on four days each week. Sauerkraut – 'a very wholesome food and a very great antiscorbutick' – was served on the days beef was offered (Tuesday, Saturday). Substitutions included sugar (1lb) and oil (one pint) served in place of butter and cheese. The diet would be altered when fish or fowl were obtained during the voyage. This diet conformed to Royal Navy regulations. Casks of beef or pork to be routinely inspected to ensure the food met the proper weight requirement and officers were to rectify any deficiencies so that the crew received the allotted portions.[19] Cook observed the antiscourbitics were similar to those on board *Endeavour*, for both general use and experiment. He believed that sweet wort was made from malt and given to those with scurvy at the direction of the ship's surgeon.

Cook considered sauerkraut as another essential means to attack scurvy, along with wort, marmalade of carrots and saloup (concentrated juice of lemons and oranges). Other food or drink included beer brewed from 'inspissated' (concentrated) juice of wort, essence of spruce and tea plants, combining boiled cabbage with peas, and wine instead of other spirits.

Through experience, Cook understood 'the People' might reject a new food such as sauerkraut. In his journal entry for 29 July 1773 he wrote,

To interduce any New article of food among Seamen, let it be every so much for their good, requires both the example and Authority of a Commander, without both of which, it will be droped before the People are Sencible of the benefits resulting from it … Many of my People, officers as well as seamen, at first, disliked Celery, Scurvy grass &c being boild in the Pease &

Wheat and some refused to eat it, but as this had no effect on my conduct, this obstinate kind of prejudice, by little by little, wore off and they began to like it as well as the others and now, I believe, there was hardly a man in the Ship that did not attribute our being so free of the Scurvy to the Beer and Vegetables we made use of at Newzealand.

Chapter 14 gives additional details about Cook's experiments to control scurvy. He noted in his journal that both *Resolution* and *Adventure* had casks on board to be filled with 4,000 gallons of Madeira wine. He observed that the sloops had 'full two years Provision on board at whole allowance of most articles and of some much more and this is exclusive of the antiscorbuticks'. Other victuals were obtained at Madeira, a regular port of call during many of Cook's voyages. For example, at Madeira on 14 September 1768 Cook recorded in his journal that *Endeavour* received fresh beef, greens and 20lb per man of Madeira onions (a total of 1.3 tons), as well as wine and water. During the voyages Cook bartered for water, wood and foodstuffs from the locations he visited, especially in the South Pacific. In the Antarctic floating pieces of ice were brought on board to be melted for water.

Supplies and Equipment on Board

In his journal Cook included a list of the supplies and equipment in *Resolution* during the second voyage. These miscellaneous items included a sea water distillation device, fishing equipment (lines, hooks, nets), trading merchandise to be exchanged for supplies with native peoples, and medals to be given to indigenous peoples (with depictions of King George III on one side and the ships on the other) as symbols of their visits.

For defence on the high seas *Resolution* was equipped with twelve 4-pounder cannon, while *Adventure* had ten. Both ships also had swivel guns (small cannon mounted to cover a wide arc) and other arms and ammunition. Marines were armed with muskets (sometimes termed 'musquetoons' in the journals). Both *Resolution* and *Adventure* had the frame and parts for a small 20-ton vessel that could be quickly assembled in case of extreme emergency. The need did not arise and no reference is made in Cook's journal to this materiel after the ships sailed from Plymouth in July 1772.

Marine Chronometers

During the second and third voyages each vessel was equipped with marine chronometers, under the supervision of the astronomers, which were to be tested for accuracy in determining longitude. John Harrison developed a working model of a chronometer for the Board of Longitude in 1730 (*see* Plate 15). The Board then asked six expert watchmakers to duplicate Harrison's the model. *Resolution* carried two chronometers, made by Lacrum Kendall and John Arnold. *Adventure* carried two Arnold chronometers. Cook often referred to them as the 'watch' or 'clock'.[20]

The Board of Longitude provided considerable guidance for the process to validate the chronometers. These instructions were given not only to Wales and Bayly but also to Captains Cook and Furneaux. Each chronometer was to be placed in a specially designed box and locked. The sloop's commander had one key, while a second was given to the first lieutenant or the officer next in charge, while the third was to be kept by either Wales or Bayly. All three persons were to be present daily for the winding of the watch and for comparing the time of the clock and observations. A daily record of the times by the clock and by observation was to be maintained.[21]

The marine chronometer is a clock that functioned on the high seas, being not affected by the ship's motion. Determining the variance in time at sea between a fixed point and the ship's position would establish longitude more accurately. While latitude (the position north or south of the equator) was determined by use of a sextant and *Maskelyne's Almanac* (1767), determination of longitude (the position east or west of a fixed point such as Greenwich) required considerable calculation time and was not always accurate.

Longitude is a function of time. Assuming the Earth to be a circle equal to 360 degrees, each degree of longitude is subdivided into 60 minutes and each minute into 60 seconds. Each day consists of 24 hours, so with 360° in a circle, the Sun crosses 15° every hour. If there is a difference of three hours between the time at Greenwich (identified by the chronometer) and the time where the observer is located, then the observer is 45° (15 × 3) west or east of the prime meridian at Greenwich. There are 180° of longitude east and 180° of longitude west of Greenwich. On some occasions Cook's journals and log books use other fixed points as reference, such as the Cape of Good Hope or Cape Palliser in New Zealand. The latter is on the southern tip of New Zealand's north island, named by Captain Cook for Sir Hugh Palliser, his long-time mentor. Today Global Positioning System (GPS) satellite technology enables even more accurate calculation of a ship's position. However, navigators are still trained in the earlier methods of calculating longitude in case modern electronics or back-up power supply systems fail. The marine chronometer was an extremely important development in navigation and it is to Cook's credit, and that of the astronomers of the second voyage, that this technological improvement was validated.

As he departed Plymouth, Cook concluded that for the second voyage, 'whatever may be the event of the expedition, the Ships are both well chosen and well provided'.[22]

PART 2

COOK'S VISITS TO TIERRA DEL FUEGO AND CAPE HORN, 1769

Tierra del Fuego, rounding Cape Horn and the Search for a 'Land of Great Extent'

December 1768–January 1769 and August–September 1769

We recommend it to you to stand well to the Southward in your passage round the Cape [Horn], in order to make a good Westing, taking care how-ever to fall into the parallel of King George's Island [Tahiti] at least 120 leagues to the Eastward of it and using your best endeavours to arrive there at least a month or six weeks before the 3rd of June next ... [After Tahiti] proceed southward in order to make discovery of the [southern] con-tinent above-mentioned until you arrive in the latitude of 40°, unless you sooner fall in with it; but not having discovered it, or any evident signs of it, in that run, you are to proceed in search of it westward, between the latitude before mentioned and the latitude of 35° until you discover it or fall in with the Eastern side of the land discovered by Tasman and now called New Zealand.

Admiralty Secret Instructions to Lieutenant James Cook, 25 July 1768

Captain Cook's search for *Terra Australis Incognita*, the unknown Southern Con-tinent, occupied two segments of the first voyage: the first part extended from 11 January to 28 February 1769 while passing through the Strait of Le Maire, rounding Cape Horn and proceeding WNW towards Tahiti. My primary focus is the difficulties encountered in passing through the Strait of Le Maire and then rounding Cape Horn, both preludes to the search for the Southern Continent. During this period of two weeks Cook's excellent seamanship in difficult seas and foul weather is on display. After several attempts, Cook passed through the Strait of Le Maire, landed to take on wood and water at the Bay of Good Success (Tierra del Fuego) and then rounded Cape Horn on 25 January, followed by sailing south-southwest to 60° south latitude in search of 'a land of great extent'. Cook decided on 28 February there was no new continent in that part of the Pacific. He then proceeded to make a 'good Westing' to 110° west longitude, as defined in the Admiralty orders.

The second phase followed observation of the Transit of Venus in Tahiti as *Endeavour* sailed 'south' of Tahiti from 9 August to 1 September 1769. *Resolution* sailed to 40° south latitude to again search for the unknown southern continent. No new continent was located. A popular assumption of the day suggested the Southern Continent was located to the south-southeast of New Zealand and was populated by a large number of persons disposed to open trade with Great Britain. Perhaps New Zealand was the 'tip' of the unknown continent? Cook's southward travels from the Society Islands to 40° south and his later circumnavigation of New Zealand (1769–1770) disproved this theory. After reaching 40° south, he sailed westward, landing in Poverty Bay, New Zealand, on 9 October 1769.

While Cook did not locate the Southern Continent, he proved it did not exist in the vast expanse of ocean in which he was directed to sail, a 'negative' conclusion, but a conclusion nonetheless, and a 'narrowing of options' in the search.[1] My primary sources of information include Cook's journal and the master's log book of *Endeavour* (presumably by Master Robert Molyneux, although his name is not identified in the log), supplemented by Joseph Bank's journal.[2]

Admiralty Instructions

In order to understand the purpose of Cook's voyages, the first place to start is the Admiralty instructions. The announced purpose of this voyage was to observe and record data about the Transit of Venus on 3 June 1769. A second set of instructions was opened by James Cook after the conclusion of the Transit of Venus. These instructions were secret, to be shared with others on the voyage only in instalments. Secrecy was to be maintained after the voyage until the Admiralty allowed disclosure.

The complete texts of the Admiralty's instructions to James Cook are located in Appendix A. In keeping with this book's focus on searching for the unknown continent, I divided the orders into six sections:

1. Cook was to sail *Endeavour* around Cape Horn to Tahiti to observe the Transit of Venus, an observation shared with astronomer Charles Green at Port Royal Harbour in King George's Island (the name given to Tahiti in 1767 by Captain Wallis in *Dolphin*). After leaving Plymouth, *Endeavour* could acquire additional supplies in Madeira (wine and foodstuffs), as well as Rio de Janeiro or alternatively Port Egmont on the East Falkland Islands.

2. While rounding Cape Horn, Cook was to navigate to 60° south latitude in search of the unknown Southern Continent. He was then to make 'a good Westing' to fall within the longitude of Tahiti. This course also was part of the search for Antarctica. The Admiralty directed Cook to arrive in Tahiti at least one month in advance of the Transit.

3. After the Transit of Venus Cook was to open the second set of secret orders (the Admiralty's 'inclosed Sealed Packet'). He was to sail *Endeavour* to 40° south of Tahiti because 'there is reason to imagine that a

continent, or land of great extent, may be found to the southward of the tract latterly made by Capt. Wallis in His Majesty's ship the *Dolphin* (of which you will herewith receive a copy) or a tract of any former navigators in pursuit of the like kind . . .'. If no land was discovered, Cook was then to proceed westward between 35° and 40° south latitude until *Endeavour* reached the east coast of New Zealand.

4. If the Southern Continent was found, Cook was to survey its coast and identify its latitude and longitude as well as other nautical and geographic features and natural phenomena. He was to record the magnetic variance of the compass, bearings, tides, currents and depth of the sea, and identify rocks, shoals and other phenomena such as harbours and bays to assist with future navigation. Assessment was to be made of the territory's soils, wildlife ('beasts and fowls'), fish, minerals (including valuable stones), trees and plants, and fruits and grains, with specimens of each to be collected and returned to England for study. The orders directed Cook to establish friendly relations with native peoples, providing them with presents ('Trifles as they may Value'). With the permission of the natives, Cook was to take possession in the name of George III and set up 'marks and inscriptions' of his visit as 'first discoverers and possessors'. He was advised to take measures for the safety of *Endeavour*'s crew. These comments will be repeated in various formulae in the other instructions for each of Cook's voyages.

5. When *Endeavour* reached New Zealand, Cook was to determine latitude and longitude and explore as much of the coast as possible, dependent upon the condition of the ship and the health of the crew. Once New Zealand had been surveyed (the detail of which was left up to Cook), *Endeavour* was to proceed to discover other islands and then return to England, either by Cape Horn or by the Cape of Good Hope.

6. The search for Antarctica is expressed towards the end of the secret orders. The Admiralty defined Cook's objective, **'which you are always to have in View, the discovery of the Southern Continent so often Mentioned'** (emphasis added). This 'land of great extent' was evidently therefore as important as observation of the Transit of Venus, the announced purpose of the voyage.[3]

From England to Rio de Janeiro

Cook took command of *Endeavour* at Deptford on 26 May. Guided by a pilot, the ship anchored along the Channel coast and reached Plymouth on 14 August, where it was provisioned. Joseph Banks and the 'scientific party' arrived the same day. On the 19th Cook read the 'Articles of War' and 'An Act of Parliament' (dealing with discipline aboard ship) and distributed two months' wages to naval personnel. Offences leading to discipline included profane oaths, cursing, drunkenness, uncleanness, 'scandalous actions in derogation of God's Honour' or 'corruption of good manners', cowardice, mutiny, desertion, using provoking speech or gestures and similar crimes or actions.[4]

Endeavour sailed from England on 25 August, first into the English Channel and then into the Bay of Biscay, reaching the harbour at Funchal, Madeira, on 12 September. There, Cook purchased additional foodstuffs, noting in his journal on 14 September that fresh beef and greens were taken on board, and casks for wine and water were taken ashore to be filled. On the 17th, 20lb of onions per man (1.3 tons) were stored away in the hold with the filled water and wine casks. The voyage crossed the Equator on 25 October and sighted the coast of Brazil on 8 November.

Endeavour arrived at the harbour of Rio de Janeiro on 14 November 1769 and departed on 2 December. Cook had anticipated a friendly reception by the Portuguese viceroy in Rio (England and Portugal have Europe's oldest diplomatic treaty of perpetual friendship, agreed in 1373 by King Edward III and King Ferdinand and Queen Eleanor of Portugal), but instead the viceroy and Portuguese officials refused to believe that the purpose of the voyage was to observe the Transit of Venus or other forms of scientific investigation. Cook was summoned in person to meet the viceroy. Cook and Banks presented documentation summarizing the scientific purpose of the voyage, details of which were ignored or not believed, much to Cook's and Banks's dismay. Banks described the government in Rio as 'despotick' in his journal entry on 7 December. *Endeavour* did not appear to be a Royal Navy ship and therefore its purpose was questioned. Perhaps it was engaged in illicit trade or smuggling. It proved awkward to obtain materials for repairs to the ship and supplies were also difficult to obtain, as Cook and others from *Endeavour* were shadowed by officials while on land and under constant surveillance while in the harbour.

Banks and other naturalists did go ashore to 'botanize', sometimes in disguise and against local government regulations. On 26 November Banks's journal contains great detail about 'parasitic' and other plants he observed, including various herbs and flowers, writing, 'the wildest Spotts here were varied with a greater quantity of Flowers as well as more beautiful ones than our best devised gardens, a sight infinitely pleasing to the Eye for a short time tho no doubt it would soon tire with the continuance of it'. Banks described birds of elegant plumage, butterflies and hummingbirds, and large crabs found along the shore, as well as grazing cattle, and commented on the extent of gardens, similar to those in Europe. On 2 December Banks wrote in his journal, 'this morn thank god we have got all we want from these illiterate impolite gentry'. A Spanish ship arrived and agreed to transmit letters to Europe, which Banks termed 'a very Fortunate circumstance'. Cook's letter to Admiralty Secretary Philip Stevens was one of the letters sent. In great detail it described the difficulties encountered in Rio de Janeiro and 'the matter we have been received & treated here is such as was never before practis'd on any English Ship which makes me think it is the more necessary that the whole should minutely be laid before their Lordship[s]'.[5]

Departing from Rio was similarly troublesome. A.B. Peter Flower fell from the ship and drowned, and the viceroy's permission to leave was granted but not communicated, so *Endeavour* could not proceed. The ship's anchor was caught on a rock and not freed until 2pm on 6 December. The pilot boat was discharged at 8pm on the 7th, at which the harbour's 'guard boat', which had shadowed *Endeavour* for over two weeks, also departed. Captain Cook then proceeded south towards Tierra del Fuego and Cape Horn.

From Rio de Janeiro to Tierra del Fuego

On most days *Endeavour* initially sailed in decent and clear weather with soft or gentle breezes. On some occasions the weather grew steadily worse during the day, ending with thunder, lightning and rain (14 December). On that day Cook recorded, 'The Caulkers Emp'd [employed] in Caulking the Decks', a task repeated frequently during all voyages. Hazy weather alternated with clear sailing, gentle breezes, then dark clouds and additional rain showers. Using data gathered from Cook's journal entries, during the two weeks from 13 to 26 December *Endeavour* travelled 1,182 miles, an average of 84.43 miles per day, with the highest total of 160 miles on the 19th but only 33 miles on the 23rd.

On 26 December Cook wrote in his journal, 'yesterday being Christmas day the People were none of the Soberest'. Joseph Banks observed in his journal on 25 December, 'Christmas day; all good Christians that is to say all hands get abominably drunk so that at night there was scarce a sober man in the ship, wind thank god very moderate or the lord knows what would have become of us.' During the second voyage the journals of J.R. and George Forster contain similar references to the crew's behaviour during Christmas celebrations. The religious significance of Christmas receives no mention in the journals of Cook or Banks, nor in the log books.

Captain Cook's plan was to sail around the tip of South America by entering the Strait of Le Maire, with Staten Island on his left and Tierra del Fuego on his right. *Endeavour* would then proceed around Cape Horn and into the Pacific Ocean (Figure 9).

As Cook approached the southern tip of South America, the weather and the ocean often proved difficult. From 27 December to 11 January (when Tierra del Fuego was first sighted), Cook's journal entries frequently reported squalls and strong gales leading to frequent adjustment and taking in, then putting out sails, then repeating the process. The weather was a mixture of haze, rain, some lightning and occasional fog, with few periods of calm or gentle breezes.

Cook observed many whales on 1 January 1769 and later numerous penguins, dolphins and seals. Hailstone showers pelted *Endeavour* on 2 January. More whales, porpoises, small red crawfish and many waterfowl are recorded during the first week of January. The presence of crawfish drew several comments, Banks calling them 'red lobsters' in his journal entry, observing 'a few hundreds of them at a time'. In the entry for 3 January, the master's log recorded 'pass'd through a

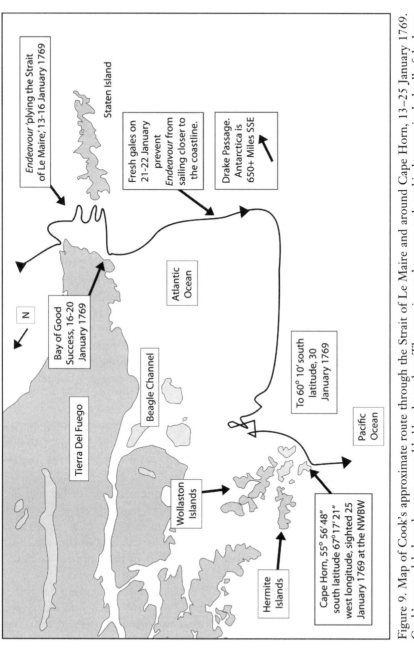

Figure 9. Map of Cook's approximate route through the Strait of Le Maire and around Cape Horn, 13–25 January 1769. Cook's route, labels and arrows are added by the author. The map is not drawn to scale and it does not include all of the bays, inlets and islands along the coastline of Tierra del Fuego. Locations identified are approximate. Landforms on the map are based upon an original design by Johntheghost (2006).

Staten Island

Endeavour 'plying the Strait of Le Maire,' 13-16 January 1769

Fresh gales on 21-22 January prevent *Endeavour* from sailing closer to the coastline.

Drake Passage. Antarctica is 650+ Miles SSE

N

Bay of Good Success, 16-20 January 1769

Tierra Del Fuego

Atlantic Ocean

Beagle Channel

To 60° 10' south latitude, 30 January 1769

Wollaston Islands

Pacific Ocean

Hermite Islands

Cape Horn, 55° 56'48" south latitude 67°17'21" west longitude, sighted 25 January 1769 at the NWBW bed of shrimps or young Crayfish of a Beautiful red Crimson colour they were so numerous as to Cause the sea to be of the same colour as far as we could see from the deck. Mr. Banks caught some of them with ease.'

At approximately noon on 4 January 'the appearance of land' was sighted from *Endeavour*. Both Cook and Banks recorded the sighting in their journals. After searching, it turned out to be the phantom 'Pepys Island', first cited in 1684 but subsequently not located by seventeenth- or eighteenth-century navigators because Pepys Island does not actually exist. During the search for Antarctica logs and journals repeatedly record 'the appearance of land', far-distant images suggesting territory, which further investigation revealed to be illusory. Banks cited a seamen's term, 'Cape fly-away' to describe the half-hour search for Pepys Island. Although the territory does not exist, it remained on maps at least until the end of the eighteenth century.[6]

The inclement weather continued, Cook writing on 6 January, 'Gave to each of the People a Fearnought Jacket and a pair of Trowers: after which I never heard one man complain of cold not but the weather was cold enough.' (A fearnought jacket is a stout woollen jacket, worn as an outer garment). On 7 January rain, strong gales and squalls led to *Endeavour* being brought to – turned into the wind, lessening headway – until the weather improved. More moderate and occasionally squally weather followed and Tierra del Fuego was sighted on 11 January, stretching from the ship's west to southeast-by-south. There was some uncertainty about *Endeavour*'s position since it was difficult to take accurate readings with the sextant. Cook also observed that he 'saw some of the Natives who made a smook [smoke] in several places, which must have been done as a signal to us as they did not continue it after we pass'd'.

The Strait of Le Maire and the Bay of Good Success

Cook observed that the Strait was about 5 Leagues (15 nautical miles) in length and width. The coastline is dotted with various bays, some providing safe anchorage, others less so. The distance is not great but the January 1769 passage proved very difficult. The crew was placed on a rotation of four hours on, then four hours off duty, repeated daily until rounding Cape Horn.

Endeavour began the attempt to pass through the Strait of Le Maire on 12 January and anchored at the Bay of Good Success on the 16th. Making his way along the coast, Cook passed first Cape St Vincent and then Cape St Diego, on the eastern tip of Tierra del Fuego. On the 12th rainy and hazy weather caused *Endeavour* to tack and stand to the northwest and by noon the following day the bark was 7 miles from entering the Strait. Additional rough weather prevailed on the 13th as Cook records:

> Plying in the Strait Le Maire ... The greatest part of the day little wind and cloudy ... kept under an easy sail until day light at which time we were abreast of Cape St Diego and then put into the Straights, but the tide soon turn'd against us and oblig'd us to haul under the Cape again and wait until

9am when it shifted in our favour. Put into the Straits again with a moderate breeze at SW which soon grew boisterous, with very heavy squalls with rain & hail and oblig'd us to close reef [reduce exposure to the wind] our top-sails.

Similar weather continued on the 14th, Cook observing, 'Kept Plying in the Straits until ½ past 4 pm at which time the Tide had made Strong against us and the wind not abating bore away intending to have hauld under Cape St Diego, but was prevented by the force of the tide which carried us past that Cape with surprising rapidity, at the same time caused a very great sea.'

Cook and others attempted to take readings to establish *Endeavour*'s position. Cook recorded in his journal the following morning that 'The Violence of the Tide of Ebb rais'd such a Sea off Cape St Diego that it looked as if it was breaking Violently on a lidge [ledge] of rocks and would be taken for such by any who knew not the true cause: when the Ship was in this torrent she frequently Pitched her bowsprit in the Water.' Likewise, the master's log recorded that 'in crossing the rippling of a strong Tide the Ship was so agitated as to Pitch the Spritsail Yard under several times & at the same time rolled surprisingly deep. This current took us out of the Strait.' At this point *Endeavour* had not yet passed through the Strait despite several attempts.

On 15 January Cook established a temporary anchorage at a bay on the east side of Cape St Vincent, which Master Robert Molyneux sounded beforehand. While the crew collected wood and water, Banks, Solander and other scientists proceeded to 'botanize'. The party returned with flowers and plants that were mostly unknown in Europe. Wild celery and scurvy grass were found in abundance which, Banks wrote, 'I believe possess as much virtue in curing the scurvy', as well as cranberries. He also observed a species of 'Antarctic birch', which he supposed might 'in cases of necessity supply topmasts'. This is an interesting observation, although it is unlikely that birch could withstand the stress of serving as a mast. Captain Cook offered a similar observation at Norfolk Island (a small Pacific island between Australia and New Zealand) in 1774, that the tall and straight Norfolk Pine could also serve as replacements for masts. However, when tried for this purpose the Norfolk Pine snapped. In the 1780s efforts to use Norfolk Island flax to make replacement sails also failed. Although these ideas did not prove useful, they raise the question as to what a vessel was to do to secure replacement masts when sailing in the Pacific, where the only port suitable for ship repair was Batavia, with its accompanying problems of disease which Cook was to discover in late 1770 (Chapter 1).

Because Cook believed Vincent's Bay was not secure, he made sail further into the Strait, anchoring in a small cove at 3am which he believed to be Port Maurice, with Cape Bartholomew (a point on Staten Island) to the east-southeast. Banks and the naturalists took a small boat to collect additional botanical specimens. Monday, 16 January greeted the ship with frequent rain and snow. By 2pm, however, *Endeavour* had passed through the Strait of Le Maire with a favourable tide and anchored in the Bay of Good Success.

Endeavour remained at the Bay of Good Success until 21 January. During the six days the crew collected wood and water and the bay was surveyed, while Joseph Banks and his party proceeded into nearby woods to collect specimens. The cold, snowy and inclement weather continued. Banks's party did not return until the 17th. The landscape was difficult to penetrate and the route taken had contained no paths. Alexander Buchan suffered an epileptic seizure and had to be carried to a temporary shelter. Banks's two black servants became drunk on his brandy, lay down in the open and refused to take another step. In his journal Banks stated that he and his companions laid the two men on a 'bed of boughs' and

> covering them over with boughs also as thick as we were able and thus we left them hopeless of ever seeing them again alive which indeed we never did ... We had spent an hour and a half expos'd to the most penetrating cold I ever felt as well as continual snow ... Now might our situation truely be call'd terrible: of twelve our original number, 2 were already past all hopes, one more was so ill that tho he was with us I had little hopes of his being able to walk in the morning, and another very likely to relapse into his fits either before we set out or in the course of our journey: we were distant from the ship we did not know how far, we knew only that we had been the greatest part of a day in walking it through pathless woods; provisions we had none but one vulture which had been shot while we were out, and the shortest allowance could not furnish half a meal; and to compleat our misfortunes we were caught in a snow storm in a climate we were utterly unacquainted with but which we had reason to believe was so inhospitable as any in the world, not only from all the accounts we had heard or read but from the Quantity of snow which we saw falling, tho it was very little after midsummer: a circumstance unheard of in Europe for even in Norway or Lapland snow is never known to fall in the summer.

On the 17th Banks sent three of his group to check on the 'poor wretches' they had covered with boughs the previous evening and subsequently learned they were both dead. The master's log recorded that Banks's greyhound had survived the night while camped near the two men. This log also noted that the servants 'had recourse to the brandy bottle by which means they became Stupid'. The weather improved and the party dressed the 'vulture' shot earlier (which Banks wrote produced three mouthfuls per man). After a three-hour walk the party reached the shore and sighted *Endeavour*.

In his journal entry for the 17th Cook recorded that the failure of Banks and his party to return as planned 'gave me great uneasiness', since they were not prepared to be gone overnight. His journal includes a short summary based on Banks's description of events. Robert Molyneux, *Endeavour*'s Master, observed that 'this was a heavy loss to Mr. Banks, they [the servants] were very useful'. Molyneux also added that Banks 'had the satisfaction in his late excursion to make a Valuable Collection of Alpine and other plants hitherto unknown to Natural History'.

Although the Bay of Good Success provided some refuge, the foul weather continued. For example, on the 18th the master's log recorded moderate, then heavy squalls of wind, snow and hail, concluding 'tho we lie very well cover'd from the wind, yet the Gale and Tides together causes such a Swell to tumble that I never knew the Ship to roll more at Sea'. The weather prevented casks of fresh water being transported from the shore to the ship. However, by 20 January, the day prior to departure, 59 tons of water had been brought aboard.

Cook's journal, the master's log book and Banks's journal contain lengthy descriptions of Tierra del Fuego, including the native peoples encountered. Initially thirty to forty natives, their numbers eventually growing to fifty to sixty, met *Endeavour*'s crew, exhibiting no hesitation in doing so. In his entry for the 16th Cook described them as

> above Middle size of a dark copper Colour with long black hair, they paint their bodies in Streakes mostly Red and Black, their cloathing consists wholly of a Guanacoes skin or that of a Seal, in the same form as it came from the Animals back, the Women wear a piece of skin over their privey parts but the Men observe no such decency. Their Hutts are made like a beehive and open on one side where they have a fire, they are made of small Sticks and cover'd with branches of trees, long grass &c in such a manner that they are neither proff [proof] against wind, Hail, rain, or snow, a sufficient proff that these People must be a very hardy race; ... they live chiefly on shell fish such as Muscles. [Guanacoes are part of the camelid family and native to South America; related to llamas, they stand 3–4ft high at the shoulder, weighing 200–300lb.]

Cook observed native bows and arrows, with some arrows bearded with glass or fine flint. A few natives visited *Endeavour* and ate some beef but after two hours made signs to be taken back to land. The Fuegians had no interest in tasting liquor and expressed little interest in the visitors' provisions.

On 20 January Joseph Banks and his party walked about 2 miles to see 'an Indian town', which was reached in about an hour. The visitors saw twelve to fourteen

> wigwams of the most unartificial construction imaginable, indeed no thing bearing the name of a hut could possibly be built with less trouble. They consisted of a few poles set up and meeting together at the top in a conical figure, these were cover'd on the weather side with a few boughs and a little grass, on the lee side about one eighth part of the circle was let open and against this opening a fire was made.

There was no furniture, Banks noting that grass laid around the edges provided both bed and chairs, while a bladder 'of some beast' was filled with water: 'in one side of this near the top was a hole through which they drank by elevating a little the bottom which made the water spring up into their mouths'. Banks remarked that the only item they accepted from the visitors were beads or anything red in colour for ornamentation, which was more of interest than a knife or hatchet.

In attempting to communicate, a commonly repeated word was 'pecheria', which the English visitors eventually – and mistakenly – used as a collective name for the natives. Tierra del Fuego was populated by many small groups of native peoples with different dialects; some were hunter-gatherers of the forests and grasslands, while others resided along the coasts and subsisted on shellfish as well as fish, seals, whales and birds. J.C. Beaglehole states that the native peoples *Endeavour* encountered are the 'Aush' people and, as will be seen, it was a different group that Cook was to encounter in December 1774 at Christmas Sound on Tierra del Fuego's western coast (Chapter 10).[7]

In observing the Fuegians, Cook noted some European items such as rings, buttons, cloth and canvas, and that the natives were familiar with firearms. They eagerly valued beads and anything red in colour. 'In a Word [Cook concluded] they are perhaps as miserable a set of People as are this day upon earth.' Both Cook and Banks described the language as 'guttural', a conclusion also noted in the master's log: 'Their language sounds very harsh in our ears & they speak it in their throats.' The temperature, Banks observed, was never lower than 38°F in the Antarctic summer (mid-January). Cook observed no discernible official leader, chief or government among the natives.

Both Banks's and Cook's journals contain detailed summaries of their observations about Tierra del Fuego gained over five days. Banks's journal contains descriptions of a sea coast covered with forests. He described the soil as 'fruitful' and of considerable depth, with small brooks running through much of the land. He observed seals and sea-lions and the footprint in a bog of an unidentified 'large beast'. The naturalists saw few birds beyond blackbirds, hawks and a vulture, but waterfowl such as ducks or geese were plentiful. There were many clams and shellfish but they were unable to catch any fish.

In regards to plants, an ecstatic Joseph Banks observed 'many species and those truly the most extraordinary I can imagine', marvelling at 'the infinite variety of Creation'. He again noted many birch trees as well as scurvy grass and wild celery. In his journal entry for 20 January Banks wrote,

> Scurvy grass is found plentifully in damp places near springs, in general every where near the beach especially at the watering place in the Bay of Good Success; when young and in its greatest perfection it lays flat on the ground, having many bright green leaves standing in pairs opposite each other with an odd one at the end which makes in general the 5th on a footstalk; after this it shoots up in stalks sometimes 2 feet high at the top of which are small white blossoms which are succeeded by long podds ... Wild Celery resembles much the Celery in our gardens only that the leaves are of a deeper green, the flowers like it stand in small tufts at the tops of the Branches and are white; it grows plentifully near the Beach, generally in the first soil which is above spring tides, and is not easily mistaken as the taste resembles Celery or

parsley or rather in between. Both these herbs we us'd plentifully while we stay'd here putting them in our soup, etc., and found the benefit from them which seamen in general find from a vegetable diet after having been long deprived of it.

Lengthy descriptions of these two antiscourbitics are included here in light of Captain Cook's efforts to control outbreaks of scurvy. The leaves of scurvy grass (*see* Plate 26) are rich in Vitamin C and may be distilled into juice or mixed with other herbs. Similar observations were made when visiting New Zealand during all three voyages, as well as Kerguelen Island during the third voyage.

For the next two days the weather at the Bay of Good Success continued to be snowy and windy, with rough seas preventing a return to sailing further along the shore of Tierra del Fuego. By the 20th the weather had moderated so Banks and the other scientists could collect shells and plants, while some of the crew were sent to collect more wood and water, as well as to cut broom (to use in sweeping the ship). Although the weather was less stormy, a kedge anchor used to hold the longboat in place was lost when the rope and buoy holding it broke in the rough seas. Cook speculated that the anchor was buried in the sand and considerable efforts were made to retrieve it. Molyneux recorded in his log: 'I was sent to sweep for it but the ground was so foul I could not find it notwithstanding I had two boats and everything fit for the purpose.'

Rounding Cape Horn

On 21 January *Endeavour* raised its anchor at 2am and left the Bay of Good Success. By noon on the 21st, the Bay was 11 leagues (33 nautical miles) to the west, due to the winds and current (meaning *Endeavour* had made no progress toward the Horn). Fresh gales and rain squalls greeted the crew on both the 21st and 22nd. Frequent sightings of landforms were recorded as *Endeavour* made its way close to the coastline of Tierra del Fuego (Figure 9). Cook observed on Monday, 23 January that the weather had improved to calm or moderate breezes and clear skies, much different for several recent days, and the ship was therefore able to proceed to Cape Horn. He continued to observe the Cape of Good Success to the northeast-by-north and Staten Island to the northeast, marking also Sugar Loaf Mountain (now Mt Campana) on Tierra del Fuego to the north-northeast. Cook observed that the mountains were topped with snow. Along the way Cook attempted to determine landmarks recorded on the charts. In the process he located an island at 55° 25′ south latitude which he named 'New Island' because it did not exist on any chart.

Cook continued to sail along the coast on the 24th, accompanied by fresh and moderate gales and rain showers. Fresh gales with rain and hail continued on the 25th in hazy weather. He sighted three islands which, based on the charts, he determined to be the Hermites, a group of islands and islets, the southernmost of which is Cape Horn (*see* Figure 9).

Cook sighted Cape Horn from 3 Leagues distance (9 nautical miles). In his journal for 25 January he described

> an Island with a very high round hummock upon it: this I believe to be Cape Horn for after we had stood to the Southward about 3 Leagues the weather clear'd up for about a ¼ of an hour, which gave us a sight of this land bearing then WSE but we could see no land either to the Southward or westward of it, and therefore conclude that it must be the Cape, but whether it be an Island of it self, a part of the Southermost of Hermites Islands or a part of Terra del Fuego I am not able to determine.

Cook remarked that the westerly winds and heavy fog took *Endeavour* away from Cape Horn and he could not therefore determine whether it was an island or part of Tierra del Fuego. Nevertheless, he fixed the position of Cape Horn at 55° 59′ south latitude and 68° 13′ west longitude from Greenwich. Cook observed that charts and accounts of the Strait of Le Maire and Cape Horn were imperfect, lacking in detail such as landforms and with incorrect latitude and longitude. Cook asserted in his journal on 25 January that 'few parts of the World are better assertain'd' than Cape Horn and the Strait of Le Maire with multiple observations by both himself and astronomer Green.

The Beaglehole edition of Cook's journal contains interesting footnotes wherein Cook reconciles his recording of Cape Horn in 1769 with that of December 1774 when he was on his way for the third leg of his circumnavigation of Antarctica. On 29 December 1774 Cook recorded Cape Horn's longitude at 67° 19′ (instead of 68° 13′ in 1769). Today the official geolocation of Cape Horn is 55° 58′ 59.9988″ south latitude and 67° 16′ 0.0012″ west longitude.

The master's log book contains two sketches of Cape Horn by artist Sydney Parkinson, as observed on 25 January. Unfortunately the log provides no commentary about the sketches, leaving them open to interpretation. When Parkinson was sketching the Tierra del Fuego coastline on the 25th, bear in mind that the weather was foggy and a clear view existed for perhaps a quarter of an hour. This likely impacted the sketches. *Endeavour* approached the Cape from the east, a distance of about 9 nautical miles. Cook's instructions were to 'stand well to Southward in your passage round the Cape, in order to make a good Westing'. The Hermite and Wollaston Islands are a group of islands and islets that are today administratively part of Tierra del Fuego. Cape Horn is located on Hornos Island, as shown in Figure 9.

I suggest the two log book sketches show a progression of images from east to west, showing partially obscured coastline views. Today's usual image of Cape Horn is a rocky point partially covered with a green moss or lichen. Plate 8 is a photograph taken by the author on 1 February 2010 with a telephoto lens at a distance of between a quarter and half a mile from the sixth deck of a large cruise ship. While the sea in 2010 produced modest 3ft-plus waves, the pressure from the winds as we sailed east to west caused the deck doors to be difficult to open so that passengers might enjoy the cool February (sub-Antarctic summer) air.

Captain Cook's detailed map of *Endeavour*'s route through the Strait of Le Maire and the rounding of Cape Horn is located in Map III, in the 'Charts and Views' drawn by Cook and his officers, published with the J.C. Beaglehole edition of Cook's journals.[8]

There is no doubt that Captain Cook endured a difficult passage through the Strait of Le Maire and around Cape Horn. Captain Alan Villiers of the Australian Navy has sailed wind-powered, deep-water ships around Cape Horn and other worldwide locations in which Captain Cook also sailed. In his biography of James Cook, Villiers writes that the passage through the Strait of Magellan was 'difficult', and that the route Cook chose through the Strait of Le Maire and around Cape Horn was much more complicated. He even suggests the route was not Cook's best choice in 1769, commenting,

> The trouble with the Horn route was that it was **too** open, for the ghastly succession of tremendous storms which raced around the world down there flung themselves upon the gaunt land which stretched its cold hand towards that home of the blizzard, Antarctica, as if they wanted to blow it over; and such a sea arose upon the banks by Diego Ramirez and all Tierra del Fuego as threatened to overwhelm the strongest ship.
>
> *All* these great storms came from the west, right in the path of ships trying to reach the Pacific from the Atlantic. The passage of these ships was often a long-continued, relentless fight against violent wind and appalling sea. A sailing ship fights thrice as hard when she must head into the wind and feels gales then infinitely more, for her sails become crude aerofoils, like a giant aircraft's wings.[9]

As well as the winds, the current flowed from west to east. There can be little doubt of Cook's sailing ability in guiding *Endeavour* through such a difficult passage.

The Search for the Southern Continent to 60° South Latitude

From 26 to 30 January Cook sailed *Endeavour* south toward 60° south latitude, following the Admiralty's instructions. During these five days he sailed 303 miles, an average of 60.6 miles per day, making approximately 1° south daily. The weather continued to be foul, with fresh gales, sometimes thick, hazy weather, some rain and hail, then sharper and cold weather. On 28 January Cook sighted an island, commenting in his journal about the two hummocks on it, matching the description of the Diego Ramirez Islands. Multiple observations were taken in attempting to reconcile differences in position due to variation. Discovered in 1619, the Diego Ramirez Islands are named after the cosmographer of the Garcia de Nodal expedition and were the southernmost islands known until Cook's discovery of the South Sandwich Islands in 1775. On 30 January Cook recorded *Endeavour*'s position at 60° 4' south latitude.

At this point, Captain Cook, Banks and Molyneux had recorded no thoughts about the search for a southern 'land of great extent'. In a letter to Admiralty

Secretary Philip Stephens, probably written in 1770 when Cook was in Batavia awaiting repairs to *Endeavour*, Cook summed up the voyage around the tip of South America, but without mentioning the difficult passage through the Strait of Le Maire or the sighting of Cape Horn, and with only a vague reference to the absence of land at 60° south:

> on the 16th of January following arrived in Success Bay in Straits Le Maire where we recruited our Wood and Water: On the 21st of the same Month we quitted Straits le Maire and arrived at Georges Island [Tahiti] on the 13th of Apl. In our Passage to this Island I made a far more westerly Track than any Ship had ever done before, yet it was attended with no discovery until we arrived in the Tropik where we discover'd several Islands ...[10]

Endeavour's Route to Tahiti, February 1769

At noon on Tuesday, 31 January 1769, *Endeavour*'s course turned to the west-northwest on its way to Tahiti. The route enabled Cook to 'make a good Westing' as directed by the Admiralty. By the end of February, after passing through somewhat rough squalls and gales, Cook concluded, 'the SW swell still keeps up notwithstand[ing] the gale has been over about thirty hours, a proof that there is no land near in that quarter [110° 38″ west of Greenwich]'. On 1 March he reflected on the lack of current at his location: 'it serves to prove as well as the repeted trials we have made when the weather would permit, that we have had no Current that hath affected the Ship Since we came into these Seas, this must be a great sign that we have been near no land of any extent because near land are generally found Currents'. These conclusions in January and March are important in 'narrowing the options' for the Southern Continent because this is one of the areas where geographers such as Alexander Dalrymple suggested that territory with significant population would be located. The other possible location was that which Dalrymple termed 'the Gulf of San Sebastian', and which Cook was to search for after departing Tierra del Fuego and Staten Island in 1775 (Chapter 11).

Moreover, as J.C. Beaglehole notes in a Cook journal footnote, Cook exceeded the longitude reached by Wallis in this latitude. Cook's reference that the 'absence of currents argued against a continent is worthy of note ... His idea that the configuration of lands round an ocean affects the direction of currents is correct ... It was right therefore to suggest that if land existed in the southern hemisphere its presence would be indicated by the deflection of the trade wind current.'[11]

Therefore, during the first voyage Cook located no Southern Continent at 60° south or at 110° west longitude, as he told Admiralty Secretary Stephens, in 'a far more westerly Track than any Ship had ever done before'.

Tahiti was first sighted on 11 April, with a landing by the ship's company at Matavai Bay occurring on the 13th. For the next three months James Cook and the visitors in *Endeavour* focused on preparations to observe the Transit of Venus on 3 June and on gathering information and botanical specimens on King George's Island.

The Search for the Southern Continent South of the Society Islands, 2 August–2 September 1769

Endeavour sailed from Matavai Bay on 13 July. Cook set a course to follow the second set of secret Admiralty instructions by which he was to sail to 40° south in search of *Terra Australis Incognita*. The ship sailed among various Society Islands, guided by the Polynesian Tupia, although Cook did not always follow his advice. Tupia was a Raiatean chief, destined to be a priest (Raiatea is the second largest of the Society Islands after Tahiti). Joan Druett, a recent biographer, describes him as a 'master navigator', whose knowledge of Pacific waters could have been valuable for Cook and *Endeavour*. Tupia possessed a 'mental navigation map', including steering directions, weather, navigation by stars, currents, ocean swells, winds, reflections of distant lagoons on clouds and flight patterns of birds. His 'navigational map' was put on paper whilst sailing in *Endeavour*, although it is believed to be 'incomplete' by English cartographical standards. It was Banks more than Cook who encouraged Tupia's presence in *Endeavour*. Tupia was also of great assistance in interpreting conversations between the English visitors and other Polynesian natives as, for example, in New Zealand, as well as in settling disputes prior to leaving Tahiti. This ability to communicate also suggested to Captain Cook that the Polynesian peoples, in spreading throughout a vast area of the Pacific Ocean, shared a common language as well as having significant navigational ability.[12] The navigational ability of Polynesians, especially Tupia, was likely underestimated by the European visitors.

Between 9 August and 2 September Cook sailed southwards in search of the Southern Continent. In contrast to the search for land after departing Cape Horn, the weather was much improved, although not without rain showers and occasional strong winds. *Endeavour* was accompanied by a variety of birds (albatrosses, shearwaters, pintados, also called cape petrels, and various other petrels), an occasional whale and sightings of seaweed and rainbows. There were other natural phenomena too, such as a waterspout on the 24th and a comet on the 30th. On 25 August Joseph Banks observed in his journal, 'It was this day a twelvemonth since we left England, in consequence of which a piece of Cheshire cheese was taken from a locker where it had been reserv'd for this occasion and a cask of Porter tapped which prov'd excellently good, so that we lived like English men and drank the hea[l]th of our friends in England.'

On 28 August boatswain's mate John Reading drank a bottle of rum during the night and, Cook wrote, 'was speechless and past recovery in the morning'. Banks mentioned the incident in his journal, suggesting it was a mystery as to where he obtained the liquor, but asserting that most of the private casks carried in *Endeavour* had been tapped, some to two-thirds of their capacity, 'to the great dissatisfaction of the owners'.

Neither Banks's journal nor Molyneux's log provides any reference to the search for the Southern Continent during the August travels. The master's log cited temperatures in the forties as *Endeavour* reached 40° south, as well as increasingly rough weather and rain showers. Cook's journal entry on 2 September summed up his search:

> At 4 PM being in the Latd of 40° 22′ S and having not the least Visible signs of land, we wore and brought too under the fore sail and reef'd the Main sail and handed it. I did intend to have stood to the Southward if the winds had been moderate so long as they continued westerly notwithstanding we had no prospect of meeting with land, rather then [than] stand back to ye northrd on the same track as we came; but as the weather was so very tempestuous I laid a side this design, thought it more advisable to stand to the Northward into better weather least we should receive such damages in our sails & rigging as might hinder the further prosecutions of the Voyage.

On 2 September *Endeavour*'s route changed from south to north. Captain Cook reached New Zealand on 7 October. In 1769–1770 he was to circumnavigate New Zealand and prove it consisted of two major islands, and that it was not the tip of the Southern Continent. A further search for the 'land of great extent' to the south would await Cook's second voyage.

PART 3

CROSSING THE ANTARCTIC CIRCLE

Chapter 5

Cook's First Crossing
17 January 1773

At about ¼ past 11 o'Clock we cross'd the Antarctic Circle for at Noon we were by observation four Miles and a half South of it and are undoubtedly the first and only Ship that ever cross'd that line.

James Cook, journal entry, 17 January 1773

The search for the Southern Continent was the purpose of James Cook's second voyage (1772–1775). *Terra Australis Incognita* was still thought to exist and also to be accessible by navigation. This meant sailing to and likely beyond the Antarctic Circle (then at 66° 32′ south latitude). Only gradually in the course of the second voyage did Captain Cook conclude that the Southern Continent surrounded the South Pole, itself encompassed by a substantial ice barrier and not accessible by navigation. During his second voyage he circumnavigated portions of Antarctica in three attempts during consecutive summer months in the southern hemisphere. The first crossing of the Antarctic Circle by *Resolution* and *Adventure* occurred on 17 January 1773. *Resolution* crossed it again on 21 December 1773 and 26 January 1774. Cook's closest point to Antarctica was at 71° 10′ south latitude on 30 January 1774.[1]

The first recorded crossings of the Circle were important achievements in exploration and navigation history and therefore I want to examine the accounts of these events. What observations were recorded? Did the writers remark on the historic importance of the first crossings? What conditions did they face? How do their writings enhance our understanding of Cook's voyages and eighteenth-century navigation and exploration? In Chapters 5 to 9 I will explore the entries made in various log books and journals during the three crossings of the Antarctic Circle, as well as two separations of *Resolution* and *Adventure* (February 1773 and October/November 1773).

James Cook informed the Admiralty by letter in February 1772 about his plan to search for the unknown Southern Continent. Previous exploration had demonstrated that no such land existed above 40° south latitude, except in 140° west longitude (which passes through Polynesia, the Yukon, Alaska and the Arctic Ocean to the North Pole). A search for the Southern Continent would therefore require circumnavigation of the globe in a higher parallel and taking an easterly course because of prevailing winds in the high latitudes. Navigation in high southern latitudes should be accomplished in the summer months, no earlier than October, to reach 60° south (or the highest latitudes that could be achieved). During the other months of the year exploration would not be possible and the ships would obtain shelter in New Zealand or Tahiti.[2]

Admiralty Instructions, Second Voyage

For Captain Cook's second voyage the Admiralty provided *Resolution* and *Adventure*, the latter captained by Tobias Furneaux, who had accompanied Wallis to Tahiti in 1767. Furneaux was under Cook's command. The Admiralty's instructions, entitled 'Secret Instructions for Capt. Cook, Commander of His Majesty's Sloop Resolution', are dated 25 June 1772 and were presented to now-Commander James Cook by Admiralty Secretary Philip Stephens on behalf of Lord Sandwich and the other Lords of the Admiralty. (The full text is in Appendix A.) This set of secret orders can be summarized in four parts:

1. The purpose of the voyage was 'to proceed upon further discoveries towards the South Pole'. This was to be accomplished by sailing from Plymouth to Madeira, where additional foodstuffs as well as wine were to be obtained, before reaching the Cape of Good Hope for additional supplies and rest before departing to high southern latitudes by the end of October.

2. The first object was to locate Cape Circumcision, first discovered by the French East India Company's navigator Bouvet in 1739 (Chapter 2). Once located, Cook was to determine if the Cape was part of the Southern Continent or an island. He was then to assess the territory, and record observations in accordance with the Admiralty's instructions to Cook during the first voyage (*see* Chapter 4).

3. Should the Cape not be located, or if it turned out to be an island, Cook was directed to circumnavigate the Southern Ocean at high latitudes and as close to the Pole as possible in search of land. This is what he did during the three Antarctic summers of 1773–1775. He was cautioned to conduct his exploration for as long as the condition of the ships, the crew's health and the sloop's provisions would allow, ensuring that there were sufficient supplies to reach a 'known port', such as the Cape of Good Hope, to purchase additional supplies to return to England.

4. During those months of the year when it was not safe to sail in high latitudes, Captain Cook was directed northwards 'to refresh your people and refit the sloops, taking care to return to the Southward as soon as the season will admit of it'. The directions required Cook to make observations on any islands not previously discovered and produce 'surveys and draughts and take possession for His Majesty'. The Admiralty's orders also noted that should emergencies arise that were not covered in the instructions, Cook was 'to proceed as you shall judge most advantageous to the service on which you are employed'.

In summary, the second voyage was intended to locate the Southern Continent, with the first objective being Cape Circumcision, and then to proceed further south making a circumnavigation of 'the Pole' in high latitudes. It was assumed that the Southern Continent was located in a navigable sea and that it was likely populated, just as Alexander Dalrymple had asserted. The navigational and scientific nature of Cook's instructions is underscored in the instructions. We will observe these details in Cook's journals, the log books and the naturalists' journals from the second voyage.

Sources for the Crossing of the Antarctic Circle

On all his voyages Cook maintained a log and a journal. In the log he wrote navigational details and described 'remarkable occurrences'. In his journal he compressed the navigational details and expanded his account of what took place. However, it appears he began a second version of the journal, rewriting earlier passages. J.C. Beaglehole, the editor of Cook's journals, believed that at one time Cook was writing three different copies or versions of his journal.[3]

For this chapter, when drawing on the handwritten copy, I used the CORRAL online version[4] as well as J.C. Beaglehole's standard edited version of Cook's journal account. This and subsequent chapters also draw upon the log books of Tobias Furneaux, captain of *Adventure*, and those of Lieutenant Charles Clerke, Lieutenant Robert Cooper, ship's Master Joseph Gilbert, Master's Mate Isaac Smith and Master's Mate John Davall Burr, all of whom sailed in *Resolution*.[5] I also used the Board of Longitude log books of astronomers William Wales and William Bayly.[6] Other sources include the journals of Johann Reinhold Forster and George Forster, the father and son team of natural scientists in *Resolution*, as well as a biography of Tobias Furneaux.[7] Other sources include Lieutenant Richard Pickersgill's journal and Midshipman John Elliott's memoirs (both in *Resolution*), 'Furneaux's Narrative', as appended to Cook's journals, and the journals of Lieutenant James Burney (*Adventure*).[8]

From England via Madeira to the Cape of Good Hope

Resolution and *Adventure* were Whitby-built sloops, similar to *Endeavour*, acquired by the Admiralty for the second voyage. In early February *Resolution* was moved from dry dock to a wet dock and provisioning of the vessel began at Deptford. *Adventure* joined *Resolution* in late April. By mid-May Cook had notified the Admiralty that the sloop was not seaworthy due to the alterations ordered by Joseph Banks. At the end of May Banks withdrew his participation in the second voyage. In early June the supernumeraries – astronomers William Wales and William Bayly, naturalists Johann Reinhold Forster and his son George Forster, and artist William Hodges – were assigned to the voyage. By early July the retrofit of *Resolution* was complete and approved by Cook. Admiralty instructions were delivered to Cook and the marine chronometers were placed on board the two vessels. The second voyage departed from Plymouth on Monday, 13 July 1772.

Resolution and *Adventure* arrived at Funchal Harbour, Madeira, on 29 July. The English ships saluted the garrison with an eleven-gun volley, which was immediately answered. Cook went ashore to meet contractors for a wine supply. The governor could not meet Cook as he was leaving the city for the country, but sent a note saying that he was welcome to purchase the supplies he needed, the only obligation being to not make drawings of Funchal's fortifications. The Forsters obtained lodgings about 2 miles out of the city and pursued botanizing, while the astronomers set up their instruments to make observations. The ships were supplied with fresh beef and a thousand bunches of onions (as on the first voyage), since Cook thought these were very beneficial for the crew's health. Water, a large supply of wine and fruit were brought on board the ships. *Resolution* and *Adventure* weighed anchor at 10am on 2 August.

The ships next anchored at Port Praia Bay ('Praya' in Cook's journal) in the Cape Verde Islands on 13 August. Empty water casks were filled and on the 14th a bullock and some hogs were brought to *Resolution* to be slaughtered. Goats and fruits were also brought on board. Additional beef that was promised did not materialize. Worse, the water sources were questionable. Cook wanted to ensure that he had a sufficient supply of water to reach Cape of Good Hope without having to ration the supply. The ships departed for the Cape on the 15th, sailing through squalls of rain. On the 25th the water distillation device was put into use, generating about 18 gallons, a meagre amount for the ship's company. Over the following week the weather cleared and temperatures rose as the sloops neared the Equator. On 5 September temperature observations were made in the open air (76.5°F), on the ocean's surface (74°F), and when submerged for 15 minutes at 70 fathoms (66°F). The second voyage crossed the Equator on 7 September.

In keeping with Cook's approach to the sloop's cleanliness, *Resolution* was 'smoaked' periodically. 'Inspissated [concentrated, thickened] Juice of Malt' (beer) left fermenting on the deck since Madeira was put into the hold after some of the casks exploded, then it was sampled and found to have a sour taste, perhaps due to a bad container of water. Cook's journal occasionally records longitudes by both observation and 'Kendall's Watch', the chronometer carried in *Resolution*. Random comparisons revealed small variations. For example, on 11 September west longitude by observation was 11° 50′ but by Kendall's Watch it was 12° 21′. On the 13th the variation was 13° 8′ by observation compared to the chronometer's 14° 20′, while on the 18th it was 16° 37′ by observation but 18° 44′ by the Watch. These differences, ranging from 0.40° to 1.87°, continued to be recorded by the astronomers during the entire voyage.

As the ships neared the Cape, increasing numbers of birds were sighted by the voyagers, including albatrosses, shearwaters, pintados and cape hens. The Cape of Good Hope was sighted on 30 October. *Resolution* and *Adventure* anchored in Table Bay about a mile from shore, firing one of the cannon as a salute to the garrison. Cook took a cutter to shore to call upon the governor and make arrangements to take on additional supplies, including wine and freshly baked bread. Astronomers Wales and Bayly set up their equipment to make observations, concluding that Kendall's Watch was functioning much better than Arnold's (in *Adventure*), which tended to lose time. Wales's log book reported on 16 November that when the chronometers were being transferred back to the ship, the cutter struck the side of *Adventure*. When the case was opened, it was discovered that the Arnold clock had stopped, perhaps because of this accident.

At Cape Town J.R. Foster met Anders Sparrman (1748–1820), a Swedish naturalist and student of Linnaeus, and invited him, with Cook's approval, to join the voyage. On the 30th Cook wrote in his journal that the People were allowed to have leave on shore in groups of ten to twelve. While at anchor, they were fed fresh beef, mutton and 'as much greens as they could eat'.

The Search for Cape Circumcision

On 23 November 1772 *Resolution* and *Adventure* left Table Bay. The first iceberg (Cook's 'ice island') was sighted on 10 December. In 1739 Lieutenant Bovet had fixed Cape Circumcision's location as 54° 00′ south latitude and 11° 20′ east longitude. Cook reached 54° 0′ south latitude 21° 9′ east longitude on 13 December. The sails and rigging were covered with ice as *Resolution* passed twenty-one ice islands and encountered more penguins. On the 14th the ships encountered a huge field of ice against which they could not proceed, nor could the sailors see the end of it. Captain Furneaux visited Cook in *Resolution* and they discussed a plan of action should the ships become separated. This was an important navigational discussion which was to be put into effect the following February when the ships became separated in an Antarctic fog (Chapter 6). The two ships proceeded along the edge of the ice, noting the appearance of open water 'ponds' from time to time. The temperature fell to 27° during the night of 15 December. Snow began to fall so that the rigging and sails were decorated with icicles. By noon the temperature on the deck was 32° and a thermometer submerged to 100 fathoms registered 34°. More snow followed the next day and the ships were accompanied by whales. By the 17th *Resolution*'s position was 55° 8′ south latitude and 23° 43′ east longitude.

The ships proceeded in fields of loose ice as well as icebergs, accompanied by seals and whales. Snow continued to fall, while foggy weather and winds rendered sailing difficult and dangerous. Anxious not to be caught in field ice, which could trap a vessel for an extended time, Cook decided to travel 30–40 leagues (90–120 miles) to the east and then turn south to determine if land could be discovered. By the 29th Cook had notified Furneaux that he planned to sail west to the 'Meridian of Cape Circumcision' (11° 20′ west). Cook sighted snow petrels and recalled that Captain Bouvet also described these birds off Cape Circumcision in 1739. On 3 January Cook recorded in his journal that *Resolution* was 1.5–2° within the longitude of Cape Circumcision. He could see a distance of 15 leagues (45 miles) with no land to be seen. He wrote in his journal, 'I am of opinion that what M. Bouvet took for Land and named Cape Circumcision was nothing but Mountains of Ice surrounded by field Ice.' He decided he would not search 'after these imaginary Lands', and expressed worry that he had already spent too much time doing so with the advance of the season for sailing in high latitudes. Cook would search again for Cape Circumcision in 1775 as he proceeded to the Cape of Good Hope after discovering South Georgia and the South Sandwich Islands.

The ships crossed 60° south latitude on 6 January and continued their southward direction in gales of varying strength, sleet, snow and fog. On 4 January Cook observed in his journal that the People stood the cold weather 'tolerable well', wearing Fearnought jackets and trousers of the same cloth with a cap of canvas and 'baise' (baize): 'These together with an additional glass of Brandy every Morning enables them to bear the Cold without Flinshing.'

On 9, 10 and 12 January floating ice was harvested for fresh water in both *Resolution* and *Adventure*. This was done by hoisting out the boats for the People to collect floating pieces, the boats then returning to the ships where the ice was unloaded and melted in copper vats, to fill the empty water casks. On the 9th, Cook observed in his journal, 15 tons of fresh water was added to *Resolution* with an additional 8–9 tons for *Adventure*. Cook wrote that the work was 'tedious' and took time, but concluded 'this is the most expeditious way of Watering I ever met with'. William Wales's entry in his log book on the 9th stated that the water was 'of much more real value than Gold'. More ice was collected and melted on the 10th, Wales writing in his log book that obtaining water in this manner was safer than filling the casks on islands such as Cape Verde. On the 12th Cook noted that *Resolution* now carried 40 tons of water and *Adventure* had filled all its empty casks. Obtaining fresh water by this method would be repeated in the following weeks in the Southern Ocean. Artist William Hodges' painting 'Ice Islands on 9 January 1773' captures the process of obtaining ice to be melted for water (*see* Plate 7).

The First Crossing of the Antarctic Circle

On Sunday, 17 January 1773 at about 11.15am *Resolution*, followed by *Adventure*, crossed the Antarctic Circle – the first recorded crossing in history. The commentary in Cook's handwritten journal also appears in the Beaglehole version, except for two sentence fragments. Cook's account begins with references to *Resolution*'s position, to the presence of ice islands and floating surface (or field) ice and to birds and whales. In his handwritten journal for the 17th, Cook wrote,

> at a quarter of an hour past 11 o'Clock on the forenoon of the 17th we cross'd the Antarctic Circle in the Longitude of 39° 35′ East for at Noon we were by observation in the Latitude of 66° 36′ 30″ South. We passed one Island of Ice about 6 o'Clock [that morning] since which time no more had been seen, so that we began to think that we had at least got into a clear Sea, but these thoughts were of short duration for at 4 o'Clock in the afternoon we discovered all at once the whole sea is in a manner covered with Ice from SE round by the South to West in which extend 38 Islands of Ice, great and small were seen from the masthead besides loose pieces, which had last

increased so fast upon us that we were obliged to loof [steer into the weather] for one and bear up for another and at ¾ past 6 o'Clock being in the Latitude of 64° 15′ South and nearly in the last mentioned Longitude, we could proceed no further, the Ice being extremely close to the South, in the whole extent from E to NSW, without the least appearance of any partition; this immense field was composed of different kinds of ice, such as high hills, loose or broken pieces packed close together, and what Greenland men call fields of ice, a float of this kind of Ice lay to the SE of us of such extent that I could see no end of it from the Masthead, and was 16 or 18 feet high at least, and appeared of a pretty equal height and surface.

William Wales recorded a corroborating description of the solid wall of ice observed on the 17th: 'A large field seemingly of fast Ice extending from ESE to WSW and seemed as high above the Water as our ship's hull, but I have often found how fallacious this appearance is. It extended further to the Southward than can be seen from the Mast Head.' Cook observed the presence of pintados or Antarctic petrels which Cook thought to be native to the area. He also noted whales surfacing or chasing each other along the edges of the ice; Wales described them as 'large whales'.

In Beaglehole's version of Cook's journal, words are inserted referencing the historic importance of 17 January: 'At about ¼ past 11 o'Clock we cross'd the Antarctic Circle for at Noon we were by observation four Miles and a half South of it **and are undoubtedly the first and only Ship that ever cross'd that line**' [emphasis added]. Cook, the increasingly successful navigator, doubtless sensed the historical significance of this event. It is interesting that Cook does not think to include *Adventure*, which was sailing right behind *Resolution* on 17 January.

Cook also added some words to his summary of why he decided not to proceed further south. 'I did not think it was **consistent with the safety of the Sloops or any ways prudent for me** to persevere in getting further to the South, especially as the Summer was already half spent and it would have taken up some time to have gotten around the Ice, supposing it had been practicable, which however is doubtfull.' Cook's addition about the safety of the ships was likely aimed at armchair explorers, such as those who criticized his decision in *Endeavour* not to explore more of eastern Australia, for example. As Cook stated, 'getting around the ice' was not possible.

Tobias Furneaux used two pages of his log book to cover the period from Sunday, 10 January to Sunday, 18 January. (He misdated his entries, omitting 15 January, but he, or another person, perhaps much later, corrected it by adding the number in small handwriting.) The latitude and longitude he initially entered for the 15th and 16th were overwritten, making them difficult to read. Perhaps he did not write his entries on a routine, daily basis but entered the information for several days at one go. Furneaux was a competent navigator so it would be wrong to think he did not know his location.

Furneaux's comments are consistently brief. In his entry for 17 January he wrote only,

> First part fresh breezes and clowdy. Passed several Islands of Ice. Variation in the Azimuth of 29°[?] at 9am. Double reefs at 8am. Squally with snow. Got down top gallant yards. Saw a number of Silver birds and Pintados. In Company with the *Resolution*.

There is no mention that it was the first crossing of the Circle, although I would have expected an experienced navigator to have remarked on it. His entry for 18 January is a very condensed account, typical of Furneaux, especially when compared to Cook's journal cited above,

> Fresh gales with sleet and snow. At 7am 23 large Islands of Ice in sight in the sea entirely covered with smaller ones so that we could proceed no further to the Southward. Tacked and stood at this hour being 67° 11′ S. Double reefs of the one main top sail. A.M. variation of the Azimuth 29° 00′ W at noon. Double Reef of the main top sail. In company with the *Resolution*.

Captain Furneaux mentions the Antarctic Circle in his narrative account of the voyage, included in Beaglehole's edition of Cook's journals. He wrote,

> We held our course southward till the 18th [sic. 17th] of January when we crossed the Antarctic Circle and entered the Frigid Zone ... We were stopt by the Ice which intirely covered the surface of the water, which obliged us to tack and stand again the Northward, their being at the same time Thirty two Islands of Ice in sight.[9]

Furneaux's view that they might have got further south had they been able to push through the ice but would likely have been hemmed in by the ice is essentially the same as Cook's conclusion.

In his log book astronomer William Bayly in *Adventure* was more descriptive than Furneaux, writing that 'At 11 this morning, Crossed the Antarctic Circle nearly in Long^d. 39° 53′ East of Green^{ch}, with the 66° 36′ South Latitude.' Bayly identified 'large Islands of Ice', noted the fresh gales and sleet, and observed a 'large flight of Pintado Birds flying towards the SE'.

A Royal Navy vessel's day began at noon. Every four hours Bayly recorded temperature readings, and for the day ending at noon on the 17th the readings recorded were: noon, 16 January (34.5°F), 4pm (34°F), 8pm (36°F), midnight (32.5°F), 4am (32°F), 8am (34.5°F) and noon, 17 January (33.5°F). On the 18th Bayly's description was similar to those of Wales and Cook, noting the sloops were 'incompassed with fields of ice drifting about the sea together with a vast number of Large islands in latitude 67° 10′ South and 39° 50′ E of Greenwich'. Unlike Wales, he does not mention the presence of whales but he notes falling sleet and snow.

In 1960 Rupert Furneaux, the great-great-great grandson of Tobias Furneaux, published a biography of his ancestor, the first navigator to circumnavigate the globe both from east to west and also from west to east. We learn that Tobias Furneaux was not advised of the Admiralty's instructions until the voyage had been under way for several days. Rupert Furneaux suggests Tobias thought the ice extended to the South Pole, and that he was of the opinion that if a Southern Continent existed, Cook would find it. However, it is doubtful whether Furneaux looked forward to sailing in the Southern Ocean. Rather, he was interested in revisiting the 'tropical paradise' of Tahiti.

As the two ships proceeded south from the Cape of Good Hope, the account in Furneaux's biography discusses the November and December search for Cape Circumcision. On 23 November 1772 the ships entered 'the thrilling region of rock-ribbed ice', although the first sighting of an iceberg was not until 10 December. While searching for Cape Circumcision at 60° 20′ he makes a passing reference to 'no land habitable in polar regions by the reason of intense cold'.

Rupert Furneaux's biography then jumps from 14 December 1772 to 1 February 1773 without any reference to the 17 January crossing of the Antarctic Circle, just as Tobias Furneaux did in his log book. The only reference in the entire book to the Antarctic Circle is a map labelled 'Antarctica', likely prepared by the publisher. Rupert Furneaux speculates that Tobias, in contrast to James Cook, did not possess the 'ruthlessness' or the 'initiative of the great explorer', nor the 'eternal curiosity by which knowledge is expanded'. After the two ships separated on 8 February, Furneaux it seems was inclined to leave behind 'the thrilling region of rock-ribbed ice' and seek more compatible anchorages in New Zealand and the Southern Pacific.

The officers in *Resolution* wrote brief log entries about the crossing of the Antarctic Circle. Lieutenant Charles Clerke wrote in his log book, 'At Noon I find by my observation which was a tolerable good one, that between 11 and 12 we cross'd the Antarctick Circle.' He then references the presence of birds such as Antarctic petrels. 'Observed Latitude 66° 36′. *Adventure* in company.' At noon *Resolution* was sailing at 4 knots, 6 fathoms (= 4.75 knots) in a 'South by Westerly course, with winds SE ½ by East'. Clerke described the weather as 'Fresh Gales and Cloudy, hazey Weather with freezing snow showers' (*see* Appendix B).

Lieutenant Robert Cooper observed 'a great number of birds' as well as 'fresh gales and hazey with sleet', later 'very hazey with frequent showers of Snow & Sleet'. For the 11am log book entry he wrote, 'About ¼ past the hour of 11 we cross'd the Antarctic Circle, the first circumnavigation that ever did ...'. He never finished his sentence. Perhaps he meant to add 'occur' or similar words. Cooper was the only officer during the second voyage to note in his log book each time *Resolution* crossed the Antarctic Circle in either direction. On 18 January he wrote, 'At ½ past 4 this morning we Cross'd the Antarctic Circle ... the Second time.' After the last crossing in January 1774 he noted he had crossed the Circle for the sixth time, a method of accounting not found in other logs.

In his memoirs Midshipman Elliott wrote briefly about the first crossing of the Circle. He had observed the cluster of ice islands from 0.5–3 miles in length and two to three times the height of *Resolution*'s mastheads. He also noted the intense cold, writing 'And the frost and cold so intense as to cover the Rigging with Ice, like compleat christal [complete crystal] ropes, from one End of her to the other, and even to stiffen our outer Coats on our backs, yet Capt. Cook would not allow any fire in the Gally, or anywhere else but at proper times in the day.' In his journal Pickersgill recognized the significance of the first crossing, 'which was never done before'. He also described *Resolution*'s position: 'We stood as far into the ice as we could, and could perceive no thing but a vast field streaching East and West with no other signs of Land.' He observed nothing in sight but ice and birds. Burney in his journal noted the crossing of the Circle and wrote that the presence of ice prevented further progress towards the South Pole.

Resolution's Master Joseph Gilbert made no reference to the Antarctic Circle in his master's log book, but he cited the ship's position at latitude 66° 36′ 22″ South, 697 Leagues from Cape Town, with 'Strong gales with sleet & snow' as well as a 'hazy view. *Adventure* in Company'. Master's Mate Smith observed 'fresh gales of hazey weather with sleet'. He noted the ship 'cross'd the Antarctic Polar Circle'. Master's Mate Burr wrote 'Cross'd the Antarctic Circle' for his entry at noon on 17 January, observing 'fresh gales, hazey weather with sleet and snow as well as ice islands'.

Wales's log book contains a wide range of data including multiple calculations of longitude, readings for the Kendall Chronometer (marked K in the log) and the Arnold timekeeper (marked A). Wales was responsible for two of the four chronometers assigned by the Admiralty to the second voyage. William Bayly, the astronomer in *Adventure*, was in charge of the other two. Wales also lists two readings for barometric pressure and temperature marked 'A' and 'B', which may refer to different, but unstated, times of the day or to the use of two barometers. His log book, unlike the others, uses a 24-hour clock to mark the ship's day. The first crossing of the Circle is found in his entry for 16 January. Wales does not identify the Antarctic Circle, but records *Resolution*'s position as 66° 36½′ south by dead reckoning and 66° 36′ 6″ by observation. Barometric pressure 'A' was 29.00 and 'B' was 29.20 (Gilbert listed it as 29.10). Wales's two temperature readings were 51 ¾° (A) and 34° (B), the latter corresponding to Gilbert's reading of 34° at noon on the 17th.

Figure 10 summarizes the four calculations of longitude in Wales's log on 17 January. The chronometer readings are based on locations east of the Cape of Good Hope. Readings by dead reckoning and observation are based on latitude east of Greenwich. To make the figures comparable to Greenwich, 18° 27′ must be added to the Kendall and Arnold readings.

Wales was puzzled by the variance in the calculated longitudes. On 14 January both Cook and Wales determined longitude with one reading by telescope and a second without a telescope. Both came up with relatively similar readings. On 15 January Wales noted in his log book that these variations between sightings by instruments compared to calculating longitude by the chronometers caused him 'much concern'. He rejected both instrument error and 'parallelism in the line of

Figure 10. Astronomer William Wales's readings on 17 January 1773, the first crossing of the Antarctic Circle, comparing longitude determined by observation, dead reckoning, and the Kendall and Arnold chronometers.

Method Used	Longitude Recorded	Longitude East of Greenwich by adding 18° to Cape of Good Hope Readings
Dead Reckoning	43° 43′ East of Greenwich	No adjustment required
Kendall's Chronometer	20° 12′ East of the Cape of Good Hope	38° 39′ East Longitude
Arnold's Chronometer	18° 32.5′ East of the Cape of Good Hope	26° 59.5′ East Longitude
Observation	39° 57′ East of Greenwich	No adjustment required

collumniation [collimation] to the phase of the Quadrant' as causes for the variation. Wales concluded that the distance to the Sun and Moon 'cannot be made with near that certainty in these high latitudes which can in lower ones. I am well convinced from experience and have made known it in the account of my voyage to Hudson's Bay' (where Wales observed the Transit of Venus in 1769). It is now understood that the curvature of the Earth at the South Pole caused his concern.

In their accounts naturalists George and J.R. Forster entered brief comments about crossing the Antarctic Circle, although J.R. Forster did not cite crossing the Antarctic Circle when he published his *Observations*. Having sailed to 70° south, he concluded that the Southern Continent, if it was discovered in the future, must lie further southward. However, in his journal (which Forster was not allowed to publish due to disputes with the Admiralty – *see* Chapter 12) his entry for 17 January stated, 'The Latitude was observed at noon 66° 36′ South, & therefore 4 miles South of the Antarctic Circle. A place where no Navigator ever penetrated, before the British nation, & where few or none will ever penetrate. For it is reserved to the free-Spirited sons of Britannia, to navigate the Ocean wherever it spreads its briny waves.'

It is generally held that J.R. Forster took no delight in English maritime achievements so, for me, this entry is somewhat astonishing. An accomplished ornithologist and naturalist, Forster's journal entries provide frequent references to birds encountered in the Southern Ocean. In a footnote, Michael Hoare suggests George Forster 'wisely omitted this patriotic outburst' in his account, in which the younger Forster observed, 'On the 17th, in the forenoon, we crossed the Antarctic circle and advanced into the southern frigid zone, which had hitherto remained impenetrable to all navigators' – a less patriotic description of the first crossing's significance.

In reading multiple log books or journals, it is often obvious that the writers tended to copy from one another's observations. One example will suffice to make this point. Earlier in this chapter a lengthy citation by Captain Cook described the sea covered with ice, with thirty-eight large and small icebergs observed from the masthead, along with loose pieces floating about, which caused the ship to repeatedly change direction in order to avoid a collision. Eventually, *Resolution* could travel no further south. In reading the log books of Clerke, Cooper and Gilbert, I found nearly identical statistics and phrases. We would expect to find generally similar observations, but many entries are word-for-word. It is not possible to decide which writer was the 'original source'. However, J.C. Beaglehole warned researchers about the 'usual copying or dog-eat-dog-process' of writing log books and journals. I believe this assertion does not apply to the journals of the naturalists or the astronomers.

Crossing the Antarctic Circle was, of course, not the discovery of the Southern Continent, only the ice barrier around it, which was a significant impediment to further progress. With the first crossing of the Circle now completed, *Resolution* and *Adventure* pulled away from the ice. By 1 February they had reached 48° 51' south latitude. In early February the second voyage encountered an Antarctic fog which separated the two sloops, discussed in the next chapter.

Chapter 6

Separated in an Antarctic Fog
8–11 February 1773

At noon Tacked ship and fired 3 guns as a sig'l to our Consort but have not
heard a single Gun returned from the first – at 8 she bore NE b N distance
I believe about 1.2 miles – We've continued our Tacks onboard – what
methods they're taking I'm at a loss to guess, but fear they hear no more of
our guns that we of theirs.

Lieutenant Charles Clerke, *Resolution* log book entry, 8 February 1773

The Admiralty sent two vessels on Captain Cook's second voyage so the sloops
could provide mutual support during the long journey, especially if one of the
ships became disabled. This decision was a result of the crisis during the first
voyage when *Endeavour* was stuck on the Great Barrier Reef for 23 hours
(Chapter 1). The events of 8–11 February 1773 provided the first opportunity to
test these plans when a heavy Antarctic fog separated *Resolution* and *Adventure*.[1]

The purpose of this chapter is to examine what happened using the journals and
log books of officers on *Resolution* and *Adventure*. The sources include the journal
of Captain Cook, the log books of Captain Furneaux, Lieutenants Clerke and
Cooper, Master Joseph Gilbert, Master's Mates Burr and Smith, and the astronomers William Wales and William Bayly, and the journals of the scientists J.R.
Forster and George Forster (references were cited in the notes to Chapter 5).

Cook's Route after the First Crossing of the Antarctic Circle

As recounted in the previous chapter, *Resolution* and *Adventure* crossed the
Antarctic Circle on 17 January 1773. The ships encountered floating pieces of ice
(the larger pieces rising 3–14ft above the water) that are sometimes referred to as
'growlers' because of the noise they make as air escapes from them). They also
encountered larger 'ice islands' and a solid barrier of ice against which they could
not proceed. The sloops sailed north-northeast not only to move away from the
very cold weather, but also to search for the islands believed to have been discovered by French navigators Marc-Joseph Marion du Fresne and Julien-Marie
Crozet (du Fresne's second in command) in January 1772. (Later that year
du Fresne was killed and cannibalized by New Zealand Maori, along with some
of his crew, while Crozet managed to escape.) In February 1772, during a separate voyage, Captain Yves-Joseph de Kerguelen had claimed discovery of the

Kerguelen Island in the vicinity of 48° or 49° south latitude and 'in the Longitude of Mauritius', said to be at 57° East. The French navigators thought these islands were close to or part of *Terra Australis Incognita*, 'the France of the South', as Kerguelen described the territory. There were many scattered islands, now known as the Kerguelen archipelago, as well as the Marion, Prince Edward and Crozet Islands, another archipelago.

In 1775 Cook met French navigator Julien-Marie Crozet at Table Bay and viewed his charts of these islands (Chapter 11). Cook finally located the islands during his third voyage, on 24 December 1776, at 46° south latitude. He also named one of the islands after Marion du Fresne. The third voyage's navigation to locate these territories (and correction of the coordinates) will be considered in detail in Chapter 13.

Resolution and *Adventure* searched to north and east for the islands until 2 February but found no territory at the expected coordinates, although there were signs of possible land, such as seaweed, penguins and other birds, probably from the nearby (but unsighted) Heard Island, which is an important seabird breeding ground. In his journal Cook records sailing through hazy, foggy weather accompanied by occasional ice islands. On 6 February Charles Clerke wrote in his log book that 'If my friend Monsieur found any land, he's been confoundedly out in the Latitude and Longitude of it for we've searched the spot he confirmed it in and its Environs too pretty narrowly and the Devil's an inch of Land is there.'

The Separation

After failing to locate the French discoveries, *Resolution* and *Adventure* took a generally southerly course, heading back towards the Southern Continent. Soon afterwards, during 8–10 February, *Resolution* and *Adventure* became separated in a thick Antarctic fog. By pre-arranged plan, James Cook and Tobias Furneaux searched for each other for approximately three days, attempting to reach, but not quite making, the point where the two ships were last in contact. Foggy, hazy, rainy conditions gradually lifted by the third day and then remained hazy at best. The two ships separated to the southwest of Heard Island[2], shown on the map in Figure 5. The wandering line around Antarctica represents the Antarctic Convergence, the area where there is much fog, rain, sleet, snow and, nearer the continent, floating ice.

By the afternoon of 10 February Cook considered the separation of the ships to be permanent, so he resumed his southerly course. On 11 February Furneaux reached the same conclusion and set sail for the pre-arranged rendezvous in New Zealand. The two ships did not meet up in the Southern Ocean. *Resolution* reached solid Antarctic ice on 24 February at 61° 21' south. By 17 March Cook had decided to proceed to New Zealand, sighting South Island on 25 March. It was not until 18 May that the ships met again at Ship's Cove, Queen Charlotte Sound.

What Caused the Separation?

Officers in the two ships record in their log books and journals fresh fair weather with strong gales for Sunday, 7 February. At 10am hammocks and bedding were placed on *Resolution*'s deck to air and the ship was cleaned and smoked between decks. Later in the day there was hazy or cloudy weather. At 4pm *Resolution* signalled to *Adventure* to keep 4 miles off starboard, and at 6pm a signal was sent to *Adventure* to come under *Resolution*'s stern.

The next day at 6am Furneaux and Clerke both noted *Adventure*'s top gallant mast was carried away (presumably by strong wind and rough seas). A new one was installed. At 8am the ocean's depth was sounded. No ground was found at 210 fathoms.[3] Penguins and other birds were seen around the ship, suggesting that land might be nearby. Cook observed that *Adventure* was approximately two points off starboard (about 1½ miles). Between 9 and 10am the vessels followed a southerly course at 6½ knots. At this point Cook wrote in his journal, 'A thick Fogg came on so that we could not see her [*Adventure*].' Furneaux's log places *Adventure* 'about 3 miles distant' from *Resolution* at the time of separation.

The heavy fog persisted through Tuesday and Wednesday, 9–10 February, along with periodic cloudy, squally weather and sometimes strong gales. Robert Cooper noted 'a great sea'. Clerke observed 'a Great Swell from the West'. Joseph Gilbert, Isaac Smith and John Davall Burr wrote similar entries. Gilbert recorded progressively fresh, moderate, strong and then hard gales from the 8th to the 10th. During the morning of the 10th the weather cleared somewhat, with Cook observing that the weather was hazy with rain, but visibility was at 3 or 4 leagues.[4] The next day Cook noted that had visibility improved and 'we could see full five leagues around us'. Furneaux noted 'fresh gales and squally weather', observing that his main top mast and stay sails were split.

William Wales recorded temperatures twice every day. Between 8 and 11 February there were 'high' temperatures from 51° to 58°F, while 'low' temperatures ranged from 40° to 45°F. These values were in contrast to the temperatures in the lower 30°s recorded by him during the first crossing of the Antarctic Circle in January. The winds were generally strong northerly, north-by-east and north-by-west winds, so that *Resolution* sailed at 6½ knots on the 7th and 8th, 4½ knots on the 9th and up to 7½ knots on the 10th. As we will see below, it was the continual wind that largely prevented a return to the point of separation.

Where was the Point of Separation?

At the approximate point of separation on Monday, 8 February, Cook entered his position as 49° 53' south and longitude 63° 39' east of Greenwich. Furneaux did not make an entry in his log at the point of separation, but his entry for noon, which was about 2 hours later, was 50° 00' south and 45° 37' east of the Cape of Good Hope. At noon Cook recorded a longitude of 45° 30' east of the Cape.

From the recorded positions at noon, I have calculated that the ships were 10.6 statute miles (17.1km) apart. Using data recorded by Cook and Furneaux,

Figure 11. *Resolution* and *Adventure*'s approximate distances apart during the separation of the two ships off Antarctica, 8–11 February 1773. Longitude is recorded east of the Cape of Good Hope. Distances apart have been calculated.*

February 1773	Resolution				Adventure				Distance Apart	
	Course	Total Miles	Latitude South	Longitude East	Course	Total Miles	Latitude South	Longitude East	Approx. Km.	Statute Miles
7 (Sun)	S. 72° E.	146	48° 49' S.	43° 25' E.	ESE	148	48° 47' S.	43° 23' E.	4	3
8 (Mon)	S. 54° E.	103	49° 51' S.	45° 34' E.	S. 50° ESE	114	50° 50' S.	45° 47' E.	17	11
9 (Tue)	S. 66° W.	5	49° 53' S.	45° 30' E.	S. 54° E.	14	50° 08' S	45° 55' E.	41	25
10 (Wed)	S. 68°	38	50° 07' S.	46° 30' E.	N. 62° E.	32	49° 53' S.	46° 39' E.	28	17
11 (Thur)	S. 54°	124	51° 25' S.	48° 57' E.	S. 6° E.	27	50° 20' S.	46° 44' E.	197	122

* This table is based upon data in the journals for 7–11 February 1773. The calculations in the columns marked 'Difference' are based upon the positions recorded at noon for *Resolution* and *Adventure*. I used formulae designed to calculate distance between points of latitude and longitude that I found at www.moveable-type.co.uk/scripts/latlong.html.

I created a table of the ships' positions and their relative distance apart. Of course, their positions were rarely static. Conclusions regarding distances between *Resolution* and *Adventure* are only relative because longitude and latitude were usually recorded only once daily, while during each 24-hour period the ships most likely would have been further apart or closer together at various points in time. Nonetheless, the data provides relative comparisons of the position of the ships during the foggy days of 8–10 February. On 7 February, sailing in hazy and windy weather, the ships were less than 3 miles apart, but they were 10.6 miles apart after encountering the thick fog on 8 February.

During the next two days, the period of thickest foggy weather, the separation was even greater: 25.3 miles on the 9th and 17.4 miles on the 10th. The weather cleared on the 10th and Cook was able to record visibility of 5 leagues (15 nautical miles), but he considered the weather probably too obscured for people in the ships to have visual contact. At noon that day Cook decided a permanent separation had occurred. He also thought he would be unable to reach the original point of separation. Thus he abandoned the search for *Adventure* and pursued a course towards the Southern Continent, so that by 11 February the ships were 122 miles apart. Cook assumed that both ships had been driven in the same direction after separation. *Resolution*'s course had been generally south, driven by a northerly wind. *Adventure*'s course had been the same until the 10th, when she struck a northerly course, heading towards the point of separation. The ships had been closest to the point of separation on Tuesday, 9 February.

The Captains' Descriptions of the Separation

After encountering thick fog on 8 February, Captain Cook concluded that the wind should have brought the ships along a common route 'directly to Windward of us, provided she [*Adventure*] kept her Wind which she ought to have done as no signal was made to the contrary. In short we were intirely at a loss, even to guess by what means she got out of hearing the first gun we fired.'

On 9 February Cook noted that the plan was 'to repair to the place where we last saw her, Captain Furneaux being directed to do the same and there to cruze [cruise] for three days'. Cook repeatedly tacked *Resolution* and made short boards during the foggy weather 'over that part of the Sea we had already made ourselves acquainted with'. False fires were displayed at the masthead and guns fired hourly (or shorter intervals), both fires and guns being used as signals to the 'other' ship.

By 10 February, despite gradually improving visibility, Cook concluded,

> for altho we laid too all the morning we could see nothing of the *Adventure* which if she had been with[in] 4 or 5 Leagues of us must have seen from the mast head. Having now spent two Days of the three assign'd to look for each other, I thought it would be to little purpose to wait any longer and still less to attempt to beat back to the appointed station well knowing that *Adventure* must have drove to leeward equally with ourselves. I therefore made sail to the SE with a very fresh gale at WBN accompanied with a high Sea.

Cook directed *Resolution* back towards the Southern Continent, where he encountered ice at 61° 52′ south latitude, and then headed for winter quarters at New Zealand.

Captain Furneaux's log book consists of his usual very brief entries, giving few details regarding Cook's ship except 'Can see nothing of the *Resolution*.' On 8 February *Adventure* fired a gun at 9am, 'in answer to one from her [*Resolution*], the report bore distant from what was expected at heading [?] East, soon after we fired another gun but heard no answer – fired every half hour. At Noon thick fog [and] could not see nor hear nothing of *Resolution*.' In his post-voyage description of the events, Furneaux stated *Adventure* 'kept the course we steered on before the Fog came on, on [*sic*] the evening it began to blow hard, and at intervals more clear, but could see nothing of her [*Resolution*] which gave us much uneasiness'. Furneaux attempted to return to the point of separation, but was prevented on the 9th by

> a very heavy gale of wind and thick weather, that obliged us to bring to and thereby prevented us reaching the intended spot, but on coming more moderate, the fog in some measure clearing away we cruised as Near the place as we could get, for three days when giving over all hopes of joining company again bore away for winter quarters distant fourteen hundred leagues, thro' a sea intirely unknown and reduce[d] the allowance of water to one quart p[er] day.[5]

Prior to the separation, Furneaux had expressed concerns about the water supply, the failure to locate land, the season of the year and the long distance to New Zealand. He restricted 'every man to an allowance of three pints of water a day'. From this we may conclude he favoured leaving the Southern Ocean for more comfortable conditions in New Zealand and the South Pacific. However, he did follow the pre-arranged plan and searched for three days after encountering the fog, one day more than Cook searched for *Adventure*.

How did the Captains Search?

Information in the log books and journals about the search methods and details are inconsistent. At first *Resolution* and *Adventure* signalled each other by the firing of cannon. The guns were also fired when the ships tacked. Signal flares (described as 'false fires') were burned at each mast head only on 10 February, according to some of the log books and journals. During the search a sailor was stationed at each mast head on *Resolution* to keep watch for any sign of the other ship. We may assume the masts on *Adventure* were also manned but there is no such reference in Furneaux's log book.

J.R. Forster (in *Resolution*) suggests a light may have been detected, in which case signal flares must have been burned on *Adventure*, although it is curious that this information is not in Furneaux's log book. Most of the log books show the guns were fired hourly, although Wales's and Cook's journals state half-hourly on 8–9 February. The methods were ineffective because the ships were too far apart, not because of the methods used.

On 9 February Furneaux observed that *Adventure* 'Fired a gun every half hour but had no answer from the *Resolution*. At times we thought we saw her bearing SE ¼ (?) at intervals clear but could see nothing of her.' However, in his post-voyage narrative he states that soon after the separation on the 8th they 'heard a Gun, the report of which we imagined to be on the Larboard [port] beam, we then hauled up SE and kept firing a four pounder every half hour but had no answer or further sight of her'. These comments make sense because, as Figure 11 demonstrates, the ships were closest together on 9 February.

In *Adventure* astronomer William Bayly documented the efforts to signal *Resolution*. On 8 February his log book recorded the weather as 'fresh gales and heavy with rain' and then fog, and *Resolution* fired a gun as a signal which was answered with a swivel gun on *Adventure*. Bayly's entry continues, 'Fir^d 3 guns within this hour [11am on 9 February] within an hour and a half as signals to the *Resolution*, but could not hear nor see anything of her. *Resolution* out of sight.' On 9 February Bayly recorded the frequent firing of guns as a signal. Between 4 and 5pm he commented, 'thought we saw the appearance of the *Resolution* bearing SE by S'. This is similar to J.R. Forster's journal observation that *Adventure* may have been sighted on the 9th. On 9 and 10 February foggy and cloudy weather continued, accompanied by 'fresh gales and squally with very rough seas'. Bayly made no reference to signal fires. Thereafter Bayly's log makes no reference to *Resolution*.

Bayly, as William Wales did in *Resolution*, recorded temperatures six times daily. For the 8–10 February period, Bayly's recordings averaged a 'low' temperature of 40° and a 'high' temperature of 43.4° which (as did Wales's recordings) averaged 10° higher than on 17 January when the sloops first crossed the Antarctic Circle. It is unsurprising that the lower temperatures occurred during the night. However, the range of lower temperatures was no more than four degrees apart.

Cook's rewriting of his journal can be seen in the events he recorded for 4pm on 9 February. The version that appears in Beaglehole's edition states, 'Mr. Forster alone thought he heard the report of another to Windward nearly in the same situation as the last, this occasioned my standing half an hour longer to the Westward in which time we fired two guns to which no answer was heard.' His handwritten journal accessible on the CORRAL website contains a differently worded entry: 'some of the People thought they heard four guns fired to leeward. This view [served] only to perplex us and made it doubtfull that any guns at all had been heard sometime after 6 & 8 o'Clock.'

Lieutenant Robert Cooper's 3pm log book entry on 9 February states, 'Heard the report of a gun to the Winward, ½ past heard another in answer to ours, which are the only ones we've heard since the fog came on, fired a gun every quarter till 5, then every half hour.' Likewise, J.R. Forster wrote in his journal on 9 February,

> We fired now & then guns till past 10 o'clock. Some believed to have seen the light & even a wild fire on the beam to leeward but I & others could see

nothing. We fired likewise a wild fire without any Answer. All night guns were fired, without any answer.

Therefore, there is conflicting log book and journal evidence as to whether guns were fired hourly, half hourly or every quarter hour. It is also unclear whether cannon signals occurred continuously when the fog was at its height on 8–10 February. Intriguingly, Forster makes no reference to hearing *Adventure*'s guns, although Cook cited Forster for this information. Forster is also the only person to report that a light might have been seen.

How much Concern did the Separation Cause?

Although the purpose of sending two ships on the second voyage was for one vessel to aid the other in case of problems, only brief concerns arising from the separation are noted in the log books and journals. As cited above, Furneaux wrote that not seeing *Resolution* 'gave us uneasiness'. I found Lieutenant Clerke's entries in his log to be quite matter-of-fact. For example, after encountering increasingly thick fog on 8 February, Clerke wrote, 'at noon Tacked ship and fired 3 guns as a sig'l to our Consort but have not heard a single Gun returned from the first – at 8 she bore NE b N distance I believe about 1.2 miles – We've continued our Tacks onboard – what methods they're taking I'm at a loss to guess, but fear they hear no more of our guns than we of theirs.' The next day he continued,

> Between 6 and 7 the weather became tolerably clear, when we every one made the best use of our Eyes in quest for our Consort but to our great mortification we found she was not within our Horizon. Continued to fire ½ hour our guns all night in case we might come by accident within hearing of each other … [at 7am the following morning] continue the ½ hour guns for the weather is still so hazey, they may be heard further than we can see …
> We can see nothing of our friends and must for the present give them over.

'Give them over' essentially means abandon the search for *Adventure*. Gilbert, Cooper, Burr, Smith and Wales recorded no concerns in their logs. Cook and Furneaux expressed relatively little worry, merely giving the conditions of weather and the ocean to explain the ships' parting. After 10 February log books on both ships contain no reference to the separation.

J.R. Forster's journal does not raise a note of alarm but cites the methods noted above on *Resolution*'s search for *Adventure*. However, considerable concern about the loss of *Adventure* was expressed by George Forster, who wrote on 10 February, the day Cook abandoned the search,

> notwithstanding all our endeavours to recover our consort, we were obliged to proceed alone on a dismal course to the southward, and to expose ourselves once more to the dangers of that frozen climate, without the hope of being saved by our fellow-voyagers, in case of losing our own vessel. Our parting with the *Adventure* was almost universally regretted among our crew, and none of them ever looked around the ocean without expressing some

concern on seeing our ship alone on the vast and unexplored expanse, where
the appearance of a companion seemed to alleviate our toils, and inspired
cheerfulness and comfort.

George Forster's remarks are typical of his more frequently recorded emotional
and fretful interpretations of events on the high seas, perhaps due to his youth
and lack of sailing experience. However, it is reasonable to assume that everyone
experienced apprehension to some degree about the separation of the vessels, but
few of their thoughts were recorded.

Conclusions

Fog, rain, sleet and snow are common features in sailing south of the Antarctic
Convergence, so it is no surprise that *Resolution* and *Adventure* came upon fog
when they did. After the onset of thick Antarctic fog on 8 February, Cook and
Furneaux proceeded according to their previously made plan. They attempted to
return to the point of separation, but were prevented from reaching it by the
strong wind. Foggy weather continued for two more days. The ships were even
further apart on 10 February when Furneaux proceeded north and Cook sailed to
the south. Signalling their position by cannon or fires was used during several
days of foggy weather, but to no avail. Tacking the ships back and forth, and
holding to, were reasonable actions under the circumstances, but did not lead to
the reunion of the ships. The journals and log books provide varying and inconsistent accounts of how frequently signals were made by cannon and flares.
Furneaux did not desert the mission: indeed, he searched for *Resolution* for one
day longer than Cook searched for *Adventure*.

It is important to place this separation of the two sloops into a broader context.
After the separation, Cook continued to sail along 60° south, often encountering
weather described as cloudy, dark and gloomy, with snow, sleet and hail, and the
continued presence of field ice and ice islands. On 17 March Cook decided to sail
for Van Diemen's Land or New Zealand, commenting

> after cruising four months in these high Latitudes it must be natural for me
> to wish to injoy some short repose in a harbour where I can procure some
> refreshments for my people of which they begin to stand in need of, to this
> point too great attention could not be paid as the Voyage is but in its infancy.

James Cook intended to return to resume the second voyage's ice edge cruise in
the summer months of 1774. As we will see, the two ships met again in May 1773,
in New Zealand.

Accounts of the Separation by Other Historians

The separation of *Resolution* and *Adventure* is included in many accounts of Cook's
voyages, with some variance in the length allotted to the events of 8–11 February
1773.[6] My expectation was that the separation would receive brief reference,
especially since there were no adverse outcomes following this event. Planning by

Cook and Furneaux likely eased serious concerns. In my opinion, the February separation of the sloops is a significant event, as well as shedding light on an interesting aspect of navigation history during adversity, but it did not rise to the highest levels of importance for the voyage or the search for Antarctica. Nonetheless, it had the potential to be dangerous since the two ships could not now rely on each other for assistance. It is also important to recognize that both Cook and Furneaux proceeded according to their agreed-upon plans should a separation occur and met up again in New Zealand later in 1773.

Secondary sources by Tobias Furneaux (1960), Villiers (1968), MacLean (1972), Beaglehole (1974), Hough (1995), Collingridge (2002), Finnis (2003) and Aughton (2004) provide accurate interpretations of the events recorded in the journals and log books, as does the account by novelist Graeme Lay (2013–2015).[7] Several authors whose emphasis is mostly on the South Pacific aspects of Cook's voyages often cited the separation with a few words or ignored the matter entirely.

However, while I found the recent Cook biography by McGlyn (2011) to be accurate in the description of the separation (cleverly commenting 'a thick fog was added to the elemental minestrone'), the writer then states the situation 'flummoxed' both Cook and Furneaux, leading to Captain Furneaux's 'sudden disappearance' for New Zealand. Moreover, he characterizes Cook's 'perseverance' in seeking Antarctica as 'monomania'. These opinions are surely overstatements. A 'flummoxed' James Cook is implausible, in my opinion. Martin Dugard's biography (2001) has Cook sailing in incorrect directions, suggesting he 'veered' up to 46° south to locate 'the French discoveries' *after*, not before, the separation (but this search ended up 200 miles short of this territory). Dugard does not mention the heavy fog, high seas or any detail about the search by both ships.

Only passing or no reference at all is made to the separation in some studies, such as those written by Alan Moorhead (1968), Tony Horwitz (2002), Nicholas Thomas (2003), Alan Gurney (2007), John Gascoigne (2007) and Dan O'Sullivan (2008). These studies are all sound accounts of Cook's voyages from a variety of perspectives, a few mainly South Pacific-focused, but the authors chose to mostly ignore the events of February 1773.[8]

This brief excursion into 'Cook Historiography' suggests that fidelity to the primary sources and historical context are essential for an interpretation of events, as is not inventing motivations unsubstantiated by the record, even the three-day 1773 separation in a thick, soupy Antarctic fog.

Chapter 7

'An agitated & tempestuous sea': the Cook Strait

October–December 1773

The fury of the winds is not yet abated & we are rolled about in an agitated & tempestuous Sea. The storm roaring in our rigging, & breaking against our Ship. The storm raises the Sea, & when she brakes over the top of the wave, the wind entirely dissolves the sea into Atoms of vapour & carries them off into the Air, like Smoke … We tried to wear ship, but the Sea & storm hindered us to do it. The Sea is mountainous & the wind rages with utmost fury.

Johann Reinhold Forster, journal entry, 26 October 1773

During Cook's second voyage *Resolution* and *Adventure* separated twice. On 8 February 1773 the two ships parted in a thick fog off Antarctica (Chapter 6). On 29/30 October 1773 they separated again in stormy weather while attempting to sail through Cook Strait to Queen Charlotte Sound, New Zealand. It was from Ship Cove that the sloops were to prepare for the second crossing of the Antarctic Circle and the search for the Southern Continent. This chapter traces the journal and log book entries by officers of the two ships from 20 October to 27 December 1773.

Introduction

Historical context is always important to understanding the sequence of events. As explained in Chapter 6, after the first separation Captains James Cook and Tobias Furneaux searched for each other for three days, attempting to reach the initial point of separation. After failing to join up in the Southern Ocean, the ships met again at Ship Cove, Queen Charlotte Sound, New Zealand, on 18 May 1773. On 7 June they departed for a four-month sweep of South Pacific islands. On 10 October the ships left Tonga for Ship Cove to prepare the vessels for a return to the Southern Ocean. This chapter further illustrates how Cook's searches for the Southern Continent formed part of larger-scope voyages to Pacific Ocean locations during months other than the Antarctic summer months (December to February).

We will first consider issues of geography and navigation, the events of 20–30 October leading to the separation, *Resolution*'s arrival at Ship Cove

(4 November) and *Adventure*'s arrival at Ship Cove (30 November). The second part will cover events affecting the ships while at Ship Cove and their separate departures. *Resolution* sailed on 25 November, searching again for *Adventure*, then headed for Antarctica. *Adventure* sailed on 23 December for Cape Horn, then on to the Cape of Good Hope and England, where she arrived in July 1774. I will also include estimates of how far apart the two ships were at the time of their 30 October separation and describe the attempts made by Cook to search for Furneaux during 25–27 November, together with a brief investigation of how these events are interpreted in selected secondary sources. After the second separation *Resolution* and *Adventure* did not sail together again during the remainder of the second voyage.[1]

In explaining these events, I used the Beaglehole edition of Cook's journals to understand day-to-day sailing conditions and also accessed the log books of *Resolution* officers Charles Clerke, Robert Cooper, Joseph Gilbert, Isaac Smith and John Davall Burr, as well as astronomer William Wales. For *Adventure*, I used the log books of Furneaux, the private journal of James Burney[2] and the log book of astronomer William Bayly, plus anecdotal information from the journals of Johann Reinhold Forster and his son George.

Geography and Navigation

The Cook Strait between New Zealand's North and South Islands links the Tasman Sea and the South Pacific Ocean. In 1769 James Cook was the first European to sail through the Strait that bears his name, proving that New Zealand consisted of main two islands (and many small islands). Cook Strait is 14 miles (22km) wide at its narrowest point. Its weather at certain times of the year is unpredictable and dangerous. To enter the Southern Pacific waters leading to Cook Strait (as did *Resolution* and *Adventure* in 1773), ships sail between Cape Palliser (North Island) and Cape Campbell (South Island), two points of land 52.6 miles (84.6km) apart. Using the mid-point on an imaginary line drawn between Capes Campbell and Palliser, I estimate the distance to Queen Charlotte Sound to be 35–40 miles.[3]

The Cook Strait's geological features comprise a deep marine canyon with steep cliffs on both sides, especially on the North Island. The Strait represents a 'gap' in the chain of mountains that extends through much of the South and North Islands. Numerous bays are located at the north end of the South Island, including Queen Charlotte Sound. The ocean is often 70 fathoms (420ft/126m) deep, although depths of 100–150 fathoms are recorded. Navigation in the Strait is difficult, with treacherous currents and fierce storms, especially in the spring-time, the season of the year in New Zealand for events covered in this chapter. Northwesterly winds predominate but south-westerly flows also occur. Winds shift quickly, and gale force winds (with gusts up to 150mph) occur in this lati-tude, 41° south, termed the 'wind belt of the Roaring Forties'.

The Strait's waters feature powerful tidal flows, resulting in strong currents. Tidal surges sometimes last 10 hours. Submarine ridges off the coasts complicate the flow of ocean water and can result in turbulence.[4] As the information in the log books demonstrates, both ships confronted ever-changing contrary winds accompanied by storms in attempting to penetrate Cook Strait from the Pacific. The map in Figure 5 identifies some of the key locations in the following narrative.

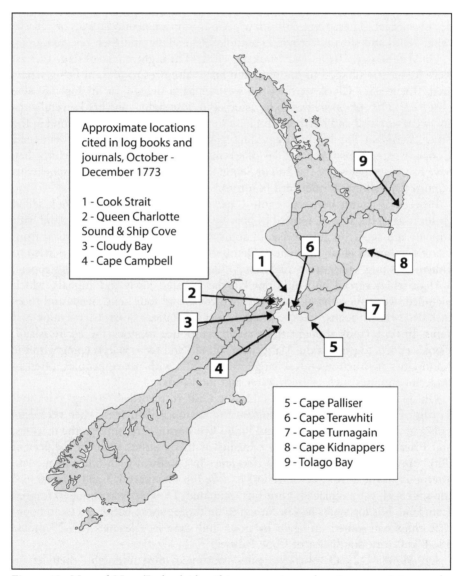

Approximate locations
cited in log books and
journals, October -
December 1773

1 - Cook Strait
2 - Queen Charlotte
Sound & Ship Cove
3 - Cloudy Bay
4 - Cape Campbell

5 - Cape Palliser
6 - Cape Terawhiti
7 - Cape Turnagain
8 - Cape Kidnappers
9 - Tolago Bay

Figure 12. Map of New Zealand identifying approximate locations pertaining to the separation of *Resolution* and *Adventure* off the Cook Strait, October–December 1773. (The map is edited by the author; the original map is by NordNordwest.[5])

Resolution and *Adventure*, 20–30 October 1773

While sailing south-southwest towards the entrance to Cook Strait, *Resolution* and *Adventure* lost sight of each other for part of the day on both 23/24 and 26/27 October, before finally becoming separated on 29/30 October. From 20 to 30 October the two ships were confronted by frequent, often strong gales, sometimes accompanied by rain, thunder and lightning and, at least on one occasion, sleet. There were only a few periods of more gentle breezes or relative calm. Gales and storms occurred continually, breaking and then resuming.

On Wednesday, 20 October Cook recorded, 'The night was so obscure that we were frequently obliged to fire guns and burn false fires to prevent being separated.' Lieutenant Clerke termed the weather as 'a deluge' in his log. He also observed, 'The *Adventure* was so far astern as to lose sight – she fired several guns and we returned 2 and burnt several false Fires.' Similar remarks are found in the other *Resolution* log books. Regarding conditions on board ship Lieutenant Cooper wrote, 'This is the last day of serving the People Fresh Pork, which they have had every day since the 2nd of September and now have several puncheons of corn [84 gallons or one-third of a ton].'

Proceeding south between Table Cape and Cape Kidnappers, Cook sailed closer to land because he wanted to provide the natives of the North Island with animals and seeds for future use. (The name Cape Kidnappers is derived from Cook's comment on an incident in October 1769 when Maori in canoes tried to kidnap a young sailor from *Endeavour*.) On 22 October, at Cape Kidnappers, a Maori chief agreed he would not kill the donated fowls and animals, which included two pairs of boars and sows, two cocks and four hens. Seeds and roots included wheat, beans, peas, cabbages, turnips, onions, carrots, parsnips and yams. In time Cook thought these could reproduce to stock the entire island. Cook's efforts to present the Maori with animals and seeds is in keeping with the Admiralty's instructions to exchange various gifts with native peoples, often in trade for supplies such as fresh water and foodstuffs.

On 23/24 October *Resolution*'s Master Gilbert recorded 'strong gales and squalls of wind off the land'. *Resolution* lost its top gallant mast, then reefed its sails and stood off Cape Turnagain. Philip Brotherson, drummer in the marines, and Private William Monk were punished with six lashes each for 'neglect of duty' (unspecified). *Resolution* and *Adventure* lost sight of each other in the late afternoon of the 23rd. *Adventure* lost its fore top mast stay sail and split its fore top sail. Both were replaced. Furneaux estimated *Adventure* was about 10 leagues from land. His log states he saw *Resolution* on the lee shore between 11 and noon. The ships had joined up again by noon and were 8–9 leagues (24–27 miles/ 38–43km) west-southwest of Cape Palliser.

On Monday, 25 October the gales continued until midnight, then let up briefly. Cook observed in his journal that *Resolution* 'loosed out the reefs out of the Top-sails and rigged top-g^t yards, with the vain hopes that the next wind which came would be favourable, we were mistaken, the wind only took this little repose in order to gain strength to fall the heavier upon us'. At this time *Resolution* was 8–9 leagues from Cape Palliser. At 11pm Cook remarked the wind

> came on in such a fury as to oblige us to take in all our sails with the utmost expedition and to lay-to under our bare poles with our heads to the SW. The brails[6] of the Mizen giving way the wind took hold of the sail and tore it in several places, we presently lowered down the yard and bent another sail. The Sea rose in proportion with the Wind so that we not only had a furious gale but a mountainous Sea also to incounter, thus after beating two days against strong gales and arriving in sight of our Port we had the mortifica-tion to be drove off from the land by a furious storm; two favourable circum-stances attended it which gave us some consolation, the Weather continued fair and we were not apprehensive of a lee-shore.

Clerke described the conditions as 'a Nasty, High, Short Sea'. Cooper described 'strong gales and very hard squally', while at 8pm Gilbert recorded 'violent hard gales handed every sail and brought to'.

These conditions continued on Tuesday, 26th and the ships separated again. Sailing conditions were difficult and the view obscure. Cook wrote in his journal, 'hazey in the horizon occasioned in a great measure by the spray of the Sea which was lifted up to a great height by the force of the wind'. By 7pm *Adventure* could not be sighted. At 8pm Gilbert recorded that *Resolution* was brought to for the night. Furneaux noted, 'also lost sight of the *Resolution*'. However, Gilbert recorded that by noon on the 27th *Adventure* 'was 5 miles astern'. With a decrease in the wind, Cook steered NBW½W for the Strait, estimating Cape Palliser to be 17 leagues (51 miles) to the north. At 3am, with a favourable change in the weather, Cook wrote, 'being near the land of Cape Campbel we tacked and stretched over for Cape Pallisser under our Close reef'd Top-sails and Courses, being as much sail as we could carry. At day-light we could but just see the *Adventure* from the Mast-head to the Southward.'

Resolution tacked about 4–5 leagues from Cape Palliser and then, with another gale, she 'stretched to the SW'. Furneaux brought to his ship, *Adventure*, estimat-ing that Cape Palliser was 10–11 leagues (33 miles) to the northeast. The next day the ocean conditions worsened. The stormy weather of 25/26 October was graphically described by J.R. Forster, who wrote of the 'fury of the winds' and of 'foul winds'. On the 26th, he wrote,

> The fury of the winds is not yet abated, & we are rolled about in an agitated & tempestuous Sea. The storm roaring in our rigging, & breaking against our Ship. The storm raises the Sea, & when she brakes over the top of the wave, the wind entirely dissolves the Sea into Atoms of vapour & carries them off into the Air, like Smoke … We tried to wear ship, but the Sea & storm hindered us to do it. The Sea is mountainous & the wind rages with utmost fury. All the night we had a tremendous tempest & the Ship rolled Gunwall to. We shipped several Seas, so that the water in the waste stood

6 or 8 inches & came through the door into my Cabin, wherein besides every thing was overturned, though ever so well lashed … At 3 o'clock the Ship wore & the wind became favourable & then I fell asleep, not being able before to sleep a winck on account of the rolling of the Ship, which very nigh flung me out of my bed, had I not been holding myself with both hands.

George Forster provided a no less colourful summary:

The aspect of the ocean was at once magnificent and terrific: now on the summit of a broad and heavy billow, we overlooked an unmeasurable expanse of sea, furrowed into numberless deep channels; now on a sudden the wave broke under us and we plunged into a deep and dreary valley, whilst a fresh mountain rose to windward with a foaming crest and threatened to overwhelm us. The night coming on was not without new horrors, especially for those who had not been bred up to a seafaring life … In the other cabins the beds were perfectly soaked in water, whilst the tremendous roar of the waves, the creaking of the timbers and the rolling motion deprived us of all hopes of repose.

J.R. and George Forster were not from a sailing background, which likely influenced their dramatic accounts, yet their comments also provide insight into the month-long saga of the ships attempting to penetrate the stormy Cook Strait.

On 28 October Cook estimated Cape Palliser was NBW½W 6 leagues (at 6pm), while Cape Campbell was 10–12 leagues to the west (at noon), with *Adventure* 4–5 miles to the leeward of *Resolution*. Furneaux, sailing in 'fresh gales and squally weather', recorded Cape Palliser as being 12–14 leagues west by north of *Adventure* at 1pm. Later in the afternoon, *Adventure*'s main top sail split. It was mended and set again.

Sometimes stormy then moderating seas continued on the 29th, with both ships sailing in company. Cooper observed 'fresh gales and squally with a large short Sea', which moderated later in the day. (In a 'short sea', waves are short, broken and irregular, producing a tumbling or jerking effect on a vessel.) Wales recorded the ever-changing weather by writing, at different times, about moderate winds, hazy conditions and brisk to strong to moderating winds.

Resolution and *Adventure* Separate

During 30 October the two ships separated for the final time. At 5pm *Resolution* was 3 leagues from Cape Palliser. At 7pm there was a north-northeasterly breeze, described by Cook as being 'as favourable as we could wish', but by 9pm it had been replaced by an ever-shifting wind from the northwest. Clerke described it as a strong gale. By midnight *Adventure* had disappeared from *Resolution*'s sight. Cook thought she had tacked and stood to the northeast. *Adventure* had, indeed, done so.

As naturalists, the Forsters took every opportunity to record scientific observations. During the stormy weather of 25–29 October, J.R. Forster wrote about some of the birds that flew around *Resolution*, including 'a black shearwater hovering over the raging ocean'. Nearly every day he noted albatrosses, pintado and other petrels. On the 29th he saw petrels (called divers) and shearwaters.

The rough ocean waves caused a sea chest to break free on the top deck, nearly crushing AB Alexander Hood. The force of the ocean's waves also broke a 'great cabin' window, freeing a scorpion stowaway, likely from the South Pacific islands visited three weeks earlier.

Courses and Distances Travelled

Astronomer Wales recorded each day his ship's course and the distance sailed. Figure 13 shows how *Resolution* travelled between 24 and 31 October as the ship was buffeted in the ocean and prevented from sailing into the Strait. The table shows that *Resolution* sailed back and forth as it tried to penetrate the Strait, buffeted by winds. The map in Figure 14 demonstrates the sloop's route during this eight-day period.

Resolution Alone

Resolution sailed through continual hard squalls. At times, Cook wrote, the wind 'blew with great fury'. On 1 November at 6pm there was 'little wind' but 30 minutes later 'it began to blow with greater fury than ever'. The weather continued to be dramatically changeable. On 2 November the ship sailed into the Cook Strait, passing Cape Campbell at a distance of a league, and remained off Cloudy Bay for the night, any advancement being halted by strong tides. Cook observed, 'our tacks were disadvantageous and we lost more on the Ebb [water flowing seaward] than we gained on the flood [water flowing inward from the ocean]'. With a clear horizon, Cook concluded that *Adventure* had already reached the Sound, but this conjecture turned out to be incorrect.

Without the strong winds, the ships' intended course would have been to round the bottom of the North Island, then sail north-northwest along Cook Strait and

Figure 13. Data from William Wales's log book showing *Resolution*'s courses and the distances travelled during the separation from *Adventure*, 24–31 October 1773.

		Miles				
October	Course	Total	North	South	East	West
25	S 32° W	55	0	43.25	0	34.25
25	S 65° W	15	0	6	0	14
26	N 10° W	53	57	0	0	9
27	S 13° W	43	0	41.5	0	9
28	N 24° E	40	37.5	0	16	0
29	S 64° W	73	0	32	0	66
30	S 58° E	19	0	10	0	16
31	N 54° W	48	28	0	0	58

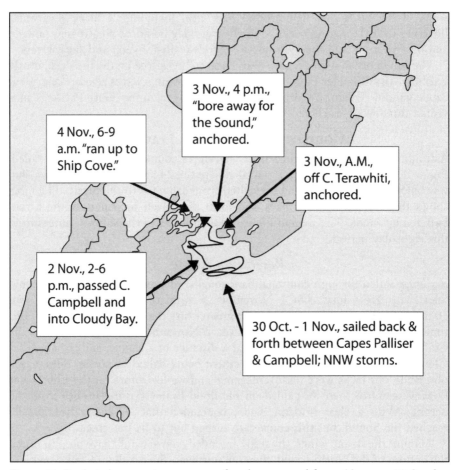

4 Nov., 6-9 a.m. "ran up to Ship Cove."

3 Nov., 4 p.m., "bore away for the Sound," anchored.

3 Nov., A.M., off C. Terawhiti, anchored.

2 Nov., 2-6 p.m., passed C. Campbell and into Cloudy Bay.

30 Oct. - 1 Nov., sailed back & forth between Capes Palliser & Campbell; NNW storms.

Figure 14. *Resolution*'s approximate course after she separated from *Adventure*, 30 October to 4 November 1773.

Queen Charlotte Sound. Instead, *Resolution* sailed southwest from the bottom of North Island for two days, then northwest, southwest, northeast, southwest, southeast and, finally, northwest along the north coast of the South Island.

On 2 November *Resolution* sailed across the Strait to reach Cape Teerawhitte (Terawhiti). A bay was found in which to anchor. As there was still no sight of *Adventure*, Cook did not explore this bay – later named Port Nicholson and now the location of Wellington. On 3 November at 3pm *Resolution* sailed away, taking advantage of a light breeze, which later turned into a fresh gale. Cook wrote,

> bore away for the [Queen Charlotte] Sound under all the sail we could bear, having the advantage or rather disadvantage of an increaseing gale which already blowed too hard; we hauled up for the Sound just at dark and after making two boards, in which most of our sails were split, anchored in

18 fathoms water … At 9 [am, 4 November] the Calm was succeeded by a breeze at NW, with which we weighed and ran up to Ship Cove where we moord with the two Bowers and afterwards unbint all our sails not having one but what wanted considerable repairs. We did not find the *Adventure* here as I expected.

Adventure Alone

After separating from *Resolution*, *Adventure* remained 3 to 9 leagues from Cape Palliser in stormy weather that lasted almost continuously from 31 October to 6 November. On 4 November natives in two canoes brought to the ship 'a large quantity of fish', which was exchanged for nails. This must have occurred when *Adventure* was closer to the shore or during a sudden, brief lull in the stormy weather. It also demonstrates the ability of the Maori to travel in stormy seas. The next day, Furneaux observed, the wind

> blew hard from WNW which again blew us off the Coast and obliged us to bring to for two days, during which time in blew one continual gale of wind with very heavy squalls of sleet, by this time our Decks were very leaky, the peoples beds and bedding wet, several of our people complaining of Colds, that we began to despair of ever getting into Charlotte's Sound or joining the *Resolution*.

On the 6th, faced with weather that Furneaux termed 'strong gales and squally with thick sleet', he sought shelter in one of the bays along the North Island, up the coast from Cape Palliser. The next day he continued his search along the coast, sailing even further away from Cape Palliser.

By 10 November *Adventure* was moored in Tolaga Bay on the North Island (38° 22′ south and 178° 18′ east), approximately 270 miles (435km) north of Cape Palliser (*see* Figure 12). This location puzzled me at first because of its distance from the Strait, so I checked several log books for an explanation. Furneaux wrote that the Bay 'affords a good riding' and that both wood and water were available; in other words it was a location that was already known to meet *Adventure*'s needs. Furneaux added that 'The natives here are the same as at Charlotte's Sound, but more numerous and seemed settled, having regular Plantations of Sweet Potatoes and other roots which are very good; they have plenty of Cray and other Fish which we bought of them for Nails Beads and other triffles at an easy rate.'

An additional reason for this location may stem from Cook's opinion of the area, which he might have shared with Furneaux. Earlier, on 22 October, Cook had written that he thought the natives in the Tolaga Bay area were 'more civilized than at Queen Charlotte's Sound'. This bay is about two days' or less sailing from Cape Palliser so the distance is not as startling as I initially thought, especially considering the stormy weather off Cape Palliser encountered in attempting to reach the Cook Strait.

Adventure sailed from Tolaga Bay on 12 November. The squally weather continued and the logs record that attempts to sail were prevented by windy and rainy weather. In his post-voyage narrative Furneaux observed,

> We were no sooner out than the wind began to blow hard dead on the shore that we could not clear the Land on either Tack which obliged us to bear away again for the Bay were [where] we anchored the next morning and rode out a very heavy gale of wind at East by South which threw in a very great sea. We now began to fear we should never join the *Resolution*, who we had reason to believe was in Charlotte's Sound and by this time ready for Sea; we soon found it was with great difficulty we could get any water, owing to the swell setting in so strong; at last, however, we were able to go onshore and got both wood and water: Whilst we lay here we were employed about the rigging which was much damaged by the constant gales of wind we met with since we made the coast.[7]

In his journal Lieutenant Burney wrote, 'The best chance of getting through Cooks Straits from the Southward is to keep close to the S.W. Shore and if Possible avoid getting to the Eastward of Cape Pallisser.' He also commented that the northwesterly winds never lasted more than three days, and are

> generally succeeded by a S.W. or Southerly wind: if it comes to blow hard at N.W. and looks very black it is almost an infallible sign of a sudden shift of wind round to the S.W. & South this we experienced several times when we were unluckily close over to Cape Pallisser or to the Eastward of it or else so far to the Southward as not to get into the Straits before the wind was spent.

Burney furthermore stated that *Adventure* could not 'carry a tolerable Stiff Sail' which would allow the ship 'to have kept our own during a N.W. Wind, and keeping to the South shore … but the Ship was in bad trim and – we not well acquainted with the Coast'. On the 29th Furneaux wrote in his log, 'little wind and thick weather' and 'put ship's company on an allowance of a quart of water per day'.

Adventure started 30 November 7 to 8 leagues off Cape Palliser. A favourable wind from the south appeared as the ship sailed into the Cook Strait, following a path similar to that suggested by James Burney. Furneaux recorded sighting the Two Brothers (two large, rocky islands in the Strait). *Adventure* turned windward and reached Long Island on the 30th, causing Furneaux to enter in his log book, in larger and more elaborate handwriting than usual, 'Turning into Charlotte's Sound.' On 1 December *Adventure* was moored in Ship Cove. *Resolution* was not waiting at anchor.

Resolution in Ship Cove, 3–25 November

During the three weeks *Resolution* was in Ship Cove, her company set to work preparing her for the next voyage to Antarctica, repairing sails, rigging, spars and iron work, as well as caulking. Lieutenant Robert Cooper's log recorded on

3 November, 'hoisted out the boats, unbent [unfasten] the sails, most of them being split & wanting repair & the remaining Rigging in general broke and not serviceable'. The men gathered wood and filled the casks with fresh water. Fresh ballast was deposited in the bilge. J.R. Forster, his son George and Anders Sparrman spent much of the stay botanizing. Astronomer William Wales set up an observation post.

Almost immediately upon the ship's arrival, Maori appeared with fish, which they exchanged for cloth. The ship's biscuit supply was in a terrible condition, part rotten and part mouldy, requiring re-baking in ovens set up ashore. Cook recorded in his journal that 3,000lb of biscuit was 'mouldy and rotten and totally unfit for men to eat' due to unseasoned (green) casks and water/dampness in the ship's hull. During their previous visit to Ship Cove, goats, pigs and fowl had been given to the Maori as well as seeds for a vegetable garden. Only one pig now survived, as did a garden, but it was much in need of tending.

On 15 November Cook, other officers and 'the gentlemen' visited a hill above East Bay, hoping to observe the Strait and catch sight of *Adventure*. While J.R. Forster obtained samples of two new plants, there was no sign of the ship. Cook recorded in his journal, ' I despair of seeing her [*Adventure*] any more but am totally at a loss to conceive what is become of her till now. I thought that she might have put into some port in the Strait when the wind came at NW the day we Anchor'd in Ship Cove and there stayed to compleat her wood and Water; this conjector is reasonable enough at first, but the elapsation of twelve days now has made it scarce probable.

Cook noted the stone marker from a prior visit had been levelled by the natives, who possibly had thought there might be something of value in it.

On the 22nd, the sailors came across signs of cannibalism. Wales observed that it was now proved the inhabitants were, 'Caniballs, which I must confess I was a little sceptical before.' Cook wrote a lengthy passage expressing his indignation, but also uncertainty about the evidence observed, such as flesh attached to thigh bones, human heads, bowels and a heart stuck on a forked stick. On the 23rd Cook concluded, 'That the New Zealanders are Canibals can now no longer be doubted.' Both the Forsters described actions of cruelty among New Zealand natives, including cannibalism, and both struggled to comprehend or explain the practice.

Resolution sailed from Ship Cove on 25 November, intending to search for *Adventure*. On the previous day Cook prepared a summary regarding *Resolution*'s arrival and departure, and his intended future route, and 'buried it in a bottle under the root of a tree in the garden in the bottom of the Cove in such a matter that it must be found by any European who may put into the Cove'. He doubted Captain Furneaux would locate the information since Cook believed *Adventure* was not anywhere in New Zealand. However, his journal entry recorded, he would search for *Adventure* where it was likely he would be found if the ship remained in the area.

Lieutenant Charles Clerke recorded in his log that *Resolution* departed Ship Cove at 3.30pm (Cook recorded 4am) and proceeded across the Strait with signal guns being fired as she went, and sailed back towards Cape Palliser on the 27th. Cooper concluded, 'Not having been lucky enough to discover our Consort or any reason to suppose her being hereabouts, therefore concluding a further search unnecessary when we bore away.' Fresh gales carried away *Resolution*'s main top mast and split another sail. The storm then carried away the main top gallant yard. In that state, *Resolution* sailed south for Antarctica.

The approximate routes of *Resolution* and *Adventure* after the separation are depicted in Figure 15.

Adventure in Ship Cove, 1–23 December

Upon arriving at Ship Cove, *Adventure*'s men made their way to a source of water near the garden planted during an earlier visit. They found a sign carved on a tree stump stating, 'Look Underneath'. A corked and waxed bottle was found with the instructions Cook had written. These provided a record of Cook's plans and left

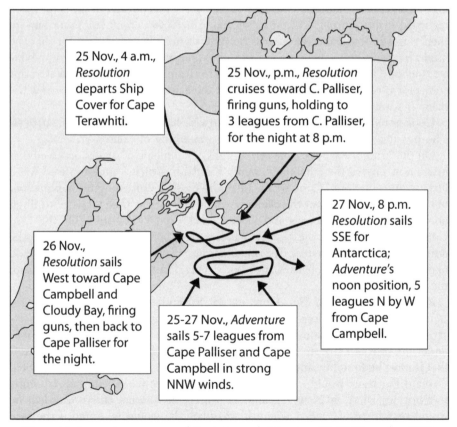

Figure 15. Approximate routes of *Resolution* and *Adventure*, 25–27 December 1773.

to Furneaux the decision of how to proceed, since Cook did not expect the ships to meet up again. Lieutenant James Burney copied Cook's instructions into his journal:

> Queen Charlotte Sound New Zealand, Nov^br 24th 1773 – His Britannic Majesty's Sloop, *Resolution*, Captain Cook – arrived last in this port on the 3^d Inst^t and Sail^d again on the date hereof. Captn Cook intended to spend a few days in the East Entrance of the Straits looking for the *Adventure* Captn Furneaux, who he parted company with in the Night of the 29th of last Month – afterwards he will proceed to the South and Eastward –
>
> As Captain Cook has not the least hopes of meeting with Cap^tn Furneaux he will not take upon him to name any place for a Rendezvous, he however thinks of retiring to Easter Island in Lat^de 27..06 So & Long^de 100°..00′ West of Greenwich, about the latter end of next March – it is even probable that he may go to Otaheite or one of the Society Isles; but this will depend so much on Circumstances, that nothing of certainty can be determined upon – James Cook

Adventure's company quickly set out to repair the ship and to lay on a supply of water, wood and food. The biscuit supply was mouldy, much like that in *Resolution*. Burney wrote that they found 'most of our Casks of Bread greatly damaged they having been buried in the Coals ever since we left England, the Damp has struck through the Casks (New Butt Ironbound) – were obliged to throw a great deal away and get the rest on Shore with our oven to bake over again'. He suspected that the same problem had occurred in *Resolution* 'for we see their oven has been set up and a good deal of bread dust lying by the place'.

On the 17th Furneaux recorded that he sent a 'large cutter up the Sound to get a quantity of Vegetables to take on sea, with my particular order to the officer not to exceed three o'clock that afternoon in his return to the Ship as I Intended Sailing next morning'. This reference to 'my particular order' is the only time I saw this term in Furneaux's log book. Usually Captain Furneaux recorded only the briefest navigational data in his log book, with virtually no personal thoughts or observations. He did so at this point, I suggest, because of the events that occurred later that day at Grass Cove. I speculate Furneaux therefore recorded his entry after word of the Grass Cove incident had been reported to *Adventure*.

The Massacre at Grass Cove occurred on 17/18 December. A detailed examination lies outside the scope of this chapter and it is well covered elsewhere.[8] James Burney's journal contains his account of the event, as he was the officer in charge of the expedition that discovered the remains of ten men killed during a period of escalating conflict between the British sailors and the Maori. Furneaux's log and post-voyage narrative both include a lengthy description of what he learned about the massacre, observing that the *Adventure*'s relief expedition found twenty baskets of human flesh, body parts and personal effects, such as clothing, of persons from *Resolution*. Some of the human remains were returned to *Adventure* and later deposited (with added ballast) in the Sound.

We will never know if Captain Cook's presence could have prevented this event – what might be termed as reckless behaviour on the part of ten men who put themselves in a defenceless position during a time of heightened tensions. The discovery came as a serious shock to *Adventure*'s personnel. Burney wrote in his journal about his expedition that returned at 8pm 'with the melancholy Account of the Cutter and her Crew being cut off by the Natives – by which dreadfull Accident we lost a good Officer & many of our best Seamen'. According to the editor of his journal, Burney was so shocked by the event he did not comment on having led the expedition on the 19th, nor would he talk about it after returning to England.

Adventure departed Ship Cove on 23 December. Furneaux recorded that the ship found a 'strong current and a good wind', although in his post-voyage narrative he says she was 'baffled by light winds for two or three days' until she 'cleared the Coast'. He sailed east to Cape Horn and then to the Cape of Good Hope, reaching England on 14 July 1774, about a year before Cook and *Resolution* returned home.

Resolution and *Adventure* – So Near, Yet So Far

Initially I intended to compare the relative positions of *Resolution* and *Adventure* during the period from 20 to 31 October to determine how far apart the ships were during the 'mini-separations' of the 23/24th and 26/27th, as well as after the final separation on the 30th. The intention was to compare the latitudes recorded by Wales in *Resolution* and Bayly in *Adventure*. This task proved more difficult than initially assumed. Comparable log book or journal data is not consistently available for all of these periods. Astronomer Wales recorded *Resolution*'s latitude and longitude in his log book on a regular basis, and Bayly did the same, except for the late November dates that I wanted to compare. For 25–27 November Bayly recorded no latitude but the phrase, 'Working the SE entrance of Cook Strait.' Once anchored at Ship Cove, Wales obviously would not record latitude or longitude on 1–4 November. However, Furneaux recorded *Adventure*'s latitude daily until 4 November, as *Resolution* searched for *Adventure*. Therefore, I have comparable latitude data for *Resolution* from Wales for the late October separation off the Cook Strait, as well as from Furneaux for both sets of data. Latitudes recorded by Bayly and Furneaux are essentially identical for dates that are comparable. For the late November dates, during which *Resolution* departed Queen Charlotte Sound and *Adventure* was attempting to reach Ship Cove, I also used data from Furneaux and Wales. This information is recorded in Figure 16.

Distances given in Figure 16 are approximate since they reflect the position of each vessel at noon after 24 hours of sailing. Of course the vessels were closer or further apart at other points during the day. The two ships separated permanently on 29/30 October. During two of the three days when *Resolution* searched for *Adventure* in late November, the two ships were between 45 and 63 miles apart.

On 3 November, when *Resolution* entered Queen Charlotte Sound and Ship Cove, *Adventure* was 7 to 8 leagues off Cape Palliser to the southwest. I estimate

Figure 16. The noon positions of *Resolution* and *Adventure* recorded in William Wales's and Rupert Furneaux's log books during separation of the ships off the Cook Strait.*

Date	*Resolution* (Wales log)	*Adventure* (Furneaux log)	Miles	Kilometres
29 October	14° 13.25' S	41° 48' S	114	183.5
30 October	42° 19' S	41° 52' S	46	74.5
31 October	41° 52' S	42° 32' S	55	88.9
25 November	41° 32' S	42° 18' S	45.5	73.4
26 November	43° 26' S	42° 34' S	63.6	102.3
27 November	44° 19' S	42° 18' S	139.9	223.5

These distances have been calculated utilizing Andrew Hedges' 'Finding Distances Based on Latitude and Longitude' (2002).

the ships were separated by about 50 miles. No comparable latitude data are available in the logs or journals to enable a good calculation.

On 25 November, when *Resolution* departed Ship Cove, *Adventure* was off the Kaikoura range of mountains (Cook named these the 'Lookers-On' Mountains in 1770).[9] At noon the next day the two ships were 45.5 miles (73.4km) apart. By noon on the 27th, by comparing latitudes recorded, I calculate that the ships were separated by 63.6 miles (102.3km). For the next day, if the entries by Furneaux and Cook were both made at noon, then the ships were separated by about 138.9 miles (223.5km).

Resolution's Search for the Southern Continent, Alone

The desired months for Antarctic exploration were December to February. Cook records in his journal that he had no anxiety about *Adventure* and supposed Furneaux, 'being tired with beating against the NW winds had taken a resolution to make the best of his way to Cape Horn or perhaps to the Cape of Good Hope; be this as it will it is not likely we shall join again, as no rendezvous was absolutely fixed upon after leaving New Zealand. Nevertheless this shall not discourage me from fully exploring the Southern parts of the Pacific Ocean.'

Although he would have preferred to sail with *Adventure*, Cook wrote that his officers all agreed that *Adventure* was not sailing along a New Zealand coast. On the 27th he recorded in his journal,

I had the satisfaction to find that not a man was dejected or thought the dangers we had yet to go through were in the least increased by going alone, but as cheerfully proceeded to the South or wherever I thought proper to lead them as if she or even more Ships had been in our Company.

As she sailed south, *Resolution* encountered ice on 15 December and crossed the Antarctic Circle again on 20 December (*see* Chapter 8).

How other Cook Biographers Described these Events

In my opinion, the best secondary source account of the events off Cook Strait during October–December 1773 is in Beaglehole's biography of Cook.[10] The story of the ships battling storms to get to Ship Cove is accurately, but only generally and briefly, cited in other studies, or barely mentioned at all. Accurate, reasonable, but often brief references are included in other biographies of Cook or books about the second voyage.[11] In his biography of his great-great-great grandfather, Rupert Furneaux describes *Resolution* and *Adventure* engaged in an 'amusing game of nautical hide and seek'.[12] Although a clever description, these two months were not a game-playing exercise and both captains expressed concern about the safety of the other. Cook and Furneaux made serious efforts to locate each other.

In his recent biography of Cook, Frank McLynn[13] suggests that Furneaux's failure to rendezvous with Cook at Ship Cove has never been satisfactorily explained, stating that '*Adventure* put into Solago Bay [*sic*, Tolaga, or *Uawa* in Maori] shortly after becoming separated from the *Resolution* and showed no particular haste to get out again.' As the log books show, after taking on food, water and wood, *Adventure* arrived at Tolaga Bay on the 10th and tried to leave on the 12th, but was prevented by storms. Furneaux departed again on the 16th, confronting storms until the 29th, disproving McLynn's assertion of Furneaux not making 'haste' or an effort to depart for Queen Charlotte Sound.

McLynn also suggests that Furneaux's arrival at Ship Cove a month late was 'just a mite convenient', since Furneaux likely did not want to return to the 'giant waves and mountainous seas of the Antarctic Ocean'. It is a reasonable argument to suggest Furneaux did not enjoy sailing in Antarctic weather. However, as seen in this chapter, the log books and journals strongly suggest *Adventure* made continuous efforts to keep up with, and rejoin, *Resolution*. The log books and journals contain references to over a dozen instances of lost and split sails, ripped brails, damaged rigging and running under bare poles, affecting both vessels confronting 'an agitated and tempestuous sea'. The battered ships were near each other but too far away to be seen in stormy weather.

During Captain Cook's next search for Antarctica *Resolution* was once again alone. In the next chapter we will study that search more closely, during which Captain Cook crossed the Circle for a second time, reaching 67° 5′ south, on 21 December 1773.

Chapter 8

Cook's Second Crossing
21–25 December 1773

the wind northerly and a strong gale attended with a thick fog Sleet and Snow which froze to the Rigging as it fell and decorated the whole with icicles. Our ropes were like wires, Sails like board or plates of Metal and the Shivers [pulleys] froze fast in the blocks so that it required our utmost effort to get a Top-sail down and up; the cold so intense as hardly to be endured, the whole Sea in a manner covered with ice, a hard gale and a thick fog: under all these unfavourable circumstances it was natural for me to think of returning more to the North, seeing there was no probability of finding land here nor the possibility of get[ting] further to the South ...

Captain James Cook, journal entry, 24 December 1773

This chapter considers *Resolution*'s second crossing of the Circle, 21–25 December 1773.[1] The second excursion in the Southern Ocean during 1773 encountered harsh weather, floating ice, the presence of numerous (and sometimes dangerous) ice islands and more Antarctic petrels, albatrosses and whales. The circumstances of the second crossing were similar to the first, as with the third crossing a month later: further progress was blocked by an impenetrable ice barrier.

The sources for this chapter are those in Chapters 5 to 7: Captain Cook's journal, the log books of Lieutenants Clerke and Cooper, Master Joseph Gilbert, and Master's Mates James Davall Burr and Isaac Smith, the journal of Lieutenant Elliott and the memoirs of Lieutenant Pickersgill, along with anecdotal observations from the journals of J.R. Forster and George Forster.

From New Zealand to the Antarctic Circle, 25 November–21 December 1773

Resolution departed New Zealand on 25 November. In passing through the Cook Strait and around Cape Palliser, the sloop fired guns as a signal to *Adventure*, but found no signs of the missing ship (Chapter 7). Course was set to the south, the ship accompanied by the usual Southern Ocean birds (various petrels, albatrosses and shearwaters), seals and penguins, the numbers of which decreased gradually. Fresh gales, some fog and haze alternated with clearer weather, then rain, snow, sleet and much colder weather. On 7 December Cook described *Resolution*'s location as precisely opposite England on the globe. On 8 December, having again sailed in waters where some thought the Southern Continent might be located, Cook noted in his journal that, having sailed south from New Zealand through that part of the Pacific, any undiscovered land must lie to the south of 60° latitude. He would reinforce that conclusion again in later 1774 on his way to Tierra del Fuego. Once again this is evidence of James Cook 'proving a negative' in searching for the Southern Continent.

Heavy snow and hail appeared on the 12th and 13th and the main topmast stay sail was, as Cook described it, 'all to raggs, it being an old sail the greatest part blew away'. On 15 December ice islands were sighted, as well as loose ice. *Resolution* steered away from the ice. At one point a huge piece of ice, described as twice the height of the ship, floated close to the sloop, creating a potentially dangerous situation. Crew members were given spars to push the ice away from the ship but, fortunately, ship and iceberg only passed close to each other. Cook observed in his journal that 'we frequently, notwithstanding all our care, ran against some of the large pieces, the shoks [shocks] which the Ship received thereby was very considerable, such as no Ship could bear long unless properly prepared for the purpose'. This situation would arise again on this segment of the second voyage. *Resolution* carried no special exterior protection against icebergs.

The Second Crossing of the Antarctic Circle, 21–25 December 1773

Sailing for several days in what Cook described in his journal as a strong gale, thick fog and sleet, 'which constitutes the very worst of weather, our rigging was so loaded with ice that we had enough to do to get our Top-sails down to double reef', *Resolution* crossed the Circle at 7pm on 21 December. In the heavy fog the ship 'came close aboard a large Island of ice and being at the same time a good deal embarras'd with loose ice we with some difficulty wore and stood to the NW until Noon when the fogg being somewhat dissipated we resumed our Course again to the SE.' During the second crossing of the Circle, the furthest point south was 67° 19′ south latitude at 138° 15′ west longitude (24 December). The weather and ice continued until *Resolution* sailed above the Circle on 25 January. The wind, fog, snow and sleet continued for several additional days. In spite of this inclement weather, the log books recorded that on the 17th and 24th boats were hoisted out to pick up floating ice to be melted for water onboard *Resolution*. With the exception of George Forster's journal, there was no mention of Christmas Day in Cook's journal or in other log books.

William Wales, astronomer in *Resolution*, described how one iceberg emerged from the fog '100 yards distant'. Although *Resolution* turned sharply away from it, another ice island quickly appeared at the same distance. During this encounter the ship was travelling at 3½ to 4¾ knots. *Resolution* then again turned sharply to avoid collision. Wales noted the helmsman had to 'drive her through a thick Field of Ice which lay between them [the icebergs] which with a few hard knocks was effected & [*Resolution*] stood to the Northward'.

On 24 December Cook entered one of his more descriptive and dramatic passages about Antarctic weather:

> with the wind northerly and a strong gale attended with a thick fog Sleet and Snow which froze to the Rigging as it fell and decorated the whole with icicles. Our ropes were like wires, Sails like board or plates of Metal and the Shivers [pulleys] froze fast in the blocks so that it required our utmost effort to get a Top-sail down and up; the cold so intense as hardly to be endured, the whole Sea in a manner covered with ice, a hard gale and a thick fog: under all these unfavourable circumstances it was natural for me to think of returning more to the North, seeing there was no probability of finding land here nor a possibility of get[ting] further to the South ...

Cook commented that he could not sail further east or south because of the ice, so *Resolution* proceeded to the northeast to unexplored ocean to determine if land could be located where he had not sailed previously.

Lieutenant Charles Clerke's log book for 21–22 December contains similar entries about the weather: 'Very Cold – the sleet as it falls freezes to the rigging in which in the first place makes it exceedingly disagreeable handling and in the next makes it so thick with ice that it is with difficulty we render the ropes through the blocks.' Clerke makes no mention of the Antarctic Circle, but records the latitude as 66° 50′ south; on the 23rd, in larger handwriting, he entered, 'Observed Latitude 67° 27′ South', with the weather 'much more favourable and visibility three to four miles'.

One of Clerke's responsibilities was to supervise collection of ice, which was melted in copper kettles ('the coppers') to make water. A painting by second voyage artist William Hodges depicts the gathering of ice in Antarctica ('Ice Islands on 9 January 1773'), a portion of which was also reproduced on a Cook Islands postage stamp (*see* Plate 14). He and Lieutenant Robert Cooper also supervised the cleansing of the air on *Resolution*'s lower decks, undertaken by the method of carrying braziers of hot charcoal infused with vinegar – an eighteenth-century version of a room air freshener. On the 20th Clerke wrote, 'Melting ice all night. Cleaned ship and smoked her with fire balls.' The ship's company counted 238 ice islands on the 27th, Cook himself recording over 200. His log also notes the presence of petrels, albatrosses and whales around the ship.

Cooper's log parallels Clerke's, with its description of cold weather, floating ice, ice islands, whales and albatrosses. Cooper also recorded melting ice – more than 6 butts in total (1 butt equalled 108 gallons). As noted previously, Cooper was the only officer during the second voyage to record in his log book each time *Resolution* crossed the Antarctic Circle, in both directions. On 21 December he wrote, 'A little past 6 we crossed the Antarctic Circle the third time.' On the 25th his log book recorded that at 9 am 'crossed the Antarctic Circle 4th time'.

During the 24 hours of *Resolution*'s day from noon on 26 December to noon on the 27th, Cooper recorded that at noon on the 26th 'the Horizon all round [was] lined with Islands of Ice, impossible to enumerate them'. Later, at 4pm, he counted 97 icebergs. On the 27th at 8am he noted 238 islands of Ice, but that number he did not think to be correct, although it matched Clerke's count. At noon on the 27th he counted 187 icebergs 'plus straggling pieces' around *Resolution*. Cooper specifically states the count of 238 was from the masthead. It is not clear in the log books if the other tabulations are from the deck or (more likely) the masthead.

Master Joseph Gilbert did not mention in his log book crossing the Antarctic Circle on 21 December, but he did record the ship's position as being 66° 50', which is below the Circle, accompanied by 'thick foggy seas with snow and hail'. A ship's master regularly recorded knots, fathoms, barometric pressure and temperature at noon. Using Gilbert's log book as a guide, when crossing the Circle at 7pm he found a 'Thick foggy view. Bore up for an ice island which could not be observed till very near us. Found ourselves much incumbered with loose Ice. Hauled [up]. The wind is to the North and stood clear of the Ice.' According to Gilbert's log at the time of the second crossing of the Circle, *Resolution* travelled at 3 knots, 4 fathoms (i.e. 3½ knots) on a northwest by north course, with winds from the northeast by north. At noon on the 22nd, the end of the 24-hour log, the barometer was at 28.70 and the temperature was 34°F, with the ship at 66° 50' south. Gilbert computed the location as 635 leagues (1,905 nautical miles) from Cape Palliser.

Wales's handwriting is both precise and relatively easy to read and his log contains data not found in the other log books. I used his data to understand the changes that occurred during the period 21–27 December and summarized them in Figure 17 below. I cannot determine at what time of the day he made his readings or where the thermometers were located in *Resolution*. Possibly, the two sets of temperature and barometric readings he records (marked 'A' and 'B') reflect the highest and lowest during each day or at the beginning and end of the ship's day (noon). The 'B' figures for barometric pressure and temperature do correspond somewhat to the readings noted by Gilbert in his log, but with small differences.

Wales's data provide an interesting glimpse into *Resolution*'s course. She did not sail in a straight line towards the Antarctic Circle but tacked according to the wind direction and ocean conditions. In the table, distances are given as north, south, east and west, representing the nautical miles travelled in these directions during the day (referred to as northings, southings, eastings and westings). Adding up the distances travelled in each direction will not produce the total distance covered because there needs to be adjustment for leeway and drift.

From Wales's data, *Resolution* proceeded in a generally northerly course with winds primarily from the north and east. She travelled at an average of 3.39 knots, totalling 427 miles, which is an average of 60.6 miles per day. The boats were hoisted out to gather floating ice for water on at least two days. This explains the shorter distances that were covered on 23 and 25 December. The ship also spent one day stuck in solid ice.

Figure 17. William Wales's log book recordings of *Resolution*'s second crossing of the Antarctic Circle, 21–27 December 1773.

Dec. 1773	Course	Wind	Knots	Fathoms	Dist. "N"	Dist. "S"	Dist. "E"	Dist. "W"	Total Dist.	Bar. "A"	Bar. "B"	Temp "A"	Temp. "B"
21	S 34° E	NEbN	3	5	–	49	33.7	–	60	28.55	28.85	55	34
22	S 69° E	NbW	3	4	–	37	97.7	–	104	28.85	29.05	50	33
23	S 8.5° W	NbW	3	4	–	6.25	–	11	13	28.80	28.80	49	32
24	N 49° E	NbE	2	4	65	–	62.7	–	83	29.30	29.30	50	34
25	N 56° E	WSW	1	1	7.7	–	11.7	–	14	29.25	29.25	56	37
26	N b S	NEbN	1	6	24.5	–	12.2	–	25	29.10	29.10	53	35
27	N 9° W	EbS	6	5	90	–	–	14	92	28.75	28.75	59	36

Figure 18. *Resolution*'s recorded positions at noon, 22 December 1773, according to Cook's journal and six log books.

Journal or Log	Course	Wind	Knots	Fath.	Distance	Latitude by Observ.	Longitude by Observ.	Barometer	Temp. (°F)
Cook	S 70° 15' E	NE	NR	NR	109	67° 27' S	141° 55' W	NR	31–33
Clerke	S 70° E	NbW	3	6	107	67° 27' S	216° 44' W	NR	34
Cooper	S 69° E	NbW	3	6	106	67° 27' S	36° 44' E	NR	33
Gilbert	SE	N	3	6	108	67° 27' S	37° 27' E	28.95	33
Smith	S 15° E	NbW	3	6	109	67° 27' S	35° 11' E	NR	NR
Burr	SE	N	3	6	106	67° 27' S	36° 44' E	NR	NR
Wales	S 69° E	NbW	3	6	104	67° 26¼' S	36° 44½' E	28.85/29.05	50/33

If my assumption is correct that the two temperature readings reflect daily high and low readings, then the average high temperature was 53.4°F and the average low temperature was 34.6°F. In general a rising barometer indicates improving weather, so the sailing conditions appear to have gradually improved during the seven days. The log books and journals record weather being at its worst from 21 to 25 December, when *Resolution* sailed below the Circle, improving gradually thereafter.

The officers in *Resolution* took their own observations to determine latitude and longitude. Minor variances in their calculations are understandable. Calculations based on dead reckoning or observations are recorded as east of the Cape of Good Hope, while longitude determined by chronometers is east of Greenwich or perhaps St Paul's Cathedral.

Most of the entries are similar (*see* Figure 18). All the latitude readings are the same, except Wales's, whose scientific precision calculated the position more accurately. The latitude cited is the furthest south during the second crossing of the Circle. Cook, Clerke and Cooper calculated longitude west of the Cape of Good Hope while Gilbert, Smith, Burr and Wales calculated longitude as east of Greenwich or 'London'.

Observations by the Naturalists

George Forster's journal provides an account of Christmas Day 1773, with sailors enjoying a double portion of pudding and the officers joining Captain Cook in the Great Cabin for a meal. He noted the crew 'saved up' their allowances of brandy for the occasion, 'being sollicitous to get very drunk' and caring little about anything else. He observed the men remained drunk on the 26th when counting 168 ice islands from the masthead. He wrote, 'The whole scene looked like the wrecks of a shattered world.' George's father, Johann Reinhold Forster, remained below in his cabin confined to his bed with 'rheumatic pains'.[2]

In his entries for 20–26 December 1773 J.R. Forster recorded temperature variances between *Resolution*'s deck and his cabin. He also wrote a lengthy observation on the quality of the food and other conditions, about illness among the company and the futility of the second voyage. During the week-long crossing of the Circle, the outside temperature varied between 32°F and 33¼°F, while it was between 35°F and 39°F in Forster's cabin. His cabin was therefore a few degrees 'warmer' than on deck, a condition likely identical in other similar quarters. On 21 December J.R. Forster enumerated a list of complaints, which included the absence of the Sun, the ever-present fog and mist, few visible birds and only 'a few solitary eremitic Whales'. The two-year-old food was 'indifferent', 'musty' and 'tasteless'. He complained about the 'tempestuous' sea, wet decks and his cold cabin (a 'subterraneous mansion for the dead'), because of the 'piercing winds', as well as being fouled by odours from 'effluvia & vapours'. Even the Great Cabin had broken window panes, with wet sails strung about, while being worked upon by the sail makers, who fouled the room with 'mephitic [noxious] Air' from the

peas and sauerkraut they consumed. The voyage, he concluded, is 'the most difficult task that could be imposed on poor mortal souls'.[3]

Although Forster often exhibited a critical attitude, these comments are interesting in understanding a supernumerary's view of the routine diet in *Resolution*.
He was also depressed by the sailing conditions and the lack of discoveries.
He also complained about his health and that of others. On 25 December he
described his 'poor & weak' condition, with others in *Resolution* also 'very ill'. On
29 December, with the outside temperature at 33°F and his cabin temperature at
43°F, Forster self-medicated himself with a 'dose of Essence of Antimony'
(a diaphoretic taken to increase perspiration), remarking that 'my cold is most
gone off', with twelve others nursing colds onboard. Five days later, at 56° 40'
south, Forster recorded that he never left his cabin, afraid his fever would return,
and again sought medication to 'promote perspiration'.

Midshipman John Elliott recalled in his memoirs that on 23 December the
boats were lowered to gather ice for water 'but it was too cold to take in much'.
He counted 300 ice islands from the masthead and much floating ice. Even in a
moderate wind he found it difficult to avoid the ice. 'But had it come on a gale of
wind we must inevitably have been lost because, at this point of the voyage, we
were a single Ship, so that should we be lost, or anything happen to the Ship, we
should never be heard of.' This comment is a reminder of *Resolution*'s position
after the second separation off the Cook Strait in October 1773.

After the second crossing, *Resolution* appeared to be sailing away from the
Circle. Elliot wrote that many hints were offered to Captain Cook that the supply
of tea, sugar and other supplies was being depleted. Cook, however, 'only smiled
and said nothing, for he was close and secret in his intentions at all times'. This is
a rare and interesting observation into Cook's relationship with his junior
officers. Very likely many in *Resolution* were eager to sail away from the ice wall,
the floating ice and temperatures that usually hovered in the lower to mid-30s°F.
The reserved, reticent Captain Cook was a person of few words and disclosed his
plans only at his pleasure.

Resolution headed north because of the ice on 27 December, Cook recording
'light airs until 4 o'Clock in the AM when meeting with a quantity of small Ice we
hoisted out two Boats and took on board sufficient to fill all our empty Casks …
This done we hoisted in the Boats again and made sail to the NW with a gentle
breeze at NE, clear pleasant frosty weather.'

The ship's company anticipated heading to New Zealand and the warmer
South Pacific. Instead, on 11 January 1774, the ship headed south again for the
third crossing of the Antarctic Circle, as described in the next chapter.

Chapter 9

Cook's Third Crossing
26 January–3 February 1774

At 8 o'Clock we were close to the edge of it [an ice field], it extended east and west far beyond the reach of our sight ... I will not say it was impossible any where to get further to the South, but the attempting it would have been a dangerous and rash enterprise and what I believe no man in my situation would have thought of. It was indeed my opinion as well as the opinion of most on board that this Ice extended quite to the Pole or perhaps joins to some land, to which it had been fixed from the creation ... I who had Ambition not only to go further than any one had done before, but as far as it was possible for man to go, was not sorry at meeting with this interruption as it in some measure relived us, at least shortned the dangers and hardships inseparable with the Navigation of the Southern Polar Regions ...

James Cook, journal entry, 30 January 1774, at 70° 10′ south latitude,
106° 45′ west longitude, Cook's 'furthest South'

This chapter covers the third time Captain Cook crossed the Antarctic Circle.[1] The journal and log book sources are the same as referenced in the chapters that covered the first and second crossings.

As explained in Chapter 8, *Resolution* reached another ice barrier on 24 December 1773. Because Cook had concluded that he could not proceed south or east in this ice field, *Resolution* sailed northeast, through up to a hundred ice islands. Fortunately, with the nearly constant daylight, the sloop avoided colliding with the floating ice, Cook observing on the 26th that 'had it been foggy nothing less than a miracle could have kept us clear of them'. Although the ice islands provided a frequent hazard, on the 27th two boats were hoisted out to gather floating pieces to fill the empty water casks. On the 31st, with a brief period of better weather providing some let-up from the frequent showers of snow and sleet, the ship's spare sails were aired and the ship was smoked between decks. Cooper observed in his log book that many of the spare sails were 'Rat eaten'.

On 1–2 January Cook recorded in his journal that the ocean swells from the east consistently indicated that no land was likely in that direction, once again 'proving a negative' about the location of the Southern Continent. At 9am on 2 January Lieutenant Clerke entered in his log 'Read the Articles of War and punished Chas Logie with 12 lashes for drawing his knife and cutting one of the

Midshipmen.' Initially a midshipman, Logie's disruptive behaviour had caused Cook to remove him from the quarterdeck. Logie subsequently got into a (perhaps) drunken fight during which he drew a knife, which led to his punishment.

Over the following eight days *Resolution* sailed 940 miles, mostly to the northnortheast, an average of 117.5 miles per day, to reach 47° south latitude. Multiple solar and lunar observations were made, weather permitting, the results causing Cook to make positive remarks about the chronometer in his journal on 8 January, commenting that the results showed 'our error can never be great so long as we have so good a guide as Mr Kendalls watch'. On 4 January Cook thought perhaps the frequent presence of blue petrels and albatrosses near *Resolution* might be a sign of land. Because of the prevailing westerly wind, he was unable to explore the ocean a further 20° to the north, which he would have crisscrossed to ensure no land was located in that direction (he was to sail in that expanse of ocean in late November 1774 on his way east to Tierra del Fuego; *see* Chapter 10). On 6 January Cook observed in his journal that his position at noon (52° 0′ south) was approximately 200 Leagues from his 1769 track to Tahiti, concluding there was no new land to be discovered in that location. He asserted this again on 10 January. With no new land to the north, once again the search for the continent narrowed.

On 11/12 January *Resolution* again turned south. This must have been a disappointment to the crew since it meant more cold weather with sleet, snow and ice (although no negative reference is found in the log books). Fresh gales appeared daily, as well as occasional high seas. On the 20th a tall ice island with a 200ft-high peak reminded Cook (and others) of the cupola of St Paul's Cathedral. The ship tacked frequently because of unsettled winds and made only 10 miles on the 21st. Then, on the 25th, no ice was observed, causing 'various opinions and conjectures' among those on the sloop as to the reason. However, on the 26th the ice islands and some whales returned as *Resolution* crossed the Antarctic Circle for the third time. Fog, snow, sleet and ice islands, one at least 3 miles in length, greeted *Resolution* over the next several days.

Astronomer William Wales daily recorded temperatures in his log book. Although the time of day at which the temperatures were recorded is not stated, we might assume the entries represent the daily high and low temperatures, or the readings may have occurred at noon and midnight. Latitude and longitude were recorded at noon, the end of the previous and the beginning of the next nautical day. On 11 January 1774 Captain Cook decided to sail back towards the Antarctic Circle, crossing it on the 26th, and reached his 'furthest south' on the 30th. *Resolution* headed north on 1 February. Figure 19 shows temperature recordings for every third day as *Resolution* moved south from 47° to 71° south, until the sloop turned north again on 4 February.

On 11 January *Resolution* was at 49° 34′ south accompanied by a range of temperatures from 63.5° to 50°F. On 26 December, the day the Antarctic Circle was crossed, the variation was 60° to 37½°F. When the 'furthest south' was reached on 30 January, the temperature fluctuation was 54° to 37°F. The lowest

Figure 19. Range of temperatures listed for every three days during *Resolution*'s third crossing of the Antarctic Circle, 11 January to 4 February 1774, recorded in William Wales's log book. Cook's 'furthest south' occurred on 17 January at 71° 10' south.

Date & Latitude South	High/Low Temp. (°F)		Date & Latitude South	High/Low Temp. (°F)	
11 January, 49° 34' S.	63.5	50	26 January, 67° 54.25 S.	60	37.5
14 January, 56° 11' S.	63.5	47.5	29 January, 70° 45' S.	56	32
17 January, 60° 55.5' S.	57.75	39.5	30 January, 69° 13' S.	58	34
20 January, 62° 27.25' S.	56	37	1 February, 67° 7.5' S.	54	37
23 January, 63° 37.5' S.	57	37	4 February, 64° 4.25' S.	58	38.5

temperature encountered was 32°F on 29 January. During this time the weather brought showers of rain, sleet and snow. On the 25th Cook observed the weather was 'very warm considering the latitude', but the next day floating ice as well as ice islands, fog (sometimes very thick fog with quarter-mile visibility), more snow and cold weather was recorded. On the 31st Cook wrote in his journal, 'Fresh breezes and thick foggy weather with Showers of Snow, piercing cold air; the Snow and Moistness of the fog gave a Coat of Ice to our rigging of near an Inch thick. Towards noon we had intervals of tolerable clear weather.' On 1 February the weather cleared, although it was 'gloomy and Clowdy, the air very Cold, yet the Sea was pretty clear of ice'.

Occasionally it is interesting to compare one of Cook's handwritten journals (which he wrote and rewrote during the voyage) with the journal edited by J.C. Beaglehole, which serves as the standard 'modern' record of Cook's voyages. In the handwritten version, he wrote,

26 January 1774. About 9 o'Clock [in the morning] we came for the 3rd time within the Antarctic Polar Circle and presently after we saw an appearance of Land to the South and SE and immediately we trim'd our sails and stretch'd towards it, a light wind to the NE. Gloomy misty weather with Sun shine. At Noon being by observation in the Latitude of 66° 36' South, Longitude 109° 31' West we sounded but had no ground at 130 fathoms [780 feet], nor had we the least sign of land, what we took for land had disappeared in the haze but we did not give it up until 8 o'Clock in the morning [of the following day].

Thursday the 27th at which time we were well assur'd the whole [?] was vanished in the clowds; we resum'd our Course to the South with a gentle breeze at NE, attended with a thick fog. Snow and Sleet meeting now and then with Islands of Ice.

In Beaglehole's edition of Cook's journal, the above passage appears as,

26 January, 66° 36' South Latitude, 109° 31' West Longitude: 'At 8 o'Clock [in the morning] we came the 3rd time within the Antarctick Polar Circle.

Soon after we saw an appearance of land to the East and SE, haul'd up for it and presently after it disappeared in the haze. Sounded but found no ground with a line of 130 fathom. A few whales and Petrels seen.

27 January, 67° 52′ South Latitude, 108° 15′ West Longitude: 'Little wind and foggy with rain and Sleet, at intervals fair and tolerable clear. Continued to stretch to the SE until 8 o'Clock am by which time we were assured our supposed land was vanished into the clowds and therefore resumed our Course to the South. A smooth Sea, what little swell we have is from the NE. A few Blue Petrels, Black Sheer-waters and Mother Carries Chickens are all the Birds we see.

Nothing significant appears altered in the two versions. It shows Cook tinkering with the wording, editing the text so there would be little opportunity to mis-construe his account. But there are minor differences. For example, 9am appears in the handwritten version, 8am in the Beaglehole edition. The spelling of Antarctic/Antarctick varies, interesting because the handwritten version contains the 'modern' spelling but the Beaglehole edition uses the common eighteenth-century version. Land disappears into the haze in the first edition but into the clouds in the second, along with references to petrels, shearwaters and 'Mother Carries Chickens' (storm petrels). When J.C. Beaglehole put together the modern edition of Cook's journals he found no single manuscript of the second voyage, only various fragments, some of which covered overlapping periods of time.[2]

Lieutenant Charles Clerke did not mark the third crossing of the Circle in 1774 with the exuberance of his entry on 17 January 1773 (*see* Chapter 5). His entry merely cited *Resolution*'s position as 66° 3′ south and 252° 12′ east longitude. His log noted that between 8 and 9am he sighted nine ice islands as *Resolution* sailed south-southeast towards the floating ice 'with the intention of taking some for water – at ½ past 9 we saw the appearance of land – so gave up the ice and made for it – Sounded. No ground at 120 fathoms. At Noon the Haze covered our supposed land. We're confoundly afraid it's nothing more [than] mere supposition.'

Lieutenant Robert Cooper and Master Joseph Gilbert also recorded 120 fathoms in their log books, but Cook's journal stated it was 130 fathoms (120–130 fathoms = 720–780ft). On 29 January and 2 February Clerke and Cooper supervised the hauling of loose ice to make water. Clerke noted that boats were hoisted from 1 to 7pm on the 29th, with the company 'pounding and melting ice all night'. Cooper observed that 'melting ice and filling the casks' occupied the entire morning on 30 January. In his journal Cook noted that the floating ice that was collected yielded, when melted, 5–6 tons of water.

Another shipboard task assigned to the lieutenants was to inspect food sup-plies. For example, on 29 January and 5 February Clerke and Cooper opened casks of meat and checked them to ensure the contents matched the provision labels on the cask. Usually the contents were short of the printed amount. Both officers noted that 'Cask of Pork No. 379' should have included 330 pieces but was actually short by twenty-eight pieces. Likewise Cask 1028 was opened and found to contain 180 pieces, two short of the total stamped on the container. On 4 February Master's Mate Burr inspected Cask 1004 to find 300 pieces of beef, short by two. Did the supplier not deliver the amount stamped on the cask, therefore 'shorting' the Royal Navy and perhaps pocketing the difference? Intriguingly, Cooper observed that his cask contained beef, whereas Clerke stated it was pork. At any rate, by 1774 the contents had been in the cask for at least 18 months, perhaps more. In his 1 August 1775 letter to the Navy's Victualling Board, Cook did not reference any shortages of beef or pork during the voyage, commenting only 'the Beef & Pork would have been thought excellent to the very last had we not lived so long upon it'. He did go into great detail about the quality of bread baked and packaged for the second voyage, recommending that bread never be packed in wet weather (because of the humidity) and that 'the Casks ought to be made of the best seasoned Wood and made very dry before the bread is pack'd in them'.[3] This was in reference to the baking/rebaking of bread for both *Resolution* and *Adventure* at Queen Charlotte Sound in November/ December 1773 (Chapter 7).

Captain Cook's 'Furthest South'

On 30 January *Resolution* reached 71° 10' south latitude, 106° 54' west longitude, Cook's furthest point south in search of the Southern Continent.[4] J.C. Beaglehole observed this was 'the furthest South anyone has ever attained by sea in this latitude',[5] an estimated 120 miles from land. In his journal Cook described the scene in great detail:

> at 8 o'Clock we were close to the edge of it [a field of ice], it extended east and west far beyond the reach of our sight. In the situation we were in just the Southern half of our horizon was illuminated by the rays of light which were reflected from the Ice to a considerable height. Ninety Seven Ice hills were distinctly seen within the field, besides those on the outside and many of them were very large and looked like a ridge of Mountains rising one above another till they were lost in the clouds. The outer or Northern edge of this immense field, was composed of loose or broken ice close packed together, so that it was not possible for anything to enter it, this was about a mile broad, within which was solid Ice in one continued compact body; it was rather low and flat (except the hills) but seemed to increase in height as you trace it to the South in which direction it extended beyond our sight ... I will not say it was impossible anywhere to get further to the South, but the attempting it would have been a dangerous and rash enterprise and what I believe no man in my situation would have thought of. It was indeed my opinion as well as the opinion of most on board, that this Ice extended quite to the Pole or perhaps joins to some land, to which it had been fixed from the creation and that it here, that is to the South of this Parallel where all the Ice we find scattered up and down to the North are first form'd and

afterwards broke off by gales of Wind or other cause and brought to the North by the Currents which we have always found to set in that direction in the high Latitudes.

This extract demonstrates Cook's mature thinking about the relationship of the ice to the Southern Continent and to the South Pole, as well as the formation of icebergs. It also appears in his journal as his 'revised' entry, recalling that Cook laboured on his journal while still on the voyage to ensure it would be accurate and not misinterpreted by an editor. *Resolution* met an impassable barrier, as Cook had done during his previous trips across the Antarctic Circle, both in East Antarctica and West Antarctica (although the 'west' and 'east' distinctions were not used in the eighteenth century). *Resolution*, Cook stated, 'could not proceed one Inch further to the South'.

At this point in his journal (30 January) Cook wrote one of his most-often-quoted comments: 'I whose ambition leads me not only further than any other man has been before me, but as far as I think it possible for man to go.' However, as observed earlier, we know that Cook reworked his journal, at times writing multiple accounts and inserting or deleting words. This well-known statement was also revised, becoming 'I who had Ambition not only to go further than any one had done before, but as far as it was possible for man to go.' The differences are small in scope and the reader may choose which version is preferred. J.C. Beaglehole explains that the small additions to the several journal versions are 'characteristic of Cook's rewriting, in his effort to get clarity and vividness, but at the same time not to overstate ...'[6]

Who in *Resolution* reached a personal 'furthest south'? A somewhat amusing interpretation of 'furthest south' arose between midshipman George Vancouver and Anders Sparrman, assistant to J.R. Forster on the second voyage. Vancouver (a 16-year-old midshipman) is said to have climbed out to the bowsprit at the moment *Resolution* tacked at 71° 10′ south on 30 January. He therefore claimed that he, personally, reached the voyage's 'furthest south'. Sparrman, however, claimed that because his cabin (presumably) was in the stern, he had been furthest south because he was below in his cabin at the time. When a ship tacks, the stern drifts away slightly before the sails fill and the ship moves ahead on its course.[7] In his account of Captain Cook at 71° 10′ south, novelist Graeme Lay depicts Cook himself as climbing out on the bowsprit to claim the honour of being 'furthest south'. Lay published an interesting series of Cook-related novels and patterned his writing closely on many details in Cook's journals and secondary sources. However, given what we know about James Cook's usual reserved behaviour, especially with the physical ailments which troubled him at times during the second voyage and especially in the weeks following late January 1774 (an account of which Lay covers admirably in considerable detail in his novel), it is unlikely that Cook would take such a risk.

In his log book astronomer William Wales gave a different description of the wall of ice, in terms of its height and extent. He stated that its height at the edge of the water was not as great as it appeared from a distance (a frequent comment in his log). Wales also suggested that 'a long ridge of prodigious high Mountains of Ice' was similarly a deception. He suggested it was not solid but an illusion probably enhanced by a fog-bank illuminated by the rays of light reflected from the ice. Wales wrote that 'we could not see over' the ice wall. However, he did not think the perceived mountains could reach the supposed height. Neither could they consist of ice or snow without 'sand under it; of which, we had no other signs'. Wales was the only man at the time to estimate the height of the ice wall and consider whether it was solid. He also used his scientist's perspective in observing the differences in appearances of objects from a distance and close up. There was no scientific European consensus about the formation of ice or ice-bergs, explaining his somewhat curious remark about the absence of sand whilst writing about ice and snow.

Lieutenant Clerke observed the huge ice wall 'extending East and West beyond the limits of our sight', his words very similar to those of Lieutenant Cooper. Joseph Gilbert noted 'a field of Ice ahead trending East and West beyond our sight at the Mast Head enclosing several mountains to the Southward', with 97 ice islands. At noon, *Resolution* 'stood to the edge of the Ice'. Burr's comments about the ice wall were similar to Gilbert's, while the CORRAL image for Smith's log is overexposed and not readable. Lieutenant Cooper recorded his 'fifth' crossing of the Antarctic Circle on 26 January and his 'sixth' crossing on 3 February.

Natural scientist George Forster recorded a phenomenon often seen at sea: the 'appearance' of land, which then vanished from sight. On 26/27 January George Forster recorded that 'we were amused with the appearance of land; for after standing on towards it for some hours, it vanished in the clouds'. This matched the journal entries of Cook and others, and recalls the 'sighting' of Pepys Island off the coast of Patagonia in 1769 (*see* Chapter 4). Forster remarked on 'the mildest sunshine we had ever experienced in the frigid zone' on the morning of the 29th and wrote, 'My father therefore ventured upon the deck for the first time after a month's confinement' (due to the cold weather's effect on his rheumatism). On 30 January George Forster's comments paralleled those of Cook and other officers in regard to 'icy masses, some of a very great height, ... irregularly piled up upon it, as far as the eye could reach' at 71° 10′ south. His father believed that solid ice covered the next 20° reaching to the South Pole. As for ice islands, he remarked that 'only the extremities [of the ice] are annually broken by storms, consumed by the action of the sun and regenerated in winter'. As far as it goes, this is a reasonably accurate description of how the floating icebergs are formed, at a time when the origins of Cook's ice islands were not generally understood.

J.R. Forster's journal is filled with comments about his personal misery in sailing in cold, damp, icy seas leading up to reaching 70° south on 30 January. His comments also provide a colourful description during rough seas. On the 16th he complained of a storm during which 'our Ship is tossed backwards & forwards, up & down the mountainous waves: each summit, from which you may overlook the vast extent of the Ocean, follows again a deep abyss, where we get hardly light in our Cabins. During night we brought to & then we felt the rolling infinitely more.' Then a 'huge mountainous Sea' brought a 'deluge' at 9 o'clock, covering the steerage table where he was sitting, putting out its candle. Even the Great Cabin as well was

> quite washed over & over by the Sea coming through the sides of the Ship. Into my Cabin came the Sea through the Skuttel [hatch or seacock] & wetted all my bed. [This tortured his arthritic body.] I did not sleep all night, my cabin being in water up to my Ankles; [if anything] fell down, it was most certainly soaked in the briny Deluge ... The Ocean & the winds raged all night.

On the 17th he complained, 'I eat little, salt meat is loathsome to me, all things look gloomy & dismall. I do not live, not even vegetate, I wither, I dwindle away.' However, he observed on the 18th that temperatures were colder (nearer the continent's ice) and the days 'grew longer, we could see at 10 o'Clock without a candle'. On the 20th the condition of the bread was mentioned once again, the bread having been packed in green casks, with the part spoiled that was next to the cask's sides and then 'rebaked' at Queen Charlotte Sound. Now the bread was 'very hard,' smelled 'musty' and crumbled when touched. Many on board were sick and Captain Cook ordered an increased bread allowance, despite its condition.

On the 27th J.R. Forster noted 'the appearance of land' although he also knew that closer inspection might prove it an illusion:

> If it be land it cannot but be hard favoured by Nature, & by no means inviting for an habitation to the human Species, & its productions must be few & of very little consequence to Great-Britain or any nation at such a distance from any Settlement, in so rigorous a Climate. The charm is gone, nothing but clouds made this appearance of land, the wind is something increased & we are gently going nearer to the pole.

On the 28th Forster observed, 'We have never before been so far South, & God knows how far we shall still go on, if Ice or Land does not stop us, we are in a fair way to go to the pole & take a trip round the world in five minutes, which is more than ever has been done for the Northpole, though so near at hand for the European nations.' ('[A] trip around the world in five minutes' refers to a circumnavigation around the Pole itself on the assumption that the Pole could be reached by a water route.)

Finally on 30 January Forster observed, 'we soon found that it was impossible to go any further South: & in good faith, I believe, it is so far South, as ever any man in future times shall choose to go, it being nearly 71° South'. The temperature in his cabin was 42°F and it snowed all afternoon, while the outside temperature was 32°F. J.R. Forster recognized the significance of 'furthest south' but he was not a happy traveller. Personal comments aside, his views shed some light on conclusions about the Southern Continent.

By Sunday, 6 February Captain Cook had determined that no land could be located south of his present location. Moreover, he concluded the Antarctic summer was too far gone to proceed to either Cape Horn or the Falkland Islands. Instead, he laid a course for Easter Island (reached 14 March), and then sailed on to the Marquesas Islands (8 April). On 22 April *Resolution* dropped anchor at Tahiti's Matavai Bay, the place where *Endeavour* had anchored in 1769 for the Transit of Venus. On the way towards the South Pacific Cook was struck down by a serious recurrence of his 'bilious cholic' which caused him to be confined to his cabin while various methods were tried to relive his extreme stomach and bowel discomfort (*see* Chapter 14).

The Three Crossings of the Antarctic Circle – a Summary

Crossing the Antarctic Circle is not the same as discovering or landing upon Antarctica. However, *Resolution* was closer to the continent than anyone in previous documented history, which was a significant achievement. The journals and log books clearly document the ship's position below the Circle and its encounter with the impenetrable wall of ice surrounding the continent. We can draw two broad conclusions from these events of 1773 and 1774:

1. The historic first of 'Crossing the Antarctic Circle' (17 January 1773) was clearly recognized by Cook, Clerke, Cooper and both J.R. and George Forster. The other observers in *Resolution* knew they were below 66° 36′ and recorded the information in their log books or journals, but did not mention being on the first ship to cross the Circle. Their subsequent crossings of the Antarctic Circle were noted in log books and journals but rarely commented upon.
2. From an historical perspective these Antarctic Circle crossings remain important 'firsts' today. They resulted from the deliberate, steady course set by James Cook and were carried out by *Resolution*'s company in a ship powered only by wind and current, sailing in uncharted and unknown waters that were sometimes dangerous because of floating ice. It might also be suggested that Cook's crossing of the Antarctic Convergence was also important, the wandering line between 50° and 60° south latitude separating oceanic regions that are significantly different.

J.C. Beaglehole describes Cook's Antarctic navigation as 'ice edge cruises'. These three episodes along the Antarctic ice barrier are important events in navigation history and helped to define the Southern Continent, even though Cook did not 'see' Antarctica, only its ice barrier.

The final leg of Cook's circumnavigation began on 3 January 1775 as *Resolution* departed from Staten Island and headed south-southeast in search of the 'Gulf of San Sebastian', which Alexander Dalrymple had suggested would lead to the

Unknown Southern Continent. Instead of Antarctica, Cook was to discover and survey the island of South Georgia and seven of the South Sandwich Islands in January and February 1775. In addition, by March he was to reach a final conclusion concerning his search for *Terra Australis Incognita* (*see* Chapter 11). However, before we review those events, James Cook and *Resolution* will once again sail the South Pacific from New Zealand towards Tierra del Fuego to rule in or out Antarctica's existence in that expanse of ocean.

PART 4

EXPLORATION OF SUB-ANTARCTIC REGIONS

Chapter 10

The Second Visit to Tierra del Fuego, Cape Horn and Staten Island
1774–1775

I have now done with the SOUTHERN PACIFIC OCEAN, and flatter myself that no one will think that I have left it unexplor'd, or that more could have been done in one voyage towards obtaining that end than has been done in this.

Commander James Cook, journal entry, 16 December 1774

As we know from Chapter 4, Cook and *Endeavour* visited Tierra del Fuego in January 1769 as the first voyage made a 'good Westing' and headed towards Tahiti to observe the Transit of Venus. In 1774 James Cook in *Resolution* visited northwestern Tierra del Fuego, then rounded Cape Horn, passing the Bay of Good Success and Staten Island in December and the first days of January 1775. We can compare the relative ease with which *Resolution* proceeded eastwards in 1774 around Cape Horn to the Bay of Good Success and then to Staten Island, with the difficult westward journey in January 1769. Christmas and the subsequent events of 1768 are a prelude to the search for Antarctica in the 'Gulf of San Sebastian', said by Alexander Dalrymple to lead to Antarctica.

Cook's second visit to Tierra del Fuego is divided into four parts: (1) departure from Queen Charlotte Sound in early November 1774 and reaching Tierra del Fuego in mid-December, (2) travelling along the western coast of Terra del Fuego in mid-December and Christmas Day, (3) sailing around Cape Horn to the Bay of Good Success (an anchorage in January 1769), to Staten Island, and (4) a further anchorage at Staten Island where wildlife was harvested for future use, and then departing for the continued search for Antarctica on 3 January 1775 (Chapter 11). The main sources for this chapter include James Cook's journal, the log books of Lieutenants Charles Clerke, Robert Cooper, the ship's Master Joseph Gilbert, and the journals of J.R. Forster and George Forster.[1]

Of course, unlike Captain Cook and the Admiralty in 1775, we know today that Antarctica lies approximately 650-plus miles through the Drake Passage, to the south of Tierra del Fuego. Cook's instructions directed him to sail to 'high latitudes' in search of the Southern Continent, which he did in January and February. We know now that he did not sail far enough directly south from Staten Island to reach Antarctica or the islands near the Antarctic Peninsula with floating or solid ice. He turned northeast instead, reaching the undiscovered South Georgia and South Sandwich Islands. As we will see in Chapter 11, he provided reasons for the course he took based on navigational and oceanic conditions.

As mentioned frequently in this study, it is important to understand that Cook's navigation in the Southern Ocean during the southern hemisphere's winter alternated with exploration of more northern parts of the Pacific during the southern hemisphere's spring, summer and autumn. In the seven months or so prior to departure for Cape Horn, Cook conducted another 'sweep' of the South Pacific, including Tahiti, where *Resolution* anchored from late April to late May. The second voyage then proceeded to visit or pass by many islands, including Niue, the Tonga group, the Fiji group, New Hebrides, Espiritu Santo and Cape Quiros (discovered by Mendaña and Quiros in the sixteenth century; *see* Chapter 2), New Caledonia and Norfolk Island.

On 21 June 1774 Cook attempted three times to land at Niue to observe the island and perhaps trade for supplies. Natives rushed the landing party, hurling rocks and spears, leading Cook to name it 'Savage Island'. At Tanna the visitors witnessed a volcanic eruption of Mt Yasur (7 August). Cook described its repeated five-minute eruptions as throwing large quantities of fire and smoke into the air, as well as ash or sand which covered everything and bothered the visitors' eyesight.

On 17 October *Resolution* sighted snow-covered Mt Edgcumbe on New Zealand's North Island and on the 18th the ship returned in very strong gales and a 'terrible sea' to Cook's favourite harbour at Queen Charlotte Sound. Cook searched for the bottle buried under a tree with instructions for Captain Furneaux (left there in November 1773). The bottle was not in that spot and Cook concluded that *Adventure* had reached the Sound after *Resolution* had departed (*see* Chapter 7).

One task was to follow up results from previous visits by *Endeavour* and *Resolution*. Cook and others attempted to find out what had happened to the animals left behind (pigs, goats and chickens) as well as the seeds that were to be planted in gardens. A few pigs and chickens appeared to be in a wild state. A sailor found fresh eggs as further proof these fowl had survived. The untended gardens proved disappointing to Cook and others in *Resolution*.

Maori behaviour was also puzzling. Conversations about *Adventure* were avoided, or contained conflicting accounts, and no real information could be obtained. The natives' behaviour was due to the 'Massacre of Grass Cove' on 17 December 1773 (*see* Chapters 1 and 7) in which ten English sailors were killed and their bodies cannibalized. Eventually Cook obtained an explanation of what happened at Grass Cove with Omai (Mai) as translator. Cook confided in his journal on 26 October that the vague, conflicting information caused unease about *Adventure*. Cook had noted on 9 October that, based on his observation of Maori behaviour, the natives were cannibals, but concluded they were of a good disposition and benign intentions. He took no reprisals against the Maori for

Grass Cove, a disappointment to *Resolution*'s crew. Cook would confirm the details from Captain Furneaux upon *Resolution*'s return to England in 1775.

The People spent the first days caulking *Resolution* for the future voyage to Cape Horn and beyond, an absolute requirement before sailing for ships and people who faced the much colder and harsher climates of high southern latitudes. The usual supply of tar and pitch was all gone so 'cook's fat and chalk' was made into putty for the purpose.

Sailing from Queen Charlotte Sound to Tierra del Fuego, 11 November–17 December

At daylight on 11 November 1774 *Resolution* weighed anchor and left Queen Charlotte Sound and by 8am was steering towards Cape Campbell at the southeast entrance to the Cook Strait. For the third time on the second voyage, Cook took his departure from his favourite anchorage and headed for 55° south latitude, intending to sail to areas unexplored previously. An occasional whale, pintados (petrels), some seals or penguins, eventually albatrosses, gales of varying strength and occasional thick fog or hazy weather accompanied *Resolution*. (The word 'gale' is open to much interpretation. Captain Cook appears to consider any wind from a gentle breeze to a strong tempest to be a 'gale', the varying adjectives determining the strength of the wind. For a sudden change in the wind's strength, perhaps accompanied by rain, Cook usually employs the word 'squall'.)

The next five weeks may be described as 'general sailing' day after day with no remarkable events beyond bursts of sudden rough weather during which *Resolution* occasionally rolled and pitched in the high seas. During November the voyage pursued, in general, a southeast-by-south route. *Resolution* was at 47° south by 15 November, 52° south on the 17th and 55° south on the 21st.

It is from log books that the historian gathers additional details (great and small) about running an eighteenth-century sailing vessel, as well as observations on the condition of the ocean and wildlife. Lieutenant Clerke's log book noted the top mast was 'carried off' and the top gallant studding sail was shredded in the late afternoon of 20 November but replaced by 3am the following day. He observed penguins, albatrosses, shearwaters and blue petrels flying around the sloop. In keeping with Captain Cook's emphasis on a clean and tidy ship, on the 22nd Clerke recorded in his log book that the ship was 'smoked' by carrying braziers of hot charcoal sprinkled with vinegar to clear the air on the lower decks. The weather was calm on that day. Lieutenant Cooper's log also referenced 'smoaking' the ship on the 22nd and caulking of a forward leak on the 23rd, while for nearly two weeks the sail-makers continued to repair *Resolution*'s sails. Clerke noted on 22 November that the *Aurora Australis* (Southern Lights) were faintly visible in the night sky.

Resolution's Master Joseph Gilbert recorded temperatures during the seven days ending on 18 November. The range was 50° to 61°F, with the average temperature 52.29°F. By comparison, during the seven days ending 27 November temperatures ranged from 43.5° to 46.0°F, with an average of 44.96°F. On the 11th Gilbert recorded 61°F. In travelling from 43° south to 55° south, temperatures dropped almost 15°F. This is not at all surprising, although temperatures were to remain in the mid-40s all the way to the arrival at Tierra del Fuego on 17 December.

By 26 November Cook concluded there was no further land to be discovered on his path towards Cape Horn. He decided to head directly for the western entrance to the Strait of Magellan. He had resolved to chart the area along Tierra del Fuego's west coast, which was not well known and would be more of a service to future navigation than searching for new territory (by which he meant the Southern Continent).

During the next two weeks, until Tierra del Fuego was sighted on 17 December, *Resolution* passed through varying gales occasionally accompanied by rain showers, with winds frequently changing direction, as the vessel generally bore east-south-east to 53° 25′ south on the 16th. Variations in the weather continued, from clear to hazy to thick foggy weather. On some days the weather prevented observations being made by a sextant to fix the ship's position. On 27 November Clerke's log book recorded that *Resolution* had travelled 183 miles, the largest total for the sloop in a single day. J.R. Forster and his son George both included that detail in their respective journals, J.R. Forster observing on the 13th that it was an 'extraordinary' passage over such a great distance.

However, both Forsters also complained about the rough passage, George writing about the 'astonishing violence' of the winds, 'the billows encreased to an immense size … sometimes several hundred yards long'. This caused *Resolution* to roll 'very disagreeably'. Both Forsters observed some signs of scurvy (e.g. swelling in their legs), for which greens brought from New Zealand as well as wort and sauerkraut were used as treatment. On 3 December Lieutenant Cooper's log book recorded another cleaning and 'smoking' of the ship. The sail-makers were noted repairing sails on nearly every day. At 10am the following day Lieutenant Clerke's log described the 'nasty, wet, foggy, disagreeable weather'.

Lieutenant Cooper's log recorded on 4 December that ocean waves caused *Resolution* to suddenly pitch and the ensign staff (carrying the national colours) fell overboard – an event also recorded by J.R. Forster. Cooper's log contained no reference that it was retrieved. Neither Cook's journal nor Clerke's log book references the incident. Clumps of seaweed were sighted during these days, suggesting that land was nearby. Astronomer William Wales recorded 'Ship's roll 38°' in his log entry for 6 December.[2] In Cook's journal entry for 17 December he described Wales's device to measure the angle the ship rolled when sailing in a heavy sea, and remarked that the greatest angle recorded was 38° on 6 December, which was likely not the 'greatest roll' made by *Resolution* during the voyage. On the 8th the top gallant sail split, requiring a new one to be bent into service. Diving petrels, penguins, an occasional seal and an increasing number of albatrosses accompanied the journey.

(*Above, left*) 1. James Cook portrait by Nathaniel Dance-Holland, *c.* 1775.
(*Wikimedia Commons*)

(*Above, right*) 2. James Cook bronze statue near Admiralty Arch on the Mall, London.
(*Author, 2011*)

(*Left*) 3. Captain James Cook Memorial Museum, Whitby, Yorkshire, formerly John Walker House, Cook's employer, 1746–1755.
(*Author, 2011*)

4. Cook's Cottage, built by Cook's father in 1755. It was moved in 1934 to Fitzroy Gardens in Melbourne, Australia. (*Author, 2006*)

5. South Georgia Island.
(*NASA, 2005; Wikimedia Commons*)

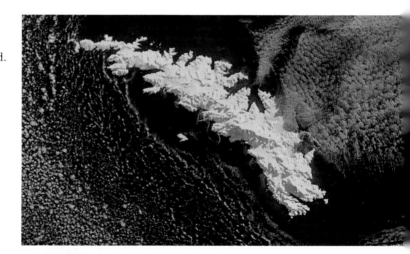

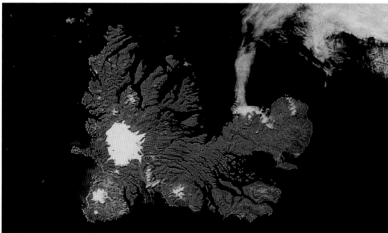

6. Kerguelen Island.
(*NASA, 2007, Wikimedia Commons*)

7. 'Ice Islands on 9 January 1773', by Wm Hodges.
(*Wikimedia Commons*)

Cape Horn.
(*Author, 2010*)

8. King penguin colony on South Georgia's Salisbury Plain and tussock grass vegetation.
(*Pismire, 2006; Wikimedia Commons*)

10. *Endeavour* and James Cook's signature. Stamp, Great Britain, 1968.

11. *Resolution* and circumnavigation of Antarctica map. Stamp, Australian Antarctic Territories, 1972. The blue line represents Cook's circumnavigation over three Antarctic summers.

12. *Resolution* at South Georgia, by Wm Hodges. Stamp, South Georgia & SSI, 2010.

13. 'Ice Islands on 9 January 1773' by Wm Hodges. Stamp, Cook Islands, 1968 (see complete sketch, Pl. 7).

14. *Resolution* and *Discovery* at Queen Charlotte Sound, New Zealand, by John Webber. Stamp, Niue, 1979.

15. Marine chronometer No. 4 by John Harrison. Stamp, Great Britain, 1993.

16. 200th anniversary, Cook at Christmas Harbour, Kerguelen, by John Webber, December 1976. (*TAAF [Terres Australes et Antarctiques Francaises: French Southern and Antarctic Territories], 1979*)

17. George Forster and tussock grass. Stamp, Falkland Island Dependencies, 1985.

18. The Arch of Kerguelen. Cook described it in December 1776 as, 'a remarkable spot, its point terminates in a high rock which is perforated quite through as to appear like the arch of a bridge'. The top of the Arch collapsed in 1908–13. (*TAAF, 2001*)

19. J.R. Forster and king penguin. Stamp, Falkland Island Dependencies, 1985.

20. Possession Bay, South Georgia (17 January 1775) by Wm Hodges. Stamp, South Georgia, 1975.

21. Joseph Banks and dove (Antarctic) prion. Stamp, Falkland Island Dependencies, 1985.

22. Macaroni penguin, South Georgia Island.
(*Andrew Shiva, 2016; Wikimedia Commons*)

23. South Georgia fur seal.
(*Brocken Inaglory, 2007; Creative Commons*)

24. Elephant seal harem, Kerguelen Island. (*Creative Commons, 2005*)

25. Kerguelen cabbage (*Chou Kerguelen*), an antiscourbitic. (*Timhaute, 2005; Creative Commons*)

26. Scurvy grass (*Cochleria officinalis*), a cabbage and antiscourbitic. (*Anne Burgess, 2007; Creative Commons*)

27. Cushion plant (*Azorela selago*). From a distance, clusters of cushion plants gave a greenish appearance to Kerguelen Island. (*Franek2, 2002; Creative Commons*)

28. Bluegrass or Cook's tussock grass (*Poa Cookii*) was used as food for cattle transported on Cook's ships in 1776. (*Franek2, 2012; Creative Commons*)

29. Wandering albatross (*Diomedea exulans*).
(Michael Clarke, 2009; Creative Commons)

30. South Georgia pipit (*Anthus antarctica*).
(ml.wikipedia, 2007)

31. Cape pigeon or pintado petrel (*Daption capense*). *(J.J. Harrison, 2011; Creative Commons)*

32 Antarctic tern (*Sterna vittata*) in the Antarctic Peninsula. *(Butterfly voyages, 2007; Creative Commons)*

The range of temperatures recorded by ship's Master Joseph Gilbert was from 43.0 to 47.75°F for the week ending on 11 December. The average temperature was 45.6°F. J.R. Forster, who did not enjoy sailing in cold weather, noted daily the variation of the temperature in the outside air compared to that of his cabin, which was only 5–7° warmer. Gilbert also noticed the increased number of birds circling *Resolution*, noting on 12 December that some were 'exceedingly large', the ornithologist J.R. Forster identifying both yellow-billed and sooty albatrosses during early December.[3]

On 16 December 1774 Cook once again concluded that the 'land of great extent' did not exist in this area of the Pacific Ocean. He made the following journal entry: 'I have now done with the SOUTHERN PACIFIC OCEAN, and flatter myself that no one will think that I have left it unexplor'd, or that more could have been done in one voyage towards obtaining that end than has been done in this.'

Cook's conclusion can be seen as a response to criticism from the first voyage that he left unexplored areas which contained *Terra Australis Incognita*. This conclusion foreshadows an even more declaratory statement on 20 February 1775 after departing the South Sandwich Islands concerning the existence of the Southern Continent (*see* Chapter 11).

However, Cook was not the only navigator who sailed in these waters. Michael Lee suggests that Captain Surville should also receive credit for disproving the existence of the Southern Continent in the South Pacific, 'east of the East Indies and West of Peru'.[4] Surville sailed the Pacific from New Zealand to Peru in 1769–1770 and drowned in a capsized skiff off the coast of Peru in April 1770.

The Western Coast of Tierra del Fuego, mid-December to Christmas 1774

On Saturday, 17 December Cook sighted Cape Deseado (Cape Pillar, *Cabo Piliar*), the northwest point of Desolation Island and the Pacific entrance to the Strait of Magellan. *Resolution* was approximately 6 leagues from the Cape at 53° 21' south latitude and 76° 17' west longitude (although Cook questioned whether he was actually a half degree more to the west). He fixed Cape Desolation's position as 53° 00' south and 74° 40' west longitude, noting the rocky and barren coastline with patches of snow. *Resolution* passed Cape Gloucester and headed for Cape Noir and then Santa Barbara Bay, which is the channel's opening to the Strait of Magellan, where the ship stood off for the night of the 18th. Cook named a small island near the shore 'Gilbert Isle' after *Resolution*'s Master.

As I have noted in prior chapters, one of the Admiralty's instructions to Cook (on all voyages) was to make observations about the islands and lands visited during his travels. I included comments from Cook, Banks and *Endeavour*'s Master Molyneux on the 1769 visit to Tierra del Fuego. We will now consider a range of observations from Cook, Lieutenants Clerke and Cooper, Master Gilbert and naturalists J.R. and George Forster during Cook's second visit to a different part of Tierra del Fuego.

During the second visit Cook wrote in his journal on 19 December that he termed Cape Santa Barbara 'Cape Desolation' because it was 'the most desolate and barren Country I ever saw'. Cook added a description of the barren coast,

> it seems to be intirely composed of Rocky Mountains without the least appearance of Vegetation, these Mountains terminate in horroable precipices whose craggy summits spire up to a vast height, so that hardly anything in nature can appear with a more barren and savage aspect than the whole of this coast. The inland mountains were covered with Snow but those on the Sea Coast were not, we judged the former to belong to the Main of Tierra del Fuego and the latter to be islands so ranged as apparently to form a Coast.

J.R. Forster also described the harsh, cold, snow-covered rocky terrain of Tierra del Fuego. The soil consisted of a thin crust and marsh. However, he was later to describe the northeast coast as less rocky and 'rich in vegetables', even though he did not go ashore on 30 December. He also commented about tussock grass (similar to that found on South Georgia in 1775) and its considerable height as protection for seals and penguins.[5] Captain Cook named a 'lofty Promontory' with two large towers not far from Gilbert Isle 'York Minster' after the great cathedral at York. Lieutenant Clerke in his log book on 19 December described the location as 'the most wretched barren looking place I ever beheld'.

The immediate task was to sound a possible bay so that *Resolution* could anchor and replenish its store of wood and water, and then make observations of this part of Tierra del Fuego. It took some time to find a suitable anchorage, in part due to the water's depth of over 170 fathoms and also because of continuous winds. A small cove was located as a temporary spot and *Resolution* anchored in water of 25–30 fathoms, moving to a better position on 21 December, a third of a mile offshore but protected from the wind. In his log entry for 21 December Lieutenant Clerke described the spot as 'conveniently located for wooding and watering'. The empty water casks were taken ashore to be filled and equipment was set up on land for astronomer Wales. Wales recorded a lengthy description in his log regarding the accuracy of the chronometer compared to astronomical sightings to determine latitude and longitude. He described a 'broken coast' of many inlets and islands. He noted quantities of wood and 'great quantities of the best wild celery I ever tasted, but a little inferior to the golden celery of England'.[6] A guard tent was set up on shore because there was some uncertainty as to the reception by natives, despite *Endeavour*'s peaceful visit in 1769.

Despite the apparently harsh environment, on 22–23 December Cook, several officers and the naturalists set off in a boat to explore the islands near *Resolution*'s anchorage. High mountains capped with snow dominated the scene, while the air was 'refrigerated' by the snow and the rays of the summer sun appeared not to penetrate much of the area. George Forster observed that some of the rocks were covered with mosses, along with some flowers and some shrubbery. A fire appeared to have burned part of the land at some point in the past. In a sheltered cove, where the water was clear and transparent as glass, the naturalists saw a large variety of birds that 'twittered around us in the sun-shine', as well as mosses, ferns and climbing vines. These, as well as flowers, were added to the scientists' specimen collections. Mussels, 'more delicious than oysters', were located on the shore, as was wild celery, which was harvested to be taken to the sloop.[7]

During 22–24 December the visitors explored the area near where *Resolution* was anchored, which was to be given the name 'Christmas Sound'. Cook observed that the country was 'a barren Rock, doomed by Nature to everlasting sterility'. The entire coast consisted of many islands of varying size. Despite the difficult topography, the visitors found ducks, shags (cormorants) and geese which were shot for food. Cook's journal noted that Marine William Wedgeborough disappeared during the night of the 22nd. Lieutenant Cooper's log book entry for the 23rd suggested Wedgeborough likely fell overboard as he was seen 'very much in Liquor at 12 o'clock' and was drowned on his way to the head. On the 24th Lieutenant Pickersgill persuaded Captain Cook to form two shooting parties to try their luck on 'Goose Island', but the rocky territory made it difficult for the hunters to progress. At the end of the day, Cook's party had taken sixty-two geese and Pickersgill's fourteen. The numbers of geese obtained were sufficient to feed the entire company for, Cook wrote, 'the approaching festival' (Christmas).

The native Fuegians appeared on 25 December. Cook decided these people were collectively the 'Pecherias', a word earlier applied by French navigator Bougainville, the 'same nation' he observed at the Bay of Good Success in 1769. However, these people were the Alacaluf, a different group, most notably because of their use of canoes, from the peoples at the Bay of Good Success.[8] Cook wrote that they were a small-sized people, 'a little ugly half starved beardless Race, almost Naked'. What clothing they had was sealskin, several skins being sewn together to make a 'cloak' worn over their shoulders. Both men and women were mostly naked except for a flap of seal skin covering the private parts of the women. They were 'dirty' and 'smelled most intolerable' of oil and general 'stench'. The smell was 'train oil' (from the Dutch *traen*, meaning 'tear' or 'drop'), produced by exudation from the blubber of marine animals such as seals or whales. J.R. Forster observed red or white paint on their bodies. Cook and Banks had also observed the red/white paint on native peoples in 1769. Forster described the natives as 'friendly and peaceable', shivering in the cold weather, and 'the most dirty of all human beings I ever saw in my Life'. Cook observed two naked children 'at the breast', thus 'they are inured from their infancy to Cold and hardships'.

Cook noted that the women remained in the canoes and tended a fire (built in earth on the canoe's floor). The natives carried fire with them wherever they travelled. Large seal hides provided shelter and protection while sailing in the canoes. They possessed bows, arrows and harpoons to kill fish, seals and whales, much like Eskimos, Cook speculated. On 27 December he concluded the natives were the 'most wretched' of all people, 'doomed to live in one of the most inhospitable climates in the world', concluding with the harsh judgement that they did not have 'sagacity enough to provide themselves with such necessaries as may render life convenient'. In an undated entry (since *Resolution* was at anchor)

Charles Clerke decided the natives' appearance 'immediately bespeaks your pity'. They were a weak, 'diminutive race – shaking and shivering' in the midsummer air. George Forster thought the natives 'seemed totally insensible of the superiority of our situation', but also observed, while noting the apparently miserable conditions in which the natives existed, that 'our civilised communities are stained with vices and enormities', so that the superior knowledge of the visitors did not make good use of their apparent advantages.[9] In his biography of Cook, J.C. Beaglehole noted that the Alacaluf people were likely no more 'primitive' than Marine Wedgeborough, who fell overboard in a drunken state on 22 December.[10] During a second visit on the 26th, Cook provided canvas and baize to provide cover for the natives in cold weather.

The Fuegians were not invited to share Christmas dinner. In his journal Cook noted, '[*Resolution*'s crew] ... we had not experienced such fare for some time, Roast and boiled Geese, Goose pies, &c.' as well as 'some Madeira Wine [which had aged well], our friends in England did not perhaps, celebrate Christmas more cheerfully than we did'.

Cook's remarks bear out the assertion by N.A.M. Rodger (cited in Chapter 3) that the standard Royal Navy diet was likely superior to the general diet consumed by *Resolution*'s contemporaries on land. J.R. Forster noted there was enough food so that one goose served four men. But he also complained that his sleep was disturbed during the night by a drunken crew, behaving like 'beasts ... soon lost in Liquor: & clamour & fighting was all over the Ship seen & heard'. George Forster echoed his father's complaint, writing that the People caroused for two days 'without intermission, till captain Cook ordered the greatest part of them to be packed off into a boat, and put ashore, to recover from the drunkenness in the fresh air'.

During the next two days more visits were paid to 'Goose Island' where additional fowl were shot and greens harvested, J.R. Forster observing that quantities of celery were added to goose soup to make an evening meal. Lieutenant Cooper's log on the 27th reported that thirty geese were shot or caught alive on the last trip before *Resolution* sailed. The Fuegians continued to visit the ship over the course of several days. One aspect of their time at Christmas Sound that met with J.R. Forster's approval was the seven new birds, three fish and twenty plants that were added as specimens to their collection.[11]

On to Cape Horn, the Bay of Good Success and Staten Island, 28–30 December 1774

The distance from Christmas Harbour to Cape Horn, Cook wrote on 30 January, was 31 leagues (93 nautical miles). At 8am on 28 December *Resolution* weighed anchor and began sailing southeast-by-east, obtaining a clear view of the St Ildefonso Islands discovered in 1619 by the navigator Diego Ramirez, a string of steep, rocky, tussock grass-covered islands that are a breeding ground for penguins and albatrosses. The voyage continued to make its way along the western coast of Tierra del Fuego, eventually reaching the west point of Nassau Bay, also known as False Cape Horn, for which Cook pinpointed its location as 55° 39′ south. *Resolution* then made 'short boards' (holding their position) until the following morning so they could obtain a clear view of Cape Horn.

At 3am *Resolution* travelled east-by-south (*see* Figure 9) and passed by Cape Horn at 7am on 30 December, thereby entering the Atlantic Ocean. In his journal Cook wrote,

> It is the very same point of land which I took for the Cape when I passed it in 1769, which at that time I was doubtfull of. It is the most Southern point of land on Hermites Islands (a group of Islands of unequal extent lying before Nassau bay) and situated in the Latitude of 55° 58′ [south] and in the Longitude of 68° 13′ [west] according to the observations made off it in 1769 …

Cook eventually decided that 67° 19' was the more accurate longitude. He described rocky hills, their sides and valleys covered with green turf and woods. A large number of birds were observed. Lieutenant Clerke observed that on the 30th at 7am Cape Horn appeared 1 league to the north-northwest and *Resolution* was sailing in 'fine smooth water these 24 hours', in contrast to the foggy conditions of 1769. The sloop made its way to the Bay of Good Success to see if there was any sign of *Adventure*. Both Gilbert and Clerke noted in their log books that, on Cook's orders, *Resolution* fired two 'guns' at 10am as a signal to *Adventure*, 'supposing her to be in Success Bay', which Captain Cook continued to think possible. A cutter was dispatched to the shore. There was no sign of *Adventure*. The Fuegian natives greeted the visitors cordially and appeared to have obtained some European-style clothing, likely Spanish, after *Endeavour*'s earlier visit. However, the visitors learned that no other European ship had visited the area in the recent past. Lieutenant Cooper noted in his log book entry on 31 December that the date of *Resolution*'s presence was carved into a tree, should *Adventure* later arrive after *Resolution*'s departure.

Resolution held its position off the Bay of Good Success until the next morning. Hundreds of seals and twenty to thirty whales surrounded the ship, the whales spouting extremely smelly 'effluvia' which, J.R. Forster noted, poisoned the air for two to three minutes at a time. He also described whales slapping their tails or fins on the water, as well as large humpback whales breaching. Forster wrote that a 40ft 'Whale fairly jumped out of the Water with the whole body & fell again into it with a loud Explosion made by his fins'.[12] In his 30 December log entry, Clerke (as well as Gilbert) wrote that there was a 'greater abundance' of seals and whales at Tierra del Fuego than anywhere else in the world.

An Anchorage at New Year's Harbour, 31 December 1774–3 January 1775

On 30 December in a calm sea (very different from January 1769), the current in the Strait of Le Maire brought *Resolution* to Staten Island. Cook decided to explore the island since it was 'little known', as with his 1769 exploration of

Tierra del Fuego. By 9am the northwesterly wind brought stormy and hazy, rainy weather. On the 31st *Resolution* proceeded along the coast in a thick haze to the east end of Staten Island. In dense fog, the presence of seals and birds was sufficient for Cook to seek an anchorage. The opportunity for fresh meat was, Cook wrote, 'a temptation too great for people in our situation to withstand, to whom fresh Provisions of any kind was acceptable'. The anchorage on an island off Staten Island would be named 'New Year's Harbour'. It positioned the sloop so that it could easily sail away with a decent wind.

From 31 December to 2 January the visitors took a huge harvest of Staten Island wildlife: seals (referred to as 'sea bears'), sea-lions, fish, penguins, ducks, geese, shags and other unspecified birds. Three boats were hoisted out from *Resolution* and made their way to the shore to obtain whatever wildlife could be found. Cook observed that the entire shore was covered by seal cows and their calves. The visitors also came across much larger sea-lions. 'They were all so tame, or rather so stupid as to suffer us to come so near as to knock them down with a stick but the large ones we shot as it was rather dangerous to go so near them.' A large number of penguins and a nesting area for thousands of cormorants (shags) were located. The boats were full of wildlife by evening when the men returned to *Resolution*.

Details about the large numbers of animals and birds killed and processed off Staten Island are amplified in the log books of Lieutenants Clerke and Cooper and ship's Master Gilbert. The 'officers and gentlemen' did the shooting, according to Gilbert. Both Clerke and Cooper record the 'killing and bringing-in' of seals and sea-lions, whose blubber was to be turned into oil amounting to 6 puncheons (Gilbert's log states 5 puncheons and 2 half-casks). A puncheon is a large cask of varying size depending on its contents. The *Oxford English Dictionary* states that the size of a puncheon varies from 72 to 120 gallons (273 to 454 litres). Assuming a puncheon is similar to a wine cask (*c.*70 gallons), the blubber harvested at Staten Island equalled perhaps 420 gallons of oil. Both Cooper and Gilbert noted the presence of a good quantity of wood and several streams with fresh water. Cooper wrote that seals and sea-lions 'entirely covered' the shore, some of the sea-lions as large as 1,000lb. George Forster estimated the size varied from 1,200 to 1,500lb, producing approximately 550lb for processing. Males were 10–12ft in length, females 6–8ft. The older bull sea-lions 'snort and roar like mad bulls or lions', while females bleat like calves and cubs like lambs.[13]

On 2 January Cooper wrote that the boats returned twice completely loaded with wildlife. Gilbert observed 'boatloads of penguins & shags' appeared on 2 January, 'which are exceeding good eating'. Both Gilbert and Cooper coordinated the work of removing the skin from the blubber so it could be reduced to oil. A 'prodigious quantity of shags and penguins, & some Ducks and geese, etc.' arrived by the boats on 2 January. That evening the penguins were 'boiled in the coppers' for the dinner of the ship's company.

The next day the ships returned to Staten Island to retrieve the seals and sea-lions from the previous night's hunting, as well as find additional wildlife. The blubber of the older seals and sea-lions was to be used for oil, since their meat was unpalatable. Cook observed that a more than necessary amount of seal and sea-lion carcasses were taken to *Resolution*, perhaps substantiating the assertion by historian Frank McLynn that perhaps a 'savage massacre' occurred.[14] On 2 January, because there was insufficient wind to sail, the men returned to find additional prey. A supply of wood and fresh water was also available at New Year's Harbour.

There is no doubt that the seals, sea-lions and penguins especially were defenceless, easy prey for the visitors. It does not appear that the wildlife was slaughtered for no purpose, especially since the meat would serve as food and the oil for other purposes during the remainder of the voyage. After a brief visit by a few people at Possession Bay on South Georgia, *Resolution*'s next anchorage was at the Cape of Good Hope on 22 March 1775.

The December/early January temperatures on both the west and east coasts of Tierra del Fuego were comparable, as seen from data in Joseph Gilbert's log book. For the seven days leading up to Christmas Day, the recorded temperatures at Christmas Sound ranged from 50 to 58.75°F, with an average of 54.4°F. For the seven days leading up to the departure from New Year's Harbour, temperatures ranged from 48.75 to 56.66°F, an average of 53.55°F. While the sloop was at anchor, J.R. Forster did not record temperatures in his cabin compared to the outside air, the main point of which was to criticize the lack of comfort of his cabin in *Resolution* after the voyage concluded during his dispute with the Admiralty over the publication of journals (*see* Chapter 12).

Resolution might have departed on 2 January but the wind was insufficient until noon, so Cook waited until 4am on 3 January to weigh anchor, taking advantage of a fresh breeze from the northwest-by-west. At Cape St John at the eastern end of Staten Island a very strong current from the south made sailing difficult for part of the day but by noon on the 3rd the seas were calm for a short time, then squalls with rain kept *Resolution* from making progress. Cook decided that he had charted the area sufficiently, also concluding that many earlier charts and records were inaccurate. He thought his fixing of longitude for Cape Horn was accurate to a quarter of a degree, concluding, 'Thus the extent of Terra del Fuego from East to West and consequently the Straits of Magalhaens will be found less than most Navigators have made it.' On 4 January 1775 Captain Cook headed east and south to determine if Dalrymple's 'Gulph of St Sebastian' was the tip of *Terra Australis Incognita* (*see* Chapter 13).

James Cook's two visits to Tierra del Fuego in 1769 and 1774 achieved a further 'narrowing of the options' in the search for Antarctica. In 1769 *Endeavour* sailed west of Cape Horn to 60° south latitude and 110° west longitude. No 'land of great extent'' was located. After observing the June 1769 Transit of Venus, he sailed 'south' of Tahiti to 40° south. Again no land was located. After the 1773 separation off the Cook Strait, Cook sailed through the far southern Pacific to search for Antarctica, sighting no continent. Again, on the October–December 1774 trek from New Zealand to Tierra del Fuego, no land of any consequence, let alone a Southern Continent, appeared. At that point James Cook concluded that his explorations of that part of the Pacific where geographers and others had speculated Antarctica might be found had proved their prognostications to be inaccurate. In addition to seeking *Terra Australis Incognita*, the two visits to Tierra del Fuego also provided descriptions of the land and peoples encountered at the tip of South America, information Cook was instructed to gather on his voyages.

Of course, there was a Southern Continent, and the next two section of this book deal with the discovery of South Georgia and the South Sandwich Islands in 1775, ending with Cook's declaration about Antarctica's location.

'Wild Rocks, Thick Fogs and Everlasting Snow': South Georgia and the South Sandwich Islands

January–February 1775

The inner parts of the Country was not less savage and horrible: the Wild rocks raised their lofty summits till they were lost in the Clouds and the Vallies laid buried in everlasting Snow. Not a tree or shrub was to be seen, no not even big enough to make a tooth-pick.

James Cook, journal entry, 17 January 1775, at Possession Bay, South Georgia

The interval of clear weather was of very short duration before we had as thick a fog as ever, attend[ed] with rain ... we spent our time involved in a continual thick Mist and for aught we knew surrounded by dangerous rocks; the Shags and Soundings were our best Pilots ...

James Cook, journal entry, 23 January 1775, at Clerke's Rocks off South Georgia

[Navigation was difficult because of] the disagreeable anxiety of being carried by the swell upon the most horrible Coast in the World ...

James Cook, journal entry, 30 January 1775, South Sandwich Islands

The Andes Mountains do not end at Tierra del Fuego (*see* Figure 20). A submarine mountainous ridge extends the range in an arc eastwards, southwards and finally westwards where it emerges in the South Orkney and South Shetland Islands and the Antarctic Peninsula.[1] The Scotia Sea forms a marine basin some 350,000 square miles (900,000 square kilometres) in area and 2,700 miles in length (4,350km). The Drake Passage forms the western end of the Scotia Sea. South Georgia and the South Sandwich Islands are located at the eastern end of this arc. Most of the Scotia Sea lies within the Antarctic Convergence, an oceanic dividing line encircling Antarctica and wandering between 50° and 60° south latitude, where the warmer waters of the Atlantic or Pacific meet the cooler waters from the south, an area often with abundant sea life.

An Overview of Cook's January and February Itinerary

During January and February 1775 Captain James Cook in *Resolution* sailed the often-stormy, sleety, snowy, cold, windy and foggy waters of the Scotia Sea

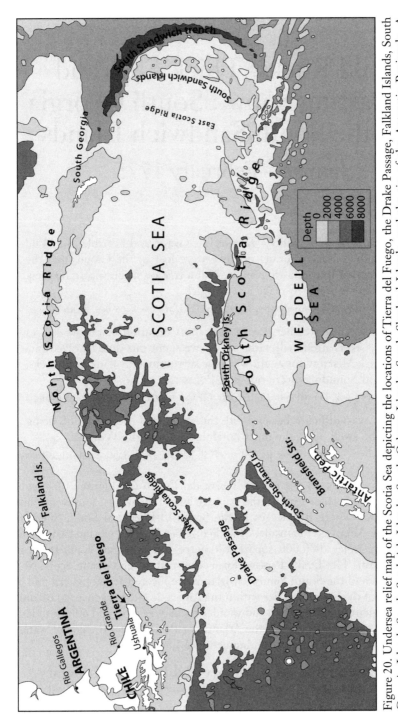

Figure 20. Undersea relief map of the Scotia Sea depicting the locations of Tierra del Fuego, the Drake Passage, Falkland Islands, South Georgia Island, South Sandwich Islands, South Orkney Islands, South Shetland Islands, and the tip of the Antarctic Peninsula. A submarine volcanic mountain chain continues the Andes Mountains in a large easterly then westerly arc around the Scotia Sea/Drake Passage and into the Antarctic Peninsula, and down the Antarctic continent, separating East and West Antarctica. The table indicates the depth of the Scotia Sea. The map is a simplified greyscale version of a map by Gi (2013).

searching for land. His purpose was to find that 'land of great extent' to see if it was part of *Terra Australis Incognita* as described in the writings of Alexander Dalrymple, perhaps also locating territory sighted by London merchant Anthony de la Roche (1675) or Jean-Baptist Bouvet (1739). Cook frequently encountered 'ice islands' and a few scattered islands, islets and rocks. Most notably he discovered and charted the northern coastline of South Georgia and parts of the South Sandwich Islands.[2]

These islands evoke sharply defined images. Cook wrote of South Georgia's 'wild rocks', its mountains whose summits are 'lost in the clouds', the 'savage and horrible' aspects of the island, with summertime valleys buried in 'everlasting snow'. He described Sandwich Land as an area of 'thick fogs, Snow storms, Intense Cold, [and] dangerous navigation'[3]. The sources for these two months of exploration in the Southern Ocean are James Cook's journals and the log books of Lieutenants Clerke and Cooper, *Resolution*'s Master Joseph Gilbert and astronomer William Wales, as well as those of J.R. and George Forster which have been referenced in other chapters. These two months of navigation complete Cook's third leg of his circumnavigation of Antarctica. The only remaining sub-Antarctic locations he sighted or visited were the Crozet and Kerguelen Islands in 1776 (*see* Chapter 13).

Cook briefly landed on the island of Georgia to claim possession, but he did not set foot on 'Sandwich Land', obtaining at best a glimpse of the islands due to ever-present fog, snow and mist, nor could he locate a safe harbour. Neither Cook nor other people in the ships noted the Sandwich Island's prominent volcanoes. In contrast, twentieth-century writers and film-makers have termed South Georgia an 'Antarctic Oasis' and a 'Living Eden, a Paradise of Ice'. Stunning panorama images are available on the island's official website.[4] The South Sandwich Islands are important breeding grounds for wildlife. Because of the important role these islands play in supporting wildlife, some references are made to later whaling and sealing activities and wildlife or sea life in these sub-Antarctic islands today.

The Gulf of San Sebastian and the Isle of Georgia, 13–17 January 1775

After Christmas and New Year anchorages in the vicinity of Tierra del Fuego, *Resolution* departed from Staten Island on 3 January 1775. During the next ten days Cook pursued an east-southeasterly route along 55° to 58° south latitude and 53° to 40° west longitude. He was in search of the 'Gulf of San Sebastian' theorized by Alexander Dalrymple to touch the Southern Continent. The coordinates cited by Dalrymple yielded sightings of seaweed, seals, albatrosses, penguins and petrels – but no land. This search recalls Captain Cook's exploration further to the east and south in search of Cape Circumcision. He was to search again for Bouvet's mysterious Cape after leaving the South Sandwich Islands in March.

On 4 January *Resolution* encountered a sudden, heavy squall which led to the loss of the top gallant mast, a studding sail boom and the fore studding sail, followed by heavy rain. Cook sailed to the southeast, following a Dalrymple chart in the 'Gulf of San Sebastian' designed to be an oceanic chart of the area between South America and Africa, based on the previous voyages of Edmund Halley (1700) and Bouvet (1738–1739), as described in Chapter 2. In his journal Cook expressed doubts that the 'Gulf' led to the coast of a continent but he was determined to explore the Southern Ocean in order to clear up speculation. On 5 January *Resolution* arrived at 58° 9′ south latitude and 53° 14′ west longitude, the area identified by Dalrymple as the south-western point of the Gulf of San Sebastian. He 'saw neither land nor signs of any'. *Resolution* then sailed to the north to be near the locations cited by La Roche (1674) as well as a Spanish ship (1756) which may have sighted snow-covered South Georgia, having been carried to the east by the winds in attempting to round Cape Horn; this information was also included in Dalrymple's chart.[5]

Over the next several days the northward route continued to 56°, then 55°, then 54° south latitude. Seals, seaweed, floating wood, albatrosses and blue petrels, all possible signs of land, were observed. *Resolution* then turned east and reached 54° south latitude and 42° 08' west longitude, said by Dalrymple to be the north-eastern point of the Gulf of St Sebastian. No additional signs of land were seen. Cook noticed an ocean swell from the east-southeast which ruled out extensive land in that direction. By midnight on the 12th the winds had abated and the seas were calm.

Today we know that at this point Cook was heading towards the Antarctic continent, about 15° further to the south. Had he continued to follow a more south-by-southeast route he would have at a minimum encountered an ice barrier. But he observed no signs that land lay to the south. He sailed in the coordinates identified by Alexander Dalrymple, found no territory, and then pursued the Southern Ocean to the east, as suggested by the Admiralty's instructions. Today we can only speculate on what oceanic conditions he would have encountered in 1775 by continuing a southward route, such as the ice Sir Ernest Shackleton encountered in *Endurance* during the Imperial Trans-Antarctic Expedition, 1914–1917.

By 13 January much cooler air and a thick fog (until 6am) greeted the crew. Cook's journal notes the air was the coolest since departing from New Zealand. At a distance of 13 leagues (about 39 miles) Cook observed an ice island as well as penguins and various petrels around *Resolution*. Uncertainty about whether a sighting was another ice island or land is reflected in Lieutenant Clerke's log book entries for 12 and 13 January. Cook eventually concluded that they had sighted land, rather than an ice island, 'wholly covered with snow'. Initial calm seas were followed by a gale with both sleet and snow.

Although it was not known for a few days, at this point *Resolution* had reached the north side of South Georgia, specifically two small islands that Cook named Willis Island (after midshipman Thomas Willis who first sighted it) and Bird Island (named for the prevalence of birds on what is today a bird and seal sanctuary). Small islands and bits of rocks protruding above the ocean are a feature of sailing near South Georgia (such as Black Rock or Shag Rocks that lie

150–200 miles off the island's coast), similar to Clerke's Rocks off the eastern coast of South Georgia that were encountered on 22 January. *Resolution* negotiated the narrow passage between Willis and Bird Islands, just 2 miles across at its widest point. Cook's journal recorded the rocky appearance of Willis Island and the flatter shape of Bird Island, covered with huge quantities of snow. As more extensive land was sighted, the excitement of exploring new territory arose. Could this, at last, be the coast of the long-sought-after Southern Continent? The land initially appeared extensive and useful for closer evaluation.

Between 13 and 17 January Cook surveyed approximately one-half of the northwestern coastline of South Georgia, as well as outlying islets. The island's coordinates are 54° 15' south latitude and 36° 45' west longitude. Naturalist George Forster's journal noted progress was slowed by a 'very boisterous' wind, cold and 'extremely foggy' weather that produced 'great falls of snow covering our decks' and a temperature of 34½°F. There were mountains of vast height covered 'by loads of snow and ice, in most places down to the water's edge', with only 'a few black and barren cliffs' in sight. Similar remarks are found in J.R. Forster's journal and 'philosophical observations'. Both naturalists observed numerous flocks of birds as well as penguins and porpoises.

Possession Bay, South Georgia

On 17 January, while *Resolution* remained about 4 miles out to sea, Cook, the scientists and an unnamed midshipman hoisted out one of the boats to venture into an inlet Cook later named 'Possession Bay'. Cook wanted to determine if detailed exploration would be of value. He found the bay to be about 2 miles wide, with no bottom located at 34 fathoms (204ft), and he described it as sheltered from the winds with sand beaches. The sloop did not sail into the bay, since Cook did not think there would be any benefit from what might be discovered. Moreover, he wanted to be sure that *Resolution* could exit the bay and not be trapped by contrary winds. We will observe Cook making this assumption several times as *Resolution* sailed both in South Georgia and the South Sandwich Islands, a reasoning likely reinforced by his contact with the ice barrier around the Southern Continent.

The landing party disembarked three times at Possession Bay. The precise locations are not known but the bay is marked in Joseph Gilbert's log book. Lieutenant Clerke's log book entry for the 17th stated, 'At 9 [am] hoisted out the Cutter for the Captain and Botanical Party went onshore to take Possession of this New Country (*Southern Continent I hope* [emphasis added]).' In his journal entry for 17 January George Forster described one location as 'perfectly sheltered from the swell, and where the land formed a long projecting point'. Cook recorded in his journal that the party 'displayed our Colours and took possession of the Country in his Majesty's name under a discharge of small Arms'.

George Forster described the act of possession in more detail: 'A volley of two or three muskets was fired into the air, to give greater weight to his [Cook's] assertion; and the barren rocks re-echoed with the sound, to the utter amazement of the seals and pinguins, the inhabitants of these newly discovered dominions.' Possession Bay is memorialized in a painting by *Resolution* artist William Hodges (*see* Plate 20). J.R. Forster, however, never enjoyed sailing in cold climates. On the 16th his journal recorded his thought that South Georgia would be useful as a prison location for officers and crew convicted of crimes, because the territory was 'inhospitable' and 'cursed'. He suggested anyone actually living in such 'terrible climates' would be 'miserable wretches'. At South Georgia his journal notes a daily difference between the temperatures on deck compared to the 5–6° 'warmer' temperatures in his cabin (in the low 40°F).

Both Cook's and Forster's journals noted the mass of ice at the end of Possession Bay, Cook writing on the 17th that the bay was 'terminated by a huge Mass of Snow and ice of vast extent, it shewed a perpendicular clift of considerable height, just like the side or face of an ice isle; pieces were continually breaking from them and floating out to sea. A great fall happened when we were in the Bay; it made a noise like a Cannon.'

George Forster observed ice in the bay similar to that observed 'floating upon the ocean in the high southern latitudes'. In his journal J.R. Foster observed that the valley was filled with snow 'changed to ice' reaching to the water's edge, 'breaking dayly off in pieces, with a great Noise'. As of yet there was no direct linkage in their journals regarding the origin of icebergs, although the example of a glacier calving at Possession Bay may eventually have helped form a more accurate theory on the origins of ice islands.

South Georgia Sealife and Wildlife

Tim and Pauline Carr assert that South Georgia contains the 'greatest concentration of Antarctic and sub-Antarctic wildlife on the planet'. One of the reasons for the large population of seals, penguins and whales is the presence of Antarctic krill, oceanic crustaceans that serve as a primary source of food. During the summer months (December–February) ocean currents close to the Antarctic Convergence bring phosphates and nitrates that feed phytoplankton, which in turn feed zooplankton, especially the krill that serve as food for sealife and wildlife in South Georgia.[6] Cook's journal entry for 17 January contains his observation of sea life, wildlife and plants that the expedition observed at South Georgia. Because observation of wildlife and other features of new territories was an important element of Cook's responsibilities under the Admiralty's instructions, the next section of this chapter includes some of Captain Cook's observations and those of the naturalists on the second voyage. A second reason is that South Georgia and the surrounding Southern Ocean is a unique and important wildlife habitat today, even with the massive harvesting of the seal and whale population in the late eighteenth and nineteenth centuries.

Seals

Cook observed that the seals and sea-lions of Staten Island were larger in size than those of South Georgia, speculating that most seen were females because 'the

Shores swarm'd with young cubs'. Seals and sea-lions are from the same family of pinnipeds. While both possess ears, sea-lions have ear flaps (*pinnae*) whilst seals have tiny openings for hearing. Sea-lion males are usually larger than seals, with longer necks and flippers which are partially covered by fur. Seals have shorter fore flippers as well as hind flippers, both with claws. While both species move quickly through water, the hind flippers of seals do not rotate, which significantly hinders land movement. Sea-lions move more easily on land because they possess rotating hind flippers.

Today, it is estimated that up to 5 million southern fur seals (*see* Plate 23) are found on South Georgia, the breeding location for 95 per cent of the total population. Seals visit other sub-Antarctic and Antarctic locations at various times of the year. The seal's undercoat is extremely thick fur which made the species valuable in the nineteenth century when they were hunted nearly to extinction. Seal blubber also produced oil. George Forster recounts the killing of a huge 13ft seal resting on the shore of Possession Bay, correctly identifying it as a seal, not a sea-lion, as seen on Staten Island, due to the 'want of external ears'. He wrote that the seals were unafraid of the visitors and were 'more fierce' than those seen on Staten Island. Seal pups barked at the scientists and tried to bite their heels. Seals gather in the summer months (the time of Cook's visit). Seals feed on krill, squid and small fish that are found in abundance in the area.[7]

Sea Elephants

Colonies of sea elephants are found in many sub-Antarctic locations, including South Georgia and Kerguelen Island, where approximately 360,000 are located today, representing the planet's largest population of this species (*see* Plate 24). These huge mammals (males range from 4,800 to 8,000lb) were valuable at one time for fur and blubber (their oil was used for lighting and lubrication). They are distinguished by the large proboscis of the males. The abundance of squid, krill, small fish and (sometimes) penguins for food make South Georgia and other sub-Antarctic islands popular breeding and birthing locations. The sea elephant feeding range extends to waters off Antarctica. It is unclear if those in *Resolution* actually saw sea elephants. Master Joseph Gilbert referenced the haunts of 'sea monsters' but with no further clarification.

Penguins

Today the king penguin is a symbol of South Georgia and the South Sandwich Islands and is included on the coat of arms that was issued by royal warrant in 1952. Captain Cook's journal records seeing the largest penguins he had ever observed. Some penguins brought on board ship weighed between 29 and 38lb. King penguins stand a little over 3ft (1 metre) tall, and can be distinguished by the bright yellow/lemon spot on each side of the head. Large colonies (over 100,000 breeding pairs) of king penguins are found today on South Georgia's Salisbury Plain (northeast coast), one of fifty colonies on the island (*see* Plate 9).

Perhaps as many as 5 million macaroni penguins are found on South Georgia, the largest concentrated population of this species in the world. Macaroni penguins (*see* Plate 22) are noted for their golden crests and deep red eyes. Their range extends far out into the ocean and they feed almost exclusively on krill. Other penguin species on South Georgia include gentoo penguins, which live in many colonies, usually not exceeding one hundred each. There are also about 2 million chinstrap penguins, as well as other species. South Georgia serves as a breeding and birthing colony. Small fish and squid are their primary food source. Macaroni and chinstrap penguins also live on the South Sandwich Islands, as well as on other sub-Antarctic islands such as the Kerguelen archipelago. King and gentoo penguins live all year round on South Georgia.

Albatrosses
Several species of albatross are found on South Georgia. The wandering albatross (*see* Plate 29) covers vast areas of the Southern and Atlantic Oceans. It is also an emblem of the Antarctic Convergence. Other albatrosses seen on South Georgia include the light-mantled sooty albatross, also known as the grey-headed albatross. The 15ft wing-span of the wandering albatross often forms a spectacular cross in the sky. Currently 1,300 breeding pairs return annually to the protected sanctuary at Bird Island, one of the first islands adjacent to South Georgia sighted by Captain Cook.

Petrels
Blue petrels, as well as other petrels, are identified in Cook's journals, usually referenced as 'divers'. Petrels found on South Georgia include the southern giant petrel and pintado (or Cape) petrel (*see* Plate 31), the South Georgia diving petrel, the snow petrel and Wilson's storm petrel among others. Millions of petrels and prions are found on South Georgia. Cook also observed a 'new White Bird', the sheathbill. Skuas, some petrels and sheathbills are scavengers.

Other Birds
Cook recorded 'common gulls', probably the southern black-billed gull, the brown skua, which Cook called 'Port Egmont Hens',[8] terns, probably the wreathed tern, and shags, perhaps the South Georgia blue-eyed shag. A small duck was sighted, the South Georgia teal, although Cook incorrectly thought it resembled a yellow-billed duck he had observed at the Cape of Good Hope. The captain dined on two of the 'Yellow-Bills', which he approvingly termed 'most delicate eating'. Land birds sighted on 17 January and labelled 'small larks' by Cook were Antarctic pipits, small wren-like birds found at various points on South Georgia (*see* Plate 30). Currently, the species is under siege in some areas because of introduced brown rats, especially in areas where whaling stations previously operated. Pipits are the only songbirds native to South Georgia.

It is entirely possible that James Cook observed only the more frequently sighted birds and sealife at South Georgia. However, it is interesting to note that when the Falkland Island Dependencies and later South Georgia and the South Sandwich Islands first issued postage stamps featuring wildlife (1963, 1985, 1987), the issues very closely matched the seals, penguins, birds and whales identified in his journal entry of 17 January 1775, perhaps reinforcing Cook's observational skills, perhaps also influenced by *Resolution*'s naturalists.

Ornithologist J.R. Forster's journal contains considerable specificity regarding birds and other wildlife encountered at Possession Bay on 17 January, describing 'innumerable Numbers of Birds of various kinds'. Prior to landing, his list included: yellow-billed and sooty albatrosses, shags, Port Egmont hens (skuas), vultures, Wilson's storm petrels (or white-rumped petrels) and blue petrels, pintados, black shearwaters, small divers (the South Georgia diving petrel) and larger petrels, gentoo penguins and king penguins, and porpoises. At Possession Bay he observed seals and sea-lions, ducks (with yellow bills and blackish-green legs), a tern and a new lark (the South Georgia pipit). On land he also identified shags, gulls, Port Egmont hens and 'Quackerbirds' (sooty albatrosses). Forster wrote that the king penguin was

> blueish-black above, below silky white, bill red below, the point of the under mandible black: behind the Ears, two large ovated Gold-yellow Spots ending in a line under the throat running out & causing a yellow Spot, which is brightest under the throat & faints away into the white colour of the belly, all the yellow included in a black line; the back towards the tail black, head & throat black, feet black, tail pointed, wings white below, with a black oblong spot at the point.

Whales

Captain Cook's journals frequently cited whales sighted in *Resolution*'s vicinity, usually referencing 'whales playing about the ship'. Neither Cook nor the natural scientists identified specific whale species. British Antarctic Survey Officer Robert Headland's account of the South Georgia whaling and sealing industry observes 'South Georgia was once the centre of the world's whaling industry', over a period of sixty years. Many whales, as well as dolphins, frequented South Georgia and South Sandwich Island waters. Species encountered in these sub-Antarctic waters include the blue whale, sei whale, fin whale, minke whale, humpback whale, southern right whale and the sperm whale. Killer whales, pilot whales and various dolphins and porpoises are also present.

Large whales, except sperm whales, feed on the abundant krill in South Georgia's waters, whilst the diet of sperm whales is squid. Exploitation in the later twentieth century, especially from factory ships, drastically reduced the population, often by depleting the krill food supply. Restoration of the whale population unfolded slowly, with some species recording measurable growth, others less so. Population totals are difficult to determine since whales are submerged most of the time. Among the whales frequenting South Georgia, the largest of all the species, the great blue whale, is thought to be in the greatest danger.

Plants

In his journal Cook noted that the naturalists located three plants at Possession Bay, although George Forster accounts for only two species since he considered one to be a moss. Most prominently, the visitors found tussock grass (*see* Plate 28), which Cook described as 'a coarse strong bladed grass which grows in tufts'. It is found on higher beach areas and slopes of the island, sometimes growing in pedestals over 5ft tall. J.R. Forster observed how penguins and seals took shelter under the grass and how shags nested in its tufts. Tussock grass serves as the main food for reindeer, introduced to the island by Norwegian whalers in 1909/1911, another species (like the brown rat) which raised havoc with South Georgia's natural wildlife in subsequent years (*see* Chapter 16).

Other plants observed by the visitors on 17 January included a South Georgia subspecies of wild burnet, a species common to sub-Antarctic islands and South America. The scientists also located a flowering cushion plant, Antarctic pearl-wort, common to sub-Antarctic and Antarctic regions. Acaena is in the genus *Rosaceae* which includes approximately a hundred species, found mostly in the southern hemisphere. In his *Observations*, J.R. Forster noted that wild burnet constituted 'one new plant peculiar to the Southern hemisphere'. He wrote that its 'starved appearance and low stature denoted the wretchedness of the country'. In the opinions of both Cook and the Forsters, the island's slate-blue rocks contained no minerals of value.

South Georgia, 17–20 January 1775

After visiting 'the barren coast of Tierra del Fuego' in December 1774, J.R. Forster wrote in his 'philosophical observations' the following January, 'we had scarce an idea of a more wretched country existing'. However, in the same latitude 'the isle of New-Georgia' now appeared 'much more dreadful'. Forster observed South Georgia as 'an island of ice' with mountains 'the most ragged and pointed on the globe', covered 'with loads of snow in the height of summer, almost to the water's edge; whilst here and there, the sun shining on points, which project into the sea, leaves them naked, and shews them craggy, black and disgustful'. Forster's descriptions in Antarctic regions are consistently negative. It must be borne in mind that he despised sailing in cold and damp weather because it affected his musculoskeletal problems and because his cabin in *Resolution* was usually only a few degrees warmer than on the deck in weather that fluctuated in the 30s and 40s.

However, the stark beauty of South Georgia is also seen in James Cook's journal entries. After completing his 17 January visit to Possession Bay, where he found floating ice islands and a glacier (though he did not specify it as such), Cook summarized his impression of South Georgia, giving rise to the subtitle for this chapter: 'The inner parts of the Country was not less savage and horrible: the Wild rocks raised their lofty summits till they were lost in the Clouds and the Vallies laid buried in everlasting Snow. Not a tree or shrub was to be seen, no not even big enough to make a tooth-pick.'

The excursion to Possession Bay occupied the morning of 17 January. From then until 20 January Cook surveyed the island's northeastern coastline, moving south-southeast, naming bays and inlets such as Cumberland Bay, Cape

Saunders, Cape Charlotte, Royal Bay, Cape George, Sandwich Bay and Cooper's Isle.[9] Cumberland Bay and King Edward Cove became the site of the whaling industry (and later South Georgia's administrative centre) at Grytviken, established in 1904. It is also the site of Sir Ernest Shackleton's grave (*see* Chapter 16). On 19 January Cook observed 'lurking rocks' and breakers off Sandwich Bay, as well as a ridge of mountains, describing their 'lofty and icy summits ... elevated high above the Clouds'. On the 18th the variable wind was matched by a 'gentle gale attended with showers of snow'. By 20 January *Resolution* had rounded the eastern end of the island at a point Cook named 'Cape Disappointment'. Nearby, a larger coastal island was named after Lieutenant Pickersgill. Master Joseph Gilbert sketched in his log book two views of South Georgia, as well as making a map of *Resolution*'s coastline survey of the newly discovered territory. His description states, 'The Country is very mountainous and intirely covered with snow. Rocky praecipes forms the shore. The land produces nothing, and only the Haunts of amphibious Birds and sea monsters. The coast forms many Bays most of which are filled with snow and Ice.' Could the 'sea monsters' refer to sightings of elephant seals?

In his log book for the hours of 9am to noon on the 17th (entered as the last four hours of the nautical day, 16 January), astronomer William Wales observed, 'Standing off ... the shore while the Capt went in the Boat to take possession of the Land ... At Noon the entrance of the Bay the boats went into bore S 60° E distance about 5 Miles ...'. On the 17th Wales described the territory:

> The Shore of the land are high Cliffs & full of Inlets, but the Inlets are all choaked up with Ice & Snow nearly level with the land. In some places the very mouths of the Bays are yet choaked up; but in others not & in those places the edge of the Ice is a perpendicular Cliff of a prodigious height & seems as if large Pieces had been broke off by the Violence of the Sea, and probably from those huge masses we call Ice Islands. It is however to be remarked that we have not seen one Ice Island in the neighbourhood of it.

After leaving Possession Bay, *Resolution* continued its coastal survey. Hopes that the Southern Continent had been located were then dashed, the name 'Cape Disappointment' serving as Cook's opinion on 20 January. Several days of anticipation ended with the realization that South Georgia was not the Southern Continent, but an island. Why? Because at 55° *Resolution*'s position was 'the very point we had seen and set the day we first came in with it and proved to a demonstration that this land which we had taken to be part of a great Continent was no more than an Island of 70 leagues in Circuit'. The area of South Georgia is 1,507 square miles (3,903 square kilometres). It is 103 miles (165km) in length and from 1–2 miles to 22 miles in width (1–35km). In his journal Cook seems amazed by South Georgia's appearance, writing on 20 January,

> Who would have thought that an Island of no greater extent than this is, situated between the Latitude of 54° and 55°, should in the very height of

Summer be in a manner wholly covered by many fathoms deep with frozen Snow, but more especially the SW Coast, the very sides and craggy summits of the lofty Mountains were cased with snow and ice, but the quantity which lay in the Vallies is incredible, before all of them the Coast was terminated by a wall of Ice of considerable height.

In order to appreciate South Georgia's snow cover, an image from space is given in Plate 5. Much like Lieutenant Clerke, Cook did think (and perhaps hoped/believed) the coast he surveyed from the 17th to the 19th 'might belong to an extensive tract and I still had hopes of discovering a continent. I must Confess the disappointment I now met with did not affect me much, for to judge the bulk by the sample it would not be worth the discovery.'

It takes not much imagination, however, to think that if South Georgia had turned out to be the Southern Continent, his attitude would have been more enthusiastic.

Astronomer Wales remarked in his log book on the 21st, 'It is worthy of remark that all the time we had the wind to the Northward [15–19 January] it was exceedingly Cold; but it became much warmer since it change[d] to the Southward: is it not rather probable from this Circumstance that there may be more Land between us and the track of Dr. Halley?' Halley's furthest south was 52.5° in 1700, while South Georgia is further south at 54° south latitude. There was 'land' to the south between *Resolution*'s position off the southeast tip of South Georgia on 20/21 January 1774 – the Southern Continent, an estimated distance of 1,000 miles.

James Cook then named the island after King George III. According to George Forster, it was his father who suggested that the land be named after the king,

> the monarch who had set on foot our expedition, solely for the improvement of science, and whose name ought therefore to be celebrated in both hemispheres – *Tua sectus orbis Nomina ducet!* ['A part of the globe will bear your name!' Horace]. It was accordingly honoured with the name of Southern Georgia, which will give it importance and continue to spread a degree of lustre over it, which it cannot derive from its barrenness and dreary appearance.

Cook theorized in his journal on 20 January about the origins of icebergs, the islands of ice which appeared frequently around South Georgia. It is known today that Antarctic pack ice sometimes reaches South Georgia. Cook believed the vast quantities of glacier ice 'broke off and dispersed over the Sea; but this isle cannot produce the ten thousand part of what we have seen, [so] either there must be more land or else ice is formed without it'. Cook was correct in his theory about iceberg formation. It is important to note that he envisioned another, yet unseen, location, perhaps a continent, as the source of the ice islands. The island's ice must, he concluded, make its bays and harbours dangerous and inaccessible most of the year, especially when the 'Ice clifts' break off into the ocean.

Cape Circumcision also remained in Cook's thoughts even as he determined South Georgia was an island. He thought Bouvet's Cape lay to the south and east, because he believed it was covered with ice and snow, as was South Georgia, 'doomed by Nature to Frigidity the greatest part of the year'. At this point *Resolution* took an east-southeasterly course. Between 20 and 24 January the ship sailed in the vicinity of the southeastern tip of South Georgia. Storms, fogs and mists accompanied the journey.

During the period 22–24 January *Resolution* circled a series of rocks approximately 35–40 miles from Cooper's Island, arrayed in a grouping some 5 miles (8km) long, at 55° 00′ south latitude and 34° 31′ west longitude. Cook named them 'Clerke's Rocks' after Second Lieutenant Charles Clerke, who first sighted them. In his 23 January log book entry Clerke complained about the 'confounded fog' which made for difficult sailing and then 'we saw a large groups of Rocks ahead'. Circling these rocks, *Resolution*'s bearings became confused and the sloop held to for the night, awaiting better visibility, since 'their appearance is totally hid from us' in a 'confused jumbled sea'. Cook recorded in his journal on the 23rd that 'we spent our time involved in a continual thick Mist and for aught we knew surrounded by dangerous rocks; the Shags and Soundings were our best Pilots'. He described 'thick Fogs', ice islands and 'a sea strewed with large and small ice', drizzling rain, sleet, hazy seas and wind, while whales and penguins accompanied the journey from 25 to 29 January as *Resolution* bore south away from South Georgia. Captain Cook's journal for the 27th recorded *Resolution* at 60° south (59° 59′ at noon), concluding he did not intend to proceed further south unless signs of land were observed.

The South Sandwich Islands, 30 January–7 February 1775

At 60° south latitude Cook began reaching additional conclusions about the Southern Continent. In his journal entry for 27 January, he concluded that although he did not intend to proceed further south unless there were signs of land, he would press on to locate Cape Circumcision. He remarked that he was tired of sailing in high southern latitudes that revealed only ice and fogs. He also expressed doubt that Dalrymple's Gulf of St Sebastian existed where it was charted. Furthermore, he doubted that la Roche 'ever saw the Isle of Georgia', but he decided not to dispute the sighting, only the incorrect coordinates published by Dalrymple and others. Sailing continued among more loose ice and more ice islands, ever-changing weather of fogs, rain and sleet, accompanied by whales and penguins.

Between 30 January and 6 February Cook sailed a north-northeasterly route along a portion of an arc of islands at 59° 27' to 56° 18' south latitude to 28° 08' to 26° 23' west longitude, recorded in his journal as 'Sandwich Land', now known as the South Sandwich Islands, approximately 320 miles (520km) south-southeast of South Georgia. The route and five of the islands are recorded on a sketch by Joseph Gilbert in his log book, which covered the sloop's passage from 59° 15′ south to 57° 15″ south latitude. Cook named some of these islands, but other names are from later European expeditions, especially the 1820–1821 voyage of Fabian Bellingshausen (*see* Chapter 16). Astronomer Wales observed on 1 February that points of land were seen at times 'through so many openings in the clouds', along with penguins, snow petrels and ice islands. Soundings determined 'no ground' at 160 and later at 220 fathoms (960/1,320ft). On 4 February Wales recorded that 'the land appears in patches. It was not possible on account of the unfavourableness of the weather & bad state of the air to determine whether they join or not. It is certain the northern parts are islands.'

Today, these eleven small islands, islets and rocks are divided into three groups. The southernmost Southern Thule group consists of Thule (Morrell), Cook and Bellingshausen Islands. The northernmost groups are the Traversay Island Group (Zavodovski, Leskov, Viskoi) and Candlemas Islands. Between these two groups lie the three largest of the South Sandwich Islands: Saunders, Montagu and Bristol. Bristol is twice the size of Saunders and Montagu at 42 square miles (110 square kilometres). Many of the Sandwich Islands contain active volcanoes.[10]

Between 30 January and 3 February Cook sighted, navigated and named islands and seas around Southern Thule, Bristol Island, Freezland Peak (an island point just off Bristol Island), Forster's Bay or Forster's Passage (the waters between Southern Thule and Bristol Island), Montagu Island, Saunders Island and Candlemas Islands. Thus he sighted more than half of the entire South Sandwich Islands. Southern Thule was so named, Cook wrote in his journal on 31 January, because it was the furthest south territory discovered, with high mountains that were covered with snow. For ancient Greek and Roman geographers, 'Thule' served as the name applied to the furthest point north (*ultima thule*). In his journal for 31 January, George Forster writes that Southern Thule's name was suggested by his father.

Difficult dark and gloomy weather with thick fog, haze, sleet and substantial ocean swells accompanied the four or five days of sailing along the South Sandwich Islands. Cook observed on 31 January that positioning the sloop in such conditions was critical because of 'the disagreeable anxiety of being carried by the swell upon the most horrible Coast in the World'. *Resolution* sailed through thick fogs and floating ice islands. Cook observed on 1 February that there was 'no anchorage, and ... every Port was blocked or filled up with ice and the whole Country, from the summits of the Mountains down to the very brink of the clifts which terminate the Coast, was covered many fathoms thick with ever lasting snow'.

Charles Clerke's log entries on 2 February described craggy rocks covered with snow with a 'dark coloured shore', an observation borne out by Gilbert's sketch, a 'murky' drawing with indistinguishable features. Clerke concluded 'the whole form a dreary disagreeable prospect in this latitude'. Lieutenant Cooper's log book entries mentioned hoisting out boats to collect floating ice for melting on 29 January and 2 February, even in foggy weather and in the presence of large ice islands. Snow fell periodically, coating the rigging with ice on 31 January.

Another of Cooper's duties was to open and inspect provisions. On 5 February he noted in his log book that he opened Cask No. 1028 and counted 180 pieces of beef, short two pieces (similar to the shortages recorded in his log during the crossings of the Antarctic Circle). He also observed a water spout for half an hour on 6 February. As *Resolution* navigated through these islands, whales and some birds accompanied the sloop in weather of rain, sleet and snow, with periodic strong gales.

George Forster observed that the ship's company was affected by 'severe rheumatic pains and colds' along with 'fainting fits' because, he concluded, 'unwholesome, juiceless food could not supply the waste of animal spirits'. The 35° temperatures, 'snow-showers and wet fogs greatly retarded the recovery of our patients', and 'another frozen country' proved disappointing. Overall climatic conditions were then, as they are now, more severe than in South Georgia.

By 2 February it was difficult to distinguish between floating ice islands and land. Cook's journal recorded two islands which 'were clear of snow and seemed to be covered with a green turf'. He later edited the entry, probably because any colour on the island's rocks was likely due to quantities of penguin guano from the many rookeries on the islands. On 3 February Cook named these small islands 'Candlemas Isles', Candlemas being 2 February when the islands were first sighted.[11] Journal entries for 4–5 February recorded 'extraordinary White Water', or a mysterious 'milkish colour' in the ocean's water, perhaps due to sharp temperature fluctuations and melting ice (*see* Chapter 14). By 5 February the sea's white colour had vanished, as did the penguins, and the ship bore eastward and away from the newly discovered islands. Now only whales accompanied *Resolution*.

Observing that he could not distinguish the land in the bays of these islands, and noting that the weather was hazy and sometimes with thick fog, Joseph Gilbert in his 3 February log book entry wrote, 'We never could see beyond two leagues and sometimes not a mile. This Country has the most dreary starved appearance that can be imagined. High spiral rocks & Scraggy praecipes from the shore [and] in land are snowy mountains of tremendous height high and above the clouds'.

On 6 February Cook named the group of islands 'Sandwich Land', although George Forster wrote in his journal that the first name was 'Snow Land'. The penguin species observed are likely to have been the gentoo, chinstrap, Adélie or macaroni penguins. The only bird identified in Cook's journal at the South Sandwich Islands is the snow petrel. However, most of the seals and birds Cook identified at South Georgia are also present on the South Sandwich Islands.[12]

The South Sandwich Islands are not only volcanic in origin but contain prominent and active volcanoes. *Resolution* sailed past several of the largest volcanoes, Mt Darnley (Bristol Island), Mt Belinda (the tallest at 4,494ft/1,370m on Montague Island) and Mt Michael (Saunders Island). Intermittent eruptions were recorded for most of these volcanoes in the nineteenth century and especially in the twentieth century as routine electronic monitoring developed.[13]

It is likely that no visible volcanic activity occurred during *Resolution*'s brief visit. J.R. Forster provides insight as to why no one observed South Sandwich Island's volcanoes: they were obscured by clouds, fog, mist and snow. Forster wrote in his *Observations* that the land, 'except for some detached rocks', was

> absolutely covered with ice and snow (some detached rocks excepted) and in all probability incapable of producing a single plant. Wrapt in almost continual fogs, we could only now and then have a sight of it, and that only of its lowest part, an immense volume of clouds constantly resting on the summits of the mountains, as though the sight of all its horrors would be too tremendous for mortal eyes to behold. The mind indeed, still shudders at the idea, and eagerly turns from so disgusting an object.

Developments in South Georgia and the South Sandwich Islands during the two centuries after Cook are briefly covered in Chapter 16.

An End to the Search for *Terra Australis Incognita*

Captain Cook's journal entries for early February include conclusions about his search for the Southern Continent, including the search for Bouvet's Cape Circumcision, and knowledge gained from his crossings of the Antarctic Circle and his navigation through portions of the Southern and Pacific Oceans. These important conclusions are worth citing in some detail. On 6 February he wrote in his journal that if there was a Southern Continent, it must be found within the Polar Circle, 'where the Sea is so pestered with ice, that the land is thereby inaccessible'. Cook remarked that the risks of exploring the coast

> in these unknown and Icey Seas, is so very great, that I can be bold to say, that no man will ever venture further than I have done and that the lands which may lie to the South will never be explored. Thick fogs, Snow storms, Intense Cold and every other thing that can render Navigation dangerous one has to encounter and these difficulties are greatly heightened by the inexpressable horrid aspect of the Country, a Country doomed by Nature never once to feel the warmth of the Suns rays, but to lie forever buried under everlasting snow and ice.

Cook sailed east and north from 6 to 27 February. On 6 February he concluded that 'it would have been rashness in me to have risked all which had been done in the Voyage, in finding out and exploaring a Coast which when done would have answered no end whatever, or been of the least use either to Navigation or Geography or indeed any other Science'. He then resumed the search for Bouvet's Cape Circumcision, often amid high seas, snow, sleet and ice islands, with temperatures rising to 36°–38°F, and an occasional gale. On 14 February *Resolution* crossed 0°, the Prime Meridian.

By 21 February Cook had reached 54° 16′ south latitude and 16° 13′ east longitude, finding no land or any birds, penguins or seals that might indicate nearby land. Cook's journal entry for 25 February noted, 'We had been a long time without refreshments, our Provisions were in a state of decay and little more nourishment remained in them than just to keep life and Soul together.' Although he believed the crew to be cheerful, Cook worried about an outbreak of scurvy and additional difficult sailing. He also stated *Resolution*'s sails and rigging were worn and they were without the materials to make replacements. George Forster had observed ten days earlier that the last of sixty 'large casks' of 'sour krout, that excellent antiscourbitic food', had been consumed. There would be no further exploration. It was time to return to England. With reference to the French discoveries, Captain Cook speculated that because of the cold weather found at that latitude the land could not be fertile. Verification of the Kerguelen Islands would await a future voyage.

Cook's journals rarely show signs of emotion or drama. However, his lengthy entry for 21 February is, in my opinion, the most assertive and triumphant statement James Cook penned during his three voyages. It declares finality to the question of *Terra Australis Incognita*:

> I had now made the circuit of the Southern Ocean in a high Latitude and traversed it in such a manner as to leave not the least room for the Possibility of there being a continent, unless near the Pole and out of the reach of Navigation; by twice visiting the Pacific Tropical Sea, I had not only settled the situation of some old discoveries but made there many new ones and left, I conceive, very little more to be done even in that part. Thus I flatter my self that the intention of the Voyage has in every respect been fully Answered, the Southern Hemisphere sufficiently explored and a final end put to the searching after a Southern Continent, which has at times ingrossed the attention of some of the Maritime Powers for near two Centuries past and the Geographers of all ages. That there may be a Continent or a large tract of land near the Pole, I will not deny, on the contrary I am of opinion there is, and it is probable that we have seen a part of it. The excessive cold, the many islands and vast floats of ice all tend to prove that there must be land to the South and that this Southern land must lie or extend furthest to the North opposite the Southern Atlantick and Indian Oceans ...

Cook's surmise that the Southern Continent lay within the Polar Circle (or nearly so) was correct. The portion of Antarctica he circumnavigated was inaccessible by sea because of the impenetrable ice barrier. Fogs, snow, cold, dangerous navigation and the 'horrible aspect' of the territory suggested a continent buried under perpetual ice and snow. In his opinion, nothing would be gained by further exploration. Other reasons for concluding the search were that *Resolution*'s provisions were low, the ship required repairs and the crew were weary ('fatigued') of sailing in cold climates. Cook's assertion that no benefit would arise from exploring the Southern Continent due to fog, snow, cold and dangerous navigation proved incorrect in later years because of Antarctic scientific research.

Cook's detailed assertions served the important purpose of answering his critics. Alexander Dalrymple in particular severely criticized Cook after the first voyage for not seeking further evidence of a southern continent beyond proving New Zealand consisted of two islands and charting the east coast of Australia. By the end of the second voyage, in addition to his 1773 and 1774 crossings of the Antarctic Circle, Cook had searched the coordinates recorded by Dalrymple and others, finding only islands such as South Georgia or 'Sandwich Land', and finding no land at all, let alone a continent, at the coordinates for Cape Circumcision. Furthermore he crossed the ocean south and east of New Zealand to disprove the existence of the Southern Continent in that location, refuting Dalrymple's conclusions. Cook did not locate Cape Circumcision but proved it was not to be found at Bouvet's coordinates.

Both Forsters generally agreed with Cook's assertions about the Southern Continent, although with various qualifications and comments. In his journal on 2 February George Forster observed that no continent was located in 'the temperate southern zone' and that in travelling to 71° south 'the space within the Antarctic circle is far from being every where filled up with land'. The idea of a vast continent is now 'invalidated', George Forster concluded, but the previous theory of its existence was based upon little data.

To sum up George Forster's conclusions, the Southern Continent did not exist in the temperate zone and whether it existed in the 'frigid zone' was based upon theory and assumption since *Resolution* met only with ice. Therefore, Dalrymple's assumptions were invalidated, yet George Forster credited the hydrographer with speculation based upon little information. He also thought that confirmation of the Southern Continent would remain undetermined 'for ages to come' due to exploration 'to those inhospitable parts of the world, besides being extremely perilous, does not seem likely to be productive to the great advantages of mankind'. Forster shared with Cook the assumption that territories in Earth's 'frigid zone' had no value.

In his 'philosophical observations' J.R. Forster observed that *Resolution*'s 'present circumnavigation … put it beyond doubt, that there is no land on this side of 60° in the Southern hemisphere, if we except the few inconsiderable fragments we have found in the Southern Atlantic ocean'. He suggested that if the theory of a southern continent to balance the northern continent was valid, 'nature has provided for this defect, by placing perhaps at the bottom of the Southern Ocean such bodies as by their specific weight will compensate the deficiency of lands; if this system of the wanted counterpoise be at all necessary'.

In mid-February Captain Cook made one final attempt to locate Bouvet's Cape Circumcision by sailing west so that he would not miss it at Bouvet's coordinates and thereby could confirm or deny its existence. A week later, on the 21st, *Resolution* sailed several degrees beyond Bouvet's coordinates and both Cook and Forster concluded it must either not exist or was an ice island. As pointed out earlier, Cape Circumcision does exist, but at different coordinates and it constitutes an island of 19 square miles in extent (*see* Chapters 1 and 2).

The last ice island was recorded in Cook's journal on 26 February as *Resolution* headed north-northeast to the Cape of Good Hope. Table Bay was sighted on 21 March. *Resolution* reached St Helena on 15 May, Ascension Island on 28 May, crossed the Equator on 11 June, sighted Plymouth on 29 July and docked at Portsmouth on 30 July 1775. One year later James Cook embarked upon his third voyage, the first segment of which was to the sub-Antarctic Kerguelen Island (*see* Chapter 13).

The second voyage was the greatest and most extensive of Cook's worldwide navigations. It crossed the Antarctic Circle three times, encountering an impenetrable ice barrier. Antarctica was clearly shown not to exist in the Pacific Ocean above 60° south latitude. The location of Cape Circumcision remained unknown. Navigation in the 'Gulf of San Sebastian' did not yield signs of that 'land of great extent'. Only the ice below the Circle had been located – Cook surmised there was a continent near the South Pole – but he concluded further exploration would yield no benefit (*see also* Chapter 14). Over the next 150 years navigators, scientists and explorers were to build upon Captain James Cook's achievements, for, as Robert Falcon Scott stated, 'James Cook defined the Antarctic Region' (*see* Chapter 16).

Chapter 12

The Second Voyage Publication Controversy

It [the second voyage journal] is a work for information and not for amusement, written by a man, who has not the advantage of Education, acquired, nor Natural abilities for writing; but by one who has been constantly at sea from his youth, and who, with the Assistance of a few good friends gone through all the Stations belonging to a Seaman, from a prentice boy in the Coal Trade to a Commander in the Navy. After such a Candid confession he hopes the Public will not consider him as an author but a man Zealously employed in the Service of his Country and obliged to give the best account he is able of his proceedings ...

James Cook, preface to his journal account of the second voyage

Nowhere in his account of the events leading up to his appointment to the *Resolution* does [Johann Reinhold] Forster mention any agreement or terms of his engagement. As we shall see this 'agreement', which Forster later persistently claimed was reached verbally with [Danes] Barrington acting for [First Lord of the Admiralty] Sandwich in June 1772, was a major stumbling block when it came to apportioning the responsibility for writing up the accounts and researches of the voyage.

Michael E. Hoare, *The Tactless Philosopher, Johann Reinhold Forster*

Controversy about publication of accounts of the second voyage developed after *Resolution* returned to England in July 1775.[1] The central figures in the dispute were John Montagu, 4th Earl of Sandwich (First Lord of the Admiralty), Johann Reinhold Forster and his son George, William Wales and James Cook. The arguments continued until 1778 (or later) and were never resolved to the satisfaction of the Forsters. Even at a distance of over 240 years, the issues surrounding the matter continue to spark interest and raise questions.

Analysis of the controversy can be divided into the following sections:

- who were the Forsters?;
- the circumstances and assumptions under which the Forsters joined the second voyage;
- the changed circumstances regarding Captain Cook's interest in publication of his journals of both the first and second voyages;

- the agreement of 13 April 1776 signed by Sandwich, Admiralty Secretary Philip Stephens, Captain Cook and J.R. Forster;
- astronomer William Wales's published challenges to the Forsters' account of the voyage; and
- the clash of personalities which coloured this controversy both during *Resolution*'s voyage of 1772–1775 and thereafter.

Who were the Forsters?

Johann Reinhold Forster (1729–1798) was descended from a royalist Scots family that had been deprived of its land by Oliver Cromwell, after which the family emigrated to Polish Prussia, territory which Russia obtained through the First Partition of Poland (1772). J.R. Forster was born near Danzig (Gdańsk) and educated in Berlin and the University of Halle (Saxony), completing theological studies in 1751. He developed interests in natural history (the natural sciences), languages and ancient history in an era when academic specialties were not as compartmentalized as they are today. After an unsuccessful commission for the Russian government to survey German settlements along the Volga River, the penniless family relocated to London in 1766. A Dissenter from the Church of England, Forster affiliated with the Warrington Academy, published scientific literature and cultivated relationships with members of the Royal Society. He was an opponent of slavery, supported the North American colonies in their war of independence and met fellow scientist Benjamin Franklin. The Royal Society connection led to participation in Cook's second voyage. After the publication controversy, the Forsters relocated in 1780 to Saxony, where J.R. Forster under-took a professorship in the natural sciences at the University of Halle. He lectured here and published until his death in 1798. Plate 19 is a sketch of Forster's profile, along with a king penguin which he described at South Georgia.

Primarily educated by his father, George Forster (1754–1794) was 18 years old when the second voyage left Plymouth. After the publication of his journal in 1777, George Forster held university positions in natural science at Kassel, Vilnius and Mainz. He emerged as a leader of German Jacobins in Mainz in the early 1790s and, as a representative of the Rhineland revolutionaries, was sent to Paris where he witnessed the Reign of Terror. Often suffering from ill-health and probably pneumonia, Forster died in Paris aged around 40.[2] Plate 17 is a sketch of George Forster, along with a drawing of tussock grass, which he and his father identified at South Georgia. An Antarctic research station commemorates George Forster, who was also marked by two East German postal stamps issued in 1979 and 1988.[3]

The Forsters Join the Second Voyage

After Joseph Banks declined to participate in Cook's second voyage, J.R. Forster was invited to join the projected enterprise in May. He understood he would be provided with an allowance of £4,000 but he had less than two months to prepare to embark. The Royal Society was instrumental in encouraging and selecting 'men of science' to accompany Cook's voyages. Daines Barrington (1727–1800), a friend and patron of J.R. Forster, invited Forster to join Cook's second voyage, apparently acting with the knowledge of the Admiralty.

Barrington, according to J.C. Beaglehole, was the son of Viscount Barrington. His brothers held positions in society, as antiquarians, in the law, in the Church of England and in the Royal Navy. Furthermore, Barrington was a friend of both Joseph Banks and Sandwich.[4] J.R. Forster could therefore assume Barrington spoke with some authority. It appears to have been only a verbal agreement, and no written documentation of responsibilities was made prior to the voyage. Captain Cook was not part of these discussions. This assumption of authority, as the extract from Michael Hoare's biography at the beginning of this chapter asserts, is the root of the controversy. J.R. Forster dined with James Cook in June 1772, their only meeting until a few days before sailing. Barrington apparently assured Forster that £4,000 would be provided to cover his expenses during the voyage. These funds were previously authorized by Parliament for James Lind,[5] the physician and specialist in naval hygiene, who was to accompany Joseph Banks until Banks withdrew from Cook's second voyage. Barrington also assured Forster that he would receive 'emolument' (payment) for publishing the history of the voyage, as well as 'a yearly provision' (pension) after the return to England – but, to repeat, there was no written agreement about these matters.

Complicating the picture was the intense lobbying conducted by Joseph Banks and his allies and aimed at factions in Parliament and the Admiralty, in a somewhat frenzied atmosphere in which time was of the essence. In his *Resolution Journal*, J.R. Forster asserts that Lord North (Chancellor of the Exchequer) told Barrington that funds (£1,795) from the King's Civil List (funds approved by Parliament for the Crown) would be provided to Forster. Consequently, Forster's 11 May journal entry states: 'From this day I could first consider myself as being appointed by his Majesty on the Expedition.' It is important to understand the significance of this to J.R. Forster as the drama of the post-voyage publication issue unfolds: *he was the King's Scientist*. On 12 June Admiralty Secretary Philip Stephens wrote to the Navy Board: 'It being His Majesty's pleasure that John Reinhold Forster and George Forster, gentlemen skilled in natural history and drawing should proceed in one of the vessels, their Lordships direct that accommodation should be made in *Resolution*.' On 15 June Cook wrote to the Admiralty, 'Understanding from Mr. Stephens that two Botanists will be sent out by the King in his Majesty's Sloop *Resolution* under my command, I pray you will be pleased to order the two fore most Cabbins under the Quarter Deck to be rebuilt for their reception, with all possible dispatch.'[6] Clearly the Forsters were now an 'official' part of the forthcoming voyage, recognized as such by the Admiralty and James Cook.

In his post-voyage published letter to the Earl of Sandwich (1 June 1778), George Forster wrote in great detail regarding the assurances repeatedly provided to his father by Barrington. These included J.R. Forster writing the official history of the voyage as well as receiving income from its publication, especially (in Forster's view) since Captain Cook 'pleaded his inability to write an account of his circumnavigation in the *Endeavour*, and had entirely given up all thoughts of becoming an author'. Barrington stated that Forster was sent out on the voyage 'as a man of letters and as an eyewitness'. Forster was to function in the same role as Dr John Hawkesworth had for Cook in editing the journal of the voyage of the *Endeavour*. Barrington also reassured J.R. Forster that the British government would support the Forster family after the conclusion of the voyage, as was customary for someone who provided such a service. The Forsters regarded Barrington as the Admiralty's 'sole agent' in working out these details.[7]

In his letter to Sandwich, George Forster detailed how the £4,000 grant was expended during the voyage. The Treasury withheld £200 for its fees in processing the grant. Instruments, books, writing paper, clothing and other expenses cost £1,200. Forster paid £750 to cover board in *Resolution* during the three-year voyage, including the cost for a servant. Another £750 was used to pay living expenses for Mrs Forster and the family of six children. Forster gave £500 to support Anders Sparrman and another £250 was allocated for skins and other materials purchased at the Cape. J.R. Forster complained that he had less than £500 remaining at the conclusion of the voyage, and that the family suffered £150 in damage after their home was broken into after their return. There was no reference to how the £1,795 sent to J.R. Forster by Lord North from the King's Civil List fitted into the £4,000 sum, whether it was an advance or a separate payment.

Money was not the end of the complaints from the chronically cash-strapped Forsters. Other complaints centred on the quarters provided in *Resolution*. The Forsters asserted that while Captain Cook, other officers and the astronomer Wales enjoyed watertight and warm 'roomy cabins on the same deck, supported by each other', the Forsters were given small, dark cabins ('these wretched hovels') in the middle of the ship, rooms that let in little light but plenty of deck water, rain and cold. This proved a hardship for Forster senior who 'was tortured with rheumatic pains, which frequently confined him to his cold damp bed', especially when sailing in high southern latitudes. They claimed their storeroom was inadequate and their supplies and specimens were often ruined.

Furthermore, it appears that the Forsters had reason for their complaints. In his journal entry for 27 November 1772 J.R. Forster points out that the ship's Master Joseph Gilbert, who occupied the cabin next to his, had the seams above his cabin carefully caulked, but the seams over Forster's cabin were done in a 'slovenly manner' so that when *Resolution* began to roll and pitch in the high seas, 'I was fairly soused.' These conditions and complaints continued for days thereafter. Discussions followed with Cook, Gilbert and others to obtain additional space for the naturalist's quarters, equipment and collections, but these issues were not resolved.[8] These factors have nothing to do with the publication issues, but they do lend context to the Forsters' attitudes.

Captain Cook's Journals

Writer and editor John Hawkesworth (1715–1773) edited Cook's journal of the first voyage and Cook obtained a copy of the Hawkesworth edition in 1775 at the Cape of Good Hope as he was heading home from the second voyage. He became quickly distressed over Hawkesworth's assertions and the liberties he had taken with Cook's account. This issue roused Cook's interest in editing his own journals. In their introduction to George Forster's journal (published in 2000), the editors comment: 'The contention concerning the writing and publication of the second voyage thus developed in the context and profound misgivings over what had happened to the history of the first.'[9] This is a critical point. For this and other reasons (such as criticism from Alexander Dalrymple about Cook's failure to locate the elusive *Terra Australis Incognita*), Cook laboured over his journal during and after the second voyage. He continued to work on the published version prior to his departure on the third voyage, attempting as far as possible to ensure that the editor of the second journal, Canon John Douglas of Windsor and St Paul's, would reflect Cook's conclusions and not his own interpretations. It is clear that Cook wanted the published version to be accurate from his perspective.

As James Cook embarked on his third voyage, he composed a paragraph about his journal from the previous voyage, trusting several friends to supervise its printing and to make corrections as were necessary but not to alter his writing style (as opposed to Hawkesworth's edition of the *Endeavour* journal). He hoped that the 'Candid and faithful manner in which [the journal] is written would counterbalance the want of stile [style] and dullness of the subject.' He then wrote,

> It is a work for information and not for amusement, written by a man, who has not the advantage of Education, acquired, nor Natural abilities for writing; but by one who has been constantly at sea from his youth, and who, with the Assistance of a few good friends gone through all the Stations belonging to a Seaman, from a prentice boy in the Coal Trade to a Commander in the Navy. After such a Candid confession he hopes the Public will not consider him as an author but a man Zealously employed in the Service of his Country and obliged to give the best account he is able of his proceedings.[10]

Cook therefore saw himself not as an author but as an experienced seaman in the service of England obliged to prepare an account of the second voyage from the point of view of its commander. His focus was navigation, based on geography explored, recorded or disproved. J.R. Forster's assumptions about Cook's interest in writing before the second voyage did not match Cook's position once *Resolution* returned to England in 1775, in good part due to the Hawkesworth edition of Cook's journal. The circumstances had changed but to J.R. Forster it appeared to make no difference. He relied upon the oral assurances and his appointment as 'the King's scientist'.

Writing the Official History after 1775

J.R. Forster advanced his rights to publish the official account of the second voyage based on his understandings with Daines Barrington before *Resolution* and *Adventure* sailed in July 1772. Discussions between the Admiralty, J.R. Forster and Captain Cook followed the return. On 13 April 1776 an agreement[11] was reached whereby Cook and J.R. Forster would receive equal shares in the profits from a two-volume published work. Cook's narrative of the voyage, his nautical observations and remarks upon customs of the peoples encountered would comprise the first volume. The second volume was to include J.R. Forster's observations on natural history, his philosophical remarks about natural phenomena and his observations of the manners, customs and languages of native peoples. Forster and Cook were to assist each other in completion of the work. They were to share in the expenses of paper and printing. The cost of engraving plates to accompany the narrative would be borne by the Admiralty and the plates would become the joint property of Cook and Forster. Cook was to provide Forster with a copy of his narrative so that he could translate the text for French and German editions, but no sooner than three months after the English edition was published. Proofing the final manuscript and the printer selected would be by persons approved by the Admiralty. Editing serves as an important point, later expanded upon and used by the Admiralty against J.R. Forster's interests.

The Forsters asserted that the April agreement amounted to a significant concession on their part since J.R. Forster was initially to be the sole author of the official version. They then argued that the April agreement was not followed. On 12 July 1776 Captain Cook left England on his third voyage to seek out further Pacific exploration, sailing from Plymouth. The Admiralty asked for a sample of J.R. Forster's writing but rejected his submission. A second specimen was similarly rejected and Forster was told that Daines Barrington would need to correct and edit Forster's material. Forster found this unjust and would not accept editorial assistance from Barrington, although the latter was a friend and patron. Moreover, Forster and Barrington had a serious falling-out over the scientific issue as to whether sea water could freeze. Barrington believed salt water would not freeze but Forster (correctly) asserted it did freeze (salt water freezes at $-2°C$ or 28.4°F). This might appear to be only an argument among naturalists, but much more importantly it left Forster without a patron.

During the ensuing months George Forster set to work writing his two-volume account of the second voyage. George Forster was not bound by his father's agreement with the Admiralty and Captain Cook. George's *A Voyage Round the World* was published in 1777, before Cook's journal was published. It is widely assumed that this book was based on J.R. Forster's notes. However, it appears likely that George and not his father wrote the work, a conclusion supported by textual analysis by editors of George's journal.[12] George Forster observed it was assumed and expected his father would produce a 'philosophical history of the voyage ... an account written upon a plan which the learned world had not hitherto seen executed'. Such an account would be a comprehensive record. In his preface, George Forster states that the British government seemed interested only in a few dried plants and butterflies collected by his father over three years.[13]

Captain Cook's published journal appeared six weeks later, offered at 2 guineas (£2.2*s*), the same price as George Forster's book. In George Forster's letter to Sandwich, it is asserted that the Admiralty provided Cook with '63 elegant copper plates engraved by the first artists' and that they priced the book unfairly to compete with George's book. Since Cook's book contained the engraved plates and was printed on more expensive paper, the Forsters claimed that the Admiralty had approved a printer offering a more expensively produced book at less than its real price and thereby reduced potential interest in and income from George Forster's publication.

In their 1778 letter to the Earl of Sandwich, the Forsters included a demand for £4,000 in unrealized compensation for the Admiralty's improper handling of the whole affair. In addition, Lord Sandwich was accused of poisoning King George III's attitude towards J.R. Forster by issuing an order that only Sandwich was to proceed with publication of Captain Cook's account of the voyage. In order to discredit and embarrass Sandwich, they drew the public's attention to his long-standing mistress Martha Ray, an opera singer (murdered by a jealous suitor in 1779). They also tried to assert that Queen Charlotte (the wife of King George III) favoured their cause. An affidavit was sworn at King's Bench by both Forsters on 26 May 1778 attesting to the misdeeds by Sandwich and the Admiralty and requesting redress of grievances. No action appears to have followed this affidavit and published letter, and the Forsters departed England for Saxony in 1780.

William Wales Joins the Fray

The personal relationship between astronomer William Wales and naturalist J.R. Forster was consistently negative during and after the second voyage. In 1778 William Wales published *Remarks on Mr. Forster's Account of Captain Cook's Last Voyage Round the World in the Years 1772, 1773, 1774 and 1775*. This letter constitutes an item-by-item refutation of many of George Forster's complaints and deals especially with the interpretation of events, the publication controversy, maps and the interpretation of maps drawn during the voyage, and many other matters, including personality and attitudes. Wales asserted that J.R. Forster was the real author of the journal and his comments about Forster's conclusions, remarks and behaviour are often devastating (although occasionally humorous to modern readers). In response to Wales's publication, George Forster, styling himself as 'Naturalist on the Late Voyage Round the world, By the King's Appointment', produced his *Reply to Mr. Wales's Remarks*, a thirty-page refutation of criticism by *Resolution*'s astronomer. The points at dispute – often matters of interpretation, a conspiracy against both Forsters, use of language, or differing impressions about facts and details – remain unresolved.

Wales objected to eighty-six items in George Forster's journal.[14] Many of these include misinterpretations of information or observation. There is something of the 'he said/you said/they said' or 'you did this/he did that' about these issues. For example, did the chronometer stop of its own accord in June 1773 or was it stopped deliberately? Wales was in charge of the chronometers in *Resolution*, so this was a personal attack on the astronomer's credibility. Did J.R. Forster's intervention at Plymouth before *Resolution* and *Discovery* sailed save the ships from crashing into rocks? Forster says yes, Wales says no, it was already being dealt with by *Resolution*'s Master, Joseph Gilbert. Forster charged that an 'unfeeling person … lured' a swallow onto *Resolution*'s deck in order to feed it to his cat. Wales said that was not at all the case. Forster wrote that the sun illuminated the bases of waterspouts off New Zealand, while Wales asserted the sun was not shining at the time. Forster also wrote of hail and lightning, but Wales stated no one else observed these. Forster wrote that it rained continually during their visit to New Caledonia, while Wales stated that rain occurred on seven out of twenty-six days, and was only heavy on five days. Forster wrote that Turtle Island was 7 miles long; Wales stated it was less than 3 miles in length. Wales charged Forster with misrepresenting an incident involving theft of Lieutenant Clerke's musket. Forster thought it a trifling matter, Wales regarded it as a serious issue.

Forster argued that South Georgia was not populated because it was too far south, while Wales remarked that Hudson's Bay in an equivalent northern latitude was inhabited. Wales thought Forster's descriptions of coastlines to be misleading and unreliable for navigators in the future. Forster did not hold a high opinion of common British sailors and frequently remarked about their uncouth behaviour, noise, singing and swearing. Wales rose to their defence: 'Who does not know that sailors will sometimes both sing and swear?' Forster complained about everything from accommodation to people, and came on board 'with very exalted notions of himself' in contrast to the officers and crew. Wales wrote:

I believe Dr. Forster never passed a week on board the *Resolution* without a dispute with one person or other: and in his part of those quarrels, he was seldom very choice either in the mildness or delivery of his expressions … There were few who would go much out of their way to oblige him in things to which their duty did not compel them. In short, before we reached New Zealand the first time, there was scarce a man in the ship whom he had not quarrelled with on one pretence or other.[15]

Wales argued that the Forsters' revenge for these unhappy circumstances was the journal produced by George Forster after the voyage.[16]

Wendy Wales, in her biography of William Wales, concludes her analysis of the 'Forster' affair by noting the importance that William Wales gave to 'put[ting] the record straight'. However, she comments that the effort must have 'seemed pretty trivial to him when on 10th January, 1780, the Admiralty broke the news from Clerke's letter that Captain James Cook was killed on 14 February 1779. The news appeared in the *London Gazette* the next day and grief swept the country – even the King had been reduced to tears.'[17]

A Clash of Personalities

Certainly a critical ingredient in the controversy was the clash of personalities, both during the voyage and long after its conclusion. George Forster asserted that rumours about his father's quarrelsome personality discouraged a potential position at the British Museum, an example of the on-going conspiracy against Forster senior. The critical views espoused by William Wales received validation and elaboration from J.C. Beaglehole in his *Life of Captain James Cook* and in his introduction to Cook's journal. Beaglehole recognized J.R. Forster's learning, range of interests and perceptiveness but he also concluded 'that for ocean voyaging no man was ever by physical or mental constitution less fitted'. He described Forster as 'dogmatic, humourless, suspicious, pretentious, contentious, censorious, demanding, rheumatic, he was a problem from any angle'. In contrast, Beaglehole describes George Forster as 'brilliantly gifted, serious, intellectually alive, romantic ... [with] a difficult parent'.[18]

These harsh comments obscure the contributions and achievements of J.R. Forster. The editors of Forster's *Observations* cite Beaglehole's lack of impartiality, observing that he adopted 'an extraordinarily opinionated and hostile attitude toward Forster'.[19] Michael Hoare's biography of J.R. Forster provides a useful counterbalance to William Wales and J.C. Beaglehole. Hoare observes that Forster established 'the foundations for ornithology' in the Antarctic and New Zealand. Hoare also cites Forster's contributions to modern geography and anthropology, and concludes that he was 'one of the most able naturalists, linguists, philologists and "polyhistors" [very learned] of his times', with considerable influence on German science and scholarship.

While Cook and J.R. Forster were different personalities, they did share some common interests, varying in degree and intensity. Both were ambitious and stubborn. This quality provided Cook with his mission-driven purpose to go beyond any other explorer. Forster, on the other hand, was interested in locating the Southern Continent but it was natural history – plants, wildlife or native peoples – which sparked his interest. He writes, 'Cook was content to zigzag across the ocean if only to disprove a point', while Forster wanted to outdo Banks and Solander in cataloguing and describing the natural world.[20] It can be argued that both Cook and Forster sought to make the second voyage the ultimate achievement of their respective careers, but Forster was dependent upon Cook to guide *Resolution* and Cook's route followed the Admiralty's instructions. Ultimately it was the navigator's orders and decisions that determined the course of the voyage, regardless of the naturalist's interests. This clash of interests also occurred with Joseph Banks during the first voyage. Cook benefited from naturalist observations but it was geography and navigation that determined the course of the voyage.

In my own work in researching Cook's travels in high southern latitudes, examining parallel accounts by Cook, George Forster and J.R. Forster yields useful, complementary material. Cook incorporated observations by naturalists into his journals during the first and second voyages and by other observers on the third voyage. We can assume he expected Forster to be a dedicated scientist, as suggested by the Royal Society. However, Michael Hoare suggests William Wales also viewed himself as a scientist, as astronomer in charge of the chronometers, while Wales perhaps regarded J.R. Forster as a well-paid scientific dilettante added at the last minute to the second voyage.[21] Wales was incorrect about J.R. Forster's abilities. However, it is not surprising that personality conflicts erupted during the second voyage.

The title of Michael Hoare's biography of Forster, *The Tactless Philosopher*, aptly summarizes the personality conflict issue. Forster presented a difficult personality to his contemporaries. After three years of global circumnavigation, often in close quarters, *Resolution*'s occupants must have grown more than a little tired of each other. J.C. Beaglehole relates that when Lieutenant James King called upon Captain Cook prior to the third voyage, and observed that no scientists were to sail, Cook replied, 'Curse the scientists, and all science into the bargain!'[22] That uncharacteristically harsh outburst should not be taken at face value, because our understanding of Cook's voyages and the works produced by J.R. and George Forster are valuable. We may conclude, however, that J.R. Forster rarely understood how to disagree without being disagreeable.

Concluding Comments

Personality issues alone are not the only reason why the Forsters fell out with Captain Cook and the Admiralty over publication. It is very clear that J.R. Forster assumed he would write and financially benefit from publishing the official history of the second voyage and receive some sort of pension after the voyage, an important factor for a large family without sufficient income. Forster was led to this conclusion by Daines Barrington, a friend, patron, person of influence and connections and Fellow of the Royal Society, but the final publication decision after the voyage fell to the Admiralty, the sponsor of Cook's Royal Navy voyages. Forster utilized funds forwarded to him by the government to pay for expenses during the voyage, including those for his son as well as a stipend for fellow naturalist Anders Sparrman. Forster purchased equipment, clothing and supplies, made provision for his family in his absence, and collected items of interest and recorded information during the three-year circumnavigation of the globe. It appears obvious that the purpose of these expenses and activities was to result in a publication about the second voyage. Why else would he undertake, on short notice, to embark on a long sea voyage?

Changed circumstances, principally Captain Cook's interest in rendering a precise account in his journals to ensure an accurate focus on navigation and geography, as well as the receipt of proceeds from publishing his account, led to different considerations at the end of the second voyage compared to the first. Cook's voyages were Admiralty projects from start to finish. The Royal Society's limited role included proposing naturalists to accompany Captain Cook for the scientific aspect of the voyages. Ultimately it was Lord Sandwich who held the authority to determine the outcome of publication. Perhaps we could also argue a divergence of interests. For the Admiralty and James Cook, the story of the second voyage was one of navigation and geography, circumnavigation at high latitudes and the identification of land and islands. For J.R. and George Forster there was greater interest in wildlife, the oceans, and the appearance and substance of land, as well as the interaction with native peoples. Scientists, not navigators, were required to understand and document these matters. Through disagreements, and perhaps because of the frailty of human interactions, the Forsters were without persons of influence to advance their cause after 1775 and this was critical to the outcome of the dispute.

Perhaps it is 'too legalistic' an argument, but J.R. Forster's verbal agreement was with Daines Barrington, not with the Admiralty and not with the First Lord of the Admiralty, Sandwich. Michael Hoare's comment quoted at the beginning of this chapter about the lack of any specific and written terms of agreement is an astute observation. But was J.R. Forster treated unfairly? It seems so, especially as it appears impediment after impediment was placed in the path of publication after the April 1776 agreement. The willingness of both Forsters to submit an affidavit carries substantial weight as to the validity of their assertions. However, the episode raises the importance of written agreements among all parties concerned, especially those empowered to make final decisions, and not merely discussions among gentlemen of the Royal Society. It is also useful to recognize that this is often how business was conducted. Eighteenth-century politics has been described as the conversion of competing interests, of often changing factions and of conversations among persons of influence (patrons and persons of influence, politicians, civil servants and others), eventually leading to decisions.[23] It is in this milieu that publication decisions affecting J.R. Forster were reached.

Johann Reinhold Forster ended his work with two injunctions. The first endorsed the idea that all mankind are 'members of one great family', capable of contributing to civilization, and knowledge about mankind ought to be peacefully pursued. Forster's second point emphasizes

> the necessity of sending out men versed in science and the knowledge of nature on all occasions to remote parts of the world, in order to investigate the powers and qualities of natural objects; and it is not enough to send them out, but they ought likewise to be encouraged in their laborious task, liberally supported and generously enabled to make such enquires as may prevent their fellow creatures in future times from becoming sacrifices to their own ignorance.[24]

This serves as a useful conclusion to the Forsters' position in the controversy. It is of little comfort to George or Johann Reinhold Forster that their observations and journals are more appreciated today than they were in the 1770s and 1780s, but we are equally (if not more so) indebted to Captain James Cook for his published journals as a source to understand his circumnavigations of the globe.

Chapter 13

Kerguelen – Cook's 'Island of Desolation'
December 1776

I found the shore in a manner covered with Penguins and other birds and Seals, but these were not numerous, but so fearless that we killed as ma[n]y as we chose for the sake of their fat or blubber to make Oil for our lamps and other uses. Fresh water was in no less plenty than birds for every gully afforded a large Stream, but I found not a single tree or shrub nor the least signs of any, and very little herbage of any sort; tho appearances had flattered us with meeting with something considerable, by observing the sides of many hills to be of a lively green, but this was occasioned by a single plant . . . I ascended the first ridge of rocks, which rise in a kind of amphitheatre one above the another, in order to have a View of the Country, but before I got up there came on so thick a fog that I could hardly find my way down again.

James Cook, journal entry, 25 December 1776, at Christmas Harbour, Kerguelen Island

The First discoveries [by Captain Kerguelen] with some reason imagined it to be a Cape of a Southern Continent, the English have since proved that no such Continent exists and that the land in question is an island of no great extent, from which its sterility I shall Call the Island of Desolation.

James Cook, journal entry, 30 December 1776, description of Kerguelen coastline

[The] Natural Dreariness of the Place . . . is still even increased by the Snow on the tops of the mountains & the Melancholy Croaking of Innumerable Penguins with which the Shore is lined.

Master's Mate Thomas Edgar, *Discovery*, 31 December 1776

The search for the Northwest Passage through North America's Arctic Ocean was the purpose of Captain James Cook's third voyage (1776–1779/1780). This attempt was to be made from the Pacific (technically making this a search for the 'Northeast Passage'), up the coast of North America, through the Bering Strait, across the Arctic Circle and around the northern tip of Russian Alaska. If successful, *Resolution* and *Discovery* would sail from the Arctic Ocean into the North Atlantic and on to England. An alternative was to search for a passage in the Arctic Ocean across Asia to the North Atlantic. The owners of the ship that first successfully navigated the passage would receive a substantial financial award of £20,000,[1] in addition to the feat's accompanying fame, and a shorter ocean route from England to the Far East would be opened up. (Chapter 1 contains a brief account of Cook's navigation in the Arctic.)

However, before the sloops searched for the Northwest Passage, Cook's course was to Table Bay at Cape Town, from where he was to sail south to 'the land recently discovered by the French', the Crozet Islands and the Kerguelen archipelago.[2] He was then to sail to New Zealand, return Mai (Omai) to Raiatea or a similar location in the Society Islands, once again visit other South Pacific islands reached on earlier voyages, and then cross the Pacific to North America. Our focus in this chapter is Cook's visit to the sub-Antarctic Crozet and Kerguelen Islands in December 1776.

Admiralty Instructions – Kerguelen

For the third voyage James Cook again sailed in *Resolution*, while Charles Clerke, a veteran of the first and second voyages, was appointed to captain *Discovery*. The sloops were to proceed to the Cape of Good Hope, stopping at Madeira, Cape Verde or the Canary Islands only if necessary for supplies, such as wine. At the Cape of Good Hope, the ships' companies were to be 'refreshed' and the sloops repaired and provided with provisions and water by late October or 1 November 1776.

The Admiralty's instructions directed *Resolution* and *Discovery* to sail south 'in search of some islands said to have been lately seen by the French in the latitude of 48° 00′ South and about the Meriden of Mauritius [57° 5′ east longitude]'. If the islands were located, Cook was to determine if there was a 'good Harbour' that would serve as a 'good port' affording 'little or nothing more than shelter, wood and water'. *Resolution* and *Discovery* were not to spend 'too much time in looking out for and examining the islands', providing only time for giving 'the sloops companies the refreshment' needed prior to carrying out further Admiralty directions.[3]

During the second voyage Cook had entertained thoughts of seeking out the 'French discoveries' but did not do so. As a prelude to the third voyage, these islands were now to be checked out but only in passing en route to New Zealand and the South Pacific.

One difference between the third voyage and the two preceding ones was that no natural scientists sailed in *Resolution* or *Discovery*. Surgeon William Anderson compiled botanical observations during the third voyage, some of which Cook incorporated into his journal. However, Anderson did not complete the voyage and died of tuberculosis (consumption) on 3 August 1778 near the Bering Strait and Cape Prince of Wales, Alaska. The primary sources for the search for the Crozet and Kerguelen Islands are Cook's journals and the log books of William Harvey, Master's Mate in *Resolution*, Thomas Edgar, Master in *Discovery*, Lieutenant James King (*Resolution*), Lieutenant John Gore (*Resolution*) and William

Bayly (*Discovery*).[4] The log book of William Bligh, *Resolution*'s Master, was lost when *Bounty* was scuttled at Pitcairn Island on 23 January 1790.[5]

The French Discoveries and Cook's Second Voyage

As stated earlier, this is not the first appearance of the Kerguelen and Crozet Islands (those 'French discoveries') in this book. Captain Cook occasionally referenced the French discoveries in the Southern Ocean during the second voyage, but they remained an unrealized target for various reasons. For example, on 3 January 1773, as *Resolution* and *Adventure* reached ice at 59° south latitude, Cook speculated on proceeding to the west or east in search of land 'said to have been lately discovered by the French' at 48° south and 57° or 58° east longitude (in a footnote J.C. Beaglehole pointed out that this territory was actually 10½ to 12½ degrees further east). On 2 February 1773 Cook recorded in his journal that the islands did not exist at 48° 36′ south and 59° 35′ east. Cook believed that the land existed but for four days the wind prevented the sloops from proceeding westwards. After conferring with Captain Furneaux, the ships sailed to north and west. By 6 February, at 48° south and 58° east, and with no land in sight, Cook decided to abandon the search.

On 11 February 1773, having separated from *Adventure* in a thick Antarctic fog (Chapter 6), Cook set a course for New Zealand and the anticipated rendezvous at Queen Charlotte Sound. At that point (50° 18′ south, 46° 55′ east), Beaglehole concluded that *Resolution* was 'not far' from Kerguelen Island, nor was he far from the sub-Antarctic Heard Island (which he did not sight). Astronomer Bayly reported that penguins with 'rose combs' were sighted, and while the description was faulty the colour matches macaroni penguins (*see* Plate 22), which are found on Kerguelen Island (as well as on the Antarctic Peninsula, South Georgia, Crozet and other sub-Antarctic islands).

On 21 February 1775, as Cook formulated his journal entries summarizing the search for the Southern Continent, he again referenced his interest in sailing in waters where the French discoveries were said to be found, which likely would lead to more cold and unproductive territory: 'but when I considered that if they had realy made this discovery, the end would be as fully answered as if I had done it my self, we know it can only be an island and if we may judge from the degree of cold we found in that Latitude it cannot be a fertile one.'

Cook concluded that he had searched the location identified by Bouvet in 1739, and if land existed there, he would have found it. He surmised that the island was only another ice island, since there were no signs of land. Pursuing the French discoveries would require an additional two months' sailing 'in tempestuous Latitude' and Cook judged *Resolution*'s sails and rigging were already worn, with no replacements available.

A remarkably fortuitous occasion arose on 21 March 1775. At Table Bay James Cook met Captain Julien-Marie Crozet, who at that time commanded *Ajax*, en route to Pondicherry (India). Crozet had sailed with Captain Marc-Joseph de Fresne when they discovered the Crozet Islands in 1772 (*see* Chapter 2). In his journal entry for 21 March 1775 James Cook described Captain Crozet as a person of good will and ability, as well as having 'the true spirit of a discoverer'. Crozet gave Cook a chart identifying their discoveries. Cook remarked that that both he and Furneaux had searched for the islands using those coordinates and did not understand how they could have missed sighting the new discoveries.

The coordinates given by Crozet about Kerguelen were not precise but Cook would put that right in December 1776. Crozet also provided information on six other nearby islands, in 46° south and 50° to 52° east, which Cook was to sight in 1776 before reaching Kerguelen; Cook named two of these islands the Marion and Prince Edward Islands. The discussion in Table Bay in March 1775 also touched upon the voyage of Captain John Francois-Marie de Surville (d. 1770) across the Pacific and near New Zealand at the same time Cook was charting and circumnavigating the North and South Islands (*see* Chapter 10). Although the two ships did not sight each other in 1769, this information and additional discussions about other South Pacific islands allowed Cook and Crozet to confirm bits of information gathered from their respective voyages, including Kerguelen-Trémarec's second voyage to Kerguelen which ended in his disgrace (*see* below).

From England to Table Bay, 8 July–1 December 1776

On 8 July 1776 Cook received the Admiralty's instructions for the voyage. Because Captain Charles Clerke could not join the voyage at that time, instructions were provided for *Discovery* to proceed later to the Cape of Good Hope. Clerke sailed from England in *Discovery* on 1 August and joined *Resolution* at Table Bay on 10 November 1776. Clerke was not available in July because was confined to King's Bench Prison, serving as a guarantor for the debts of his brother Sir John Clerke.[6] While in prison, Clerke contracted consumption (tuberculosis). When Cook was killed on 14 February 1779, Clerke took overall command of the third voyage but died, as explained in Chapter 1, on 22 August near Kamchatka, a peninsula in Siberia off the North Pacific and the Sea of Okhotsk.

Captain Cook and *Resolution* sailed from Plymouth on 12 July. On 30 July the ship anchored at Tenerife (the largest of the Canary Islands) to take on supplies, primarily because there was a more abundant supply of food for the livestock carried in the sloop. While at Tenerife, Cook obtained beef, pork, sheep, goats and poultry. He purchased live animals (observing in his journal that this was a wrong decision on his part, because of the greater cost). In addition, various fruits and Indian corn (maize), as well as onions and potatoes were added to the ships' stores. Cook observed that pumpkins, onions and potatoes could be kept in good order during the long sea voyage. The wine at Madeira was superior to that of Tenerife and the small beer too strong, Cook concluded, but the prices of food and drink were lower at Tenerife. Some corn (wheat or barley) and straw were also purchased for the livestock carried in *Resolution*.

Captain Cook and *Resolution* reached Table Bay on 18 September. In separate letters written on 26 November 1776 to First Lord Sandwich and Joseph Banks from the Cape of Good Hope, Cook remarked 'Nothing is wanting but a few females of our own species to make *Resolution* a Compleate ark,' having added four horses to 'keep Omai happy'. *Resolution* also carried sheep, goats, pigs, rabbits and poultry. A peacock and a hen were donated by the Earl of Bessborough (a Lord Commissioner of the Admiralty). At Cape Town the sheep were off-loaded for a spell on land, but dogs attacked and killed four sheep and drove away the others, most of which were rounded up later.[7] In addition, King George III donated a bull, two cows and their calves, carried in *Resolution*, destined for Tahiti.[8] This donation was in keeping with the king's interest in improving agriculture and livestock, earning him the sobriquet 'Farmer George'. Despite the good intentions, some of the animals did not survive the voyage to reach their South Pacific destinations (*see* below).

On 4 August Cook weighed anchor and proceeded south, crossing the Equator on 1 September; on the 17th they sighted the Cape of Good Hope, where *Resolution* anchored the next day. Captain Clerke and *Discovery* arrived fifty-three days later on 10 November, at which time both ships were provisioned and caulked for the journey ahead. Cook provided Clerke with a copy of the Admiralty's instructions, along with orders regarding a plan should the sloops become separated during their travels. Although the Admiralty's instructions encouraged Cook to depart by early November, the voyage was a month late in leaving the Cape for the sub-Antarctic. This delay (and other factors occurring later in the South Pacific) further prevented Cook and Clerke from seeking the Northwest Passage until the summer of 1778.

From the Cape of Good Hope to the Crozet Islands, 2–15 December 1776

Resolution and *Discovery* sailed southeast on 2 December. *Resolution* lost its mizzen top mast on the 5th. Strong gales and high seas caused the ship to roll, which created difficulty in caring for the cattle on board. Some of the sheep and goats died, mostly from the increasingly cold weather. Cook sighted two islands on 12 December, between 46° 53′ south/37° 46′ east and 46° 40′ south/38° 08′ east. He estimated the largest of the islands was 15 miles in circumference, while the smaller was about 9 miles around, separated by about 5 leagues. Master's Mate William Harvey (*Resolution*) observed the presence of both porpoises and dolphins on 12 December, while Lieutenant Gore sighted a whale on the 14th. Cook observed the islands through a telescope, noting that neither appeared to have trees or shrubs but had 'a rocky and bold shore' and, except for the southeast, contained 'barren mountains which rise to a considerable height and whose summits and sides were covered with snow, which in many places seemed to be of considerable depth'. Cook named the larger island Marion, after Captain Marion de Fresne, and the smaller island after Prince Edward, the fourth son of George III. On the 13th Gore thought there might be an 'appearance of some verdue' but the islands were very barren. He observed a 'remarkable Steeple Rock' on the east side of Marion Island and thought that location might serve as a safe harbour. The Crozet Islands lie 9–12 degrees of longitude east of Prince

Edward and Marion Islands, which Cook passed to the southeast. Cook described the weather as similar to that of an English winter.

The shipboard routine continued even in the increasingly cold weather. Lieutenant Gore recorded that on the 12th the ship was aired between decks and on the 15th 'Clean'd & Smoak'd Ship below', while on the 14th the wet sails were taken from storage and dried on deck. The colder weather is also observed in various log books. In his log book entry for 14 December Thomas Edgar (*Discovery*) wrote, 'Serv'd out Magellan Jackets and Trowsers to the People.' (Magellan jackets are composed of thick and dense wool with a hood, roughly the same construction as Fearnought jackets or trousers.)[9] Because of the 'squally weather', including hail and sleet, Lieutenant King (*Resolution*) commented in his log book entry on 13 December that it was difficult to observe the islands in detail, also noting that there was no adequate anchorage. On the 15th King also commented that four goats and 'all the young kids' died, despite the great care Captain Cook took to preserve all the animals. King also remarked that no one knew what purpose these animals were intended for, but 'all on board feels for the Accidents befalling them'. Other concerns were recorded by King regarding *Resolution*: 'We have also serious concerns on our own Account, for the Cabbins & all between Decks leak as bad as before we go to ye Cape. We did hope ye caulking the Ship had there, would have remov'd that Evil, which altho' not a pressing One, leaves room for Anticipation.'

This recalls the frequent comments from J.R. Forster and George Forster about cold, leaky conditions during the Antarctic portion of the second voyage. Both Lieutenant King and Midshipman Harvey entered in their logs on the 15th that, in the midst of strong gales and variable weather, *Resolution* was cleaned and smoked between decks, Harvey adding that the wet sails were brought on deck to dry out. *Resolution* and *Discovery* continued to the south in what Cook termed 'Strong gales' and 'indifferent weather' in search of Kerguelen's land.

Yves-Joseph de Kerguelen-Trémarec and the Discovery of La France Australe

The European discovery of the uninhabited Kerguelen Islands on 12 February 1772 is credited to Captain Yves-Joseph de Kerguelen-Trémarec (1734–1797) aboard *Fortune*, one of two ships of the French royal fleet. The islands were claimed for France in the name of King Louis XV. Lieutenants Charles-Marc du Boisguehenneuc (d. 1772) and François-Alesno de St-Allouran (d. 1778) in *Gros Ventre* landed for quarter of an hour on 14 February 1772, establishing France's initial claim. They buried documents in a glass bottle at the Baie du Lion Marin (also known as the Baie du Gros Ventre) on the Loranchet Peninsula, the 'top-most' promontory of the island, near the bay Cook named 'Christmas Harbour' in 1776 and across from the Arch of Kerguelen (Figure 21).

Upon his return to France, Kerguelen presented glowing, exaggerated reports about the island's significance, describing the land as *La France Australe* ('France of the South'). Apparently the 'green' he sighted through a telescope (the cushion plant, *see* below) led to the false assumption about trees and rich vegetation. Cook's 1776 observations proved this inaccurate. Some contemporaries thought of Kerguelen as a 'new Columbus'. A rivalry with French marine explorer Alexis-Marie du Rochon, salon gossip and perhaps court intrigue all affected accurate understanding about the territory. It appears Kerguelen began to believe (or not dispute) the exaggerated accounts.

Alaine Boulaire, a Kerguelen biographer, recounts the claims promoting the 'France of the South': its congenial temperature, great natural fertility and green forests. Kerguelen stated he was convinced the territory was not inhabited because of the birds' lack of timidity around the landing party. On 25 July 1773 Kerguelen was presented to Louis XV, to whom he recounted the 'marvellous richness of the continent'. The king promoted Kerguelen to the grade of captain (*Captaine de vaisseau*) and bestowed on him the Order of the Cross of Saint-Louis, a reward given to exceptional officers. An August memorandum prepared for Louis XV by the Secretary of State for the Navy cited Kerguelen's discovery as the territory on the *cote du cercle polaire antarctique* and insisted it represented positive advantages for both commerce and navigation to the Indies. Kerguelen's discovery, however, was not the coast of the Antarctic Circle but a large sub-Antarctic island.

Kerguelen's promotion created envy among more senior officers who had been passed over for promotion. The glowing reports served to promote a second voyage to the southern oceans. In December 1773–January 1774 Kerguelen reluctantly returned to the islands. Three ships sailed on this voyage: *Le Rolland*, *l'Oiseau* and *La Dauphine*. Kerguelen (in *Le Rolland*) again did not land on the island during the second voyage, probably due to rough seas and his apparent reluctance to set foot on the uninviting territory. Captain de Rochegude (in *l'Oiseau*) landed on 6 January 1774, leaving documents in a glass bottle at the Baie de l'Oiseau (Cook's Christmas Harbour), again claiming the territory for France. Cook opened these documents on 27 December 1776 and added his own inscription, then sealed and returned the bottle to a prominent location in a cairn above Christmas Harbour.

Captain Kerguelen forced his officers to swear to false information regarding his decision to stop further exploration and *Le Rolland* returned to France – effectively abandoning the voyage and disobeying his naval instructions. Other difficulties arose: scurvy affected the crew; Kerguelen is said to have treated fellow officers in an arrogant manner; and the officers quarrelled among themselves. At least four women had been smuggled aboard *Le Rolland* and Kerguelen refused to share one of them, his 16-year-old mistress Louise Segun, with the other officers. Upon his return to France, Kerguelen appeared before a naval disciplinary tribunal for violations of naval regulations and personal conduct.

Because of his conduct in disobeying orders (and perhaps the earlier exaggerated assertions about the islands), in May 1775 Kerguelen was imprisoned for a term of six years in the Loire Valley chateau at Saumur, but he was released by order of King Louis XVI in August 1778. During the wars associated with the

French Revolution, Kerguelen pursued a career as a privateer (*liber navigateur*), then was restored to the navy with the rank of Admiral and was subsequently captured and briefly imprisoned by the British. A native of Brittany, he concluded his career as commander of the port at Brest. Kerguelen died on 3 March 1797.[10]

Captain Cook at Kerguelen Island, 21–30 December 1776

After sighting and sailing past the Crozet Islands, on 16 December *Resolution* and *Discovery* began to see signs of land, such as penguins, diving birds (likely petrels) and sea weed. On the 21st a large seal was sighted. Cook's journal recorded foggy weather as well as 'tedious and dangerous' navigation.

The Kerguelen archipelago is of volcanic origin and consists of some 300 islands, islets, reefs and rocks covering 2,786 square miles (7,215 sq. km) in the south Indian Ocean. Kerguelen, the largest island, is located 3,293 miles (5,300km) from the southeast tip of Africa and approximately 684 miles (1,100km) from the Antarctic Circle (*see* Plate 6). Today Kerguelen is part of the French Southern and Antarctic Territories (*Terres Australes et Antarctiques Françaises*, or TAAF). Although only France claimed the Kerguelen archipelago, TAAF honoured Captain James Cook by issuing several postage stamps, including a painting of Christmas Harbour by John Webber (*see* Plate 16) marking Cook's 'passage' at Kerguelen Island (1976). A TAAF triptych issued in 1997 on the 200th anniversary of Kerguelen's death commemorates Cook's presence at Kerguelen, along with a sketch of Captain Kerguelen and his coat of arms. It is suggested that the reason Cook was so honoured is that he did not insist on the use of his phrase 'Island of Desolation' as the name of the island but favoured using Kerguelen's name, as first discoverer.[11]

The archipelago lies along the Antarctic Convergence where the cold waters of the Antarctic mix with the warmer waters of the Indian Ocean. The islands are classified as sub-Antarctic. The surrounding ocean waters do not freeze. Kerguelen Island (*Grande Terre*) occupies 1,318 square miles (3,414 sq. km). Rain, sleet or snow (or combinations thereof) fall on 300 days annually, thick fogs frequently surround the ocean and island, and fierce winds (averaging 62mph/100kph) blow almost continually.

In December 1776 Cook visited Kerguelen Island for six days. *Resolution* first sighted land on 24 December. Cook's journal contains numerous descriptions of difficulty encountered in sailing near Kerguelen and nearby islands – the same difficulties that had affected Captain Kerguelen's earlier voyages. Intermittent foggy weather obscured vision. Persistent winds increased the risks of sailing along a coastline with rocks lurking amidst shoals that could damage ships. On the 24th Cook wrote, 'if there was no passage or we should meet with any sudden danger, we should not be able to get off, as the wind was right on and there ran a prodigious sea what broke on all the shores with a frightfull surf'.

On the 24th Lieutenant King described the approach to Kerguelen in his log book: 'At 6 we were within 2 or 3 Leagues of the first Land we saw. No Trees or Shrubs to be seen, but patches of a beautifull green which we Supposed [to be] moss.' By the 25th the fog had cleared and the sighted land appeared to be 'of a considerable extent'.

Using Crozet's maps (which included Kerguelen's discoveries), Cook searched for the 'Isle of Rendezvous' but, after searching among possible points of land in fog and windy weather, he wrote in his journal on 24 December, 'I know nothing that can Rendezvouz at it but fowls of the air, for it is certainly inaccessible to every other animal.' Lieutenant Gore's 24 December log book entry stated that with the thick weather Captain Cook did not think it safe to land, so the ships stood off until the morning. Eventually, a calm harbour was located on the tip of the island near where Kerguelen's ships had landed in 1772 and 1774. Cook dispatched *Resolution*'s Master William Bligh to sound the potential anchorage. Bligh reported that the harbour was, as Cook wrote, 'safe and commodious with good anchorage in every part, and great plenty of fresh Water, Seals, Penguins and other birds on the shore but not a stick of Wood' – a conclusion which immediately met the Admiralty's purpose in visiting Kerguelen Island. Cook named the location 'Christmas Harbour' two days later. The location is the Baie de l'Oiseau ('Bay of Birds') from Kerguelen's second voyage (Figure 21).

Cook first landed on Kerguelen on 25 December. A painting by John Webber depicts *Resolution* and *Discovery* anchored in the bay with various penguins on the shore (*see* Plate 16). Across the bay (lower left horizon) is the Arch of Kerguelen. The ships' companies celebrated Christmas on 27 December by making excursions in different directions from the harbour, Cook himself remarking on the 'desolate and barren' land. In his journal Cook described Kerguelen:

> I found the shore in a manner covered with Penguins and other birds and Seals, but these were not numerous, but so fearless that we killed as ma[n]y as we chose for the sake of their fat or blubber to make Oil for our lamps and other uses. Fresh water was in no less plenty than birds for every gully afforded a large Stream, but I found not a single tree or shrub nor the least signs of any, and very little herbage of any sort; tho appearances had flattered us with meeting with something considerable, by observing the sides of many hills to be of a lively green, but this was occasioned by a single plant ...
> I ascended the first ridge of rocks, which rise in a kind of ampitheatre one above the another, in order to have a View of the Country, but before I got up there came on so thick a fog that I could hardly find my way down again.

When boats were sent ashore, one of the first tasks was to obtain fresh water and also fresh food. In a rather brutal entry for Christmas Day, Lieutenant Gore entered in his log, 'Slew all the Principal Inhabitants for their Oil, Seals, & Sea Lyons or rather Sea Bull Doggs, hear [*sic*] in a Great Number. Of Penguins three different sorts. Pintado Birds, Petterels of different sorts & a white long shore bird, the (?) Common Pidgeon without webb feet, [and] no other land bird of any sort.'

Gore also observed ducks 'of very good eating', as well as 'Skaggs'. It was the time of the season when seals and penguins 'bring up their young & through off

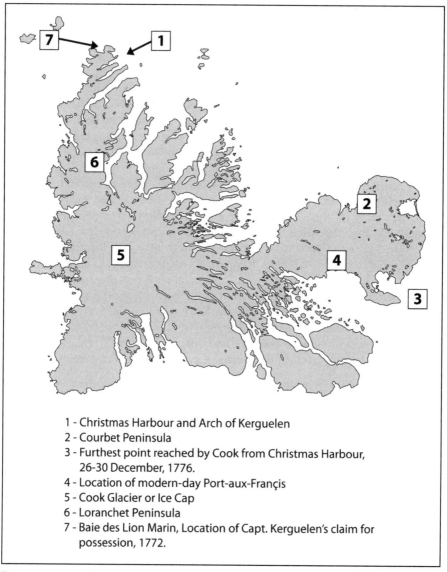

Figure 21. Map of Kerguelen Island showing the approximate location of features referenced in the text associated with Cook's 1776 visit. This is a greyscale version of an
original outline map by Rémi Kaupp (2009).

their winter cloathing', since Gore observed seals and sea-lions lying on the shore
'with new coats without fur'. Lieutenant Gore described his excursion of several
miles at Kerguelen on 25 December. In his log book entry he wrote that the land
was barren and rocky, with water everywhere, and numerous shallow bogs. The
birds made use of a moss 'to furnish their nests in holes of the rocks'.

On 27 December, during a Kerguelen excursion, one of 'the People' discovered a glass bottle attached to a rock on the north side of the harbour. Documents in the bottle, dated 1773, revealed it to be the bottle left by Captain de Rochegude on 6 January 1774. It stated, '*Ludovico XV galliarum rege. et d. de Boynes regi a Secretis ad res maritimas annis 1772 et 1773*' ('In the reign of Louis XV, King of France, the lord de Boynes being Secretary of the Marine, in the years 1772 and 1773'). Cook assumed incorrectly that it referred to Kerguelen's first voyage in 1772. He placed an inscription on the reverse side of the 1774 French and Latin text, stating, '*Naves Resolution & Discovery de Rege Magnae Britaniae Decembris 1776*' ('The ships *Resolution* and *Discovery* of the King of Great Britain November 1776'). Lieutenant Gore referenced the discovery of the bottle and its message and noted that Cook added some 'Latin writing' and placed a 1772 silver two-pence coin in the bottle. The bottle was sealed with a lead cap and placed in a cairn, described by Cook as 'a pile of stones erected for the purpose on a little eminence on the north shore of the harbour and near to the place where it was first found'. On 27 December the Union Jack was displayed at the site and the area was given the name 'Christmas Harbour'. No reference is made in Cook's journal to this serving as an assertion of 'possession'.[12]

In his journal Captain Cook described the inlet on which the Arch of Kerguelen is located: 'its south point terminates in a high rock which is per[f]orated quite through so as to appear like the arch of a bridge'. This inscription is also located on the selvage of a 2001 TAAF miniature sheet containing comments from navigators about the Arch from 1774 to 1931 (*see* Plate 18). The log book description by astronomer Bayly read 'At the entrance is a high Rock resembling part of an old wall with a hole right through it.' He provided a tiny sketch of the Arch in his log book but its pen-and-ink depiction is too dark for reproduction in this book. After anchoring in Christmas Sound on 25 December, Lieutenant John Gore observed 'a Remarkable Tower Rock with a pass thro it like an Arched gate' about 2 miles in the distance. The Arch stands 112.67yd high (103m). As shown in Plate 17, its top portion collapsed between 1909 and 1914. It is one of the most remarkable topographic features Cook encountered during his three voyages.[13]

During his six-day visit Captain Cook charted only approximately one-third of Kerguelen's coastline. He sailed from Christmas Harbour on the northeastern tip of the Loranchet Peninsula, across the Bai des Baleiners ('Bay of Whales') and around much of the Courbet Peninsula to the Baie Norvegienne ('Norwegian Bay') and the Ile du Prince de Galles ('Prince of Wales Island') on the southeastern coastline. *Resolution* and *Discovery* did not proceed into the Golfe du Morbihan which today leads to the administrative centre at Port aux Français (*see* Figure 21). In searching for locations on Kerguelen maps, one of the difficulties is that Cook or later navigators named points of interest using different names. Cook did not circumnavigate Kerguelen Island because the Admiralty's instructions required only information about safe anchorage, wood and water, which limited Cook's time in this area.

On 30 December Captain Cook described the Bay of Isles, off the Baie des Baleiners, in the northeast of Kerguelen:

in and before the entrance of this bay are several low islands, rocks and those beds of Sea Weed, but there seem'd to be winding Channels between them. After continuing our Course half an hour long we were so much imbarrassed with these shoals that I resolved to haul off to the Eastward to endeavour by this Course to extricate our selves from the danger that threatened us. But so far was this from answering the intended purpose that it brought us into more, so that I found it absolutely necessary to secure the Ships, if possible, in some place before the night, as the weather was now become hazey and threatened us with a fog ... Captain Clerke made the Signal for having discovered a harbour in which, about 5 o'clock we anchored in 15 fathom water over a bottom of fine dark sand. The North point of the Harbour bore NBE ½ E one mile dist^t and the small islands lying in the entrance, within which we anchor'd, extended from East to SE. The Ships were no sooner secured than it began to blow very strong ...

Once the weather had relented, the Masters from *Resolution* and *Discovery* sounded the Channel. Later Cook, Lieutenant Gore and astronomer Bayly landed and made observations of the bay, identifying the shoals that caused navigation to be dangerous. Unfortunately there was no food or shelter for the cattle and Cook realized that they would soon perish. There were many penguins as well as seals and other birds. Later in the day Captain Cook named the landing place as Port Palliser in honour of his mentor in Newfoundland and at the Admiralty.

Edgar's commentary about *Discovery*'s coastline survey from 26 to 30 December includes the following observations of Kerguelen Island, which in three paragraphs sum up the more extensive remarks by Cook and Anderson:

This Land has an Aspect Extremely barren & Desolate being a continued Lump of Rocks, without either tree or bush, what little soil there is from the Continual Rains [and it] is too Rotten to bear a man's weight. In this latitude even in the midst of Summer is very often Wet & Foggy which over not a little Contribute to the Natural Dreariness of the Place. This is still even increased by the snow on the tops of the mountains & the Melancholy Croaking of Innumerable Penguins with which the Shore is lined.

Nature seems to have designed this Land solely for the use of Sea Lions, Seals and Penguins. [Of the] Fowl, the Penguins fare by much the most. The most frequent being there three kinds. There is a few Wild Duck or rather a kind of Teal, [and] fish we saw none.

This Land appears to be a large group of Isl [Island] Rocks extending from the Latitude of 48° 24′ 30″ to 51° 30′ south latitude & Longitude from 68° 21′ to 70° 15′ East of the Meridian of Greenwich. As we ran down surveying the shore we passed several very deep Bays. The Land having a great many Openings that seem to afford very good Anchorage and Shelter, but no appearance of Trees or Verdue. The Land high and uneven until we came off the S[outh] end. There the Land ran low and level for some miles to the Westward.

As *Resolution* sailed along the coast, Lieutenant King observed many inlets with deep bays which would likely be suitable for anchorage and shelter, along with numerous islands. Both ships encountered 'patches of Rock Weed; we for some time tried to avoid them'. The sloops also encountered 'dangerous & sunken Rocks'. Cook encountered intermittent and sometimes thick fog, a coastline of rocky fiords with 'craggy precipes' and some hills covered with snow. The island provided 'neither food nor water for cattle'. Kerguelen's shores were 'barren and rocky without the least sign of tree or shrub but very little Verdue [green vege-tation] of any sort'. He described the high mountains of 'naked rocks whose summit were cap'd with snow'.

The ocean yielded great clumps of seaweed. Cook described the Bay of *Fucus giganticus*, containing seaweed 'of a most enormous length' which grew at an acute angle up to 60 fathoms (320ft). On the 30th William Harvey on *Resolution* recorded in his log that 'a great number of very long weed is around us ... [It] Obliged us to frequently run thro' great beds of weed, as the surface in most places was covered with it which required us to Luff up [turn into the wind] and bore away frequently to gain clear water'. On the 29th Wales recorded crossing 'beds of Sea weed of great extent' growing 3–4 miles off shore. The seaweed also obscured shoals and breakers, making for cautious sailing, with the ships about half a mile apart.

Lieutenant King provided an interesting comparison, writing in his log on the 30th that 'We know of no island so desolate in such extent in this Latitude. In the Last Voyage they discovered ye Island of Georgia and South[ern] Thule which are still more so; but they are in a much higher latitude.' Also on the 30th astron-omer Bayly summed up the island with 'neither tree nor shrub of any kind what-ever ... The islands ... are the habitation of Seals, Sea Lyons and Sea fowls only.'

Cook made it very clear that Kerguelen was not the Southern Continent, as claimed by French discoveries, writing on 30 December that Kerguelen was an 'island of desolation': 'The First discoverers [Kerguelen] with some reason imagined it to be a Cape of a Southern Continent, the English have since proved that no such Continent exists and that the land in question is an island of no great extent, from which its sterility I shall Call the Island of Desolation.'

Kerguelen's grasses and water did assist, to some degree, in replenishing the sloops' provisions, as previously cited in Lieutenant Gore's log book entry on 25 December. Master's Mate Harvey recorded in his log for 26 December that 'Party's onshore Cutting Grass for the Stock, killing, skinning blubber of the Sea Lyons & Seals for Oil'. These tasks continued on the 27th. Harvey observed that Christmas was celebrated on the 27th: 'Kept this day for the 25th [and] served a double allowance of brandy to the Ship's Company.' By the 29th Harvey reported that a ton of water had been put in the casks and blubber filled three puncheons.

Kerguelen Flora

During the three days of sailing along part of Kerguelen's northeastern coast, Cook's journal entries contain a wealth of observations about the island as he searched for trees, driftwood, grass or plant life, and fresh water and food for the livestock on board the sloops. In many respects his observations here could be described as among his best among all his voyages, being often thoughtful and detailed, largely based upon Surgeon William Anderson's account. A distillation of these comments follows, taken from his 30 December journal entries about Kerguelen's flora and fauna and the island's physical characteristics.

The cushion plant, *Azorella selago*, 'grows in large spreading tufts to a considerable way up the sides of the hills'. If stepped upon, 'one sinks a foot or two at every step'. Cook described the plant turning the hillside into 'a lively green', which is likely the green colour Captain Kerguelen thought were trees, shrubs or plants (*see* Plate 27). Log book entries pointed out how from a distance Kerguelen's hills had a notable greenish colour but up close the colour was due only to the single plant and certainly not to trees or shrubs, the assumption made by Captain Kerguelen through his telescope in 1772. The only use for the plant would be, Cook speculated, to dry it and use it for fuel (perhaps an important consideration since there was no wood on the island).

Another plant was thought to be similar to a garden cress. A 'coarse grass' and 'goose grass', perhaps *Cotula pulmonosa* and *Poa cookii*, growing in limited areas, were harvested for the cattle. *Poa cookii* (*see* Plate 28), a short tussock grass (*Poa flabellata*), was named after Captain Cook by Joseph Dalton Hooker, a nineteenth-century botanist.[14] Tussock grass is also located on South Georgia. Moss and lichens were also observed. Most significantly, the Kerguelen cabbage (*Pringlea antiscorbutica*), described in Cook's journal as 'plentifully scatered about the boggy declivitys', with leaves growing up to 2ft long, was perhaps adaptable, Cook thought, to English kitchen gardens. As an antiscourbitic, the cabbage was consumed raw because it acquired 'a rank flavour by being boiled' (*see* Plate 25).

At Christmas Harbour Bayly also identified watercress and 'a Plant somewhat resembling a Broccoli Cabbage'. This is similar to Lieutenant Gore's log book entry on the 25th concerning quantities of 'pepper grass' which, along with an unnamed plant, made for 'an agreeable sallad'. Another plant, which must be the Kerguelen Cabbage, was likely a good antiscourbitic in Gore's opinion. The ship's company was divided over whether it was better raw or boiled, but Gore preferred it in its raw state. The Kerguelen cabbage and scurvy grass (*see* Plates 25 and 26) found in Tierra del Fuego and New Zealand served as examples of the visitors' discoveries which were part of the overall scheme to combat scurvy.

Kerguelen Fauna

Kerguelen Island provided a variety of wildlife, both on land and at sea. Cook observed that seals, including the Kerguelen fur seal, were most numerous, along with sea-lions (sometimes referred to as 'sea bears' by explorers). Seals and sea-lions are now considered the same species. Cook also identified 'Ducks, Petrels, Albatrosses, Penguins, Shags, Gulls, Sea Swallows, etc. . . . Penguins form by far the greatest number of birds here and there are three sorts', identified later as the king penguin, the gentoo penguin and the rockhopper penguin. His journal also observed that the wildlife was similar to that observed in other sub-Antarctic islands such as South Georgia or the tip of South America. Some fish were caught using a seine net near the shore but only a few were caught with a fishing line. Surgeon Anderson located shellfish and mussels, starfish and sea anemones in coastal waters. Cook concluded Kerguelen had a large array of animals but he thought the marine animals used the island for breeding purposes, not as a permanent habitation. Species identified by Cook in his journal correspond with the southern hemisphere's late spring and early summer.

Sea-lions/Seals/Sea Leopards/Sea Elephants
Sea-lions and seals refer to the same species of pinnipeds. Cook observed the Kerguelen fur seal 'shedding its hair and so fearless that we killed what number we chose'. The species is now referred to as the Antarctic fur seal. These seals nearly became extinct in the later eighteenth and nineteenth centuries, but protection from sealing led to increased numbers.[15] Sea elephants and sea leopards represent the largest of the seal species, both commonly found in sub-Antarctic waters and observed both at sea and on shore. Visitors to Kerguelen today remark that this island is the only location with a 'Sea Elephant Crossing' sign on the island pathways. Lieutenant Gore used the phrase 'sea bull doggs' to describe some of these animals.

Penguins
Considerable detail is provided in Cook's journal regarding Kerguelen's numerous penguins. Cook and the naturalists also saw the king penguin when visiting South Georgia in January 1775. The king penguin is the largest penguin found at Kerguelen. Cook described it as 'The head is black, the upper part of the body a leaden grey, and the under part white with black feet. It has two broad stripes of fine yellow beginning at the sides of the head, and, descending by each side of the Neck, meet above its breast.'

Astronomer Bayly's log book for 22 December noted 'This Afternoon we saw some penguins with beautiful yellow heads.' Were these king penguins or was he referring to the brilliant yellow crest of macaroni penguins? Cook also described the gentoo penguin which 'scarcely exceeds half the size of the former [king penguin]. The upper part is blackish grey, with a white spot on the upper part of the head, growing broader at each side. The Bill and feet are yellowish.' Cook wrote that the rockhopper penguin was

> never seen by any of us before. Its length is 24 inches the breadth 20. The upper part of the Body and throat are black; the rest white, except the upper part of the head which has a fine yellow arch looking backwards, and ending on each side in along soft feathers which it can erect as two crests . . . [Rock

Hoppers] were only found by themselves, but in great numbers on the outer shores of the harbour. They were breeding at this time, and lay only one white egg, larger than a Ducks, on bare stones.

It is possible the rockhopper penguin was confused with the macaroni penguin, today the island's most numerous penguin species. King and gentoo penguins are found together on the beach and are also to be found in the hills. All the penguins were very tame and the crew used only their hands to catch them. Cook does not mention whales in his journal but on the 30th Lieutenant King recorded in his log that he saw 'many whales' (unspecified), perhaps in the Bay of Whales off the northeastern coast.

Other Birds and Ducks

Cook described ducks as plentiful (such as the Kerguelen pintail), which were shot and tasted good, without any 'fishy taste'. Petrels also frequented the island, such as the giant petrel, the cape petrel and Wilson's storm petrel. Cook compared the giant petrel to 'Seaman Mother Carey's goose'. Petrels 'were so tame we could kill them with a stick on the beach', and he noted they fed on dead seal or bird carcasses found in the ocean. Albatrosses seen included the sooty albatross, also observed in other southern latitudes. The wandering albatross and grey-headed albatross are also identified in the journal, along with the Kerguelen cormorant and the sheathbill, a scavenger seen in other Antarctic locations.

Insects and Fish

No insects are included in Cook's journal entries even though the visit occurred in the spring and summer. Biologists observe that Kerguelen insects crawl or hop rather than fly because of the continual strong winds on the island. Plants have adapted to pollination by wind rather than insects. A few fish that were seined seemed similar to haddock, Cook observing in his journal that the fish were of a different species than seen before: 'the snout is lengthened, the head armed with some strong spines, and the rays of the back fin very strong and long. The belly is large and the body without scales.' The description suggests the crocodile rockfish (*Chaenichthys rhinoceratus*), which is found in the Southern Ocean and waters surrounding Kerguelen.

The Animals in *Resolution*

On 12 December, as *Resolution* and *Discovery* sailed past the Crozet Islands, Cook wrote in his journal about the failing condition of the animals in *Resolution*. Over two weeks later Lieutenant James King summarized the issue in his log book entry for 30 January:

I cannot leave this Place without taking Notice of what has befallen our Stock & which will be considered a real misfortune. During our stay here our two young bulls and one of the two heifers purchased at the Cape of Good Hope died. We partially attribute this to ye grass given them which was fouled with Dung of Penguins & part to the usual want of attention, all hands being busy in Ships' duty. By this Accident is Capt. Cook deprived of leaving a pair at Van Damien's Land as he intended & He is doubtful whether he can now have [leave?] a pair at New Zealand, for there is only 1 Bull and a Bull calf. Everyone will make his own reflections upon what Effect ye cattle might have in changing ye shocking customs of ye New Zealanders & that opportunity is now perhaps for ever lost.

Judging by King's analysis, the livestock appear to have died from both scarce or poor quality food and the lack of attention. Although some animals survived to be deposited at various locations in the South Pacific, the variety carried by *Resolution*'s 'ark' was much reduced as the sloops bore east on New Year's Day 1777.

Kerguelen Geography and Topography

Kerguelen Island totals 2,400 square miles (6,200 sq. km); for comparison, the state of Rhode Island is 1212 square miles (3,144 sq. km). The two main Falkland Islands are approximately 3.6 times larger than Kerguelen Island. The Cook Glacier, which once covered the entire island, occupies about 500–550 sq. km, although some estimates are larger (*see* Plate 6). The island's highest point is Mt Ross, named after the nineteenth century British explorer James Clark Ross, whose name is also given to the Antarctic's Ross Ice Shelf. The other significant geological feature is the Arch of Kerguelen, described earlier.

Cook and Anderson reported that the island's rocks yielded no 'ore or metal'. Quartz and sandstone were located and some stone had been smoothed in brooks by flowing waters. The island's rocks and hills were compared to those of Scotland, Sweden, the Canary Islands and the Cape of Good Hope. Cook observed dark blue and hard stone with veins of quartz as well as a brittle and brownish stone. The quartz would likely be feldspar or zeolite. More recent explorations identified other minerals on Kerguelen, including minerals formed in volcanic cavities such as analcime, consisting of hydrated sodium aluminium silicate crystals.

The Kerguelen Islands occupy part of the Kerguelen–Gaussberg Ridge, which is part of the massive 'Kerguelen Mini-continent' or plateau which formed 100–200 million years ago and subsequently sank, the plateau bottom resting 1–2km below sea level. The island's sedimentary rocks are similar to those of India and Australia and it is thought that perhaps these territories were once connected 50 million years ago. Volcanic eruptions began approximately 40 million years ago. Mt Ross is the highest (1,850m) and the youngest of the volcanoes, of which there are three on the island. No eruptions have occurred in the historic era, the last eruption being dated to approximately 26,000 BC. Fumaroles and hot springs are also found on Kerguelen.[16]

*   *   *

Resolution and *Discovery* sailed from Kerguelen Island on 30 December 1776. In his journal Cook observed that the livestock were in need of water and hay, and many of the animals that left England had perished. The sloops were also in need of wood for fuel. *Discovery*'s Master Edgar's log book stated that between 3am and noon on the 31st, the ship 'weighed and came to Sail under single Reef'd top sail. Got up Top Gall't Yards, Haul'd up and bore away occasionally to keep clear of the Weeds at the Northernmost points of the Bay. *Resolution* in Company.'

He bade farewell to Kerguelen: '[The] Natural Dreariness of the Place ... is still even increased by the Snow on the tops of the mountains & the Melancholy Croaking of Innumerable Penguins with which the Shore is lined.'

In *Resolution* Master's Mate Harvey observed, 'Fresh gales and squally with showers of hail. At 5 [a.m.] Squally with thick Snow Carried away the Larboard fore Topmast Stud sail Boom. Haul'd down the studding sails ... Carp[enters] making New stud sail booms ... *Discovery* in Company.' In his final log entry for 1776, Lieutenant Gore wrote, 'Bore away & took our leave of this Cold Blustering Wet Country of Islands, Bays & Harbours ... Whoever Comes to this French Land and wants a Harbour, need only get on the East Side of it and Open his Eyes.'

Cook's visit to Kerguelen is a relatively small footnote to his three voyages. He accomplished the Admiralty's assignment, to determine if there was a safe harbour and supplies of wood and water for future voyages. His short stay also allowed the first significant exploration of a portion of Kerguelen's coastline, as well as documentation of the island's flora and fauna, some of its terrain and severe climatic conditions. Unlike Captain Kerguelen, no effusive description followed in the wake of the 1776 visit.

Few people will ever visit the Kerguelen archipelago and, like South Georgia, there is no tourist accommodation available today, but Cook's account of his six-day visit serves as another of his remarkable adventures in geography and navigation. Kerguelen may be remote and inhospitable, but topographical desolation offers its own unique beauty, as well as having a curious impact on the imagination. An account of Kerguelen after Cook is given in Chapter 16.

Cook's third voyage then sailed east, stopping at Tasmania (visited by Captain Furneaux in 1773), and arriving in Queen Charlotte Sound in February 1777.

PART 5

NATURAL SCIENCE, COOK'S ACHIEVEMENTS AND ANTARCTICA AFTER COOK

Chapter 14

Natural Science and Cook's Journals

It is wonderfull to see how the defferent Animals which inhabited this little spot [Staten Island] are reconciled to each other, they seem to have entered into a league not to disturb each others tranquillity. The Sea Lions occupy most of the Sea Coast, the Sea bears take up their aboad in the isle; the Shags take post on the highest clifts, the Penguins for their quarters where there is the most easiest communication to and from the sea and the other birds chuse more retired places ... I am neither a botanist nor a Naturalist and have not the words to describe the productions of Nature either in the one Science or the other.

James Cook, journal entry, 3 January 1775, leaving Staten Island and
Tierra del Fuego on the third leg of his circumnavigation of Antarctica

As *Resolution* departed Staten Island, James Cook wrote lengthy observations in his journal on the natural history encountered at Tierra del Fuego and Staten Island, including the relationships among species. He compared what he observed to domestic cattle and poultry in a farmyard of his youth near Marton, Yorkshire. Cook was neither botanist nor natural scientist in the same sense as Joseph Banks, Hermann Spöring, Anders Sparrman, Johann Reinhold Forster or George Forster, but I suggest he was a 'natural scientist' in the sense that, through experience, observation and study, he became an astronomer, a master surveyor and a ship's captain who attended to the health of sailors with a general understanding of eighteenth-century dietary requirements. As a navigator he had to understand weather and its impact on the oceans. He was a master of 'navigation science', practical knowledge gained through two decades of service in commercial vessels and in the Royal Navy. Moreover, the Admiralty required Cook to make observations about new lands he visited to document the physical geography, rocks, minerals, plants, vegetation and wildlife on land and in the seas, as well as native people encountered and their relationships to their physical environment. Natural science is in great part based upon observation and description. Cook's powers of observation, and those of the naturalists and officers who sailed in *Endeavour*, *Resolution*, *Adventure* and *Discovery*, are apparent from the journals and log books from all three voyages.

This chapter summarizes the scientific observations based upon those journals and log books.[1] It requires a study of Cook's voyages not in terms of a chronological narrative but as a topical approach to certain scientific information. It will begin with comments about eighteenth-century science and then focus on six topics:

- Navigation and astronomy
- Health and medicine on the high seas
- Temperatures during Antarctic summers
- The Southern Ocean
- Plants and vegetation
- Wildlife

Eighteenth-Century Natural Science

Eighteenth-century science included observation and classification, for which Swedish scientist Karl Linnaeus may be the foremost example. Naturalists directly or indirectly influenced by the Linnaean methodology participated in Cook's first two voyages. During the eighteenth century the scientific advances of the sixteenth and seventeenth centuries (from Galileo to Newton) were applied to the natural world. Scientific knowledge became not only part of culture but public knowledge through the filter of educated elites. During the later eighteenth century scientific work in botany and taxonomy made progress, areas of inquiry pursued by naturalists in this book such as Joseph Banks and J.R. Forster. Both production and consolidation of scientific knowledge had a significant impact upon society.

During the eighteenth century a transformation of knowledge occurred in natural history and geography, with 'a systematic analysis of virtually all the accessible parts of the planet' through scientific exploration. These activities were sometimes cooperative (such as the observation of the 1769 Transit of Venus), but they were also very competitive in commercial, political and imperial contexts. As we have seen, Captain Cook's Admiralty instructions were secret, with many details confined to a very few persons, even among those who sailed with him. Captain Cook's three voyages were a critically important part of this transformation of knowledge. The countries chiefly involved in this endeavour were Great Britain, France, Russia and Spain. Institutional support for such activities can be traced in the development of various scientific societies, such as the Royal Society for the Improving of Natural Knowledge and its counterparts in France, Berlin, St Petersburg and elsewhere.[2]

During Cook's voyages 'scientists' were referred to as 'naturalists' or 'botanists' and sometimes 'scientists', or collectively the 'scientific party'. Their written work was referred to as 'philosophical observations'. 'Natural science' included anything not made by humans, from the Earth to the Heavens, and was intermixed with philosophy and religion. As historians of science assert,

> Few people made an absolute divide between religion, the stuff of belief, and what was called natural philosophy, the stuff of experiment and analysis. Nor was natural history fully divisible from religion. Natural theology, or

the study of the relationships between God and the natural world, continued to be pursued well into the nineteenth century.[3]

Today, scientific disciplines are highly compartmentalized and specialized. In the eighteenth century the study of biology or botany was not included in the traditional classical college curricula. To study botany at Oxford University, 'gentleman-scientist' Joseph Banks sponsored a series of lectures focused on botany by a professor then affiliated with Cambridge University.[4] Banks became a Fellow of the Royal Society in 1766. After Cook's first voyage, Joseph Banks went on to organize collections from his travels at the British Museum and to develop the Chelsea Physic Garden and the Royal Botanical Garden at Kew. Johann Reinhold Forster was sent on Cook's second voyage on the recommendation of the Royal Society to prepare 'philosophical observations' of what he observed. As a student, Forster had studied languages, natural history and theology. He became a respected ornithologist, as testified by his numerous journal entries about bird species observed.

Navigation and Astronomy (The Marine Chronometer, *Aurora Australis* and Navigational Data)

The Marine Chronometer

Captain Cook's journals for the summer months of 1772–1774 contain documentation of longitude determined by both observation and the chronometer. Cook usually described the chronometer as 'the clock', or 'Mr. Kendall's Clock'. (An example of a chronometer by watchmaker John Harrison is shown in Plate 15.) Larcum Kendall[5] prepared two of the chronometers which travelled on the second voyage, during which the reliability of the devices was evaluated.

Cook often daily recorded longitude and latitude in his journal, sometimes by both observation and the chronometer. Comparisons of longitude determined by observation and the chronometer demonstrated only a very small variance, as shown in the following table showing comparisons from 11 December 1772 to 23 March 1773.

During this nearly four-month period Cook recorded in his journal longitude by both observation and the chronometer on thirty-eight occasions. Zero variance occurred on 11 December 1772. The greatest variance was 1.74° on 22 March 1773. A variance of less than half a degree is noted on seventeen occasions and a variation of less than one degree was recorded on twenty-eight occasions (*see* Figure 22). A table with similar conclusions can be produced for the same-time frame for 1773–1774, also in the Southern Ocean. The chronometer was therefore evaluated as accurate in determining longitude, and moreover was functional regardless of oceanic conditions.

On 14 March 1773 Cook recorded in his journal that the variance 'has not much exceeded two degrees'. On 8 January 1774 he wrote, 'indeed, our error can never be great so long as we have so good a guide as Mr. Kendall's watch'. In his letter of 19 March 1775 to Philip Stevens, Secretary to the Admiralty, Cook

Figure 22. Comparison of longitude by observation and the marine chronometer, first crossing of the Antarctic Circle, 1772–1773. James Cook did not record longitude by both observation and the chronometer on every day in his journal. (Data examples: 25.28 = 25° 48')

Date	Longitude Observ.	Longitude Chronom.	Variance	Date	Longitude Observ.	Longitude Chronom.	Variance
11-Dec-72	25.28	25.28	0	28-Jan-73	51.46	51.33	-0.13
14-Dec-72	22.13	22.1	-0.03	31-Jan-73	56.48	56.49	0.01
17-Dec-72	23.43	23.28	-0.15	2-Feb-73	59.35	59.33	-0.02
21-Dec-72	29.24	29.23	-0.01	6-Feb-73	58.22	58.32	0.10
24-Dec-72	31.19	31.3	0.11	7-Feb-73	61.48	61.47	-0.01
2-Jan-73	9.45	10.17	0.72	10-Feb-73	64.53	64.49	-0.04
3-Jan-73	9.35	10.6	1.25	12-Feb-73	70.20	70.10	-0.10
7-Jan-73	28.03	28.08	0.05	13-Feb-73	72.34	72.24	-0.10
8-Jan-73	33.02	32.38	-0.64	18-Feb-73	83.44	83.00	-0.44
10-Jan-73	36.07	35.48	-0.59	19-Feb-73	87.43	86.59	-0.84
12-Jan-73	38.14	37.47	-0.67	20-Feb-73	91.44	90.56	-0.88
14-Jan-73	39.38	38.36	-1.02	25-Feb-73	95.15	94.27	-0.88
15-Jan-73	39.38	38.35	-1.03	26-Feb-73	97.52	97.07	-0.45
16-Jan-73	39.35	38.32	-1.03	3-Mar-73	109.59	109.15	-0.44
19-Jan-73	40.12	39.9	-0.22	6-Mar-73	117.59	117.19	-0.40
22-Jan-73	43.25	42.35	-0.9	7-Mar-73	120.15	119.36	-0.79
23-Jan-73	46.15	45.31	-0.84	8-Mar-73	121.9	120.60	-1.3
27-Jan-73	50.46	50.32	-0.14	14-Mar-73	135.51	134.42	-1.09
11-Dec-72	25.28	25.28	0	20-Mar-73	51.46	51.33	-0.13

concluded, 'Mr. Kendalls Watch has exceeded the expectations of its most Zealous advocate and by being now and then corrected by Lunar observations has been our faithfull guide through all the vicissitudes of climates.' This is high praise indeed from a navigator who asserted he could find his location accurately anywhere on the ocean using only traditional methods of observation.

The *Aurora Australis*

The astronomical phenomenon of the Southern Lights was observed several times in February 1773. Cook's entry on 17 February indicates that the lights were similar to those known as the Northern Lights but he did not recall previous voyages referencing them in the southern hemisphere. In a revised journal entry Cook commented that, 'the officer of the Watch observed that it sometimes broke out in spiral rays and in a circular form, then its light was very strong and its appearance beautifull, he could not perceive it had any particular direction for it appear'd at various times in different parts of the Heavens and difused its light throughout the whole atmosphere'.

Similar observations are found in Lieutenant Charles Clerke's log book, as well as in the journals of J.R. and George Forster. The latter described 'long columns of clear white light, shooting up from the horizon to the eastward, almost to the zenith, gradually spreading on the whole southern part of the sky'. He concluded that the southern lights differed from those in the north, 'being always of a whitish colour, whereas ours assume various tints, especially those of a fiery and purplish hue'.

In his 16 February journal entry, astronomer William Wales remarked that he asked the officers to notify him if they observed an 'extraordinary or uncommon appearance in the heavens'. Lieutenant Pickersgill told Wales that on the night of the 16th 'he had seen something like the *Aurora Borealis*', but it then vanished into the clouds. On the 17th Wales's journal entry compared the *Aurora Australis* with the *Aurora Borealis*:

> At 1 a.m. Mr. Clerke informed me that the same appearance Mr. Pickersgill had seen was very bright. I got up and found it the very same that we call the northern lights in England. [Wales further described the scene to the southeast] ... for about 10° high above the horizon was a whitish haze through which Stars of the third Magnitude were just discernible. All round the horizon was covered with thick clouds out of which rose streams of a pale reddish light that ascended towards the Zenith. These Streamers had not the motion they are sometimes seen to have in the Northern Parts of England, but were perfectly steady except just toward their edges, where they had a small, tremulous kind of motion.

On the 25th Wales recorded in his journal that the 'Southern Lights [are] very bright', and on 6 March he observed that they sometimes appeared through the clouds. On 15 March Wales remarked on, 'The Southern Lights very bright and exceeding beautiful, the colours as various and vivid as I have ever seen in the

North. The motion was also quick and very [curious?].' The lights appeared again on 18 March. Wales observed,

> the Southern Lights exceeding bright and beautifull. They formed a kind of semi-circular, or rainbow like form, the two Extremities of which were nearly in the East and West points of the horizon. This bow when it first appeared, passed a considerable way to the Northward of the Zenith; but rose by degrees, turning, as it were on its diameter; and passing through the Zenith, descended and [settled ?] towards the Southern horizon. These lights at one time were so bright that we could discern our shadows on the deck.

As explained in Chapter 6, *Adventure* and *Resolution* separated in the fog during the period 8–11 February 1773. Like Wales, William Bayly in *Adventure* (at 51° 10′ south latitude and 114° 2′ east longitude of Greenwich) also observed the *Aurora Australis*. On the 26th he wrote in his journal, 'This Evening saw the Aurora Australis, the Southern Lights, which was so bright you might see to read good print. This is the first time I have seen them.' (When Bayly completed this entry, *Resolution* was at 60° 24′ south and 104° 27′ east longitude, according to William Wales's journal.) In researching this phenomenon, Cliff Thornton concluded that the Southern Lights were particularly bright in February/March 1773 due to sunspot activity which resulted in solar storms reaching Earth with the aurora appearing and observable over a wide geographic area.[6]

Navigational Data
Cook sailed over 200,000 miles during his three voyages, covering 140 of Earth's 180 degrees of latitude. What does this mean on a daily basis, for example while crossing and sailing along the Antarctic Circle? This information is found in Cook's journal. Of course, the miles travelled were not subject to a specific requirement or timetable. In addition to the overall course set for the day (or weeks) ahead, distances covered each day were affected by the wind and weather, the condition of the ocean and any stops to gather floating ice for water, as well as observation and charting of territory.

Figure 23. *Resolution*'s Antarctic mileage totals during various months of 1772–1774 during the search for the Southern Continent.

Mileage Totals	3 December 1772 to 25 March 1773	29 November 1773 to 17 February 1774
Total Miles Recorded	8,776	7,416
Days Sailed	113	81
Average Miles Per Day	77.75	91.55
Median	71	94
Five Highest Daily Totals	163, 162, 158, 158, 155	184, 171, 161, 158, 158
Five Lowest Daily Totals	0, 2, 5, 13, 16	9, 10, 17, 20, 20

Figure 23 tracks *Resolution*'s daily distances travelled above 45° south (an arbitrary point). Antarctic summer voyages during 1772–1773 were about thirty days longer than those in 1773–1774. *Resolution* averaged 113 miles per day during the first leg of the Antarctic circumnavigation and 81 miles per day on the second leg. The data also covers those days in February 1773 when *Resolution* and *Adventure* became separated in an Antarctic fog, during which attempts were made to return to the point of separation. Distance was also affected by the time spent in searching for Cape Circumcision, as well as the need to complete sailing in high southern latitudes during the southern hemisphere's summer months.

Health and Medicine on the High Seas: Controlling Scurvy, Smoking the Ship, Cook's 'Billious Colick' and Sailing in Cold Weather

Controlling Scurvy

Captain Cook's efforts to prevent outbreaks or treat scurvy occurred during all three voyages. These methods included using a variety of foods and other methods to ward off the disease which imperilled many vessels on long-distance navigation. For example, during the search for Cape Circumcision, Cook' journal entry for 20 December 1772 records,

> Also began to make Wort from the Malt and give to such People as had symptoms of the Scurvy; one of them indeed is highly Scorbutick although he has been taking of the Rob [concentrated lemon or orange juice] for some time past without finding himself benefited therefrom, on the other hand the *Adventure* has had two men in a manner cured by it who came, even, from the Cape highly Scorbutick.

Wort is the sweet infusion of malt (before it ferments into beer). This sweet liquid was thought to cure scurvy and was favoured by Cook in treating the disease. *Resolution* carried 80 bushels of malt and 19 half-barrels of concentrated juice of malt when it departed Plymouth in 1772. Note that Cook judged the concentrated orange or lime juice as ineffective in this experiment.

George Forster graphically described his own onset of scurvy, writing in his journal on 1 March 1774,

> Excruciating pains, livid blotches, rotten gums and swelled legs, brought me extremely low in a few days, almost before I was aware of the disorder; and my stomach being very weak, through abstinence from the unwholesome and loathed diet, I could not take the wort in sufficient quantity to remove my complaint.

Forster judged the wort to be ineffective (although it was Cook's favourite remedy), and also commented that others 'crawled about the decks with the greatest difficulty'. Both Forsters preferred sauerkraut, 'that excellent antiscourbitic food'.

In his journal entry on 11 April 1769, Joseph Banks commented upon his personal efforts to ward off scurvy at Tahiti during the first voyage. He consumed 'Sower crout'

> constantly till our salted Cabbage was opened which I preferred as a pleasant substitute. Wort was served out almost constantly, of this I drank from a pint or more every evening but all this did not so entirely check the distemper as to prevent my feeling some small effects of it. About a fortnight ago my gums swelled and some small pimples rose in the inside of my mouth which threatened to become ulcers. I then flew to the lemon Juice which had been put up for me ... Every kind of liquor which I used was made sour with the Lemon juice No. 3 so that I took near 6 ounces a day of it. The effect was surprising, in less than a week my gums became as firm as ever and at this time I am troubled with nothing but a few pimples on my face which have not deterred me from leaving off the juice entirely.

For Banks, sauerkraut and lemon juice served as successful treatments while wort partially masked the effect of the disease.

Although Captain Cook achieved success in combating scurvy in *Endeavour* and *Resolution*, this practice did not occur routinely on *Adventure*. When the ships met up in Queen Charlotte Sound in July 1773, Cook learned that *Adventure*'s crew 'were sickly'. On the 29th he hoisted out one of the boats and visited *Adventure*, recording his observations and actions in his journal. He discovered that the sloop's cook had died and around twenty People had signs of 'Scurvy and Flux' (dysentery), with others showing symptoms. Cook ordered use of wort, marmalade of carrots and rob of lemons and oranges. He sent a written memorandum to Captain Furneaux ordering measures to be taken. The proposed solutions were to

> Brew Beer of the Inspissated juce of Wort, Essence of Spruce and Tea plants [all of which he had aboard] for all hands, if he could spare Water, if not for the Sick, to inlarge their allowance of Sour Krout, to boil Cabbage in their Pease, to serve Wine in lieu of spirit and lastly to shorten their allowance of Salt Meat.

Cook speculated that *Adventure*'s crew was more scorbutic when they arrived in New Zealand and spent their time there eating few if any vegetables.

Lieutenant Clerke's log book entry at Dusky Sound, New Zealand, on 28 March 1773 summed up Cook's efforts to maintain the crew's good health:

> in the best Order that I believe ever was heard of after such a long Passage at Sea [from the Cape of Good Hope to New Zealand] – particularly if we come to consult Climates; this happy state of Health was certainly owing to the Extraordinary indulgencies of Governt of Crowt [sauerkraut], Wheat, Malt, &c &c together with the strickt attention paid by Capt Cook to the Peoples Clenliness.

In addition to the curiously phrased 'extraordinary indulgences of Government of Crowt', salted cabbage prepared in casks was boiled and served as an alternative to sauerkraut to determine if it was beneficial to combat scurvy.

A new diet was something that seamen would often reject out of hand. In a revised addition to his 29 July 1773 entry, Cook outlined the role of a naval commander:

> To interduce any New article of food among Seamen, let it be ever so much for their good, requires both the example and Authority of a Commander, without both of which, it will be droped before the People are Sencible of the benefits resulting from it ... This obstinate kind of prejudice, by little and little, wore off and they began to like it as well as the others and now, I believe, there was hardly a man in the Ship that did not attribute our being so free of the Scurvy to Beer and Vegetables we made use of at Newzealand.

Through example (and psychological insight), Cook wrote in a note to his journal, he seldom had to order anyone to gather or eat vegetables which we know as a source of Vitamin C.

On 5 February 1775, in a lengthy journal passage, J.R. Forster extolled the use of sauerkraut:

> we are come to the last Cask of *Sower-krout*, the best preventative against the Scurvy ... We found the *Sowerkrout* so good, that we emptied about 60 Casks & 60 boxes of portable Soup, of 2 Canisters each at 25 lb. Which clearly proves, how much prejudice can operate upon the minds of people: In the *Endeavour* but few would eat Sowerkrout, but as some of the Crew in the *Endeavour* came into the *Resolution* they set the Example to the Rest & all ate very heartily both portable Soup with Pease & Sowerkrout, to which latter we must ascribe the preservation of the Crew from the Scurvy, though we have been longer out at Sea, from any European Port or Settlement & Refreshments, than any other ship whatsoever.

Forster's conclusions surely arose from a conversation with Cook or other officers. In Chapter 3 examples of foodstuffs including antiscourbitics are listed, including the quantities carried on *Resolution* and *Adventure*. In addition to malt and sauerkraut, other antiscourbitics included salted cabbage, portable broth (dehydrated meat extract or bouillon cubes), saloup (concentrated orange and lemon juice), mustard and marmalade of carrots. Mustard was intended for general use and was considered then as an antiscourbitic. Marmalade of carrots – carrot juice concentrated to the consistency of honey – was given in a dose of one spoonful mixed with water as a cure for scurvy.

Captain Cook held that wort was the best antiscourbitic. In his letter (probably dated 1 August 1775) to the Admiralty Secretary summarizing the foodstuffs sent on the voyage and the overall diet, Cook commented on the value of wort, 'sour krout', 'portable broth' and 'robs of lemon or orange'. He remarked that wort 'is without doubt one of ye best Antiscourbitic Sea Medicines', sauerkraut 'can never be enough recommend[ed]' and broth was 'very nourishing & valuable' (and also 'kept good to ye last)'. Cook deferred an assessment about concentrated lemon and orange juice since it was under the surgeon's care. However, on 10 March 1772 Cook requested the Navy Board provision *Resolution* and *Adventure* with robs of lemons and oranges because they were useful in *Endeavour*.[7]

Cook's letter also disclosed his opinion on foodstuffs available during the voyage. He believed sugar prevented scurvy but oil encouraged it, as fat produced by beef and pork. Cook proudly asserted that no 'Scourbitic people' were in *Resolution* from its journey from Queen Charlotte Sound to Tahiti but in *Adventure* 'many of her best men' were 'far gorne [gone] in that disease', once again indicating that Captain Furneaux did not assiduously follow through on Cook's directives. He observed that at Queen Charlotte Sound, *Resolution*'s crew lived 'on Fish, Spruce beer & Vegetables for upwards of two Months which eradicated every seed of ye Scurvy, & this was not ye only time we received this Benefit during the Voyage'.[8]

The absence of Vitamin C (ascorbic acid) causes scurvy. Providing foods with Vitamin C both cures and prevents the disease. Captain James Cook experimented with a variety of methods to prevent any outbreak of the disease. He also placed an emphasis on cleanliness, a useful practice to combat any disease. Naval historian N.A.M. Rodger points out that although scurvy occurred on long voyages, the 'real killers at sea' were typhus, malaria and yellow fever or other tropical diseases. By the end of the eighteenth century 'a healthy diet, including fresh meat and vegetables was indispensable'.[9] Prevention and cure were joined in 1795 when the Royal Navy ordered that the sailors' daily grog was to include ¾oz lemon juice. Admiral Edward Vernon ('Old Grog') ordered the daily ration of rum to be diluted with water in 1740. After 1795 grog was a mixture of rum, water and lemon juice. Lime juice was substituted in the mid-nineteenth century.[10]

Smoking the Ship
Cook routinely assessed the overall health and routine of his crew. He summarized his actions in a letter to Admiralty Secretary Philip Stephens, dated 1 August 1775. Cook stated that the crew were usually on a three-watch schedule,[11] except in unusual circumstances, and 'never broke their rest & were seldom Wet, consequently had always dry cloaths [clothes] to shift themselves'. The crew's hammocks, bedding and clothes were 'kept constantly clean & frequently examined into, especially after Wet rainy weather'. If clothing was wet, it was placed on the deck to air.[12]

Cook also believed that a clean ship would help maintain the health of the crew. Periodically the ship was 'smoked', when braziers of charcoal or smoking vinegar-flavoured gunpowder were carried between decks to relieve foul odours. Lieutenant Clerke recorded in his log one such occurrence on 21 December 1773: 'Clean'd ship and smok'd her with fire balls.' Cook recorded another example on 22 July 1776, 'Smoked the ship with Gunpowder, moistened with vinegar.' On Friday, 31 December 1773 Cook observed 'PM little wind with showers of snow and sleet. Middle fresh gales, latter [later] gentle breeze and clear pleasant weather; this gave us an opportunity to air the spare Sails and to clean and smoak the Ship betwixt decks.' As *Resolution* sailed past the Crozet Islands, Lieutenant Gore noted in his log book that on the 12th the ship was aired between decks and on the 15th they 'Clean'd & Smoak'd Ship below'. Master's Mate William Harvey in *Resolution*, as the sloop bore east from Kerguelen Island on 2 January 1777 recorded that they 'Clean'd and Smoak['d] between decks'. In his 1775 letter to the Admiralty, Cook stated the ship was smoked once or twice per week in both hot and cold weather. This process, he asserted, must not be neglected to eliminate 'putrified Air and a disagreable Smell below which nothing but fire & smoak will purify'. In insisting upon a clean ship, including clothes and hammocks, Cook's leadership was matched by other progressive commanders in the later eighteenth century whose actions limited the spread of disease.[13]

Sailing in Cold Weather

Travelling in the cold weather of Antarctic summer required suitable clothing. On 20 December 1772 Cook's journal describe how he 'set all the Taylors to work to lengthen the Sleves of the Seamaens Jackets and to make Caps to shelter them from the Severity of the Weather, having order'd a quantity of Red Baize [coarse woollen cloth] to be converted to that purpose'. William Hodges' painting 'Ice Islands on 9 January 1773' (*see* Plate 13) shows a sailor clad in baize harvesting ice. At 58° 55' south Cook wrote on 4 January,

> strong gales attended with thick Fogg Sleet and Snow, all the Rigging covered with Ice and the air excessive cold, the Crew however stand it tolerable well, each being cloathed with a fearnought Jacket, a pair of Trowsers of the same and a large Cap made of Canvas and Baise. These together with an additional glass of Brandy every Morning enables them to bear the Cold without Flinshing.

There can be little doubt that in high southern latitudes, in 30° and 40° weather, accompanied by rain, sleet, hail, snow, floating ice and ice islands, maintaining the ongoing operation of a sailing vessel must at times have been a difficult task for officers and the People. To furl or unfurl sails, the rigging must be climbed, whether or not it is encased in ice, and whether or not the ship is rolling on the high seas. Wet sails must be dried and stored, or repaired. Providing suitable clothing to match the severity of the weather is a further example of James Cook's attention to the health of sailors.

Cold also affected the animals. Sailing in the Antarctic Convergence at 58° 59' south on 28 February 1773 Cook's journal chronicled the birth and subsequent sudden death of a nine-piglet litter, 'notwithstanding all the care we could take of them', due to the cold (the journal recorded the noon temperature at 36½°F). He also recorded that 'several People on board have their feet and hands chilblain'd from the circumstances a judgment may be formed of the summer weather we injoy here'. Chilblains (inflammation of small blood vessels due to exposure to cold) may also be a manifestation of scurvy. Cook included himself among those affected by the Antarctic cold weather, a rare personal reference in the journals. During the third voyage some of the animals bound for the South Pacific died due to fouled food, cold weather and the lack of attention while at Kerguelen Island.

Medicine on the High Seas – Cook's 'Billious Collick'
A glimpse into eighteenth-century medical treatment for ailments is seen during Cook's serious attack of 'billious collick' (his term) from December 1773 to February 1774. On 27 December George Forster described Cook's condition: 'Captain Cook himself was likewise pale and lean, entirely lost his appetite and laboured under a perpetual costiveness [constipation].' Cook's bilious complaint continued through January and into February. On 8 February George Forster observed that Cook was confined to bed with 'violent pains' and loss of appetite, but the serious condition 'was concealed from every person in the ship' (presumably 'the People' rather than the officers with whom Cook was in regular contact). Cook was given no food, then purged (an enema), which led to 'violent vomiting'. He was also treated with opiates and hot baths and 'plasters of theriaca'[14], a universal curative, were applied to his abdominal area.

Despite these measures, Cook's discomfort continued. On 24 February he hiccupped for 24 hours. Forster wrote that Cook's 'life was entirely despaired of'.[15] Forster observed that the baths and plasters relaxed the patient during the week the captain was in 'imminent danger'. Shortly afterwards J.R. Forster's dog was butchered to provide broth and meat. Cook gradually recovered. On 27 February 1774 he wrote his only journal reference to this episode that lasted over two months, commenting that he 'was taken ill of the Billious colick and so Violent as to confine me to my bed'. In a revised journal entry, Cook also commented that Forster's dog 'fell a Sacrifice to my tender stomack; we had no other fresh meat whatever on board, and I could eat of this flesh as well as broth made of it, thus I received nourishment and strength from food which would have made most people in Europe sick, so true that is it that necessity is govern'd by no law'.

While Cook was out of action, Lieutenant Richard Cooper was in charge of *Resolution*. On 27 February Cook acknowledged Cooper's work as satisfactory. He also described *Resolution*'s surgeon James Patten as 'not only a skilfull Physician but a tender Nurse'.

In a study marking the 200th anniversary of Cook's voyages (1979), physician James Watt examined the medical aspects of the second voyage and concluded that a parasitic infection in the lower ileum of the intestine caused Captain Cook's distress. His symptoms included fatigue, digestive disturbances, fever, vomiting and constipation. Cook likely received the parasite, probably a roundworm, as a result of eating tainted meat in Tahiti. The recurrence of 'bilious colick' reappeared during the third voyage negatively affecting Cook's behaviour, causing irritability, outbursts and loss of concentration, among other symptoms.[16]

Temperatures While Sailing in the Antarctic Summer

Log books contain daily records of the weather at noon and other factors such as barometric pressure. Cook recorded some of the daily temperature readings in his journal during the Antarctic portions of his travels. These are summarized in Figures 24 and 25.

These tables demonstrate that the temperatures hovered in the 30°s Fahrenheit during December and January. The fluctuations are explained by following *Resolution*'s track across the Southern Ocean. Cook sailed south across the

Figure 24. Temperatures recorded in Cook's journal sailing towards the Antarctic Circle, December 1772 to February 1773. Data was not recorded every day. (Data examples: 43.53° = 43° 52')

Date	South Latitude°	Temp. (F)	Date	South Latitude°	Temp. (F)
2 Dec 1772	43.52°	49.5	6 Jan 1773	60.18°	34.5
3 Dec 1772	44.28°	49.0	8 Jan 1773	61.22°	35.5
4 Dec 1772	45.46°	43.0	9 Jan 1773	61.36°	35.0
6 Dec 1772	48.11°	38.0	11 Jan 1773	63.12°	35.5
7 Dec 1772	49.32°	42.5	13 Jan 1773	64.18°	36.0
8 Dec 1772	49.36°	40.0	16 Jan 1773	64.31°	34.0
9 Dec 1772	49.48°	36.0	17 Jan 1773	66.36°	34.0
10 Dec 1772	50.57°	36.5	23 Jan 1773	60.04°	32.0
11 Dec 1772	51.37°	34.0	24 Jan 1773	58.24°	34.5
12 Dec 1772	52.56°	31.0	26 Jan 1773	57.10°	35.0
13 Dec 1772	54.00°	31.5	27 Jan 1773	56.28°	35.0
14 Dec 1772	54.55°	29.0	29 Jan 1773	52.29°	38.0
15 Dec 1772	55.10°	30.0	30 Jan 1773	51.34°	39.5
16 Dec 1772	55.08°	32.0	1 Feb 1773	48.51°	41.5
17 Dec 1772	55.16°	33.5	6 Feb 1773	48.06°	43.5
18 Dec 1772	54.57°	31.0	7 Feb 1773	48.49°	45.0
20 Dec 1772	54.00°	31.0	8 Feb 1773	49.05°	40.5
21 Dec 1772	54.10°	31.0	10 Feb 1773	50.07°	40.5
22 Dec 1772	54.34°	31.0	11 Feb 1773	51.25°	40.0
23 Dec 1772	55.26°	32.0	12 Feb 1773	52.48°	38.0
24 Dec 1772	56.31°	31.0	13 Feb 1773	53.54°	36.0
25 Dec 1772	57.50°	31.0	14 Feb 1773	55.23°	35.0
26 Dec 1772	58.31°	31.0	15 Feb 1773	56.52°	36.5
27 Dec 1772	58.19°	31.0	18 Feb 1773	57.57°	30.0
28 Dec 1772	58.44°	35.0	19 Feb 1773	58.30°	33.0
29 Dec 1772	59.12°	31.0	21 Feb 1773	59.00°	36.0
30 Dec 1772	59.23°	36.0	23 Feb 1773	61.00°	35.0
31 Dec 1772	59.58°	31.0	25 Feb 1773	60.40°	35.0
1 Jan 1773	60.12°	31.0	26 Feb 1773	61.08°	33.0
2 Jan 1773	59.12°	31.0	27 Feb 1773	60.28°	35.0
3 Jan 1773	59.18°	31.0	28 Feb 1773	59.58°	36.5

Figure 25. Temperatures recorded in Cook's journal sailing towards the Antarctic Circle, December 1773 to February 1774. Data was not recorded every day. (Data examples: 47.04° = 47° 04′)

Date	South Latitude°	Temperature (F)	Date	South Latitude°	Temperature (F)
1 Dec 1743	47.04°	49.0	9 Jan 1774	48.17°	51.3
2 Dec 1773	48.23°	46.0	10 Jan 1774	48.07°	52.5
3 Dec 1773	48.56°	47.0	11 Jan 1774	47.51°	50.0
5 Dec 1773	50.15°	47.0	12 Jan 1774	49.23°	56.0
6 Dec 1773	50.50°	49.0	13 Jan 1774	52.00°	52.5
7 Dec 1773	55.07°	49.0	14 Jan 1774	53.54°	51.3
12 Dec 1773	62.46°	32.0	15 Jan 1774	56.04°	51.0
13 Dec 1773	63.42°	32.0	16 Jan 1774	56.19°	47.8
14 Dec 1773	64.55°	32.0	18 Jan 1774	60.54°	40.0
15 Dec 1773	65.52°	31.0	20 Jan 1774	62.34°	40.0
16 Dec 1773	64.16°	31.0	21 Jan 1774	62.26°	37.0
17 Dec 1773	64.41°	33.8	22 Jan 1774	62.09°	37.0
20 Dec 1773	65.57°	33.0	23 Jan 1774	62.22°	38.5
21 Dec 1773	66.50°	33.0	24 Jan 1774	63.40°	39.0
22 Dec 1773	67.27°	31.0	25 Jan 1774	65.24°	42.0
23 Dec 1773	67.12°	33.0	26 Jan 1774	66.36°	40.0
24 Dec 1773	67.19°	32.0	27 Jan 1774	69.35°	37.5
25 Dec 1773	66.23°	34.0	28 Jan 1774	69.35°	36.0
26 Dec 1773	65.15°	37.0	29 Jan 1774	70.00°	36.5
27 Dec 1773	65.53°	35.0	30 Jan 1774	70.48°	32.5
28 Dec 1773	64.20°	35.0	31 Jan 1774	69.13°	34.0
30 Dec 1773	61.05°	33.8	1 Feb 1774	68.01°	35.0
31 Dec 1773	59.46°	31.5	2 Feb 1774	67.07°	37.0
1 Jan 1774	59.09°	36.5	3 Feb 1774	66.25°	33.0
2 Jan 1774	57.58°	38.5	4 Feb 1774	65.42°	34.5
3 Jan 1774	56.46°	36.0	5 Feb 1774	64.06°	38.5
4 Jan 1774	54.55°	46.3	6 Feb 1774	63.54°	39.5
5 Jan 1774	53.43°	46.8	7 Feb 1774	61.06°	40.0
6 Jan 1774	52.00°	47.0	8 Feb 1774	58.05°	41.5
7 Jan 1774	50.36°	50.0	9 Feb 1774	55.39°	47.0
8 Jan 1774	49.07°	49.8	10 Feb 1774	53.37°	47.0

Antarctic Circle (66° 36′ south) until he met the impassable ice barrier surrounding the continent in those three locations reached in January and December 1773 and January 1774. *Resolution* retreated from the ice barrier northwards and then approached the Circle again at high latitudes. During the first two legs of Cook's Antarctic circumnavigation, thirty-two days were spent at temperatures below 40°F, and on eight days temperatures were between 30° and 32°F. Below the Antarctic Circle, temperatures of 31° to 33°F were recorded on four days, with a further eight days from 35½° to 37°F. In a sense, the Antarctic ice barrier func-

Figure 26. Temperatures recorded in Cook's journals at South Georgia and the South Sandwich Islands (1775).

Date	Temperature(s) in Fahrenheit	Date	Temperature(s) in Fahrenheit
14-Jan-75	35–37.5	10-Feb-75	34.5
15-Jan-75	35.5	11-Feb-75	35.66
20-Jan-75	39–41	13-Feb-75	29
28-Jan-75	35	14-Feb-75	32
6-Feb-75	38	17-Feb-75	32
9-Feb-75	40		

Figure 27. Temperatures recorded in Cook's journal at Kerguelen Island, December 1776.

Date	Temperature(s) in Fahrenheit	Date	Temperature(s) in Fahrenheit
23-Dec-76	44–49.5	28-Dec-76	44.5–57
24-Dec-76	40–47.5	29-Dec-76	44.5–50
25-Dec-76	43–50.5	30-Dec-76	45–48
26-Dec-76	45–50.5	31-Dec-76	40–45.5
27-Dec-76	43.5–52.25		

tioned in a similar way to an ice cube in a glass of liquid, cooling everything in which it came into contact. As ships moved away from the ice barrier, temperatures became warmer, as illustrated in the tables.

Temperature data were also recorded at South Georgia, the South Sandwich Islands and during the search for Cape Circumcision where thermometer readings fluctuated between 30° and 40°F, as seen in Figure 26, during January and February 1775. The daily data in Figure 27 are from Master Joseph Gilbert's log book. Temperatures at Kerguelen Island (23–31 December 1776) ranged from 40° to 50°F.

The Southern Ocean: Ice, Ice Islands, Frozen Salt Water and the 'Milkish Sea'

Ice and Ice Islands

Cook's travels in the Southern Ocean make frequent reference to ice in various forms: floating ice on the seas gathered for water, larger and dangerous pieces of floating ice known as growlers, and icebergs, sometimes over a mile in length, some with jagged features reminiscent of English cathedrals or other architecture. Cook called icebergs 'Ice Islands'. The *Oxford English Dictionary* identifies 1774 as the first use of the word 'iceberg' in English. Cook encountered his first ice island on 10 December 1772 at 50° 57′ south, 20° 45′ east, and saw his final iceberg on 28 February 1775 at 50° 52′ south and 26° 31′ east. His journal records ice islands ranging in size from 100 to 400ft high, and 1 to 3 miles 'in circuit'. Both tabular (flat) and perpendicular icebergs are cited. At times more than two hundred ice islands were sighted in a single day.

In describing ice islands, Cook used more colourful language than was typical. For example, at 61° south on 24 February 1773 he remarked that the pieces which break from larger ice islands

> are more dangerous than the Islands themselves, the latter are generally seen at a sufficient distance to give time to steer clear of them, whereas the others cannot be seen in the night or thick weather till they are under the Bows: great as those dangers are, they are now become so familiar to us that the apprehensions they cause are never of long duration and are in some measure compensated by the very curious and romantick Views many of these islands exhibit and which are greatly heightened by the foaming and dashing of the waves against them and into the several holes and caverns which are formed in the most of them, in short the whole exhibits a View which can only be described [by] the pencle [pencil] of an able painter and at once fills the mind with admiration and horror, the first is occasioned by the beautifulness of the Picture and the latter by the danger attending it, for was a ship to fall aboard one of these large pieces of ice she would be dashed to pieces in a moment.

Astronomer William Wales provided vivid examples of sailing among ice and ice islands on 17 February 1773. In the late morning *Resolution* sailed near an iceberg to obtain ice to be melted into water. In his log book Wales wrote that the sloop was

> by some kind of indraught or some how or other, sucked so near so I did not think there was the least possibility of Escaping without being drove against it which must have meant inevitable destruction; but, through the miraculous interposition of Providence, I believe, for the means were Unknown, as these which set us on, we got clear of it, and was not a cable's length off when a piece as big as the Ship broke off from that very part we were so near to. This piece soon broke into lesser ones by being drove against the Island, and as soon as the Ship was got to a convenient distance, the boats were hoisted out to pick it up; after which they were hoisted out again, and we made sail.

This is reminiscent of the William Hodges ice islands painting (*see* Plates 7 and 13) depicting sailors in boats gathering ice for water, picking up pieces of ice with their bare hands and using a pick axe to break the bigger pieces, while officers are shown standing in small boats and firing at ducks or other sea fowl. The sailors obtained several tons of fresh water by this method.

Captain Cook's thoughts on the formation of icebergs matured during the second voyage. He initially thought they formed in rivers and bays, and then floated into the ocean. However, at Possession Bay, South Georgia, on 17 January 1775 he observed ice falling from a glacier into the bay that 'made a noise like a cannon': this was an example of an iceberg calving. As for the many icebergs encountered on his journey of circumnavigation, Cook wrote, 'but this isle [South Georgia] cannot produce the ten thousand part of what we have seen, either there must be more land [somewhere else] or else ice is formed without it'. One month later, during the final search for Bouvet's Cape Circumcision, Cook formed a more definite opinion, concluding, 'the snow may fix and consolidate to ice to most of the other coasts and there also form Ice clifts. These clifts accumulate by continual fall of snow and what drifts from the Mountains till they are no longer able to support their own weight and then large pieces break off which we call Ice Islands.'

In January 1773 Cook fretted about spending time searching 'after these imaginary lands'. After reaching Bouvet's coordinates again on 21 February 1775 he concluded that Bouvet's Cape was 'nothing but an Island of Ice'. If it was land, Cook confidently asserted it would not have been missed. Moreover there was no proof of land such as seals, penguins or birds. Cook speculated that 'Ice hills had deceived us as well as Mr. Bouvet'. This is a rare instance in which Cook was incorrect. British whalers located Cape Circumcision thirty-three years later (1808) and fixed its coordinates at 54° 26′ south latitude, 3° 24′ east longitude. Cook missed Bouvet's Island 19 square mile (49 sq. km) ice-filled crater by about three degrees in 1775. Certainly Bouvet's Island resembles one of Cook's Ice Islands.

Frozen Salt Water

An unresolved issue in the eighteenth century was whether or not salt water would freeze. We now know that it does freeze at 28.4°F (-2°C). Cook's thinking about this issue is reflected in his journal. For example, on 13 January 1773 Cook wrote, 'Some curious and interesting experiments are wanting to know what effect cold has on Sea Water in some of the following instances: does it freeze or does it not? If it does, what degree of cold is necessary and what becomes of Salt Brine? For all the Ice we meet with yields Water perfectly sweet and fresh.' At this point Cook did not distinguish between ice calved from glaciers to eventually form ice islands and ice that might be formed by freezing surface sea water. This matter also led to disputes among scientists and their supporters. As we saw in Chapter 12, this very issue led to a separation between J.R. Forster and Daines Barrington at the conclusion of the second voyage.

Mystery of the 'Milkish Sea'

An unusual oceanic phenomenon occurred in February 1775. On the night of 4 February, as *Resolution* sailed along the South Sandwich Islands, the ship encountered a 'Milkish Sea'. At 57° 11′ south and 27° 6′ west, a portion of the sea turned white as milk. Cook recorded in his journal that this 'Alarmed the officer of the Watch [Lieutenant Clerke] so much that he tacked the ship instantly'. This was no reflection of the clouds upon the ocean, Cook concluded, and it was something he had never seen before. Clerke gave a descriptive account in his log book:

> Just before 12 this Evening I saw a change in the colour of the Water that a good deal alaurm'd me – it was a large patch of [water] perfectly white as milk about 100 yards in estimate – The weather was Cloudy and very dark and when we first observ'd this extraordinary appearance it was close under the SW bow – I immediately put the ship helm down [tacked] for I apprehended danger from it, but what with the large swell she missed stays and of course fell round off into it – I threw over the lead but could find no Ground – I took up a bucket of water upon supposition it might be small Ice – but there was not a particle of Ice, or any other perceptible matter in the water, so what could occasion this strange a change in the Colour of it I'm still at a loss to divine – some might be of opinion it might be the spawn of fish – possibly it might – but for my own part I've frequently seen large quantities of spawn which in the Night was a very extraordinary show in the water – but I never had any idea and have very little now of its affecting so very great a change as we last night met with.

Notice the quick succession of actions and both the urgency and bewilderment this phenomenon caused at the time: an immediate tack of the ship to avoid danger, an attempt to find ground, examining a bucket of ocean water, and then guesses as to what the sudden change in the colour of the ocean meant. J.R. Forster must have been in his cabin at the time but he makes no reference to the 'Milkish Sea'. He reported the temperature on the deck was 37° and 41° in his cabin, but he did not identify the time of day. Similarly, there is no reference in George Forster's journal or Lieutenant Robert Cooper's log book. Master Joseph Gilbert's log book carries an entry indicating that the ship was tacked to avoid ice; this may refer to the incident since it was recorded in the late evening of 4 February. Captain Cook returned to the incident in his 5 February journal, stating he could not account for the ocean's colour.

The cause of the 'Milkish Sea' was the microscopic bacterium *Vibrio harveyi*. Between 4° and 35°C these bacteria colonize and emit a bluish light, which often appears white on the ocean's surface. It is primarily an Indian Ocean phenomenon, whereas the South Sandwich Islands lie in the far South Atlantic Ocean. Ocean temperatures were in the mid- to high 30° range during *Resolution*'s visit to the South Sandwich Islands. The 'Milkish Sea' was a one-day phenomenon. After 5 February the ocean resumed its normal colour and *Resolution* continued sailing through the South Sandwich island chain. More recently, examples of bioluminescence have been documented from space.[17]

Plants and Vegetation

A reading of Cook's journals suggests that the sub-Antarctic islands are windblown, treeless landscapes. However, the Southern Ocean expeditions did find some plant life. During the brief visit to Possession Bay, South Georgia, one moss

Common Name/location	Cook's Journal Description	Scientific Name
Cushion Plant Kerguelen Island	"Saxifrage which grows in large spreading tufts to a considerable way up the sides of the hills"	*Azorella selago*
Kerguelen Cabbage Kerguelen Island	Like a small cabbbage, eaten raw as an antiscourbitic. Similar to "New Zealand scurvy grass." "We frequently eat it raw … rank in flavour by being boiled." Perhaps introduce as a "Pot-herb in our kitchen gardens"	*Pinglea antiscorbutica*
Cress Kerguelen	Like garden cress. Very fiery in taste	*Ranunculus crassipes*
Antarctic Water Starwort Kerguelen	Very small androgynous plant	*Callitriche antarctica*
Tussock Grass South Georgia	Coarse grass cut as food for cattle	*Poa flabellata*
Moss (unspecified) South Georgia	"Plant like Moss which grows on rocks"	Probably a cushionry flower plant, *Colobanthus crossifolius (Beaglehole)*
Lichen Kerguelen Island	"A beautiful species of lichen. Grows upon the rocks higher up"	*Neuropogen taylori*
Wild Burnet South Georgia	Wild Burnet	*Acena adscendens*
Grass "A" – Kerguelen	A coarse grass cut for cattle	*Poa cookii*
Grass "B" – Kerguelen	A "smaller sort which is rarer." Perhaps Antarctic Hair Grass	*Deschampsia antarctica*
Grass "C" – Kerguelen	"a sort of Goose Grass"	*Cotula pulmssa*

Figure 28. Plants identified in Cook's journals at South Georgia (1775) and Kerguelen Island (1776).

and two plants were identified. In his journal entry for 17 January 1775 Cook identified wild burnet and tussock grass ('a coarse bladed grass which grows in tufts'). Moreover, Chapter 11 recounts J.R. Forster's colourful description of tussock grass providing cover for seals and penguins and nesting places for shags. The soil of the country, he suggested, is improved by dung from the animals that find cover in the tussock grass.

Captain Cook's description of South Georgia's plants shows he used a layman's approach to botany, as opposed to using the system developed by Linnaeus or others (J.C. Beaglehole's version of Cook's journals inserts the Latin nomenclature as journal footnotes). The plants identified in Cook's journal at Kerguelen and South Georgia, with his description and their scientific names are given in Figure 28 (*see* Plates 25–28).

As referenced in Chapter 13, in 1772 Captain Kerguelen assumed (or wanted to believe) the 'green colour' of the island he is credited with discovering, as viewed from a telescope, was due to trees and shrubs. Four years later Captain Cook identified the 'lively green' as due to the cushion plant, in which 'one sinks a foot or two at every step', and which might serve as fuel if dried. One of the grasses, *Poa Cookii*, was named after Cook. The other plant of note is the Kerguelen Cabbage, an antiscourbitic.

Wildlife: Whales, Seals, Penguins and Oceanic Birds

Cook's journals and other sources frequently cite 'whales playing about the ship' during the circumnavigations of Antarctica, visits to South Georgia and the South Sandwich Islands, occasionally during the coastline survey at Kerguelen Island, and during the search for Cape Circumcision. The whale species are not identified. Seals and sea-lions were noted at Staten Island and South Georgia, the latter producing the planet's largest annual quantity of seals. Elephant seals are not specifically cited, but 'large' seals are mentioned at both South Georgia and Kerguelen Island, where significant colonies are located. *Resolution*'s Master, Joseph Gilbert cited 'Haunts of . . . sea monsters' in his 20 January 1775 log book entry, which might refer to the huge male southern elephant seal.

Penguins are frequently mentioned. I conclude that eighteenth-century sailors found penguins as fascinating as we do today. J.R. Forster is credited with naming two penguin species, the chinstrap (1788) and the rockhopper (1781). King penguins were sighted (and eaten) at South Georgia. Other penguins likely seen were the gentoo (Antarctica, South Georgia, South Sandwich Islands and Kerguelen) and the chinstrap (Antarctica, South Georgia and South Sandwich Islands). Antarctica is also home to Adélie penguins (not classified until 1840) and Cook sighted a 'yellow-eyed' penguin in New Zealand waters. The emperor penguin is native to Antarctica and its scientific name acknowledges J.R. Forster (*Aptenodytes forsteri*, 1844); he may have seen emperors off Antarctica but considered them to be king penguins instead.

Cook's journals refer to thirteen families of birds in Antarctic and sub-Antarctic waters (*see* Plates 29–32). His journals cite six varieties of albatross, skuas (Cook's

'Port Egmont Hens'), eight varieties of petrel, shearwaters, fulmars and prions, the Dominican gull (also called the southern black-backed gull or kelp gull), two varieties of tern, two varieties of shag (cormorants) and one songbird, the South Georgia pipit (which Cook termed a lark), the only songbird native to South Georgia. Cook occasionally recorded sighting an 'Egg Bird' which J.C. Beaglehole suggests is the sooty tern.[18] Captain Cook held favourable opinions about Port Egmont Hens and cited their presence frequently. For Cook, Port Egmont Hens and 'Egg Birds' suggested the ship was near land. Port Egmont is the location of the first British settlement on the West Falkland Islands (1765). Although Cook never visited the Falklands, he was familiar with Commodore Byron's account of his circumnavigation in *Dolphin* (1764–1766) and his visit to Port Egmont.

Conclusions

Journals and log books from the second voyage yield a good deal of scientific information based upon observation and recording of data. Readings from the marine chronometers were compared to observational data, proving the usefulness of the chronometer. Attempts to control scurvy were made and the results reported to the Admiralty. Phenomena such as the *Aurora Australis* and the 'milkish sea' were observed and recorded. A growing catalogue of plants, vegetation and wildlife was documented, with samples returned to England for study. Ice and ice islands were similarly described, while debating whether salt water could freeze and how icebergs formed. Documented daily temperatures from this era are investigated today to determine changes in climate.

In terms of geography, Cook crossed the Arctic Circle three times. Moreover, the mystery of *Terra Australis Incognita* ended with Cook's voyages, the 'great object you are always to have in view' during his travels. Except for Tierra del Fuego, the sub-Antarctic islands Cook visited were uninhabited, ruling out contemporary theories. Artists William Hodges and John Webber produced the world's 'first paintings' of South Georgia and Kerguelen Island and the log books provided various sketches of anchorages. At the end of Cook's first 'ice edge cruise', J.C. Beaglehole observed, 'To complete four months in high latitudes in a small ship would in itself be an achievement; to navigate without accident in one of the stormiest oceans of the world, hampered by fog, and constantly among icebergs, was a very remarkable achievement of seamanship indeed.'[19]

Cook's memorials may be 'geography and navigation', but the scientific information from the journals and log books also make an important contribution to our knowledge about the Southern Ocean and the area below the Antarctic Convergence, information that was useful in the eighteenth century and remains so today.

Chapter 15

Cook's Search for Antarctica – Navigation in High Southern Latitudes

I who had Ambition not only to go further than any one had done before, but as far as it was possible for man to go ...

Captain James Cook, journal entry, 30 January 1774

No previous navigator had contributed voyages of such length; remained at sea for such long periods, or brought back so much accurate knowledge of such an immense extent of the Earth.

A. Grenville Price, *The Explorations of Captain James Cook in the Pacific*

He was (and he still is) the meticulous and infinitely careful explorer by sea, the most consistent and the greatest sailing ship seaman there ever was.

Captain Alan Villiers, *Captain James Cook*

He recorded his discoveries with an exactness which raised exploration to the dignity of a science.

Ian Cameron, *Lodestone & Evening Star: The Epic Voyages of Discovery, 1493 B.C.–1896 A.D.*

There are statues and inscriptions; but Geography and Navigation are his memorials ... If we wish for more, an ocean is enough, where the waves fall on innumerable reefs, and a great wind blows from the south-east with the revolving world.

John Cawte Beaglehole, *Life of Captain James Cook*

As the Admiralty's instructions for the *Endeavour* voyage emphasized, the discovery of the Southern Continent was the objective James Cook was 'always to have in view'. During the first voyage he sought Antarctica in the vicinity of Cape Horn (to 60° south) as well as 40° south of Tahiti. Location of the unknown Southern Continent served as the main purpose of the second voyage. Cook verified Kerguelen Island's location at the beginning of the third voyage, tasked with assessing its potential as a safe harbour and a source of water and wood. But the major (secret) goal of the third voyage was finding the Northwest Passage, 140° to the north of Antarctica. Navigation in high latitudes, both south and north, served as critically important features of Cook's three voyages. A glance at a world map tracing the three voyages (*see* map, p. xiv) shows the vast extent of his travels, delineating the Pacific and Southern Oceans as never before. Historical context is very important. We must measure Cook's achievements based upon eighteenth-century knowledge about the globe, as well as the entire context of his three voyages, and not in the light of our present-day understanding about Antarctica or its location.

This study concludes that James Cook's navigation in high southern latitudes represent accomplishments that can summarized in thirteen categories, the last three of which apply to Cook's voyages overall, as well as to the search for Antarctica.

1. Extending the Legacy of Past Navigators

'Endurance' is the watchword for navigators/explorers, often in the face of difficult odds. It applies to Antarctic explorer/navigator James Cook as well as to many others. Navigation not only required endurance but navigators faced ever-present danger as well as disease. Captain Cook, of course, was killed by a Polynesian warrior in Hawai'i in 1779. Of contemporary French navigators, Jean-Francois-Marie de Surville died in a skiff accident off Peru (1770), Marc-Joseph Marion du Fresne was killed by Maori in New Zealand (1772), Julien-Marie Crozet died at sea in the Indian Ocean (1780) and Jean-Francois de La Pérouse died in a storm off the Solomon Islands (1788). Others also died on Cook's voyages. A partial list includes Charles Clerke from tuberculosis off Siberia (1779), artist and epileptic Alexander Buchan (1769), artist Sydney Parkinson off Batavia (1771), astronomer Charles Green after departing Batavia (1771), Surgeon William Anderson from tuberculosis off Alaska (1778), Surgeon Monkhouse off Batavia (1770), the Tahitian prince and master navigator Tupia and his servant off Batavia (1770), and Banks's two servants at Tierra del Fuego (1769). The Massacre at Grass Cove resulted in the deaths of two Maori and ten British sailors in *Adventure* (1773). As this list shows, navigators faced dangers from storms, accidents, disease and violence. Other deaths occurred during the exploration of Antarctica as recently as a century ago (*see* Chapter 16). As we have seen in the foregoing chapters, James Cook and other navigators endured numerous challenges in exploring the Southern Ocean. Cook followed in the wake of 250 years of navigation which began with Ferdinand Magellan's discovery of the South American strait that bears his name (1519) and the subsequent realization that Tierra del Fuego was not connected to *Terra Australis Incognita*. In 1578 Francis Drake was driven eastwards in his efforts to round Cape Horn (how far is not known), giving his name to the Drake Passage between South America and Antarctica. In April 1675 London-born merchant Antonio de la Roché was blown south and east of Cape Horn, eventually taking refuge in a bay surrounded by snowy mountains, perhaps South Georgia. In 1699–1700 Edmund Halley conducted research in compass variations to 50° south in an effort to calculate accurate longitude. In 1739 John-Baptiste Bouvet de Lozier sighted an island he called Cape Circumcision, thought perhaps to be the tip of Antarctica. In

February 1772 Captain Yves Kerguelen-Trémarec sighted the sub-Antarctic island that bears his name, exaggerated by some reports to be the 'coast of the polar Antarctic circle'.

Between 1773 and 1775 Captain James Cook circumnavigated the Southern Ocean, at times searching for the elusive Cape Circumcision, crossing the Antarctic Circle three times to encounter ice beyond which the ships could not travel and reaching 70° south. The voyages of *Endeavour* and *Resolution* are records of endurance, little by little clarifying – and extending – understanding of the Southern Ocean and the continent at the South Pole. The voyages lay the groundwork for future navigation and exploration of Antarctica over the following 150 years.

2. 'Negative Discovery'

Cook's voyages 'narrowed the options' regarding the location of the Southern Continent. He began this process during the first voyage, when he sailed to 60° south and 110° west longitude after rounding Cape Horn, locating no new territory. After concluding the observation of the Transit of Venus (June 1769), *Endeavour* sailed south to 40° south, proving that no large territory was to be found south of Tahiti and the Society Islands. On the second voyage, as Cook prepared for the third leg of his circumnavigation of Antarctica, he once again sailed to the south and east of New Zealand, definitively declaring that the Unknown Continent was not in that area of the Pacific. These explorations proved that the assumptions about the Southern Continent's existence 'south' of the known Pacific Islands or New Zealand were incorrect. Cook's conclusion was that Antarctica must exist above 60° south. Historian Michael Hoare remarked on Cook's willingness to pursue a zigzag, criss-cross course across vast tracts of ocean to prove the existence (or non-existence) of land. Historian Daniel Boorstin calls this the achievement of 'negative discovery'.

3. Crossing the Circle

James Cook, *Resolution* and *Adventure* crossed the Antarctic Circle for the first time in recorded history on 17 January 1773. *Resolution* crossed the Circle again on 21–25 December 1773 and 26 January–1 February 1774. Crossing the Antarctic Circle is not the same as 'discovering' Antarctica. He did not set foot on the continent and very likely did not 'see' Antarctica beyond the impenetrable wall of ice which surrounded it at the three locations he reached in 1773 and 1774. The ice prevented Captain Cook from getting any closer than around 75 miles from Antarctica (January 1773). Nonetheless, these are historic 'firsts'. Cook pushed back the assumptions about the continent's location, reaching the ice that surrounded it. His three circumnavigations of the Southern Ocean in January–February 1773, December 1774, January–February 1774 and January 1775 narrowed the options about the continent's location.

4. What if?

As a historian, I believe my primary obligation is to discover, verify and explain what Captain Cook actually did in regard to the location of the Southern

Continent, rather than speculate on what he did not do. But what if he had kept sailing 'south' in the Drake Passage after departing from Staten Island in January 1775 in search of Dalrymple's 'Gulf of San Sebastian'? He did not do this because he concluded the ocean's condition indicated there was no land to the south. But, had he continued 'south', would he have eventually come across islands in West Antarctica such as the Orkney or the South Shetland Islands, or the Weddell Sea? That sea too has an ice shelf 'barrier', but in the Antarctic summer it is possible to reach the South Shetlands, the Antarctic Peninsula and the sea coast of the Weddell Sea. This is the location where 140 years later, in 1915, Sir Ernest Shackleton and *Endurance* became locked in ice which eventually crushed the vessel and sent it to the bottom. Where would *Resolution* have encountered floating ice in 1775? Would there again be a barrier of ice beyond which *Resolution* could not travel? Where was the pack ice in 1775? We know now it was said 'sometimes' to reach to South Georgia in the winter season, as Shackleton found in 1915. The prevailing winds blow from west to east in the Drake Passage. How would that affect Captain Cook's course in 1775? We do not and cannot know the answers to these questions. We can only ask 'what if'? Captain Cook turned north on 7 January 1775 because as he interpreted the ocean at 57° south and 30° 16′ east longitude (Lieutenant Clerke's logbook coordinates for noon), he detected no signs of land. He explored the territory of the supposed 'Gulf' as included in the Admiralty's instructions, finding no signs of land but only rolling seas, which he thought unobstructed by a then-unknown continent.

5. The Impenetrable Wall of Ice
Cook encountered floating ice, ice islands and a wall of ice that no eighteenth-century ship could sail through: this barrier greeted *Resolution* in Antarctica at 70° 10' south (30 January 1774) as well as in the Arctic Ocean at 71° 44′ north latitude (August 1778). Yet in a curious sense Cook did reach Antarctica in 1773 and the eventually discovered water route to the Arctic's Northwest Passage at Icy Cape in 1778. It was Captain Cook's fate that, in both instances, his further progress was prevented by ice.

6. Exploding the *Terra Australis Incognita* Myth
Maps from the sixteenth to the early eighteenth century depicted a vast white space at the bottom of the globe where Antarctica was assumed to exist. After Cook, and further navigation and exploration, world maps became more accurate and depictions of Antarctica became 'smaller' in size. The Unknown Southern Continent was not populated by millions of people who sought commerce with Great Britain. Cook's navigation, as he said, put an end to navigational exploits by maritime nations over two centuries and the speculations of geographers of all ages. Moreover, James Cook's views about the continent's existence matured through knowledge and experience gained over the course of three voyages from speculating that it might not exist at all to declaring that if land existed, then it did so at the South Pole. His views changed because of his voyages and not through speculation. Although he never located Bouvet's Cape Circumcision, the tiny

island's re-discovery thirty-three years later showed it was 1,100 miles (1,700km) from Antarctica.

7. A Verifiable Record
The documentation of Cook's achievements is seen both in his journals and the log books of those who sailed with him. In addition, Cook's navigation established accurate coordinates in the Antarctic, Pacific and Arctic Oceans. Captain James Cook was a master navigator as well as a surveyor/cartographer. He accurately calculated latitude and longitude of the territories he visited. It is said his maps were surpassed only by modern geo-location technology of the later twentieth century. His rare errors in fixing coordinates or landforms are so few as to generate surprising 'Cook erred' articles in our own day. In addition to exact latitude and longitude, log book sketches also verified views of Tierra del Fuego, South Georgia, the South Sandwich Islands and Kerguelen Island.

8. Island Discoveries
In the Southern Ocean James Cook is credited with the discovery of South Georgia and the South Sandwich Islands, locations with no human inhabitants, but home to penguins, seals and whales along with flocks of oceanic birds and a few Antarctic-area plants. These locations became important during the sealing and whaling seasons from the later eighteenth to the early twentieth century. In the twenty-first century South Georgia is infrequently visited, to be preserved rather than exploited, considered an island oasis often of spectacular beauty.

9. Delineation of the South Pacific
Cook's Antarctic voyages must be seen against the context of his navigation in the southern Pacific Ocean where he travelled at times other than the southern hemisphere's summer months of December, January and February. In what he termed 'the Pacific Tropical Sea', he stated he had confirmed prior discoveries and made many new ones, concluding there was little more to be done by way of future exploration. Other navigators sailed the Pacific previously but none so thoroughly, nor did they leave such a complete and accurate record.

10. Confirmation of 'Lands Discovered by the French'
The visit by *Resolution* and *Discovery* to the Crozet and Kerguelen Islands confirmed their existence and, in the case of Kerguelen, assessed its value in terms of wood, water and harbour for future navigation. Captain Cook left a message marking his December 1776 visit and displayed British colours, but acknowledged Captain Kerguelen as its first discoverer.

11. Natural Scientific and Other Observations
Cook's journals and those of natural scientists, as well as the various logbooks, serve as useful resources for the identification of the territories he visited. Logbook information is currently being evaluated by meteorologists studying climate change over centuries, just as they are useful references for maritime historians. His journals provided an exhaustive record of his travels and are an example of

popular eighteenth-century travel literature. As such they represented a further understanding of previously remote or unknown locations on the globe and were an important contribution to the reading public of his day.

12. Navigation – Marine Chronometer

Cook's second voyage validated the use of the marine chronometer to provide a means of accurately determining longitude. The testing of this device on Cook's ships was an important step in proving the chronometer's usefulness, a valuable contribution to science associated with navigation, both in the Southern Ocean, the South Pacific and the Arctic Ocean.

13. The Health of Seamen

It has long been claimed that no one died from scurvy during Cook's voyages, a plague that typically affected long sea voyages. Captain Cook experimented with a variety of means to cure scurvy. Although he maintained wort was the preferred method, he also saw the value in concentrated lemon and orange juice and vegetables, along with leafy greens gathered during his voyages (e.g. scurvy grass, Kerguelen cabbage), sauerkraut and spruce beer, all of which seemed to combat the disease. While Cook did not 'cure' scurvy, he contributed to understanding how to combat it when its signs appeared. Prevention and cure were realized as one and the same within a decade and a half after his death. Cook also insisted on a clean ship as a means of preventing unhealthy living conditions, which included smoking the sloop to clear foul air. Cook's letter to Sir John Pringle on the measures taken to improve the health of seamen earned him the 1775 Copley Medal and election to England's Royal Society.

*   *   *

When Captain James Cook began his voyages of navigation and exploration, Antarctica was *Terra Australis Incognita*, a land of mystery and speculation, an idea represented as an imaginative white space on maps. After the conclusion of Cook's three voyages, the world's maps were revised. There was land near the South Pole covered with and surrounded by ice. Cook narrowed the options by pursuing 'negative discovery' as to the location of Antarctica. He laid a trail to Antarctica, documented his voyages in his published journals and provided answers to questions which drew the attentions of geographers of all ages and the interests of the great maritime powers of his day and, in the process, brought to light considerable information about 'an immense extent of the earth'.

If the wandering albatross is a symbol of the Antarctic Convergence, it is also a symbol of Cook's Antarctic voyages, the criss-crossing of vast expanse of oceans, engaged in 'negative discovery' and leading to more accurate conclusions about *Terra Australis Incognita* and the Southern Ocean.

Chapter 16

Antarctica and Sub-Antarctic Islands after Cook

We all assembled about the Norwegian flag – a handsome silken flag – which we took and planted all together and gave the immense plateau on which the Pole is situated the name of King Haakon VII's Plateau.

Roald Amundsen, 14/15 December 1911, *The Antarctic Exploration Anthology*

We took risks, we knew we took them; things have come out against us and therefore we have no cause for complaint, but bow to the will of Providence, determined still to do our best to the last ... Had we lived, I should have had a tale to tell of the hardihood, endurance and courage of my companions which would have stirred the heart of every Englishman.

Robert Falcon Scott, 29 March 1912, letter to the public

We had pierced the veneer of outside things. We had 'suffered, starved and triumphed, grovelled down yet grasped at glory grown bigger in the bigness of the whole'. We had seen God in his splendours, heard the text that Nature renders. We had reached the naked soul of men.

Ernest Shackleton, after crossing the mountains of South Georgia from King Haakon Bay to Stromness whaling station, 20 May 1916. *South*, The *Endurance Expedition*

Navigation in the Southern Ocean and exploration of the Antarctic continent involved great risks, skilful navigation, thorough planning, often extreme hardships, valiant struggles against the odds and significant honours (even in the face of failures). Some of these efforts resulted in obtaining useful scientific information about Antarctica. For those who came after Cook and landed on Antarctica to pursue the 'race to the Pole', establishing supply depots and employing the best equipment were paramount considerations, as well as timing the effort to match the short season for traversing part of the continent. James Cook led the way to Antarctica. Others followed, building upon previous navigators and explorers, often with interesting parallels with James Cook.

This chapter will provide brief sketches of selected events in Antarctic navigation and exploration during approximately 150 years after James Cook, to the end of the 'heroic age' of Antarctic exploration (*c.*1917). The intent is not to provide a comprehensive account of all Antarctic exploration, explorers and navigators, but to focus on vignettes of the following topics and individuals: the sealing and whaling industries, navigators Fabian Bellingshausen and James Weddell, and

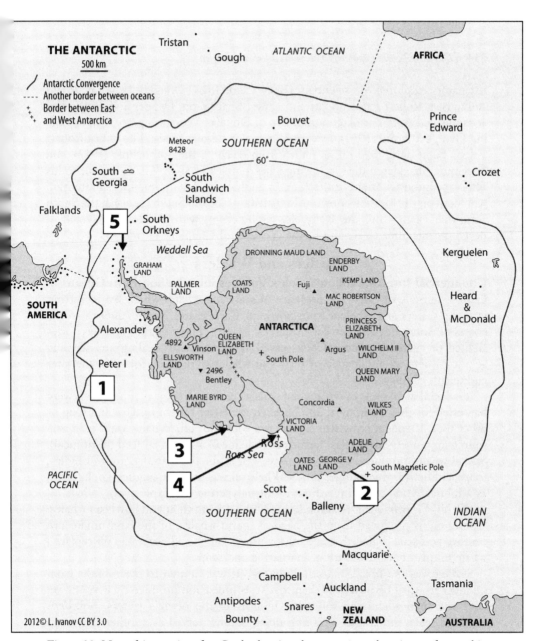

Figure 29. Map of Antarctica after Cook, showing the *approximate* locations referenced in Chapter 16 such as (1) the Sea named after Bellingshausen, (2) the area where Mawson was 'alone on the ice', (3) Amundsen's base camp, (4) Scott's base camp, and (5) Elephant Island (Shackleton). The Ross Sea (and Ross Ice Shelf) are named after James Clark Ross. All of the Sub-Antarctic locations visited by Cook are identified on the map: Tierra del Fuego, South Georgia, South Sandwich Islands, the Crozet and Kerguelen Islands. Bouvet's Island (which Cook did not locate) and the Weddell Sea are also identified on the map. Many of the islands identified served as sealing and whaling locations. The original map is by L. Ivanov & N. Ivanova (2012).

navigators, explorers or scientists James Clark Ross, Douglas Mawson, Roald Amundsen, Robert Falcon Scott and Ernest Shackleton. Danger and deaths also accompanied Antarctic exploration: two of Douglas Mawson's party died exploring George V Land (1912), leaving Mawson alone on the ice. The entire Robert Falcon Scott party died on its return from reaching the South Pole (1912), and Sir Ernest Shackleton died following a heart attack in South Georgia prior to his fifth expedition to Antarctica (1922). In addition to Antarctica, special attention will focus on the locations previously visited by Cook in South Georgia, the South Sandwich Islands and the Kerguelen archipelago, with a follow-up sketch of developments after Cook and to the contents of Chapters 11 and 13.

Sealers and Whalers

Commercial Interests follow Cook's Voyages into the Southern Ocean

Cook's journals revealed the presence of seals and whales which led to further visits by sealers and whalers from northern Europe and North America to the coasts of Antarctica and the sub-Antarctic islands. Those islands and territories sighted or visited by James Cook served as locations for sealing and whaling activity, where an abundance of seals and whales were to be found in the later eighteenth century.

It is said that all parts of whales and seals were used in some manner. Seals were harvested for their skin, meat and blubber, the latter turned into oil and soap or other uses. Elephant seals also served as a source of oil. Whales were used as a source for corsets, umbrellas, fertilizer (bone meal) and animal feed (meat meal). Sperm whales produced oil for lamps as well as for the manufacture of candles, soaps, cosmetics, glue and perfumes. Whale oil was used for candles, cooking oil, as a lubricant and as an ingredient in nitroglycerine (for explosives). Whale oil ('train oil')[1] is produced from rendering blubber from right and bowhead whales. 'Sperm oil' is produced from the head of sperm whales. In the later nineteenth century kerosene replaced whale oil for use in lamps and vegetable oil replaced whale oil in the manufacture of margarine and soap.[2]

Sealing was the first 'Antarctic industry'. It was limited to the months from October to April because it is then that seals breed and produce their young on land and then spend the following months in the ocean's waters. Southern elephant seals, sometimes weighing up to 4 tons, served as another target for sealers. A ton of seal blubber produced a ton of oil. There were large fluctuations and shifts in the numbers of seals harvested, largely due to the lack of any regulations about harvesting seal populations. Polar researchers Bamberg and Headland summarized sealers and the industry:

> The majority of the sealers were from Britain and United States (New England). They took fur seals first (for the fur) and later elephant seals (for the oil). The most important markets were in Britain (London), the US (New York) and Canton (China) where the furs were remunerative for hats and other clothing. The markets for oil were mainly the first two.

Sealing accelerated after information from Cook's second voyage became widely known. The harvesting of seals brought the Antarctic fur seal to the edge of extinction.

Sealers and whalers operated in four main areas, several of which are directly tied to James Cook: (1) the South Orkney Islands, South Shetland Islands and the Antarctic Peninsula (including its islands); (2) South Georgia, the South Sandwich Islands and Bouvetøya (Bouvet Island) in the South Atlantic; (3) Prince Edward Island, Crozet Islands, Heard Island and the Kerguelen Islands in the southern Indian Ocean; and (4), Campbell, Auckland and Macquarie Islands, south of New Zealand. Other areas included the Falkland Islands and Tierra del Fuego.³

The mid-nineteenth century was the highpoint of 'traditional' whaling based on seasonal visits to high northern or southern latitudes. Ports such as Whitby in Yorkshire (where James Cook learned to sail in the commercial navy, and where a huge whalebone arch still stands, framing both the North Sea and Whitby Abbey, a landmark for sailors entering the port), New Bedford and Nantucket, Massachusetts, were three of the most important centres from which whalers weighed anchor. South Georgia's initial whaling activity was seasonal, but became permanent from 1904. It included both onshore and floating factories. Norwegians and Swedes were among the most numerous nationalities involved. Grytviken ('Pot Bay' in Swedish), located at King Edward Cove and Cumberland Bay, served as the main centre of South Georgia's whaling activity. Some Antarctic islands, as well as Kerguelen, featured shore factories for processing whales. Abandoned factories are located today at both South Georgia (nine sites) and Kerguelen (two sites). Whales were also processed on ships. The seas surrounding these islands are filled with food for whales such as zooplankton ('krill' in Norwegian), as well as fish, shrimp and other food sought by seals, which is why South Georgia especially was a prime sealing and whaling centre.

Sealing and whaling at South Georgia expanded into Antarctic waters and the continent's surrounding islands, including the South Shetland Islands (1819), the Antarctic Peninsula (1820), the South Orkney Islands (1821), Macquarie Island (1821) and the Weddell Sea (1831). In 1820 Royal Navy master Edward Bransfield (d. 1852) charted part of the tip of the Antarctic Peninsula (Trinity Peninsula) and the South Shetland Islands (including the largest island named for King George III), and sighted other points such as Deception Island and the later-named Elephant Island (*see* Figure 29). The Bransfield Strait separates the South Shetlands and the tip of the Antarctic Peninsula. In the twentieth century the northern part of the Antarctic Peninsula was named 'Graham Land' after Sir James R.G. Graham, First Lord of the Admiralty at the time the area was explored by John Biscoe. An English sealer/whaler, Biscoe (1794–1843) completed the third circumnavigation (after Cook and Bellingshausen) in 1832–1833. The southern part was named 'Palmer Land' after Nathaniel Palmer, an American sealer whose log records landing on Deception Island (South Shetlands) in 1820. Another sealer, John Davis from Connecticut, born in England, is suggested as the first person to actually land on Antarctica (Hughes Bay) in 1821. It is entirely possible that other sealers landed earlier but the logs of Palmer and Davis offer written documentation.[4]

Fabian Gottlieb von Bellingshausen (1778–1852)
The Second Circumnavigation of Antarctica
It is generally held that Fabian Gottlieb von Bellingshausen, a Russian navigator of German heritage, first sighted the land of Antarctica on 27 January 1820. Tsar Alexander I (1801–1825) commissioned Bellingshausen to conduct a mission with two ships, *Vostro* ('*East*') and *Marni* ('*Peaceful*'), sailing in 1821. Bellingshausen completed the second circumnavigation of Antarctica, the first since Captain Cook (whom Bellingshausen greatly admired). Other parallels with Cook included the attention paid to supplying the vessels for a long voyage, and the making and recording of scientific observations. In London Bellingshausen purchased maps and navigational equipment (such as chronometers). He also visited Joseph Banks, *Endeavour*'s naturalist and President of the Royal Society. Bellingshausen used a three-watch system and insisted on a clean ship. As did Cook, supplies were purchased in Tenerife as well as Rio de Janeiro.

Between mid-December and mid-January 1820 the ships reached South Georgia (surveying the southern coast) and then sailed southeast to the South Sandwich Islands, naming Lysol, Vasuki and Zavodovski Islands before landing on Zavodovski, an active volcano. (Cook never landed on the South Sandwich Islands because he found no safe harbour.) During the voyage the crews harvested floating ice for water as did Cook's crew in *Resolution*. On 15 January 1820 Bellingshausen crossed the Antarctic Circle but, as with Cook, progress was stopped by ice. The voyage continued to the south, again crossing the Circle and reaching 69° 07′ south before being halted again by ice. Bellingshausen attempted to replicate Cook's 'furthest south' but ceased just short of that position (71° 10′ south).

The ships then visited several South Pacific locations before returning to Antarctica in 1821 and making their way to the northwestern part of West Antarctica. At 68° 57′ south, 90° 46′ west Bellingshausen sighted land, an island he named after Tsar Peter I, the Great (1682–1725), the founder of the Russian Navy. Additional land was sighted later, named Alexander I Land (Figure 29). He then set course for the South Shetlands and by February was heading north to Rio de Janeiro, thus completing a circumnavigation of Antarctica. The results of Bellingshausen's activities disappeared into Russian bureaucracy and were not followed up.[5]

James Weddell (1787–1834)
Penetration of the Weddell Sea to 74° 15′ South
James Weddell, a Scot holding the rank of master in the Royal Navy, pursued sealing and exploration after the end of the Napoleonic Wars (1815). A sealing voyage to the South Orkneys and South Georgia (1820–1822) was followed up in 1822–1824 in *Jane* and *Beauvoir*, again sailing in the Southern Ocean. After

leaving the Falkland Islands, Weddell pursued a route similar to that taken by Cook and Bellingshausen to South Georgia and the South Sandwich Islands, reaching 74° 15′ south, 30° 15′ west, waters eventually named the Weddell Sea (*see* Figure 29). He returned to England and published accounts of his exploration. Weddell continued sailing into the 1830s in both the Atlantic and Pacific (Australia, Tasmania). He died in London in relative poverty, but leaving to posterity his name for the Weddell Sea as well as his record as 'furthest south'.[6]

Weddell's achievement, author Alan Gurney suggests, derived from the variable condition of the sea ice in the Weddell Sea. He had the good fortune to sail in the sea during a season of much less ice in 1823. Other navigators were less successful in this body of water. Alan Gurney provides an especially descriptive statement about the Weddell Sea and the Antarctic Peninsula, writing,

> A glance at a map of Antarctica shows the Antarctic Peninsula rising like a splinted thumb from the clenched fist of the continent. Close to the rim of the continent the prevailing winds blow counter clockwise, herding the sea ice, shelf ice and icebergs into the bight of the Weddell Sea. Here the ice is stopped by the Peninsula and the southwest and western areas of the sea become virtually impassable for ships.

The ice forms pressure ridges and the only escape is for the ice to move to the north and into the open waters at the tip of the Antarctic Peninsula, where easterly winds continue the circular route to the southeast. The Weddell Sea contained over 100,000 square miles of pack ice which is impossible for a ship to enter.[7] As Shackleton found in 1915, the pressure of packed ice can trap and then crush a ship and send it to the ocean's bottom.

The 1830s–1840s witnessed follow-up activity. In January 1840 American navigator/explorer Charles Wilkes (1798–1877) gave his name to Wilkes Land. French naval officer/explorer Jules-Sebastian Dumont d'Urville (1790–1842) named a stretch of southern coastline after his wife Adélie in 1837–1838 (Adélie Land, today part of the French Southern and Antarctic Territories (TAAF)). Both Wilkes Land and Adélie Land are identified in Figure 29.

James Clark Ross (1800–1862)
Magnetism and Scientific Studies in the Southern Ocean, 1839–1843

James Clark Ross led *Erebus* and *Terror* in search of Antarctica's Magnetic Pole in 1841. His name is given to both the Ross Sea and the Ross Ice Shelf, which he attempted to penetrate. It was off the Ross Sea and its ice that James Cook's 'Furthest South' occurred in January 1774. Ross also explored the Arctic in the 1820s, reaching the North Magnetic Pole in 1829–1831. He later conducted an unsuccessful search for Sir John Franklin in 1848 in the Arctic's Baffin Bay.[8]

Ross's expedition occurred during 1839–1843. Admiralty instructions directed Ross to complete a series of observations of magnetism in high southern latitudes for the purpose of improving 'practical navigation'. These observations were to occur at multiple locations: St Helena, the Cape of Good Hope, Kerguelen

Island and Van Diemen's Land (Tasmania). In the summer of 1841 *Erebus* and *Terror* were to sail to Antarctica 'in order to determine the position of the magnetic pole, and even to attain it if possible, which it is hoped will be one of the remarkable and credible results of the expedition'.[9] Ross commanded *Erebus* while his trusted friend Commander Francis Crozier took charge of *Terror*. Great attention was paid to provisioning. In addition to fresh or salted foodstuffs, canned provisions were also carried on the voyage, a recommendation Ross made to the Admiralty and which was eventually adopted in 1847.[10]

Following Cook's earlier route, Ross stopped at both Madeira and the Cape of Good Hope. He then sailed for the Marion and Crozet groups of islands, arriving in late April 1840, and charted the coastline. By 5 May the expedition had reached the Kerguelen Islands, eventually anchoring in Christmas Harbour, with a week's delay due to bad weather. (Cook also experienced brief weather-related anchoring difficulties in 1776.) Master C.F. Tucker's log book on *Erebus* from 5 to 12 May consists of constant soundings and descriptions of the black sand bottom as *Erebus* and *Terror* made their way into Cook's Christmas Harbour, concluding at midnight on the 12th.[11] An observatory was then set up on the shore.

The expedition spent sixty-eight days at Christmas Harbour, with nearly constant gales, rain or snow. There were routine sightings of meteors, sometimes labelled 'falling stars' in the log. The temperature of the water was tested often, with 'sea temperature' ranging from 40° to 46°F during May. The Kerguelen Cabbage (noted by Cook in 1776) was the only fresh vegetable available, becoming a dietary item during the stay on Kerguelen. No signs of scurvy were observed during the visit. On 3 June the log recorded that a container of lime juice was opened, reflecting the now-routine carrying of lemon or lime juice as an antiscourbitic, about forty years after Cook's voyage. The log makes no reference to the Kerguelen Arch in the logbooks, visible from and located a short distance from Christmas Harbour.[12] Much later, Kerguelen's highest mountain was named after Ross, just as Cook's name was given to its glacier (or ice cap).

Erebus and *Terror* departed Kerguelen Island and sailed to Van Diemen's Land (Tasmania) to conduct additional magnetism and astronomical studies. In November Ross sailed for the Auckland Islands and then to Antarctica in search of the South Magnetic Pole. By 12 December 1840 *Erebus* and *Terror* had reached Campbell Island,[13] encountering icebergs and pack ice on 1 January 1841 which they sailed along or through for the next ten days, a major navigational achievement. A biography by Ross's great-grandson describes the 'first penetration of the Antarctic pack ice' as 'one of the most remarkable events in the history of exploration. The ships might almost have been in another world: similar to *Resolution*, they had no means of communication with civilization, and there was no ship in the southern hemisphere capable of passing through the pack ice to search for them.'[14]

The Master's logbook from *Terror* records multiple sightings of land and soundings to determine ocean depth, noting the extent of the ice as the two ships moved slowly through the pack ice, a quarter of a mile apart, on a daily basis from

12 to 22 January 1841. Whales, penguins, occasional seals and birds such as cape pigeons and petrels accompanied the ships. Eventually the ships emerged from the pack ice, the master's log in *Terror* recording on the 23rd 'no land or ice in sight'.[15]

After sailing into the pack ice *Erebus* and *Terror* found open sea, later named the Ross Sea. Land was sighted on the 11th in the shape of mountains, their peaks covered with snow. Later these were named the Admiralty Range. The South Magnetic Pole was located over 500 miles to the southwest. On 23 January an active volcano (named Mt Erebus) was sighted; later, another nearby volcano was named Mt Terror. The voyage continued into February encountering a high and lengthy ice wall, eventually arriving at a bay Ross named McMurdo Bay (later McMurdo Sound, named for a lieutenant in *Terror*). The sound served as a location for later expeditions by Shackleton and Scott. *Erebus* and *Terror* continued along the Antarctic coast into late February and March, heavy snow and fog making observations difficult. In April the ships returned to Tasmania.

Ross and Crozier returned to Antarctica in December 1841. At 146° 43' west longitude the ships again encountered the ice barrier, crossing the Antarctic Circle on New Year's Day 1842. Into late January the ships were tied into an ice floe drifting northwards, then freed, then caught in a gale and crashing ice which smashed the rudders of both ships. By early February the voyage reached its furthest south at 78° 9' 20" south, 161° 27' west, a record that stood for fifty years. By 1 March the two ships had reached the most westerly point of the pack ice and then steered north and east to Cape Horn.

On the night of 12 March 1842 the two ships collided while steering to avoid an iceberg, resulting in the temporary disablement of *Erebus*, then manoeuvring to avoid crashing into other ice islands. Entries in logbooks from *Erebus* and *Terror* describe this sequence of dramatic events in a sea filled with many icebergs:

[*Erebus*] A large Berg was seen close on the S [Starboard] Bow, hauled to port; obs^d the Terror on the St^bd bow under her Topsails and Fore Sail, moving across us. Hove all aback, and immediately afterwards the two ships came in Violent Collision, the *Terror* Striking us hard and remained Entangled about 10 minutes. The __ [sails, unreadable] carried away our bowsprit, 1 Top Sail, Fore Top Yard but binding we could not weather the Berg, and not heavy cause to wear bound (?) the yards and set the Main, making three broad perpendicular ____ and the spray breaking on board of us, the strong draw back alone keeping the ship off it [the iceberg] – at 1:30 nearly cleared the front of it [the iceberg] – filled and saw a channel between the Bergs, obs^d the *Terror*'s light NW, – burned a blue light [flare] which was answered. Hove to until daylight.[16]

[*Terror*] 12:30 observed an Iceberg bearing ENE. 12:52 observed another 20 yards ... *Erebus* crossing, the bow got athwart ___ and carried away [sails entangled on both ships] ... the two ships slackening very heavy, set the fore sail, ahead the *Erebus* ... between two large icebergs – about 25 yards apart ahead. The bergs braced up and fast track – close – close to a large Berg, Lit a Blue Light [flare] ... heavy sea. 5 Bergs bearing, the first about 2 miles long, SE, S. SBN, SBW, SBS, Erebus sail split.[17]

After partially repairing the damage, *Erebus* and *Terror* sailed east and landed at Port Louis on East Falkland on 5 April. Additional magnetism studies were conducted on East Falkland while *Erebus* was careened for further repairs.

Early in December 1842 *Erebus* and *Terror* departed from the Falklands for Antarctica, passing the South Shetlands on the way to the Weddell Sea. They attempted to travel south but encountered pack ice at 64° south. Land was sighted but it could not be reached since the ships were in pack ice. A typical *Erebus* logbook entry on 16 January stated,

> 4 p.m., Ice closely packed all around. 6 p.m., tide turned out, set to the NW, Ice close and heavy all around ... 4 a.m., Ice slackening to the NE, Received ice, one ton [for water]. 9:45 a.m., The Ice to which the ships were fast parted in 3 places was fixed and made fast to the remaining part to which were fast before – *Terror* fast to another part ... Drifting to the NE. *Terror* NEBN 1' – Ice close and heavy all around.[18]

Summer temperatures were in the 50s and low 60s. By 1 February Ross decided to give up after six weeks of travelling in and next to the ice since he could not travel further south than 65° 13'. Log books in *Erebus* and *Terror* record the ships on the edge but free of the ice on 31 January and 1 February. Additional sailing along the ice continued into March, but by 4 April the ships were back at the Cape of Good Hope, reaching England in early September 1843.

Ross's 1840–1843 voyages obtained considerable geographic and oceano-graphic knowledge. Place names were given to mountains as well as 'Victoria Land' and McMurdo Sound. Seventy years later the Ross Ice Shelf was the depar-ture point for both Amundsen and Scott in their 'race to the South Pole'. Both Cook and Ross faced the ice barrier, and both recorded observations at Kerguelen Island. Ross achieved the first penetration of the pack ice in the Ross Sea. *Erebus* and *Terror* 'were the first and last ever' to navigate the Ross Sea under sail alone. In his biography of his great-grandfather, Maurice Ross cites a conclu-sion from Robert Falcon Scott: 'It might be said that it was James Cook who defined the Antarctic Region and James Ross who discovered it.'[19] In a similar vein, Apsley Cherry-Garrard (1886–1959), a member of Scott's *Terra Nova* Expe-dition, remarked, 'Cook, Ross and Scott: these are the aristocrats of the South'.[20]

Sir Douglas Mawson (1882–1958)

Things look bad, but I shall persevere.

Douglas Mawson, 12 January 1912

Alone on the Ice

Douglas Mawson was born in Yorkshire. In 1884, when he was 2 years old, his family moved to Sydney, Australia. Mawson studied mining engineering at the University of Sydney, and subsequently joined Ernest Shackleton's British

Antarctic Expedition (BAE) in *Nimrod* (1907–1909) as a physicist, because he wanted to study the geological aspects of glaciation. During the expedition he was one of the first to climb Mt Erebus, named by James Clark Ross in 1840. The expedition reached the vicinity of the South Magnetic Pole in the summer of 1908.

Douglas Mawson is best known for the 1911–1914 Australasian Expedition, of which he was the chief organizer. The goal was scientific, encompassing geology, meteorology, geomagnetism and biology (zoology, botany). The expedition sailed in December 1911 and established three main research bases: (1) Macquarie Island (which also served as a radio relay station), (2) Commonwealth Bay (which was the main base and Mawson's headquarters (Figure 29), and (3) the Western Base on the Shackleton Ice Shelf under the direction of Frank Wild, who subsequently served as second-in-command to Shackleton on the *Endurance* expedition of 1914–1918. Frank Hurley served as photographer, a task he also performed later in *Endurance*.

At Commonwealth Bay the expedition put together three-man sledging teams for exploration. Mawson, Xavier Mertz and Lieutenant Belgrave Edward Sutton Ninnis departed in November 1912 to survey King George Land. Unfortunately Ninnis, his dogs and his sled (containing most of the team's supplies, including protective gear) fell into a deep crevasse and disappeared about 310 miles from the base camp. Mawson and Mertz then decided to return to Commonwealth Bay. The two men were weakened by exertion and lack of food, the bitterly cold weather and winds that reached 40mph taking a heavy toll. Because much of their food supply had been lost, they began to kill and eat their dogs to survive. Some of the meat was also consumed by the remaining dogs, their number also dwindling over time. It was not known then that consumption of quantities of dog liver was toxic and it is believed this led to the weakening of both explorers, Mertz especially becoming more debilitated daily. On 28 December the last dog died from exhaustion. It was then up to Mawson and the increasingly weak Mertz to drag the sledges but their slow progress meant they could not reach the base before their remaining food ran out. Mertz died on 8 January 1913. Mawson recorded in his diary that his companion died from weather, exposure and lack of food. He was now 'alone on the ice'.

Using a serrated pocket knife, Mawson cut his sledge in half and discarded everything except his geological notes and specimens, Mertz's diary, and pictures of Mertz and Ninnis. He then began dragging the sledge the remaining 100 miles (161km) to the base camp. His feet were raw, the skin layers separated. He used lanoline and bandages to bind the 'old and new skin', wearing six pairs of woollen socks and his crampon overshoes (to grip snow/ice). He described 'treading like a cat' to reduce the pain in his feet and pressed onwards. He faced 45mph winds and snow. On 13 January he sighted the Mertz Glacier, with the base camp located beyond the glacier. Knowing he was on the correct path, he wrote in his diary, 'Things look bad, but I shall persevere'. He tumbled into a crevasse on 16/17 January but his sledge acted as an anchor and he gradually extricated himself. He fashioned a rope ladder connected to his sledge in case he fell into another crevasse. In his diary Mawson wrote that he 'had hopes of pulling through ... I trust in Providence, however, who has so many times already helped me'. He avoided additional crevasses in the 'valley of crevasses', traversing the Mertz Glacier by 20 January. His physical condition was deteriorating and during 25–26 January he faced a blizzard with 60mph winds. Base camp was now about 48 miles ahead.

On 29 January Mawson sighted in the distance blocks of snow with a flapping black cloth. Reaching the spot, he found food and a note stating that it had been left just six hours earlier by McLean, Hodgeman and Hurley from the base camp. They were out searching for Ninnis, Mertz and Mawson, all of whom had been scheduled to be at the base camp by 15 January, two weeks earlier. The note also gave directions to 'Aladdin's Cave', where food was located. From that location, base camp was only 5 miles' distant, but the surface was half-ice and half-snow and additional crevasses lay ahead.

On 1 February 1913 Mawson reached Aladdin's Cave to find oranges and a pineapple. For the next six days a blizzard prevented Mawson from making any progress so he rested at Aladdin's Cave and made new crampons for the final trek to base camp. Even with the food from the two depots, Mawson continued to feel his body weakening and thought he might be developing signs of scurvy because of the weakness in his joints. As he proceeded down the slope to the base camp he saw a speck on the ocean which turned out to be the supply ship *Aurora*. He was eventually sighted on 8 February, the five men at the camp racing out to meet him (and to discover who he was – Ninnis, Mertz or Mawson). No longer alone on the ice, Mawson and the five others then remained at the base camp until December 1913.[21]

The scientific information gathered by the Australasian Expedition, which covered George V, Queen Mary and Adélie Lands, was subsequently published over the next four decades. It included geography, a description of the Antarctic continental shelf, biology on land and sea, as well as geomagnetism studies at Commonwealth Bay. The Australasian Expedition is regarded as perhaps the greatest reconnaissance expedition to Antarctica. Mawson was knighted in 1914 and was nominated a Fellow of the Royal Society in 1923. His efforts mirror Shackleton's *Endurance* expedition as an example of heroic battling of individuals against great odds in confronting the ice and snow of Antarctica.

Roald Engelbregt Gravning Amundsen (1872–1928)

So we arrived and were able to plant our flag at the geographical South Pole. God be thanked!

Roald Amundsen, diary, 14 December 1911

Roald Amundsen explored both the Arctic and Antarctic and led the expedition which was first to reach the South Pole (1911). Amundsen also led a three-year nautical expedition that was the first to cross the Northwest Passage (1903–1906) from the Atlantic to the Pacific Oceans, passing Icy Cape which marked James Cook's furthest progress in search of the Passage in 1778. During this expedition, and because of impenetrable ice, Amundsen spent two winters at King William Island, where he studied survival skills by the native Inuit, including the use of sled dogs and furred animal skins for protection (instead of woollen clothing). In 1918–1920 Amundsen sailed the Northeast Passage (west to east) through the Arctic Ocean, much of the time stuck in ice even during the short season when Arctic pack ice melts. Amundsen disappeared in June 1928, presumably in an airplane crash in the Arctic.[22]

The ship Amundsen used in Antarctica was *Fram* ('*Forward*'), which had been used from 1893 to 1912 in the Arctic by Norwegian explorers such as Fridtjof Nansen. Amundsen landed at the Bay of Whales, a natural ice harbour, at one extremity of the Ross Ice Shelf to set up his base camp (Figure 29), a bay named by Ernest Shackleton in 1908. Amundsen named the camp 'at' Framheim' ('home of the *Fram*') in mid-January 1911. A series of depots were stocked with supplies at various points from 80° to 82° south on a line towards the Pole. His first attempt to reach the South Pole did not succeed. The second attempt began on 19 October 1911. In addition to Amundsen, the polar party included Olav Bjaaland, Helmer Hanssen, Sverre Hassel and Oscar Wisting, using four sledges and accompanied by fifty-two dogs.

In order to reach the South Pole from Framheim, the expedition needed to cross the Trans-Antarctic Mountains separating East and West Antarctica (first sighted by James Clark Ross in 1841) and then proceed onto the polar plateau. The party reached it on 21 November, Amundsen describing it as a 'frozen sea, a domed cupola of ice'. They faced blizzard after blizzard, with winds at 30 knots or more, with the landscape 'boiling with snow'. With temperatures ranging from −20° to −4°C (28.8° to −4°F), Robert Huntford writes 'the fact that Amundsen could travel at all was due to the Eskimo cut of his clothes and the furs around his face'. Amundsen termed crevasses 'The Devil's Dance-Floor'. Sledge-runners and dogs occasionally crashed into the bottomless pits. In addition to blizzards, occasional fog and crossing 'a minor jungle of *sasturgi*'[23] (ridges formed in the snow parallel to prevailing winds), Amundsen and his party now had a 'straight run' to the South Pole. On 7 December the party crossed 88° south, therefore exceeding Ernest Shackleton's position on the British National Antarctic Expedition of 1901–1904.[24]

On a brilliant summer's day on 14/15 January 1911, at approximately 3pm, Amundsen and his team arrived at the South Pole (90° 0' south). (Because the western and eastern hemispheres and the International Date Line meet at the two Poles, either 14 or 15 December 1911 may be used to mark the day on which Amundsen reached the South Pole.) In his diary, Amundsen wrote,

> at three o'clock in the afternoon we halted, as according to our reckoning we had reached our goal.

We all assembled about the Norwegian flag – a handsome silken flag – which we took and planted all together, and gave the immense plateau on which the Pole is situated the name of King Haakon VII's Plateau.

It was a vast plain of the same character in every direction, mile after mile.

Over the next two days Amundsen's team took multiple observations to determine 'True South'. On 16 December twenty-four observations were made, one for each hour of the day, and the group moved 5.6 miles (9km) from their position on 14 December to the calculated True South. At that point, on the 17th, they again raised the Norwegian flag and a pennant from *Fram*, naming the location 'Polheim'. The location was 870 'English miles' (1,400km) from the base camp, so Amundsen's party had averaged 15 miles per day to the Pole.[25]

On 14/15 December Scott's party was 360 miles behind, climbing the Beardmore Glacier. Thirty-four days later, on 17 January 1912, Robert Falcon Scott and his party reached the South Pole. For Amundsen, the return to the Bay of Whales began on 17 December. The group reached Framheim on 25 January 1912, completing a round-trip journey of 1,400 miles.[26]

Robert Falcon Scott (1868–1912)

Had we lived, I should have had a tale to tell of the hardihood, endurance and courage of my companions which would have stirred the heart of every Englishman.

Robert Falcon Scott, final message, 29 March 1912

The British Antarctic (*Terra Nova*) Expedition, 1910–1913

Robert Falcon Scott, a British Royal Navy officer and explorer, led the Royal Geographic Society's 'Discovery Expedition' (1901–1904), sailing in Royal Research Ship (RRS) *Discovery*. Its goal was to perform geographical and scientific research (including geology, meteorology and magnetism, as well as botany and zoology). Ernest Shackleton served as one of the expedition officers, along with Frank Wild and Tom Crean, who also served on Shackleton's *Endurance* expedition of 1914–1917.

The Discovery Expedition reached 82° south on Christmas Day 1902 but, suffering from frostbite, snow blindness, signs of scurvy and exhaustion, the party returned to the base camp in early February 1903. Shackleton and several others departed on the expedition ship *Terra Nova*. An attempt was made the next year to cross the Antarctic Mountains to reach the South Magnetic Pole, the party returning to the base camp by mid-December to find *Discovery* locked in ice; the ship was freed by the use of dynamite to reach *Terra Nova* in mid-February 1904. A rivalry emerged between Scott and Shackleton. Subsequently Shackleton's Nimrod Expedition (1907–1909) set off to reach the Pole. It reached 88° 25' south in 1907, while an allied party reached the South Magnetic Pole.

Scott then began planning for the *Terra Nova* Expedition (1910–1913) with the goal of reaching the South Pole. Scott's base was Cape Evans on Ross Island in the Bay of Whales, on the opposite side of the Ross Ice Shelf from where Amundsen's

Framheim base was located (Figure 29). In order to reach the Pole the path lay across the Ross Ice Shelf, over the mountains to the Beardmore Glacier and then onto the polar plateau, a distance of approximately 870 miles (1,400km). After eight months of preparation Scott's party departed on 1 November, thirteen days later than Amundsen's party and late in the Antarctic exploration season. Ponies, motor sledges and dogs were used for the first stage. Once at the glacier, the sledges would be moved only by men (whereas Amundsen used dogs as part of his plan to reach the Pole). Both Amundsen and Scott established supply depots as they proceeded towards the Pole. The use of motorized sledges and ponies proved unsuccessful. The sledges broke down and, with no spare parts, were abandoned. The ponies were unsuited to Antarctic conditions and required a food supply that needed to be transported during the trek.

Polar author Roland Huntford writes that the problems with motorized equipment and ponies reflected 'Scott's inability to grasp the implications of the cold, storms and unpredictable surfaces of the Antarctic world'. Some of the equipment and clothing was of little use or poorly designed. Huntford concludes, 'where transport was concerned, Scott trusted neither ponies, nor skis, dogs or sledge, in truth all he really believed in was human effort'.[27] Eventually Scott's party utilized only 'man-haul' sledges. The dogs were sent back to the base camp. In addition to Scott, the team consisted of Henry Bowers, Edgar Evans, Lawrence Oates and Edward Wilson.

On 9 January Scott exceeded Shackleton's 88° south but faced blizzards blowing at 25 knots (28.8mph). By departing so late from base camp, Scott was approaching the South Pole at a time of colder temperatures than those faced by Amundsen. Scott and his companions were not only physically weak but dehydrated and suffering from vitamin deficiencies. On the return trip from the South Pole, Robert Huntford suggests, the Scott party's calorie intake was about 1,500 calories per day too low.

Robert Falcon Scott's party of five reached the South Pole at 6:30pm on 17 January 1912, thirty-four days after Amundsen. The temperature was −30°C (−22°F). It was a terrible disappointment to the five men. Inside Amundsen's tent was a short note addressed to Scott and a document to be sent to King Haakon VII (as proof of Amundsen's arrival at the Pole). The party erected a cairn marking their visit and hoisted the Union Jack.

Blizzards, ice and extreme cold hampered the return journey. There was no safety margin. When he crossed the Beardmore Glacier on the outward journey, Scott left behind no bearings for the route through the 'labyrinth of crevasses'. Rations were cut, which reduced the party's strength as they attempted to reach their supply stations. Edgar Evans died from injuries and exhaustion in February. Edward Wilson died from exhaustion in March. In his diary Scott recorded that Wilson began to grow weaker as they first approached the South Pole, then on the return trip suffered frostbitten fingers and a fall on a glacier's ice, during which he may have hit his head. On 17 January Wilson became unconscious, then comatose and died at 12:30am. Scott observed that 'Providence' removed Wilson at a 'critical moment. He died a natural death, and we did not leave him till two hours after his death.'

As January turned into February and then into early March, the four remaining team members kept moving towards their supply stations and ultimately their base camp as best they could, but cold weather and snow and ice were a constant problem. Their sleeping bags were always damp. Foot problems and frostbite were increasingly severe for all but especially for Lawrence (Titus) Oates. On the 14th Scott wrote he had 'no idea there could be temperatures like this [−43°F] at this time of the year with such winds. Truly awful outside the tent. Must fight it out to the last biscuit, but can't reduce rations.' Oates suggested the team just leave him in his sleeping bag, but that was unacceptable to his companions. Scott wrote that he wanted it known that Oates's final thoughts were of his mother and how proud his regiment would be 'in the bold way in which he met his death. We can testify to his bravery. He has borne intense suffering for weeks without complaint.' In the morning of 15 March Oates told the others, 'I am just going outside and may be some time.' Scott recorded that Oates 'went out into the blizzard and we have not seen him since'.[28] Scott's party now consisted of three persons. On 16/17 March Scott wrote in his diary, 'We knew that poor Oates was walking to his death, but though we tried to dissuade him, we knew it was the act of a brave man and an English gentleman. We all hope to meet the end with a similar spirit, and assuredly the end is not far.'

Scott and the others feared their frostbite was severe enough to warrant eventual amputation. Faced with blizzards during which they could not proceed, and −30° to −40°C (−22° to −40°F) temperatures, with their food running out, and suffering from snow blindness, injuries, scurvy and frostbite, on or about 29 March the remaining three perished from cold, exhaustion and starvation. On 22/23 March Scott's diary recorded that they faced a blizzard, Wilson and Bowers were unable to proceed and tomorrow was their final chance with no fuel and two days of food remaining. He wrote, 'must be near the end. Have decided it will be natural – we shall march for the depot with or without our effects and die in our tracks.'

Scott, his feet also now frostbitten, maintained his diary until he died. His final entry was written on 29 March 1912. Declaring that he could not go on, Robert Falcon Scott stated in a general letter to be published at some future time,

> We took risks, we knew we took them; things have come out against us and therefore we have no cause for complaint, but bow to the will of Providence, determined still to do our best to the last . . . Had we lived, I should have had a tale to tell of the hardihood, endurance and courage of my companions which would have stirred the heart of every Englishman. These rough notes and our dead bodies must tell the tale, but surely, surely, a great rich country like ours will see that those who are dependent on us are properly provided for.[29]

Their last location was approximately 12.5 miles (20km) from a supply depot.[30] Cherry-Garrard stated that Scott's party had travelled 721 statute miles from the South Pole and were 177 miles from their base camp on 29 March.[31]

At the base camp the remaining expedition members grew uneasy when Scott and his party did not return by March and the onset of the 'autumn and winter' seasons. Scientific work continued until mid-October, when the weather allowed a search party to set out. On 12 November 1912 Scott's tent was discovered, along with the remains of the three team members. The relief party erected a snow cairn over the tent, topped with a cross. The team's letters to their families, sponsors and others, their diaries and their research notes and specimens were taken back to the base camp. The other members of the original five-man team were never located. *Terra Nova* left Antarctica for the final time on 13 February 1913 for New Zealand, where the shocking news of the ill-fated expedition reached the outside world. The *Terra Nova* Expedition returned with thousands of specimens, including new geological and zoological discoveries. As for its legacy, the Antarctic Heritage Trust concludes, 'The scientific programme undertaken by the *Terra Nova* Expedition was at the time one of the broadest and most comprehensive ever conducted in Antarctica.'[32]

Sir Ernest Henry Shackleton (1874–1922)

Shackleton – An exceptional leader and a born survivor.

Fergus Fleming, introduction to Shackleton's diary *South, The* Endurance *Expedition*

The *Endurance* Expedition, 1914–1917

Sir Ernest Shackleton is for ever linked with the heroic Imperial Trans-Antarctic Expedition of 1914–1917 which aimed to achieve the first land crossing of the Antarctic continent. Shackleton's earlier attempts to reach the South Pole included the British National Antarctic Expedition of 1901–1904, led by Robert Falcon Scott (82° 17′ south), of which Douglas Mawson was a member, and the Nimrod Expedition (88° 25′ south), 112 miles (180km) short of the Pole.

The plan for Shackleton's Imperial Trans-Antarctic Expedition was to cross the Antarctic continent from the Weddell Sea to the Ross Sea, also reaching the South Pole during the trek. Shackleton and the 'Weddell Sea Party' sailed in *Endurance*, with Frank Wild as his second in command, and Frank Worsley as captain of the vessel. Frank Hurley served as photographer. His photos and film were salvaged from the *Endurance* expedition for posterity. Fergus Fleming summed up the expedition as 'the most comprehensive scientific and topographical analysis of Antarctica to date, a sensational attainment of the Pole, and the news that the Union Jack flagged resolutely at the bottom of the world'.[33]

While the Weddell Sea Party was laying plans to cross the continent (the first continental crossing), the ship *Aurora* was to establish a series of base camps on the Ross Ice Shelf and further inland for the use of the Weddell Sea Party on the last leg of their cross-continental journey. Attempts to complete these supply stations occurred between 1913 and 1915 with both failures and successes. The

Aurora party, their ship entrapped in ice and marooned on land, was not rescued until 1917, with Shackleton among those on the rescue vessel.

The expedition's departure occurred in the final weeks leading up to the First World War. Although Shackleton was the owner of *Endurance*, some of her crew had naval or military commitments, and England was about to be placed on a wartime footing. After consultation with Winston Churchill, First Lord of the Admiralty (1911–1915), it was determined the expedition would proceed. King George V presented Shackleton with a Union Jack and Queen Dowager Alexandra presented a Bible to be carried on the voyage. *Endurance* sailed on 4 August. Great Britain entered the war at midnight on 4 August.

Endurance reached Grytviken, South Georgia, on 5 November. After a month's preparation, the expedition departed from Grytviken whaling station on 5 December 1914, but quickly encountered loose ice and icebergs, with pack ice at 57° 26′ south, not expected at this location. From early December to late February *Endurance* battled the ice in the Weddell Sea, making slow progress south to 76° 34' south latitude and 31° 30′ west longitude. On 21 February the ship began to drift with the pack ice, gradually heading in a northward direction.

By mid-April Shackleton (called 'the Boss' by the crew) realized that the pack ice was piling up and *Endurance* might be crushed from the building pressure. During the winter months of May to July the weight of new snow and the slow breaking-up of the pack ice brought severe pressure to bear on the ship and Shackleton ordered *Endurance* to be abandoned on 27 October (at 69° 05′ south and 51° 30′ west). Supplies were salvaged from the vessel, including films of the expedition. The ship sank into the Weddell Sea on 21 November, Shackleton observing the vessel sank bow first before being lost under the ice.[34]

The crew established 'Ocean Camp' on the ice on 27 October 1915. Termed by Shackleton 'a floating lump of ice', it was about one square mile in the beginning but gradually diminished. It served as the expedition's base for two months. Food consisted of penguin and seal meat, in addition to supplies salvaged from *Endurance*. The distance to the mainland was approximately 300 miles. On 26 December 'Patience Camp' was established. The expedition attempted to march across the ice and drag the three small boats to open water. The vessels were named after three of the expedition's sponsors, *James Caird*, *Dudley Docker* and *Stancomb Willis*. On 8 April the expedition reached open water, boarded the boats and began the journey towards land. Deception Island was the first target, but on 15 April it was decided to land at Elephant Island (61° 08′ south, 55° 07′ west), about 170 miles off the tip of the Antarctic Peninsula.

A camp was established on the uninhabited Elephant Island (Figure 29), under the command of Frank Wild. It was to be a base for most of the Weddell Sea Party during the next four months. Two of the ships were inverted to give protection from the weather. By trial and error the men constructed an adequate shelter around the boats for protection from the snow and wind and the ever-present dampness and cold.

The central issue facing the expedition now was rescue from Elephant Island. The best option for was for several of the crew to sail *James Caird*, the largest of the three boats at 22ft long, to South Georgia, 800 miles (1,300km) across the Drake Passage. Although the Falkland Islands and Cape Horn are closer in distance (Figure 29), the prevailing winds ruled out those locations. In addition to the prevailing wind, the easterly current in the Drake Passage is said to travel up to 60 miles per day.[35] Shackleton and five others (Frank Worsley, Tom Crean, Henry McNish, John Vincent and Timothy McCarthy) sailed from Elephant Island in *James Caird* on 24 April.

During the dangerous, perilous voyage across cold, rough seas (which made Worsley's sextant observations very difficult), and with at least one monstrous wave which miraculously did not overwhelm the vessel, *James Caird* reached King Haakon Bay[36] on the southern coast of South Georgia on 10 May. By now the boat was no longer seaworthy. After a brief rest, eating a stew of boiled albatross to gather strength, Shackleton, Worsley and Crean decided to cross the glaciers and mountains to Stromness whaling station on the other side of the island. Once there, a rescue boat would be sent to pick up Vincent, McNish and McCarthy, who were in poor physical shape and remained in 'Peggotty Camp',[37] close by a large elephant seal colony.

No one had previously crossed South Georgia's mountains. In preparation for the trek, nails were driven through the soles of their boots to give grip in the ice and snow (a primitive form of crampon, similar to that which Douglas Mawson created). On 19–20 May the three men crossed the mountains (about 5 miles from James Cook's 1775 Possession Bay), then turned eastward towards Stromness. They fought wind, cold and weariness, and at one point had to backtrack on their route. At 7.00am on the 20th they heard the work-day whistle at the whaling station. Shackleton remarked there could have been 'no sweeter music' to the three climbers. After sliding down a snow-covered mountain and through a waterfall, the group made their way to the whaling station.

The three men were unrecognizable, and there was initial disbelief when it was learned the three had traversed the mountains from South Georgia's southern coast.

'Who are you?' he [the wharf manager] asked.
'We have lost our ship and come over the island, I [Shackleton] replied.
'You have come over the island?' he said in a tone of entire disbelief.[38]

Frank Worsley summed up the 'tramp' across South Georgia: 'Without sleep, and halting only for meals, we had crossed South Georgia in thirty-six hours. True they had been hours of unremitting effort, of risks, anxiety and misadventure, but we had succeeded, and that was all that mattered.'[39]

In 1995 a British survey team of professional climbers, with appropriate modern equipment, made the second crossing of South Georgia, following Shackleton's route. Their leader, Duncan Carse, remarked, 'I do not know how they did it, except that they had to – three men of the heroic age of Antarctic exploration with 50 feet of rope between them – and a carpenter's adze.'[40]

Having reached safety, Ernest Shackleton immediately began planning to rescue the remainder of the Weddell Sea Party marooned on Elephant Island. On the next day, 21 May, the three sailors from *James Caird* were rescued from Peggotty Camp. Shackleton made four attempts to reach Elephant Island, the first three stopped by impenetrable pack ice. *Southern Sky* from South Georgia could get no closer than 70 miles in late May/early June. A request for a ship from England met with a refusal due to wartime naval requirements. A second attempt in a Uruguayan trawler failed to reach Elephant Island in June, also because of ice. A third attempt with a vessel from Punta Arenas, Chile, in July resulted in the same fate. Finally, in August, another attempt in a Chilean vessel, *Yelcho*, reached Elephant Island on 30 August 1916 and rescued the remaining crew from *Endurance*, all of whom survived their four months on the island.

The rescue party's arrival was timely, because rations were short, as Shackleton relates:

> All were naturally weak when rescued, owing to having been on such scanty rations for so long, but all were alive and very cheerful, thanks to Frank Wild. August 30, 1916, is described in their diaries as a 'day of wonders'. Food was very short, only two days' seal and penguin meat being left, and no prospect of any more arriving [due to the season]. The whole party had been collecting limpets [aquatic snails] and seaweed to eat with stewed seal bones.[41]

Within an hour the Elephant Island group was transferred to *Yelcho* and the vessel headed north to Punta Arenas.

In subsequent months members of the expedition returned to England and members of the crew then began service in the army or navy, with several being killed and others wounded during the remaining months of the First World War. Shackleton himself led the rescue of the Ross Sea Party in December 1917. Overall, the Imperial Trans-Antarctic Expedition was not a success. However, its record is one of heroic survival against great odds. The entire project was fraught with great risk. Shackleton, Fergus Fleming concludes, was 'an exceptional leader and a born survivor'.[42]

Ernest Shackleton's fifth expedition to the Antarctic, the Shackleton-Rowell Expedition in *Quest*, 1921–1922, was intended to explore Enderby Land in East Antarctica, southwest of the point where James Cook first crossed the Antarctic Circle on 17 January 1773. However, on 5 January 1922, before setting out for Antarctica, Shackleton died at Grytviken from a congenital heart condition. He is buried at Grytviken Cemetery at King Edward Point, overlooking the bay.[43] The *James Caird* may be seen today at Dulwich College, London. Frank Wild died in South Africa in 1939. In 2011 his ashes were taken by his granddaughter and several of his relatives to be buried at Grytviken alongside Shackleton's grave; in life and death he was Shackleton's 'right-hand man'.[44]

South Georgia after Captain James Cook

Following Captain Cook's January 1775 visit to South Georgia and the South Sandwich Islands, sealers and whalers accounted for the next chapter of human contact with these territories. Sealing began in the 1780s and continued to ebb and flow during the nineteenth century and into the early twentieth. The impact on the seal and whale populations of South Georgia was catastrophic. However, spectacular seal population recovery occurred in the later twentieth century and today seals may total 5 million or more. The first whaling station was established at Grytviken in 1904, through leases granted by the British Governor of the Falkland Islands, with both floating and shore-based factories. The last station at Grytviken closed in 1965. Whaling became less important when petroleum-based and other products came into use, and because the overall whale population was declining. An international convention on whaling in the 1930s was replaced by the International Convention for the Regulation of Whaling, which was signed in 1946 and came into effect in 1948. Its purpose was the conservation of whale populations.

During the 1982 invasion of the Falkland Islands, the Argentine military junta also dispatched troops to South Georgia. A detachment of twenty-two Royal Marines defended their positions at Cumberland Bay and King Edward Point during a two-hour battle on 3 April. The Marines, along with thirteen scientists from the British Antarctic Survey (who sought refuge in the church at Grytviken), then surrendered on the same day. The Marines and scientists were initially placed under guard around Grytviken's central flag pole, before being imprisoned on an Argentine naval vessel and eventually released in Uruguay. Scientific data and related resources on the island were damaged or destroyed by the invasion force. Three weeks later, on 25 April, British forces restored control of South Georgia after a brief assault. An Argentine naval weather station on Southern Thule (South Sandwich Islands) was closed by the Royal Navy in *Endurance* on 20 June and later destroyed by bombardment from a Royal Navy vessel in January 1983. The four scientific stations established at scattered South Georgia locations were not seized during the 1982 conflict, and the counting of wildlife and associated activities were not interrupted.

From 1908 the Falkland Islands administered South Georgia and the South Sandwich Islands as a dependency, which is why postage stamps for these areas were labelled 'Falkland Island Dependencies' (until 1985). In 1985 the islands were organized as the territories of South Georgia and the South Sandwich Islands, with the governor of the Falklands continuing to provide administrative authority. The detachment of Royal Marines was withdrawn from South Georgia in 2001 but British Antarctic Survey scientists provide local administrative contact at Grytviken, in addition to continuing scientific observations.

South Georgia today is a location for limited ecotourism during the Antarctic summer months. Scientists occasionally connect data at the Sandwich Islands. The island is accessible by boat only. There are no roads or facilities for air travel, and no over-night visitor amenities are available on the island. Day visits increased after the conclusion of the Falkland Islands conflict, and small cruise ships occasionally visit the harbour at Grytviken. Travellers may visit the South Georgia Museum, located in the former whaling manager's house, where Shackleton and the South Georgia rescue party were welcomed on 20 May 1916, as well as Shackleton's grave. The museum contains exhibits on whaling and the exploration by Shackleton and others. Another site to be visited is a church building (originally built in the early twentieth century for use by Norwegian whalers). Extensive regulations are in place to preserve the island's ecology. Two webcams operate daily providing views of the bay and recording occasional visits by seals, penguins, small cruise ships and a few small icebergs.[45]

Unintended consequences from whaling or sealing plagued South Georgia. Rats that arrived on ships spread on the island, endangering, among other wildlife, the South Georgia pipit, the island's only songbird. Rats also destroyed the eggs of birds such as albatrosses, skuas, terns and petrels, which nested on the ground because there are no native trees. An extensive campaign to eradicate rats on the island began in 2010 and was described as an 'unqualified success' in 2018 by the South Georgia Heritage Trust. Helicopters dropped 300 tonnes of poison bait to combat the rodents. The $13 million decade-long project is termed 'the largest rodent eradication programme of all time'. The pipit is now reported to be making a comeback. Monitoring of results will continue indefinitely.

Reindeer are another introduced species, brought to South Georgia as an alternative source of meat for Scandinavian whalers/sealers, and only periodically controlled by seasonal hunting. Reindeer tended to eat and thereby destroy the tussock grass which served as protection for birds and penguins. A reindeer eradication programme began after 2010. 'Rounding up' reindeer proved impossible because of the mountainous terrain. The eradication programme included shooting reindeer and processing the meat for food, marketed primarily in Scandinavian countries.[46]

The Kerguelen Archipelago after Captain Cook

The Kerguelen Islands received infrequent attention in the nineteenth century. As described above, British ships commanded by James Clark Ross (*Erebus*) and Francis Crozier (*Terror*) carried out magnetic, astronomical and scientific observations in 1840. A French expedition in *Challenger* visited the Kerguelen and Crozet Islands in 1872–1876. French sovereignty was reasserted in 1893.

Whaling and sealing began around the Kerguelen archipelago and the Crozet Islands in 1790. The two main centres were at Port Jeanne d'Arc and Port Couvreux, and by the early nineteenth century the Kerguelen fur seal population was severely endangered. Commercial interests then turned to elephant seals. Sealing continued until 1927. Whaling at Kerguelen was not as extensive as at South Georgia and ended in 1963. Abandoned sites still remain on Kerguelen Island. Large 'freezer-trawler ships' from the Soviet Union, Poland and Japan operated in the 1970s to harvest seafood, an activity which also occurred off South Georgia (mostly without governmental approval). In 1978 France established a 200-nautical mile zone around Kerguelen to prevent further exploitation and unrestricted fishing near the islands. These activities in remote locations are sometimes difficult to monitor. A resources management plan is in place to monitor future economic activity.[47]

Several sheep and cattle farming endeavours failed, as did attempts to establish settlements, such as the colonization efforts by Henry and Rene Bossiere at Port Couvreux in the 1920s. In 1928 a government-sponsored lobster cannery was established on Saint-Paul Island and then forgotten about until a relief vessel arrived in December 1930 to find three survivors. Colonization and agricultural efforts ended in 1931. Wild sheep and reindeer are now found on the island. The islands were completely charted only in 1913–1914 on a second visit to Kerguelen by Captain Rallier du Baty, who also recorded the collapse of the Arch of Kerguelen. Salmon farming began in the twentieth century. Several German naval cruisers were moored at Kerguelen in 1940–1941 (during Vichy France) to obtain water or supplies and to be camouflaged.

French officials on Madagascar initially administered the islands and the first postage stamp (1 January 1955) is a Madagascar overprint. After 1955 France administered the islands as part of the autonomous *Terres Australes et Antarctiques Francaises* (French Southern and Antarctic Territories, TAAF), which also includes the Crozet archipelago, the Amsterdam/St-Paul Islands and Adélie Land in Antarctica. France also used the island to track test missiles in the 1960s and joint French-Soviet Union magnetosphere research missile tests were conducted over Kerguelen and the Antarctic in the 1960s. The first ascent of Mt Ross by French mountaineers occurred on 5 January 1975.

An oceanographic research vessel, *Marion du Fresne*, today visits the islands several times annually with supplies and crews of scientists who, on a rotational basis, staff the research station at Port-aux-Français. The vessel is named after the explorer who first sighted the Crozet Islands (1772). A nature reserve was established in the Crozet Islands in 1938, and a permanent scientific research station was built in 1963 at Port Alfred on Il de la Possession, the largest island. At the Kerguelen research station (Port aux Français) the population of scientists and engineers varies from fifty to a hundred persons. Feral cat and rabbit populations now exist on the island, descendants from expeditions in prior centuries. Cats were introduced to control the rats which also arrived earlier by ship. Introduced animals such as cats, rabbits, reindeer and the Kerguelen Sheep negatively impacted native birds and flora, especially the Kerguelen cabbage and the cushion plant referenced in James Cook's journals. Attempts to restore vegetation proceed very slowly due to the sub-Antarctic climate's brief 'growing season'. Scientific activities based on the island accelerated in the twentieth century at several locations. The Arch of Kerguelen continues to serve today as a geological symbol and a source of 'mystery' for Kerguelen Island.[48]

Conclusion

It was the great English navigator James Cook who laid the foundations of
our knowledge.

Ashley Cherry-Garrard, Introduction to *The Worst Journey in the World*,
The Antarctic Exploration Anthology

As Cherry-Garrard suggests, Captain James Cook laid the foundation for knowledge about Antarctica. Although he never set foot on the continent, he played a
pivotal role in turning *Terra Australis Incognita* into modern-day Antarctica. The
150 years before and the 150 years after Cook's travels in the Southern Ocean
demonstrate how the results of navigation and exploration build upon each other.
After serving as a centre for sealing and whaling, South Georgia became a location for small-scale ecotourism, recognized for its stark beauty, its wildlife (with
information tracked by its scientific stations) and the remarkable recovery of the
South Georgia fur seal. Kerguelen and the surrounding archipelago experienced
similar sealing and whaling activities, but no ecotourism. Some economic development opportunities emerged and mostly failed.

Antarctic scientific research today includes approximately forty-five year-round
bases plus thirty summer stations. Some of these bases are named after persons
referenced in this book: Amundsen-Scott, Bellingshausen, George Forster,
Halley, Mawson, McMurdo, Scott Base, Vostok and Weddell. Sub-Antarctic
research stations include Alfred Faure (Il de la Possession (Crozet archipelago),
Bird Island (South Georgia), Campbell Island (New Zealand), King Edward
Point (South Georgia), Marion (Prince Edward Island) and Port-aux-Français
(Kerguelen).

Antarctic exploits continue today. In November–December 2018 an American
and a Briton completed the first crossing of Antarctica on skis, tracked by GPS
but alone and unaided, during a 54-day, 1,000 mile (1,600km) race, crossing from
the Weddell Sea to the South Pole and then to the Ross Ice Shelf. In addition,
a British marine archaeologist is using an icebreaker to locate the remains of
Endurance, Shackleton's ship, in the Larsen-C Ice Shelf in the Weddell Sea.
Attempts by teams of 'adventurers' to cross the 600-mile (965km) Drake Passage
in rowing boats were made in 1988 and 2019, crossing from Tierra del Fuego to
the Antarctic Peninsula. The 1988 effort used a boat with a sail, while the 2019
attempt used a specially designed craft powered by 'human effort only'.[49] *Terra
Australis*, no longer *Incognita*, thanks to Cook and those who followed him, continues to draw explorers and scientists into the twenty-first century.[50]

Admiralty Instructions for Captain James Cook's Three Voyages[1]

First Voyage – *Endeavour*

By the Commissioners for executing the Office of Lord High Admiral of the United Kingdom of Great Britain and Ireland, etc.

'Whereas we have, in obedience to the King's commands, caused His Majesty's Bark the *Endeavour*, whereof you are commander, to be fitted out in proper manner for receiving such persons as the Royal Society should think fit to appoint to observe the passage of the Planet Venus over the disk of the sun on the 3rd of June 1769 and for conveying them to such place to the southward of the Equinoctial Line as should be judged proper for observing that phenomenon, and whereas the Council of the Royal Society have acquainted us that they have appointed Mr. Charles Green, together with yourself, to be their Observers of the said phenomenon, and have desired that the observation may be made a Port Royal Harbour in King George's Island [Tahiti] lately discovered by Capt. Wallis in His Majesty's ship the *Dolphin*, the place thereof being not only better ascertained than any other within the limits proper for the observation, but also better situated, and in every other respect the most advantageous; you are hereby required and directed to receive the said Mr. Charles Green, with his servant, instruments and baggage, on board the said Bark, and proceed in her, according to the following instructions.

'You are to make the best of your way to Plymouth Sound, where we have ordered the crew of the Bark to be paid two months' wages in advance.

'When they have received the same you are to put to sea with the first opportunity of wind and weather, and make the best of your way to the Island of Madeira, and there take on board such a quantity of wine as you can conveniently stow for the use of the Bark's company.

'Having so done you are to put to sea and proceed round Cape Horn to Port Royal Harbour in King George's Island aforesaid, situated in 17 degrees and 30 minutes of South Latitude, and 150 degrees of Longitude West of the Meridian of the Royal Observatory of Greenwich.

'You are at liberty to touch upon the Coast of Brazil or at Port Egmont in the Falkland Isles, or at both in your way thither, if you find it necessary, for completing your water and procuring refreshments for the Bark's company.

'We recommend it to you to stand well to the Southward in your passage round the Cape, in order to make a good Westing[2], taking care however to fall into the parallel of King George's Island at least 120 Leagues to the Eastward of it, and using your best Endeavours to arrive there at least a month or six weeks before the 3rd day of June next, that Mr. Green and you may have leisure to adjust and try your instruments before the observation. And for your guidance in entering Port Royal Harbour, as well as for your more general information of the figure and extent of the island itself, you will herewith receive copies of such surveys, plans and views of the island and harbour as were taken by Capt. Wallis and the officers of the *Dolphin*, when she was there.

'You are to Endeavour by all proper means to cultivate a friendship with the natives, presenting them such trifles as may be acceptable to them, exchanging with them for provisions (of which there is great plenty) such of the merchandize you have been directed to provide, as they may value, and shewing them every kind of civility and regard. But as Capt. Wallis has represented the island to be very populous, and the natives (as well there as at the other islands which he visited) to be rather treacherous than otherwise you are to be cautious not to let yourself be surprised by them, but to be constantly on your guard against any accident.

'You are at all opportunities with the service upon which you are employed will admit of it, to make such father surveys and plans and take such views of the island, its harbours and bays as you conceive may be useful to navigation, or necessary to give us a more perfect idea and description than we have hitherto received of it.

'But whereas the Council of the Royal Society, although they have named King George's Island, yet, to provide against any accident which may prevent the observers from being landed there, have transmitted to us a table of limits drawn up by the Astronomer Royal, within which some other place that will be proper, may, in that case, be sought for. We have hereunto annexed a copy of the said Table of Limits and in case you shall not be able to effect a landing on King's George's Island, require and direct you to search for some other place within those limits where the observation may be made, and to make it there accordingly. When this service is performed, you are top put to sea without loss of time, and carry into execution the Additional Instructions contained in the enclosed sealed packet.

'But in case of your inability to carry out these our instructions to you into execution, you are to be careful to leave them, as also the additional instructions above-mentioned, with the next officer in seniority, who is hereby required and directed to execute them in the best manner he can.

'Given &c. the 30th of July 1768.

E[d]. Hawke[3]

P[y]. Brett[4]

C. Spencer[5]

To Lieut. James Cook, Commander of His Majesty's Bark the *Endeavour*, in Galleons Reach.

By &c. Ph^p. Stephens[6]

The Astronomer Royal's Limits for the Southern Observation of the Transit of Venus which will happen on the 3rd of June 1769.

Latitude Limit of Longitude

South	West of London
5 from	124 to 187
10 from	126 to 185
15 from	128 to 183
20 from	130 to 181
25 from	133 to 178
30 from	136 to 175
35 from	139 to 172

Additional secret instructions to Lieut. James Cook, Commander of
His Majesty's Bark the Endeavour

'Whereas the making discoveries of countries hitherto unknown, and the attaining a knowledge of distant parts which though formerly discovered have yet been but imperfectly explored, will redound greatly to the honour of a nation as a Maritime Power, as well as to the dignity of the Crown of Great Britain, and may tend greatly to the advancement of trade and navigation thereof; and whereas there is reason to imagine that a continent, or land of great extent, may be found to the southward of the tract lately made by Capt. Wallis in His Majesty's ship the *Dolphin* (of which you will herewith receive a copy) or of the tract of any former navigators in pursuits of the like kind; you are therefore in pursuance of His Majesty's pleasure hereby required and directed to put to sea with the bark you command, so soon as the observation of the transit of the planet Venus shall be finished, and observe the following instructions.

'You are to proceed to the southward in order to make discovery of the continent above-mentioned until you arrive in the latitude of 40°, unless you sooner fall in with it; but not having discovered it, or any evident signs of it, in that run, you are to proceed in search of it to the westward, between the latitude before mentioned and the latitude of 35° until you discover it or fall in with the Eastern side of the land discovered by Tasman and now called New Zealand.

'If you discover the continent above-mentioned, either in your run to the southward, or to the westward, as above directed, you are to employ yourself diligently in exploring as great an extent of the coast as you can; carefully observing the true situation of both in latitude and longitude, the variation of the needle, bearings of headlands, height, direction, and course of the tides and currents, depths and soundings of the sea, shoals, rocks &c., and also surveying and making charts, and taking views of such bays, harbours and parts of the coast as may be useful to navigation.

'You are also carefully to observe the nature of the soil and the products thereof, the beasts and fowls that inhabit or frequent it, the fishes that are to be found in the rivers or upon the coast and in what plenty; and in case you find any mines, minerals, or valuable stones, you are to bring home specimens of each, as also such specimens of the seeds of the trees, fruits and grains as you may be able to collect, and transmit them to our Secretary, that we may cause proper examination and experiments to be made of them.

'You are likewise to observe the genius, temper, disposition and number of the natives, if there be any, and Endeavour by all proper means to cultivate a friendship and alliance with them, making them presents of such trifles as they may value, inviting them to traffic, and sewing them every kind of civility and regard, taking care however not to suffer yourself to be surprised by them, but to be always upon your guard against any accidents.

'You are also with the consent of the natives to take possession of convenient situations in the country, in the name of the King of Great Britain; or, if you find the country uninhabited, take possession for His Majesty by setting up proper marks and inscriptions, as first discoverers and possessors.

'But if you should fail of discovering the continent before-mentioned, you will, upon falling in with New Zealand, carefully observe the latitude and longitude in which that land is situated, and explore as much of the coast as the condition of the Bark, the health of her crew, and the state of your provisions will admit of, having always great attention to reserve as much of the latter as will enable you to reach some known Port where you may procure a sufficiency to carry you to England, either round the Cape of Good Hope, or Cape Horn, as from circumstances you may judge the most eligible way of returning home.

'You will also observe with accuracy the situation of such islands as you may discover in the course of your voyage that have not hitherto been discovered by any Europeans, and take possession for His Majesty and make surveys and draughts of such of them as may appear to be of consequence, without suffering yourself however to be thereby diverted from the object with you are always to have in view, the discovery of the Southern Continent s so often mentioned.

'But for as much as in an undertaking of this nature, several emergencies may arise not to be foreseen, and therefore not particularly to be provided for by instructions beforehand, you are, in all such cases, to proceed, as upon advice with your officers, you shall judge most advantageous to the service on which you are employed.

'You are to send by all proper conveyances to the Secretary of the Royal Society, copies of the observations you shall have made of the transit of Venus, and you are at the same time to send to our Secretary, for our information, accounts of your proceedings, and copies of the surveys and drawings you shall have made. And upon your arrival in England you are immediately to repair to this office in order to lay before us a full account of your proceedings in the whole course of your voyage, taking care before you leave the vessel to demand from the Officers and Petty Officers the log books and journals they may have kept, and to seal them up for our inspection, and enjoining them, and the whole crew not to divulge where they have been until they shall have permission so to do.'

Given, etc., the 30th of July 1768

E$^{d.}$ Hawke

P$^{y.}$ Brett

C. Spencer

To Lieut. James Cook, Com$^{r.}$ of His Majesty's Bark the *Endeavour*.

By, etc.

'Whereas we have directed Lieut. James Cook to proceed in His Majesty's Bark the *Endeavour* upon a particular service, you are hereby required and directed not to demand of him a sight of the Instructions he has received from us for his proceedings on the said service, nor upon any pretence whatever to detain him, but on the contrary to give him any assistance he may stand in need of, towards enabling him to carry the said instructions into execution.'

Given, etc., the 30th of July 1768

E$^{d.}$ Hawke

P$^{y.}$ Brett

C. Spencer

To The Flag Officers, Captains & Commanders of His Majesty's Ships and Vessels to whom this shall be exhibited.

By &c.

Ph$^{p.}$ Stephens

Second Voyage – HM Ships *Resolution* and *Adventure*

Secret Instructions for Capt. Cook, Commander of His Majesty's Sloop Resolution

By, etc.

'Whereas several important discoveries have been made in the Southern Hemisphere in the voyages performed by the *Dolphin* under the command of Captain Byron, and afterwards under that of Captain Wallis, by the *Swallow Sloop* under the command of Captain Carteret, and by the *Endeavour Bark* commanded by yourself; and whereas we have, in pursuance of His Majesty's pleasure signified to us by the Earl of Sandwich, caused the *Resolution* and *Adventure* sloops to be fitted out in all respects proper to proceed upon further discoveries towards the South Pole, and from the experience we have had of your abilities and good conduct in your late voyage, have thought fit to appoint you to command the first mentioned sloop, and to intrust you with the conduct of the present intended voyage, and have directed that Capt. Furneaux, who commands the other sloop, to follow your orders for his further proceedings, you are hereby required and directed to proceed with the said two sloops to the Island of Madeira, and there take on board such quantities of wine as may be proper for their respective companies.

'Having so done you are to make the best of your way to the Cape of Good Hope, where you are to refresh the sloops companies, and take on board such provisions and necessaries as you may stand in need of, and may be able to procure.

'You are if possible to leave the Cape of Good Hope by the end of October or the beginning of November next, and in proceeding to the Southward Endeavour to fall in with Cape Circumcision[7] which is said by Mons[r.] Bouvet[8], to lie nearly in the latitude of 54° 00′ South and in about 11° 20′ of longitude East from Greenwich.

'If you discover Cape Circumcision you are to satisfy yourself whether it is a part of that Southern Continent which has so much engaged the attention of Geographers and former Navigators, or part of an Island. If it proves to be the former you are to employ yourself diligently in exploring as great an extent of it as you can, carefully observing the true situation thereof both in latitude and longitude, the variation of the needle, bearings of headlands, height, direction and course of the tides and currents, depths and soundings of the sea, shoals, rocks, etc., and also surveying and making charts and taking views of such bays, harbours and different parts of the coast and making such notations thereon as may be useful either to navigation or commerce. You are also carefully to observe the nature of the soil and the produce thereof, the animals and fowls that inhabit or frequent it, the fishes that are to be found in the rivers or upon the coast, and in what plenty; and in case there are any which are peculiar to that country you are to describe them as minutely and to make as correct drawings of them as you can. If you find any mines, minerals, or valuable stones you are to bring home specimens of each, as also of the seeds of trees, shrubs, plants, fruits and grain peculiar to the country, as you may be able to collect, and to transmit them to our Secretary that we may cause proper examination and experiments to be made of them. You are likewise to observe the genius, temper, disposition and number of the natives or inhabitants, if there be any, and endeavour by all proper means to cultivate a friendship and alliance with them, making them presents of such trinquets as they may value, inviting them to trafick and showing them every kind of civility and regard, but taking care nevertheless not to suffer yourself to be surprised by them, but to be always on your guard against any accidents.

'You are with the consent of the natives to take possession of convenient situations in the country in the name of the King of Great Britain, and to distribute among the inhabitants some of the medals with which you have been furnished to remain as traces of your having been there. But if you fund the country uninhabited you are to take possession of it for His Majesty by setting up property marks and inscriptions as first Discoverers and Possessors.

'When you have performed this service, if the state of your provisions and conditions of the sloops will admit of it, you are to proceed upon further discoveries, either to the Eastward or Westward as your situation may then render most eligible, keeping in as high a latitude as you can, and prosecuting your discoveries as near to the South Pole as possible; and you are to employ yourself in this manner so long as the condition of the sloops, the health of their crews, and the state of their provisions will admit of it, having always great attention to the reserving as much of the latter as will enable you to reach some known port where you may procure a sufficiency to carry you to England.

'But if Cape Circumcision should prove to be part of an Island only or if you should not be able to find the said Cape from Mons[r.] Bouvet's description of its situation, you are, in the first case, to make then necessary surveys of the Island, and then to stand on to Southward so long as you judge there may be a likelihood of falling in with the Continent, which you are also to do in the latter case, and then proceed to the Eastward in further search of the said Continent, as well as to make discovery of such Islands as may be situated in that unexplored part of the Southern Hemisphere, keeping in as high latitudes as you can and prosecuting your discoveries as before directed as hear to the Pole as possible until by circumnavigating the Globe you fall in again with Cape Circumcision, or the spot where it is said to be situated, from whence you are to proceed to the Cape of Good Hope, and having there refreshed your people and put the sloops into condition to return to England, you are to repair with them to Spithead where they are to remain till further order.

'In the prosecution of these discoveries whenever the season of the year may render it unsafe for you to continue in high latitudes, you are to retire to some known place to the Northward to refresh your people and refit the sloops, taking care to return to the Southward as soon as the season will admit of it.

'You are to observe with accuracy the situation of such Islands as you may discover in the course of your voyage, which have not hitherto been discovered by any Europeans, and to make surveys and draughts and take possession for His Majesty of such of them as may appear to be of consequence in the same manner as directed with respect to the Continent.

'But for as much as in an undertaking of this nature several emergencies may arise not to be foreseen, and therefore not particularly to be provided for instructions beforehand, you are, in all such cases, to proceed as you shall judge most advantageous to the service on which you are employed.

'You are by all proper conveyances to send to our Secretary, for our information, accounts of your proceedings and copies of the surveys and drawings you shall have made. And upon your arrival in England you are immediately to repair to this office in order to lay before us a full account of your proceedings in the whole course of your voyage, taking care before you leave the sloop to demand from the Officers and the Petty Officers the Log Books and Journals they may have kept, and to seal them up for our inspection, and enjoining them and the whole crew not to divulge where they have been until they shall have permission so to do. And you are to direct Capt. Furneaux to do the same with respect to the Officers, Petty Officers and crew of the *Adventure*.

'If any accident should happen to the *Resolution* in the course of the voyage so as to disable her from proceeding any further you are, in such case, to remove yourself and her crew into the *Adventure*, and to prosecute your voyage in her, her Commander being hereby strictly required to receive you on board and to obey your orders the same in every respect as when you were actually on board the

Resolution. And in case of your inability or sickness or otherwise to carry these instructions into execution, you are to be careful to leave them with the next officer in command who is hereby required to execute them in the best manner he can. Given &c. the 25th of June 1772'.

Sandwich[9]
Lisburne[10]
Hervey[11]
Thos. Bradshaw[12]
By command of their Lordships.
Php. Stephens

Third Voyage – HM Ships *Resolution* and *Discovery*

Secret Instructions for Capt. James Cook, Commander of His Majesty's Sloop the Resolution

By &c.

'Whereas the Earl of Sandwich has signified to us His Majesty's pleasure that an attempt should be made to found out a Northern Passage by sea from the Pacific to the Atlantic Ocean, and whereas we have in pursuance thereof caused His Majesty's sloops Resolution and Discovery to be fitted in all respects proper to proceed upon a voyage for the purpose above mentioned, and from the experience we had had of your abilities and good conduct in your late voyages, have thought fit to intrust you with the conduct of the present intended voyage, and with that view appointed you to command the first mentioned sloop, and directed Capt. Clerke, who commands the other, to follow your orders for his further proceedings; you are hereby required and directed to proceed with the said two sloops directly to the Cape of Good Hope, unless you shall judge it necessary to stop at Madeira, the Cape de Verd, or Canary Islands, to take in wine for the use of their companies, in which case you are at liberty to do so, taking care to remain there no longer than may be necessary for that purpose.

'On your arrival at the Cape of Good Hope you are to refresh the sloops' companies, and to cause the sloops to be supplied with a much provisions and water as they can conveniently stow.

'You are if possible to leave the Cape of Good Hope by the end of October, or the beginning of November next, and proceed to the Southward in search of some Islands said to have been lately seen by the French in the latitude of 48° 00' South and about the Meridian of Mauritius. In case you find those Islands you are to examine them thoroughly for a good Harbour, and upon discovering one make the necessary observations to facilitate the finding it again, as a good port in that situation may hereafter prove very useful, although it should afford little or nothing more than shelter, wood and water. You are not however to spend too much time in looking out for those Islands, or in the examination of them if found, but proceed to Otaheite [Tahiti] or the Society Isles (touching at New Zealand in our way thither if you should judge it necessary and convenient) and taking care to arrive there time enough to admit of giving the sloops companies the refreshment they may stand in need of before your prosecute the further object of these instructions.

'Upon your arrival at Otaheite, or the Society Isles, you are to land Omiah [Omai] at such of them as he may chuse and to leave him there.

'You are to distribute among the Chiefs of those Islands such part of the presents with which you have been supplied as you shall judge proper, reserving the remainder to distribute among the natives of the countries you may discover in the Northern Hemisphere; and having refreshed the people belonging to the sloops under your command, and taken on board such wood and water as they may respectively stand in need of, you are to leave those Islands in the beginning of February, or sooner if you shall judge it necessary and then proceed in as direct a course as you can to the Coast of New Albion [Likely modern-day Point Reyes, north of the Golden Gate in California, named by Francis Drake in 1579], endeavouring to fall in with it in the latitude of 45° 00′ North; and taking care in your way thither not to lose any time in search of new lands, or to stop at any you may fall in with unless you find it necessary to recruit your wood and water.

'You are also, in your way thither, strictly enjoined not to touch upon any part of the Spanish Dominions on the Western Continent of America, unless driven thither by some unavoidable accident, in which case you are to stay no longer there than shall be absolutely necessary, and to be very careful not to give any umbrage or offence to any of the inhabitants or subjects of His Catholic Majesty. And if in your further progress to the Northward, as hereafter directed, you find any subjects of any European Prince of State upon any part of the coast you may think proper to visit, you are not to disturb them or give them any just cause of offence, but on the contrary to treat them with civility and friendship.

'Upon your arrival on the Coast of New Albion you are to put into the first convenient Port to recruit your wood and water and procure refreshments, and then to proceed northward along the coast as far as the latitude of 65°, or further, if you are not obstructed by lands or ice, taking care not to lose any time in exploring rivers or inlets, or upon any other account, until you get into the before-mentioned latitude of 65°, where we could wish you to arrive in the month of June next. When you get that length you are very carefully to search for and to explore such rivers or inlets as may appear to be of a considerable extent and pointing towards Hudsons [Hudson's] or Baffins [Baffin's] Bays; and, if from your own observations, or from any information you may receive from the natives (who, there is reason to believe, are the same race of people and speak the same language, of which you are furnished with a vocabulary, as the Esquimaux [Eskimos]) there shall appear to be a certainty, or even a probability, of a water passage into the aforementioned bays, or either of them, you are, in such case to use your utmost endeavours to pass through with one or both of the sloops, unless you shall be of the opinion that the passage may be effected with more certainty, or with greater probability by smaller vessels, in which case you are to set up the frames of one or both the small vessels with which you are provided, and, when they are put together, and are properly fitted, stored and victualled, you are to dispatch one or both of them under the care of proper officers, with a sufficient number of Petty Officers, men and boats, in order to attempt the said passage; with such instructions for their rejoining you, if they should fail, or for their further proceedings if they should succeed in the attempt, as you shall judge most proper. But nevertheless if you shall find it more eligible to pursue any other measures than those above pointed out, in order to make a discovery of the before mentioned passage (if any such there be) you are at liberty, and we leave it to your discretion, to pursue such measures accordingly.

'In case you shall be satisfied that there is no passage through to the above-mentioned bays sufficient for the purposes of navigation you are, at the proper season of the year, to repair to the Port of St Peter and St Paul in Kamtschatka [Kamchatka Peninsula, separating the Pacific Ocean from the Sea of Okhotsk] or wherever else you shall judge more proper in order to refresh you people and pass the winter; and in the Spring of the ensuing year, 1778, to proceed from thence to the Northward as far as, in your prudence, you may think proper in further search of a North East, or North West Passage, from the Pacific Ocean to the Atlantic Ocean, or the North Sea. And if, from our own observations or any information you may receive, there shall appear to be a probability of such a passage you are to proceed as above directed, and, having discovered such as passage, or failed in the attempt, make the best way back to England by such route as you may think best for the improvement of Geography and navigation, repairing to Spithead with both sloops, where they are to remain till further orders.

'At whatever places you may touch in the course of your voyage where accurate observations of the nature hereafter mentioned have not already been made, you are, as far as you time will allow, very carefully to observe the true situation, the variation of the needle, bearings of headlands, height, direction and course of the tides and currents, depths of soundings of the sea, shoals, rocks, etc, and also to survey, make charts, and take views of such bays, harbours and different parts of the coast, and to make such notations thereon as my be useful either to navigation or commerce. You are also carefully to observe the nature of the soil and the produce thereof, the animals and fowls that inhabit or frequent it, the fishes that are to be found in the rivers or upon the coast and in what plenty, and, in case there are any peculiar to such places, to describe them as minutely, and to make as accurate drawings of them as you can and if you find any metals, minerals, or valuable stones, or any extraneous fossils, you are to bring home specimens of each, as also of the seeds of such trees, shrubs, plants, fruits and grains peculiar to those places as you may be able to collect, and to transmit them to our Secretary that proper examination and experiments may be made of them. You are likewise to observe the genius, temper, disposition and number of the natives and inhabitants, where you find any, and to endeavour by all proper means to cultivate a friendship with them, making them presents of such trinkets as you may have on board, and they may like best, inviting them to traffic and shewing them every kind of civility and regard, but taking care nevertheless not to suffer yourself to be surprised by them, but to be always on your guard against any accidents.

'You are also with the consent of the natives to take possession in the name of the King of Great Britain of convenient situations in such countries as you may discover, that have not already been discovered or visited by any other European power, and to distribute among the inhabitants such things as will remain as traces and testimonies of your having been there. But if you find the countries so discovered are uninhabited you are to take possession of them for His Majesty by setting up proper marks and inscriptions as first discoverers and possessors.

'But for as much as in undertakings of this nature several emergencies may arise not to be foreseen, and therefore not particularly to be provided for by instructions beforehand, you are, in all such cases, to proceed as you shall judge most advantageous to the service on which you are employed.

'You are by all opportunities to send to our Secretary, for our information, accounts of your proceedings and copes of the surveys and drawings you shall have made; and upon your arrival in England you are immediately to repair to this office in order to lay before us a full account of your proceedings in the whole course of your voyage, taking care before you leave the sloop to demand from the Officers and Petty Officers that Log Books and Journals they may have kept, and to seal them up for our inspection, and enjoining them and the whole crew not to divulge where they have been until they shall have permission so to do. And you are to direct Capt. Clerke to do the same with respect to the Officers, Petty Officers and crew of the *Discovery*.

'If any accident should happen to the *Resolution* in the course of the voyage so as to disable her from proceeding any further you are, in such case, to remove yourself and her crew to the *Discovery* and to prosecute your voyage in her, her Commander being strictly required to receive you on board and to obey your orders the same in every respect as when you were actually on board the *Resolution*; and in case of your inability by sickness or otherwise, to carry these instructions into execution, you are to be very careful to leave them with the next officer in command, who is hereby required to execute them in the best manner he can.'

Given, etc, the 6th day of July, 1776.

SANDWICH

C. SPENCER

H. PALLISER[13]

By command of their Lordships.

Ph^P. Stephens. Sent the same day to him at Plymouth by Butler the Messenger at ¼ before 5 o'clock P.M.

29th July, 1776. An attested copy of the above Secret Instructions was this day delivered to Capt. Clerke, of the Discovery Sloop sealed up, with an order of this date, directing him not to open the above pacquet, unless he is not able to join Capt. Cook according to the rendezvous he has left for him.[14]

By, &c.

You will herewith receive a sealed pacquet addressed to yourself containing a copy of our secret instructions to Capt. Cook of the Resolution sloop, which pacquet if you are not able to join Captain Cook according to the rendezvous he has left for you, you are to open and carry into execution to the best of your ability the above mentioned instructions; but in case you shall join Captain Cook you are then to deliver the said pacquet to him unopened.

Given , &c., 29th July, 1776

SANDWICH

C. SPENCER

H. PALLISER

To Captain Clerke, Commander of His Majesty's sloop Discovery.

By &c.

Ph^{p.} Stephns

(In red).

Delivered to him the same day in town.

Appendix B

Journals and Log Books

In Cook's journals, historian Dan O'Sullivan explains, we learn of Cook's 'sterling qualities – his sense of duty and determination, his methodical approach and obsession with accuracy, his desire for continuous activity, his ambition and his personal courage'.[1] The New Zealand historian J.C. Beaglehole edited Cook's journals for publication for the Hakluyt Society by Cambridge University Press, 1961–1968. His editions of Cook's journals and his *Life of Captain James Cook* together represent one of the greatest contributions to twentieth-century history writing. Beaglehole's contributions are further recognized by many honours given to him, such as Queen Elizabeth II's award of the Order of Merit in March 1970 and an honorary D.Litt. from Oxford University (1966). In attempting to understand James Cook it is useful to understand how the modern edition of his journals was compiled. In his biography of his father, Tim Beaglehole explains how J.C. Beaglehole completed this monumental task. Initially, Beaglehole thought the original text could be 'typed out', cheaply printed and then worked on by historians or anyone. This 'simple, straightforward' approach proved impossible, because there was no single 'plain text'. Instead there were multiple fragmentary drafts and copies. Therefore, Beaglehole's first task was 'to establish an accurate text'. Insofar as possible, his editorial approach was to maintain Cook's original spelling and punctuation. For clarity, Beaglehole inserted valuable footnotes to further explain Cook's entries.

After assembling versions of the journals located in Australia and England, Beaglehole eventually worked with three versions of Cook's journals. Cook himself edited his journals during the voyages, so there is more than one account of entries that required reconciliation. In the final draft Beaglehole sometimes included alternate entries to show Cook's development of conclusions about his observations. Tim Beaglehole describes 'the immensity of the labour' required for the project,

> from the tracking down of material in archives, libraries and private ownership in many parts of the world and the painstaking decisions about spelling and punctuation in eighteenth-century documents to the innumerable hours spent in collating and checking texts against the originals or photocopies of the originals, even more time in research for the introductions and explanatory notes and an almost interminable process of proofreading and correcting.

Beaglehole also travelled around New Zealand and Australia, as well as New Caledonia, the New Hebrides, Hawai'i and Vancouver (Nootka Sound),[2] visiting locations associated with aspects of Cook's voyages.

Log Books

Log books provide useful day-by-day information: a ship's course, wind direction, temperature, barometric pressure, daily changes in weather, ocean conditions (including ice and icebergs), the ship's speed (hourly), longitude and latitude at the end of the day, compass variations, daily distances travelled, and distance from a fixed point (Greenwich, or the last major land sighted, such as the Cape of Good Hope, Cape Palliser, etc.). Until Greenwich became the English standard in 1851, St Paul's Cathedral, 30 seconds west of Greenwich, might serve as the fixed point. Other information included 'remarkable occurrences' during the day, the latter category often being most interesting to an historian. It is here where comments about coastline sightings, vegetation, wildlife, floating ice and ice islands and other observations are located. Captain Cook's journals (and those of others) include only some of this information.[3]

Interpreting log book handwriting is sometimes difficult. Logs record daily nautical and other operational information about the running of the ship. Although 'nautical' in origin, these are historical documents but they not written for the amusement of later historians. Originally the property of the Admiralty, they are now housed in national archives. Log book compilers tended to copy from one another, so sometimes there is little variation in information.

Log book pages were either blank or pre-printed. Grids were used for the insertion of information. The grids varied, as did the size of the books. Occasionally sketches were included. Entries were written in black ink and errors were corrected by overwriting entries. Abbreviations and symbols abound, as do contracted words such as Wea'^{thr} (weather), Gall't (top gallant), sig'l (signal), Ad'^{re} (*Adventure*) or T'kd (tacked). In Cook's era there appears to have been no required format for a log, except general Admiralty comments for a ship's master. Each officer compiled his log with much the same information. In completing this study, I often found the master's log the most valuable because he was responsible for the running of the ship, although logs by the first and second lieutenants are also useful. In order for officers to draw their pay, log books were submitted to the Admiralty at the end of a voyage. The log books remained the property of the Admiralty and the contents could not be divulged without permission. Portions of Cook's log books were lost during the editing of his journals. Digital copies of logs, such as those obtained online through the CORRAL site for this book, must be enlarged 150 per cent or more on a monitor for accurate reading or transcription.

During the years Cook sailed, the nautical day began at noon and ran for twenty-four hours until noon on the following day. Therefore the log for 17 January 1773, the date of the first crossing of the Antarctic Circle, began at noon on 16 January and ended at noon on 17 January. That is also why in Cook's journal the description of events during the afternoon (16 January) precedes that of the following morning (17 January). The 'ship's day' was usually divided into three parts: noon to 8pm, 8pm to 4am and 4am until noon. In October 1805 British log books began conforming to the hours of the civil day.

Log books also record magnetic variations of the compass. This is because 'True' North and South vary from 'Magnetic' North and South, as do the North and South Magnetic Poles and the North or South Poles. An azimuth compass was used to measure the magnetic azimuth, the angle across the horizon between the position of the sun or another object (such as Jupiter's moons) and Magnetic North. This led to determining magnetic declination, the amount by which a ship's compass must be adjusted to give a true reading. Magnetic variation therefore is the angle between Magnetic North/South and True North/South. Compass readings are also affected by the presence of magnetic rocks (e.g. when compass readings are taken on land) and by magnetic storms due to excessive Sunspot activity.[4]

How was Log Book Data Obtained and Recorded?
A ship's course and the wind direction (based on the direction winds were blowing from) were determined by a 32-point compass (although 8- and 16- point compasses were also used). Adjustments to a vessel's direction were made due to leeway, the degree to which a vessel's course was altered by lateral pressure of wind on the hull and sails, as well as the variation between Magnetic North (or South) and True North (or South). A vessel's course 'made good' was determined between two successive noon-day positions, after applying corrections for leeway and drift (the influence of currents and tides). Distance was listed in nautical miles.

A vessel's speed in knots was determined by a log line that had a large knot every 50ft with seven fractional knots. The log line was cast into the sea and the line run out for 30 seconds, the time being measured by sand falling in a glass. The number of knots run out was then counted. The fractional knots measured fathoms, with seven fathoms to a knot in Cook's day. This data was recorded under the H(our), K(not) and F(athoms) columns in the log book. A log book record of 6 knots and 4 fathoms indicated a speed of 6.5 nautical miles per hour. A fathom is also a measure of the depth of the water under the ship (1 fathom = 6ft). Wales and Bayly also maintained astronomical data in separate logs.[5]

*　*　*

Log book information adds specificity to our understanding of journal accounts. The 'observations and comments' include personal insights and provide historians with greater detail and interest, especially those by Lieutenants Clerke and Cooper and *Resolution*'s Master Gilbert. Some variations are seen, for example, in calculating latitude and especially longitude, or miles travelled daily. Differences (usually minor) in knots, fathoms, temperature, wind direction or course at noon are the result of multiple persons interpreting and entering information at different times of the nautical day.

It is through log books that we observe a brief glimpse into the running of the ship, such as hoisting boats to gather floating ice, bringing ice onboard, then breaking and melting it in 'the coppers' and storing it in butts (casks). We also see the cleaning and smoking of the ship below decks with braziers of charcoal and vinegar, as well as counting the contents of casks of pork or beef to ensure accurate provisioning by the Royal Navy's contracted suppliers. Also noted are descriptions of conditions on board *Resolution* through the eyes of both J.R. and George Forster, especially how 'non-sailors' describe sailing below the Circle.

The observation of 'hard' facts as well as the observer's remarks and occurrences of the day in log book entries allow us to understand the demands involved in sailing below the Circle. *Resolution* and *Adventure* faced rain, sleet, hail, snow, haze, fog, floating ice, icebergs often of huge dimensions, and a wall or barrier of unending, impenetrable ice. Low temperatures below the Circle ranged between 32° and 37°F at the height of the Antarctic summer. Petrels, albatrosses and other seabirds and seals, whales and penguins were often present. Facing often-difficult and dangerous conditions, in a ship not well insulated from the elements, and often without a companion vessel for aid and assistance, Cook, the officers, the company and supernumeraries achieved (and recorded) the historic first crossings of the Antarctic Circle, as well as the discovery of new territories such as South Georgia and the South Sandwich Islands.

One Day in Antarctica Recorded in Lieutenant Charles Clerke's Log Book
Lieutenant Charles Clerke's entries for the twenty-four hour period ending at noon on 17 January 1773, recording the first crossing of the Antarctic Circle, is transcribed below, revealing the array of information generated from a log book.

Navigational data: At 1 pm on 16 January, *Resolution* was proceeding at 3 knots, 6 fathoms, heading south by west with easterly winds. The weather was described as 'Fresh Gales and Cloudy Wea^thr'. At 12 pm she was sailing at '4 knots, 6 fathoms, in a south by westerly course and with winds SE ½° by E'. Clerke described the weather as 'Fresh Gales and Cloudy, hazey Weather with frequent snow showers'. He wrote two observations regarding adjustments to the main topsail and the mizzen topsail. The variation by azimuth was recorded as '27° 18' W'sterly', the difference between True South and Magnetic South.

'Remarkable occurrences' on 17 January: 'At Noon I find by my observation which was a tolerable good one, that between 11 and 12 we cross'd the Antartick Circle – We've seen this morning many Flocks of Birds in a good deal like the Pintado, or Cape Pidgeon, & about its size. We've met with many of these before in high Southern Latitudes, but this morning they flew about absolutely in Flocks – the upper Edge of the wing along the Pinion [outer edge of the wing including feathers] from the body to the extreme end is brown, the lower part all white – for distinctions sake I'll here after call these Antartick Petrels – a good deal of sea going grampuses [dolphins]. Observed Latitude 66° 36′ South, *Adv*^{ture} in Company.'

Weather: At noon (the end of the 'nautical day'), 'Fresh Gales with Flying Clouds. Haze & Showers.' At 12 noon on 17 January *Resolution* was sailing at 6 knots, 4 fathoms, heading South ½° East, having travelled 127 miles over the previous twenty-four hours. The ship's position was 66° 36′ south, so below the Antarctic Circle. The longitude was 40° 46′ east of Greenwich. The air temperature was 34°F. The course was north by northwest. The total distance travelled from the Cape of Good Hope (the last port and point of departure for the Southern Ocean) was 707 leagues (about 2,121 nautical miles).

Data grids: The left columns in the log book contain hourly entries for the H(our), K(nots), F(athoms), Courses, Winds and Weather during the 24-hour period. The ship's speed is measured in knots and fathoms. Running across the bottom of each day are grid lines and boxes for (left to right): Course (direction of the ship over the day), Distance (in nautical miles from the previous day), Latitude, Longitude, Thermometer (temperature), Course at Noon, and distance travelled from a fixed point (1 league equals 3 nautical miles or 5.6km).

Notes

Introduction

1. The 28 October 1728 date is based on the Julian Calendar, replaced in many parts of Europe after 1582. The Gregorian Calendar began to be used in Great Britain and its colonies in 1752. The Gregorian Calendar date for Cook's birth is 7 November, but most sources continue to refer to 28 October as the date for Cook's birth.

2. The third voyage ended when *Resolution* and *Discovery* returned to England on 7 October 1780, *Resolution* docking at Deptford, *Discovery* at Woolwich. James Cook, however, was killed in Hawaii on 14 February 1779. Therefore the dates of the third voyage are often listed as 1776–1779/1780.

3. The 'ice edge' term is from J.C. Beaglehole, the editor of Cook's journals and a biography of James Cook.

4. For the trans-Atlantic Enlightenment-era community see Thomas J. Schlereth, *The Cosmopolitan Ideal in Enlightenment Thought, Its Form and Function in the Ideas of Franklin, Hume, and Voltaire, 1694–1790* (University of Notre Dame Press, South Bend, IN: 1977), chapter 1, especially with reference to Cook, pp. 22 and 30. The map on the dust jacket of Schlereth's book traces the three voyages of James Cook, likely modelled after a similar map produced by Henry Roberts, who sailed as a lieutenant in *Discovery* during Cook's third voyage, performing cartographic and related tasks.

5. For Constantine Phipps' Arctic exploration in 1773, see Ann Savours, Sophie Forgan and Glyn Williams, *Northward Ho! A Voyage to the North Pole 1773*, Catalogue to the Exhibition at the Captain Cook Memorial Museum (Whitby: 2010).

6. David Nicandri, 'Influences of Captain Cook on Lewis and Clark', *Cook's Log*, vol. 41, no. 2 (2018), pp. 15–19. See also Nicandri's expanded article, 'The Literature of Captain Cook and Its Influence on the Journals of Lewis and Clark', in *We Proceed On*, located online at www.lewisandclark.org/wpo/. For Lewis and Clark see Stephen E. Ambrose, *Undaunted Courage: Meriwether Lewis, Thomas Jefferson, and the Opening of the American West* (Touchstone/Simon & Schuster, New York: 1996), p. 28. Cook references are also located on pp. 54, 69, 70, 74, 76, 139, 212, 216, 410 and 474.

7. Access to the Captain Cook Society stamp checklist is at https://www.captaincooksociety.com/home/collectables/stamps. The current list was last updated in 2011, but *Cook's Log* contains quarterly updates of worldwide Cook-related issues.

8. The site is now undergoing archaeological examination in search of artefacts.

9. James C. Hamilton, 'Exploring the possible Remains of *Endeavour*', *Cook's Log*, vol. 36, no. 1 (2013), pp. 15–18. See also separate articles by James Hamilton and Phil Parent, 'Exploring the Possible Remains of *Endeavour*', *Cook's Log*, vol. 39, no. 3 (2016), pp. 6–7, and James Hamilton's update with the same title, *Cook's Log*, vol. 41, no. 4 (2018), p. 39; *Cook's Log*, vol. 42, no. 4 (2019), p. 62.

10. N.A.M. Rodger, *The Wooden World: An Anatomy of the Georgian Navy* (W.W. Norton & Company, New York: 1996), pp. 60, 86–7.

11. For possible Spanish visits to Hawaii, see Donald Cutter, 'The Spanish in Hawaii: Gaytan to Marin', a paper presented to the Pacific Coast Branch of the American Historical Association in August 1979, available at https://core.ac.uk/download/pdf/5014742.pdf. For Polynesian navigation to the Southern Ocean, see S. Percy Smith, 'The Polynesians as Navigators', *in Hawaiki: The Original Home of the Maori, with a Sketch of Polynesian History* (Whitcombe & Tombs Ltd,

Christchurch: 1904), p. 129, available at http://nzetc.victoria.ac.nz/tm/scholarly/tei-SmiHawa-t1-body-d7-d8.html. For a brief reference to Polynesian navigation to the Southern Ocean see Arthur B. Ford, 'Antarctica, History', in *Encyclopedia Britannica* (Chicago: 1987), vol. 13, p. 858.

Chapter 1.   The Three Voyages of Captain Cook

1. J.C. Beaglehole, *The Life of Captain James Cook* (Cambridge University Press for the Hakluyt Society, Cambridge: 1974), p. 6.
2. *Streoneshalch* is the Anglo-Saxon name for Whitby. The Northumbrian King Oswiu founded *Streoneshalch* Abbey in 657, the site of the 664 Synod of Whitby. It was a 'double abbey' with separate wings for women and men. The Danes sacked it in a series of raids in the late 860s. The abbey was rebuilt in the eleventh/twelfth centuries and was closed in 1540 during the Dissolution of the Monasteries. The site, including a museum which houses some artefacts, is managed by English Heritage.
3. John Robson, *Captain Cook's War and Peace: The Royal Navy Years, 1755–1768* (Annapolis, Naval Institute Press, 2009), pp. 2–3. See also Stephen Baines, *Captain Cook's Merchant Ships, Freelove, Three Brothers, Mary, Friendship, Endeavour, Adventure, Resolution, and Discovery* (History Press, Stroud, Gloucestershire: 2015), pp. 122–3 and chapter 13, *passim*.
4. The Captain Cook Memorial Museum website is http://www.cookmuseumwhitby.co.uk/.
5. See 'Where did Cook Stay When in Whitby?', by Sophie Forgan and Stephen Baines, *Cook's Log*, vol. 39, no. 3 (2016), pp. 21–3.
6. Beaglehole, *Life*, p. 7.
7. See Baines, *Captain Cook's Merchant Ships*, for Cook's service in Walker's merchant fleet. Muster rolls are not always accurate or complete, perhaps leaving gaps about ports Cook may have visited.
8. Robson, Captain *Cook's War and Peace*, p. 18.
9. Frederick Quinn, *The French Overseas Empire* (Praeger Publishers, Westport, CT: 2002), pp. 69–71; for St Pierre and Miquelon, see James C. Hamilton, 'St. Pierre and Miquelon', Parts 1–4, *The New Carto-Philatelist*, no. 48 (January 2015), pp. 4–6, no., 49 (April 2015), pp. 5–6, no. 50 (July 2015), pp. 3–4, and no. 52 (January 2016), pp. 3–4).
10. Andrea Wulf, *Chasing Venus: The Race to Measure the Heavens* (Windmill Books, London: 2013), pp. xxix–xxx.
11. Today the average distance from Earth to the Sun is stated at 92,955,807 miles (149,597,870km), a distance also known as an astronomical unit. For modern-day calculation of the distance from Earth to the Sun (http://curious.astro.cornell.edu/about-us/41-our-solar-system/the-earth/orbit/87-how-do-you-measure-the-distance-between-earth-and-the-sun-intermediate). James Cook's journals cited in this book include the following: J.C. Beaglehole (ed.), *The Journals of Captain James Cook*. Vol. I: *The Voyage of the Endeavour, 1768–1771*; Vol. II: *The Voyage of the Resolution and Adventure, 1772–1775*; Vol. III: *The Voyage of the Resolution and Discovery, 1776–1780* (Cambridge University Press for the Hakluyt Society: 1968). Hereafter cited as Cook, *Journal*, vol. I, II or III. See Beaglehole's introduction (*Journal*, vol. I, p. cxliv) for an interpretation of data associated with the 1769 Transit.
12. Queen Charlotte (1744–1818) was the wife of King George III. They married in 1761.
13. Michael Lee, 'Endeavour and St Jean Baptiste', *Cook's Log*, vol. 41, no. 4 (2018), pp. 48–53.
14. Regarding the settlement of Australia, see Robert Hughes, *The Fatal Shore: the Epic of Australia's Founding* (Alfred A. Knopf, New York: 1987). Colonization of New Zealand began after 1840.
15. Letter from James Cook to Philip Stevens, Secretary to the Admiralty, 23 October 1770, cited in A. Grenfell Price (ed.), *The Explorations of Captain James Cook in the Pacific: As Told by Selections of His Own Journals, 1768 – 1799* (New York, Dover Publications, 1971), p. 89.
16. Philip Edwards (ed.), *James Cook: The Journals* (Penguin Books, London: 2003), Introduction, p. 12.
17. Beaglehole, *Life*, p. 257. One of *Endeavour*'s bower anchors was lost at the Reef. It was discovered and relocated to a Cooktown Museum and commemorated by an Australian postage stamp issued in 2015.

18. French explorer Jean-Francois de la Perouse's comments praising Cook are cited in Grenfell Price, *Explorations*, p. 192.

19. A copy of a portion of Cook's letter to Sir John Pringle and the document proposing Cook ('a worthy and useful member') as a Royal Society Fellow is found in 'Captain Cook and the Royal Society, National Museum of Australia,' located at www.nma.gov.au/exhibitions/exploration_and_Endeavour/worthy_useful_member.

20. See James Watt, 'Medical Aspects and Consequences of Cook's Voyages', in Robin Fisher and Hugh Johnston (eds), *Captain James Cook and His Times* (Seattle, WA, University of Washington Press: 1979), pp. 129–57; Stephen R. Brown, *Scurvy, How a Surgeon, a Mariner, and a Gentleman Solved the Greatest Medical Mystery of the Age of Sail* (Thomas Dunne Books, New York: 2003), especially chapter 7.

21. For the 1779 visit to Kamchatka, see Glyndwr Williams, Geoff Quilley, Arutiunov and Sophie Forgan, *Smoking Coasts and Ice-Bound Seas: Cook's Voyage to the Arctic*, Catalogue to the Exhibition at the Captain Cook Memorial Museum (Whitby: 2008).

22. Alan Villiers, *Captain James Cook* (Charles Scribner's Sons, New York: 1968), p. vii.

23. Beaglehole, *Life*, p. 694.

24. References for Elizabeth Cook and the family of James and Elizabeth Cook are Beaglehole, *Life*, pp. 689–95 and John Robson (ed.), *The Captain Cook Encyclopedia* (Chatham Publishing, London: 2004), pp. 65–6.

25. Graeme Lay, *The Secret Life of James Cook, A Novel; James Cook's New World, A Novel; James Cook's Lost World, A Novel* (Fourth Estate/Harper Collins, Auckland: 2013–2015).

26. Lashings were administered by a cat-o-nine-tails, a whip with nine thongs. During the second voyage lashings were administered for five instances of theft, five for unauthorized leaving the ship, including failure to post a sentinel on shore, four for drunkenness, four for insolence, and disobedience (for neglect of duty or rioting). There were miscellaneous charges of mutiny and desertion, removal of water from the ships' hold, losing tools on a shore excursion, and one charge for throwing an 'old chew' into victuals. Lashes were administered in multiples of six, with a total of 1,506 lashes administered during the nine years of Cook's three voyages; twelve lashes per incident appears to be the most common, with six lashes as the least and twenty-four as the most (1779). See Allan Arlidge, *Captain Cook's Discipline*, privately published, New Zealand: 2013.

27. Beaglehole, *Life*, especially pp. 712–13.

Chapter 2. *Terra Australis Incognita*

1. Susan Woodburn, 'John George Bartholomew and the Naming of Antarctica,' *CAIRT*, Newsletter of the Scottish Maps Forum (National Library of Scotland, no. 13, July 2008), pp. 4–6.

2. James C. Hamilton, 'An Atlas of Vatican City Cartophilately – Part I', *Vatican Notes*, Journal of the Vatican Philatelic Society, vol. 59, no. 348, 2nd Quarter, 2011, pp. 11–18.

3. Jerry Brotton, *Great Maps* (Dorling Kindersley Ltd, London: 2014) for the Smithsonian Museum, pp. 24–7.

4. J.H. Parry, *The Age of Reconnaissance* (Mentor Books, New York: 1963), p. 17.

5. Ian Cameron, *Lodestone and Evening Star, The Epic Voyages of Discovery 1493 B.C.–1896 A.D.* (E.P. Dutton & Co. Inc., New York: 1966), pp. 102–4.

6. Peter Russell, *Prince Henry 'The Navigator'; A Life* (Yale University Press, New Haven: 2001).

7. Daniel J. Boorstin, *The Discoverers* (Random House, New York: 1983), pp. 282–3.

8. Rob Iliffe, 'Science and Voyages of Discovery', in Roy Porter (ed.), *The Cambridge History of Science*, vol. 4, *Eighteenth Century Science* (Cambridge University Press, Cambridge: 2003), pp. 618, 644.

9. Alan Gurney, *Below the Convergence: Voyages Toward Antarctica, 1699–1839* (W.W. Norton & Company, New York: 1997), p. 55.

10. For Halley's 1699–1701 voyage, see *The Complete Dictionary of Scientific Biography*, located at https://www.encyclopedia.com/people/science-and-technology/astronomy-biographies/edmond-halley#2830901830; Gurney, *Below the Convergence*, pp. 68–85.

11. Bouvet's 24 June 1739 letter to the French East India Company, cited at http://www.south-pole.com/p0000067.htm.

12. The text of Dalrymple's *A Historical Collection of Voyages ...* is located at https://archive.org/details/cihm_35630. The text cited here is found on pp. xxiv–xxx.

13. J.C. Beaglehole, *The Exploration of the Pacific*, 3rd edition (Stanford University Press, Stanford, CA: 1966), pp. 231–2.

14. See Gurney, *Below the Convergence*, for Dalrymple's reaction to Cook's first voyage, pp. 16–18, 21.

15. Alexander Dalrymple in *Australian Dictionary of Biography*, vol. 1 (1966), located at http://adb.anu.edu.au/biography/dalrymple-alexander-1949.

16. History of the Royal Society, located at https://royalsociety.org/about-us/history/.

17. William C. Lubenow, '*Only Connect*', *Learned Societies in Nineteenth-Century Britain* (Boydell Press, Woodbridge, Suffolk: 2015), pp. 81, 88, 272.

18. James McCellan III, 'Scientific Institutions', in Porter, *The Cambridge History of Science*, vol. 4, *Eighteenth Century Science*, p. 93.

Chapter 3.   Ships and the Ships' Companies

1. Villiers, *Captain James Cook*, pp. 83–4. See also Villiers' Appendix, 'The Sense of the Sailing Ship', pp. 284ff. For details about Cook's ships see also 'Cook's Ships' located on the Captain Cook Society website at https://www.captaincooksociety.com/home/cook-s-ships. See also Baines, *Captain Cook's Merchant Ships*, chapters 15–17.

2. Karl Heinz Marquardt, *Captain Cook's Endeavour, Anatomy of a Ship Series*, revised edition (London: 2010), p. 18.

3. Cook, *Journal*, vol. I. *Endeavour*'s specifications are listed on p. ccxiv. See also the detail and sketches in Marquardt, *Captain Cook's Endeavour*, pp. 7–22.

4. Cook, *Journal*, vol. II.

5. Villiers, *Captain James Cook*, p. 182.

6. *Resolution* and *Adventure* data based upon Cook, *Journal*, vol. II, pp. xiv–xv. For Banks' alterations to *Resolution*, see Beaglehole, *Life*, pp. 291–7.

7. *Discovery* data based on Cook, *Journal*, vol. III, p. lxix.

8. Information for the Rhode Island Marine Archaeology Program's (RIMAP) search for *Endeavour* is available at www.rimap.org. See also Hamilton, 'Exploring the Possible Remains of *Endeavour*'; Parent, 'Exploring the Possible Remains of *Endeavour*', *Cook's Log*; Hamilton, 'Exploring the Possible Remains of *Endeavour*', update, *Cook's Log*, vol. 41, no. 4 (2018), p. 39.

9. *Endeavour Replica* at the Australian National Maritime Museum; information is located at http://www.anmm.gov.au/whats-on/vessels/hmb-Endeavour.

10. Cliff Thornton, 'Stockton's Endeavour Replica Moves to Whitby', *Cook's Log*, vol. 41, no. 3 (2018), pp. 24–5; 'Whitby's Endeavour Replica', *Cook's Log*, vol. 41, no. 4 (2018), p. 37.

11. For *Endeavour* at the California Science Center, see https://californiasciencecenter.org/exhibits/air-space/space-shuttle-Endeavour. See also James C. Hamilton, '*Endeavour*'s Future Home in California', *Cook's Log*, vol. 35, no. 3 (July 2012), pp. 45–6 and vol. 35, no 4 (October 2012), p. 37.

12. For the fate of *Adventure* and *Discovery*, see an explanation on the Captain Cook Society website at https://www.captaincooksociety.com/home/detail/Discovery and https://www.captaincooksociety.com/home/detail/Adventure.

13. Brian Lavery (ed.), *Shipboard Life and Organisation, 1731–1815* (Ashgate, Aldershot, Hampshire: 1998), pp. 25–7.

14. Lavery, *Shipboard Life*, pp. 23–5.

15. Rodger, *Wooden World*, pp. 68–71.

16. Nat Weddell, http://blog.wellcomelibrary.org/2013/07/youve-goat-to-be-kidding/.

17. Identification of those persons who sailed on all three of Cook's voyages is located in the Appendices to the Beaglehole editions of Cook's journals under the title 'The Ships' Company'.

18. Reay Tannahill, *Food in History* (Stein & Day, New York: 1973), pp. 270–1.

19. Lavery, *Shipboard Life*, pp. 17–18.

20. Information on daily food allowances, description of certain foodstuffs, supplies and equipment is located in Cook, *Journal*, vol. II, pp. 14–17; Cook's journal entry for 13 July, the start of the second voyage.

21. Wendy Wales, *Captain Cook's Computer: The Life of William Wales, F.R.S., 1734–1798* (Hame House, Yorkshire: 2015), pp. 129–30. Hereafter cited as Wales, *William Wales*.

22. Cook, *Journal*, vol. II, p. 16.

Chapter 4.   Tierra del Fuego, rounding Cape Horn and the Search for a 'Land of Great Extent'

1. A portion of this chapter was published as 'Search for the Southern Continent, January 1769', in *Cook's Log*, vol. 42, no. 1 (2019), pp. 7–13. Additional material especially in reference to Joseph Bank's botanizing and Captain Cook's and Banks' descriptions of native peoples are included in chapter 4.

2. Cook, *Journal*, vol. I; Master's Log, *Endeavour*, ADM55, Log 40, accessed via Colonial Registers and Royal Navy Log Books (CORRAL), http://archive.ceda.ac.uk/cgi-bin/corral/view_images/a=55/l=39/p=1/; Joseph Banks, *The Endeavour Journal of Joseph Banks, 25 August 1768–12 July 1771*, 2 vols, downloaded from the website of the Mitchell Library, State Library of New South Wales, Sydney, Australia, and included in the Cook's Log CD-Rom, version Y2012#12a (January 2013).

3. W.G. Perrin et al. (eds), 'Admiralty Instructions to Captain Cook for his Three Voyages', *The Naval Miscellany* (Navy Records Society: 1927), pp. 343–50. See also Cook, *Journal*, vol. I, the Admiralty's Instructions, pp. cclxxix–cclxxxiv.

4. The 1749 Naval Act, 22 George II, c. 33. The full text is located at http://www.pdavis.nl/NDA1749.htm.

5. Cook, *Journal*, vol. I, 'Letter to the Admiralty Secretary, 30 November 1768,' Appendix I, Letter no. 3, pp. 481–6.

6. Banks, *Journal*, vol. I, 3 January 1769; Cook, *Journal*, vol. I, entry for 4 January 1769. J.C. Beaglehole's note on Pepys Island is in Cook, *Journal*, vol. I, p. lxxi. A useful reference to Pepys Island is Kathleen Parker, 'Pepys Island as a Pacific Stepping Stone: the Struggle to Capture Islands on Early Modern Maps', *British Journal of the History of Science*, vol. 57, no. 4 (December 2018), pp. 659–77. Pepys Island's location was said to be at 47° south latitude and off the Patagonian coast.

7. Beaglehole, *Life*, p. 427. See also 'South American Nomad Cultures', *Encyclopedia Britannica*, vol. 13 and 'Yamana South American Peoples', *Encyclopedia Britannica*, vol. 12.

8. R.A. Skelton (ed.), *The Journals of Captain James Cook on His Voyages of Discovery. Charts & Views Drawn by Cook and His Officers and Reproduced From the Orignal Manuscripts* (Hakluyt Society: 1955). Map III.

9. Villiers, *Captain James Cook*, p. 117.

10. Cited in Cook, *Journal*, vol. I, pp. 499–500.

11. Cited in Cook, *Journal*, vol. I, pp. 62–3.

12. Joan Druett, *Tupia: Captain Cook's Polynesian Navigator* (Praeger, Santa Barbara, CA: 2011).

Chapter 5.   Cook's First Crossing

1. A version of this chapter was published in *Cook's Log*, vol. 38, no. 3 (2015), pp. 3–8. The text has been revised and extended for this book.

2. James Cook's letter to the Earl of Sandwich, First Lord of the Admiralty, 6 February 1772, cited in Cook, *Journal*, vol. I, pp. cciii–cxiv, and also cited in vol. II, Introduction, pp. xx–xxi.

3. Cook, *Journal*, vol. II, pp. cxv–cxxiii.

4. The CORRAL site journal is in the hand of Cook's clerk, William Dawson, the journal copy sent to the Admiralty in March 1775 from the Cape of Good Hope.

5. Log books are located at the National Archives Image Library, accessed through the Colonial Registers and Royal Navy Log books (CORRAL), www.archive.ceda.ac.uk/corral, and include: Log of Captain Tobias Furneaux (ADM55, Log 1); Master's Log, *Endeavour* (ADM55, Log 39);

Lieutenant Charles Clerke Log (ADM55, Log 130); Lieutenant Robert Cooper Log, November 1771 to April 1774 (ADM55, Log 131), Master's Mate Isaac Smith Log (ADM55, Log 132); Master's Mate John Davall Burr Log (ADM55, Log 133); Master Joseph Gilbert Log (ADM55, Log 134); Journal of Captain James Cook, handwritten (ADM55, Log 135), Lieutenant Robert Cooper Log, April 1774 to May 1775 (ADM55, Log 136).

6. Log books by William Wales and William Bayly are the property of the Board of Longitude and accessed through Cambridge University: William Wales, *Log Book of HMS 'Resolution'*, RGO 14/58, located at https://cudl.lib.cam.ac.uk/view/MS-RGO-00014-00058/15; William Bayly, 'Observations on HMS *Adventure*', RGO 14/57, located at https://cudl.lib.cam.ac.uk/view/MS-RGO-00014-00057/1, used by permission from the Syndics of Cambridge University Library.

7. Rupert Furneaux, *Tobias Furneaux, Circumnavigator* (Cassell, London: 1960); Michael E. Hoare (ed.), *The Resolution Journal of Johann Reinhold Forster, 1772–1775*, vols 1–4 (Cambridge University Press for the Hakluyt Society, London: 1982), hereafter cited as J.R. Forster, *Journal*; Johann Reinhold Forster, *Observations Made During A Voyage Round the World*, ed. Nicholas Thomas, Harriet Guest and Michael Dettelbach (University of Hawai'i Press, Honolulu: 1996); George Forster, *A Voyage Round the World*, ed. Nicholas Thomas and Berghof, vols I–II (University of Hawai'i Press, Honolulu: 2000).

8. Beverley Hooper, *With Captain James Cook in the Antarctic and Pacific: The Private Journal of James Burney, Second Lieutenant* (National Library of Australia, Canberra: 1975); Christine Holmes (ed.), *Captain Cook's Second Voyage: The Journals of Lieutenants Elliott and Pickersgill* (Caliban Books, Dover, NH: 1984).

9. 'Furneaux's Narrative' in Cook, *Journal*, vol. II, Appendix IV, p. 730.

Chapter 6.   Separated in an Antarctic Fog

1. Part of this chapter was published in *Cook's Log*, vol. 39, no. 2 (2016), pp. 17–21. The material has been revised and extended for this book.

2. See the 1997 Expedition to Heard Island, at www.cordell.org/HI/.

3. One fathom is 6ft or 1.8m.

4. One league is 3 nautical miles or 5.56km.

5. Furneaux's comments are located in Cook, *Journal*, vol. I, Appendix IV, p. 731.

6. The author's more detailed discussion of other accounts of the February separation is in *Cook's Log*, vol. 39, no. 3 (2016), pp. 28–32.

7. Authors referenced include Furneaux, *Tobias Furneaux*, pp. 99–103; Villiers, *Captain James Cook*, pp. 196–7; Alistair MacLean, *Captain Cook* (Doubleday & Company, New York: 1972), pp. 116–17; Beaglehole, *Life*, pp. 318–19; Richard Hough, *Captain James Cook, A Biography* (W.W. Norton, New York: 1994), pp. 202–6; Vanessa Collingridge, *Captain Cook, A Legacy Under Fire* (Lyons Press, Guilford, CT: 2002), pp. 202–6; Bill Finnis, *Captain James Cook, Seaman and Scientist* (Chaucer Press, London: 2003), pp. 135–6; Peter Aughton, *Resolution: Captain Cook's Second Voyage of Discovery* (Weidenfeld & Nicholson, London: 2004), pp. 46–7.

8. Authors referenced include Alan Moorhead, *The Fatal Impact* (Harper & Row, New York: 1966); Tony Horwitz, *Blue Latitudes*; Nicholas Thomas, *Cook: The Extraordinary Voyages of Captain James Cook* (Walker & Company, New York: 2003); Gurney, *Below the Convergence*; John Gascoigne, *Captain Cook*; Dan O'Sullivan, *In Search of Captain Cook, Exploring the Man Through his own Words* (I.B. Tauris, London: 2008),.

Chapter 7.   'An agitated & tempestuous sea': the Cook Strait

1. This chapter was originally published in two parts in *Cook's Log*, Part 1 in vol. 40, no. 1 (2017), pp. 18–23 and Part 2 in vol. 40, no. 2 (2017), pp. 18–22. The text has been revised and extended. The author thanks Captain Cook Society member and Cook novelist Graeme Lay who suggested I investigate the ships' second separation because of its long-term implications (e.g. the Massacre at Grass Cove) which were more serious than the separation off Antarctica the previous February.

2. Hooper, *With Captain James Cook in the Antarctic and Pacific*.

3. Cape Palliser is a point of land at the southern tip of the North Island, at 41° 43′ 39.2″ south and 174° 16′ 31.7″ east. Cape Campbell is a point of land on the northeast tip of the South Island at 41° 36′ 49.2″ south and 175° 17′ 23.8″ east. In calculating distances, I utilized Andrew Hedges's online calculator, *Finding Distances Based on Latitude and Longitude*, at http://andrew.hedges.name/ experiments/haversine/. Other measurements are based on *The Times Atlas of the World* (1967).

4. For information on the Cook Strait see the online *Encyclopaedia of New Zealand* at http://www.teara.govt.nz/en/1966/cook-strait.

5. New Zealand map by NordNordWest (2008), in the public domain through Wikimedia Creative Commons, located online at https://commons.wikimedia.org/wiki/File:New_Zealand_location_ map. svg, a blank map edited by the author.

6. Brails are small ropes attached to certain sails to truss them up during the process of unfurling.

7. Furneaux's post-voyage narrative is located in Cook, *Journal*, vol. I, Appendix IV, pp. 742–3.

8. For example, see Beaglehole, *Life*, pp. 446–7; Anne Salmond, *The Trial of the Cannibal Dog: the remarkable story of Captain Cook's encounters in the South Seas* (Yale University Press, New Haven: 2003), pp. 2–3, 228–30, 314–17; Nicholas Thomas, *Cook: The Extraordinary Voyages of Captain James Cook* (Walker & Company, New York: 2003), pp. 252–6.

9. In 1770 fifty-seven men in double canoes sailed towards *Endeavour* to a stone's throw distance, and 'After looking at [us] for some time the[y] pull'd in for the land . . .' 15 February 1770 journal entry in Cook, *Journal*, vol. I.

10. Beaglehole, *Life*, pp. 446–7, 521–2.

11. Examples of brief accounts are found in Vanessa Collingridge, *Captain Cook: The Life, Death, and Legacy of History's Greatest Explorer* (Ebury Press, London: 2003); Hough, *Captain James Cook*, pp. 231–3, 296–7; Aughton, *Resolution*, pp. 96–8.

12. Furneaux, *Tobias Furneaux*.

13. Frank McLynn, *Captain Cook: Master of the Seas* (Yale University Press, New Haven: 2011), pp. 224–5, 291–4, 311–12.

Chapter 8.   Cook's Second Crossing

1. A version of this chapter was published in *Cook's Log*, vol. 38, no. 4 (2015), pp. 4–9. The text has been revised and extended for this book.

2. G. Forster, *Voyage*, vol. I, pp. 289–90.

3. J.R. Forster, *Journal*, vol. III, p. 438.

Chapter 9.   Cook's Third Crossing

1. A version of this chapter was published in *Cook's Log*, vol. 39, no. 1 (2016), pp. 10–14. It has been revised and extended for this book.

2. Cook, *Journal*, vol. II, p. cxvii. See also Beaglehole, *A Life of J.C. Beaglehole*, commentary in Appendix B.

3. Cook, *Journal*, vol. II, pp. 955–6.

4. Although 71° 10′ south is always noted as Cook's 'furthest south', his 30 January journal also cites 70° 48′ south and 70° 23′ south as *Resolution*'s positions at various occasions during that day.

5. Cook, *Journal*, vol. II, p. 322.

6. *Ibid.*

7. David Seymour, 'Vancouver Day, Western Australia', in *Cook's Log*, vol. 4, no. 2 (1981), p. 108; Graeme Lay, *James Cook's New World, A Novel*, p. 215.

Chapter 10.   The Second Visit to Tierra del Fuego, Cape Horn and Staten Island

1. Cook, *Journal*, vol. II; Log of Lieutenant Charles Clerke (ADM55 Log 130); Log of Lieutenant Robert Cooper (ADM55 Log 131); Log of Joseph Gilbert (ADM55 Log 134); J.R. Forster, *Journal*, pp. 687–90; Forster, *Observations*; G. Forster, *Voyage*, vol. II, pp. 618–19. In order to avoid repetitive log book notes, Cook's journals and the Clerke, Cooper and Gilbert log books are cited in the text by date of entry only.

2. Wales, *Log Book*, entry for 6 December 1774.
3. J.R. Forster, *Journal*, vol. IV, pp. 687–90; G. Forster, *Voyage*, vol. II, pp. 618–19.
4. Michael Lee, *Endeavour* and *St Jean Baptiste*, p. 52.
5. Forster, *Observations*, pp. 118–19, 43.
6. Wales, *Log Book*, entry for 26 December 1774; a brief entry about the device to measure a ship's roll is in Wales, *William Wales*, p. 245.
7. G. Forster, *Voyage*, vol. II, 621–4.
8. Beaglehole, *Life*, p. 426.
9. G. Forster, *Voyage*, vol. II, p. 630–1.
10. Beaglehole, *Life*, p. 426.
11. J.R. Forster, *Journal*, vol. IV, p. 698–700, 702; G. Forster, *Voyage*, vol. II, p. 632.
12. J.R. Forster, *Journal*, vol. IV, pp. 702–3.
13. G. Forster, *Voyage*, vol. II, p. 638.
14. Frank McLynn, *Captain Cook*, p. 258.

Chapter 11.   'Wild Rocks, Thick Fogs, and Everlasting Snow': South Georgia and the South Sandwich Islands

1. The map of the Scotia Sea is based on a design of an undersea relief map by Gi (2013), accessed in *Wikimedia Creative Commons*.
2. The Isle of Georgia, named by Cook in honour of King George III, was eventually designated South Georgia to distinguish it from the American colony founded in 1732. Sandwich Land (named in honour of John Montagu, 4th Earl of Sandwich and First Lord of the Admiralty) was designated the South Sandwich Islands to distinguish them from the Pacific islands of Hawai'i, and named the Sandwich Islands by Cook in 1778. George Forster termed the former 'Southern Georgia', while J.R. Forster labelled the island 'New Georgia'. The Scotia Sea was named after the expedition vessel *Scotia* from the Scottish National Antarctic Expedition, 1902–4.
3. Chapter 11 is revised and extended from a two-part article published in *Cook's Log* as 'Wild Rocks, Thick Fogs, and Everlasting Snow': part 1, *Cook's Log*, vol. 34, no. 1 (2011), pp. 3–9; part II, vol. 34, no. 2 (2011), pp. 3–9.
4. A collection of photography and descriptive text concerning South Georgia is found in Tim and Pauline Carr, *Antarctic Oasis: Under the Spell of South Georgia* (W.W. Norton, New York: 1998). A video about South Georgia produced by Alastair Fothergill is *Living Edens: South Georgia Island, Paradise of Ice* (Public Broadcasting System: 1999). Photographic and panoramic views are available on the South Georgia official website located at www.gov.gs. A webcam located at King Edward Point and Larsen House transmits images 24/7, which are updated every 10 minutes. Depending upon the season and time of day penguins and seals are imaged on shore, as are occasional small icebergs that enter King Edward Cove at Grytviken and a few small cruise ships that provide day-trip excursions to South Georgia.
5. Dalrymple's chart is reproduced in the Beaglehole edition of Cook's *Journal*, vol. II, p. 617.
6. Carr & Carr, *Antarctic Oasis*, pp. 9, 23.
7. References for flora and fauna at South Georgia include Robert Headland, *The Island of South Georgia* (Cambridge University Press, Cambridge: 2009), chapter 8; Carr & Carr, *Antarctic Oasis*; *The Seal Conservation Society*, located at www.pinnipeds.org/; *Penguin World*, located at www.penguinworld.com/types/king.html.
8. Port Egmont was the first port established on West Falkland Island at Saunders Island and was recorded by navigators who visited the Falklands, whose journals Cook was familiar with. Cook did not visit the Falkland Islands during his voyages, although it remained an option during his exploration of the Southern Ocean.
9. These inlets and bays were named for the Duke of Cumberland (King George III's brother), Admiral Sir Charles Saunders (under whom Cook served in the St Lawrence in 1759), Queen Charlotte, King George III, the Earl of Sandwich and First Lord of the Admiralty, and Robert Palliser Cooper, *Resolution*'s First Lieutenant.

10. A submarine volcano, Protector Shoal, lies 31 miles (50km) off Zavodovski Island in the Traversay Group. Its base is 3,900ft (1,200m) below the ocean's surface, rising to 180ft (55m) below the surface. The South Sandwich Islands are scattered over approximately 1,450 square miles (3,756 sq. km).

11. Candlemas is 2 February on the Christian religious calendar, the date of Christ's presentation in the Temple, thirty-three days after his circumcision; it is also the feast of the Purification of the Blessed Virgin Mary, and a day for the blessing of candles.

12. A source of information about current wildlife on land and sea at the South Sandwich Islands is http://ngm.nationalgeographic.com/2006/12/south-sandwich/holland-text/2.

13. The Smithsonian Institution's Global Volcanism programme provides data about eruptions at www.volcano.si.edu/world/find_erruptions.cfm.

Chapter 12.   The Second Voyage Publication Controversy

1. A version of this article was published in *Cook's Log*, vol. 33, no. 4 (2010), pp. 34–9. It has been revised and extended for this book.

2. References for biographical data on the Forsters include Gerrit Schaefer, 'George Forster: Scientist, Democrat, Revolutionary', *Cook's Log*, vol. 31, no. 4 (2008), p. 5; Ian Boreham, 'John Reinhold Forster', *Cook's Log*, vol. 8, no. 3 (1985), p. 368.

3. James C. Hamilton, 'George Forster and his Antarctic Research Station', *Cook's Log* vol. 40, no. 4 (2017), pp. 10–11.

4. Cook, *Journal*, vol. II, p. lxiv.

5. For James Lind and his importance in naval hygiene, including experiments to prevent scurvy, see Brown, *Scurvy*.

6. Cook, *Journal*, vol. II, Appendix VIII, letters of 12 June: Admiralty Secretary to Navy Board, and 15 June: Cook to Navy Board, p. 940.

7. G. Forster, *Voyage*, vol. II, 'A letter to the Right Honourable the Earl of Sandwich,' pp. 785–806.

8. J.R. Forster, *Journal*, vol. II, entries for 27–30 November 1772.

9. G. Forster, *Voyage*, vol. I, Introduction by the editor, p. xxvii.

10. Cook, *Journal*, vol. II, p. 2.

11. For the text of the 13 April 1776 agreement see G. Forster, *Voyage*, vol. II, Appendix D, pp. 805–6.

12. G. Forster, *Voyage*, vol. I, editor's introduction, p. xxvii.

13. *Ibid.*, pp. 5–6.

14. Wales's entire letter is located in G. Forster, *Voyage*, vol. II, Appendix B, pp. 699–718. Subsequent letters between the Forsters and Wales follow, in Appendices C and D, pp. 718–806. A condensed summary of Wales's criticisms is in Wales, *William Wales*, Appendix VII.

15. William Wales, 'Remarks on Mr. Forster's Account of Captain Cook's Last Voyage Round the World', in G. Forster, *Voyage*, vol. II, Appendix B, p. 701.

16. A short summary of 'The Forster Affair' is in Wales, *William Wales*, chapter 13.

17. *Ibid.*, p. 322.

18. Cook, *Journal*, vol. II, p. xlii; Beaglehole, *Life*, p. 303.

19. Nicholas Thomas, 'John Reinhold Forster and his Observations', introduction to Forster, *Observations*, p. xviii, note 4, p. 402.

20. Michael E. Hoare, *The Tactless Philosopher: Johann Reinhold Forster* (Hawthorn Press, Melbourne: 1976), p. 102.

21. *Ibid.*, pp. 78–9.

22. Cook, *Journal*, vol. II, p. xlvi.

23. Lewis Namier, *The Structure of Politics at the Accession of George III*, 2nd edition (Macmillan & Company: London: 1961).

24. Forster, *Observations*, p. 376.

Chapter 13.   Kerguelen – Cook's 'Island of Desolation'

1. *Discovery of the Northwest Passage Act*, 1744 (18 George II, chapter 7). The £20,000 prize was perhaps the equivalent of £3.1 million in 2018.
2. A portion of this chapter was originally published as 'Kerguelen: Captain James Cook's "Island of Desolation"' in *Cook's Log*, vol. 31, no. 1 (2009), pp. 13–24. It has been revised and extended for this book.
3. W.G. Perrin et al. (eds), 'Secret Instructions for Capt. James Cook, Commander of His Majesty's Sloop the *Resolution*', *Naval Miscellany*, pp. 357–64.
4. Cook, *Journal*, vol. III; Log of the *Discovery* by Thomas Edgar, Master (ADM55, Log 21); Log of the *Resolution* by William Harvey, Master's Mate (ADM55, Log 110); Log of the *Discovery* by William Bayly, Astronomer (ADM55, Log 20); Log of the *Resolution* by Lieutenant James King (ADM55, Log 116); Log of Lieutenant John Gore, *Resolution* (ADM55, Log 120).
5. Anne Salmond, *Bligh: William Bligh in the South Seas* (University of California Press, Berkeley: 2011), p. 483, note 50.
6. A brief biography of Charles Clerke is found in Robson, *Captain Cook Encyclopedia*, pp. 61–2. Clerke's brother's debts amounted to £4,000. See also Clerke's entry in the *Dictionary of Canadian Biography* located at www.biographi.ca/en/bio/clerke_charles_4E.html.
7. Cook to Sandwich, 26 November 1776, and Cook to Joseph Banks, 26 November 1776, in Cook, *Journal*, vol. II, pp. 1520–1.
8. A brief list of animals and fowl carried on *Resolution* is found in Beaglehole, *Life*, p. 508.
9. See 'Fearnought Jackets and Trousers', at http://southseas.nla.gov.au/biogs/P000127b.htm.
10. Sources for Kerguelen-Trémerac and for Kerguelen archipelago include: Alain Boulaire, *Kerguelen: le phenix des mers australes [Kerguelen: Phoenix of the Southern Oceans]* (France-Empire, Paris: 1977), pp. 81–90, 215–16; Jean-Paul Kaufmann, *The Arch of Kerguelen: Voyage to the Islands of Desolation*, trans. Patricia Clancy (Basic Books, New York: 2000); Cook, *Journal*, vol. III, especially notes on pp. 31–2; references to Kerguelen Island, Kerguelen Cabbage, polar physiology and geology, and the Kerguelen Plateau in *Encyclopedia Britannica* (Encyclopedia Britannica Inc., Chicago, IL: 1987), vols 6, 17, 25. Similar information on the Crozet Islands and Crozet Basin is located in *Encyclopedia Britannica*, vol. 3, p. 76,1 and vol. 25, p. 191. A topographical map of the ocean floor identifying the Crozet and Kerguelen Islands is located in vol. 25, pp. 192–3. Other sources include the Kerguelen entry located at https://earthobservatory.nasa.gov/images/89328/kerguelen-islands.
11. This interpretation of the inscription on the view of Christmas Harbour is based on correspondence by the author with Captain Cook Society member M. Alain Melaine of Rouen, France, regarding the meaning of Cook's 'dedication' found on the 1997 triptych stamp issue.
12. Cook, *Journal*, vol. III. The entry for 27 December contains footnotes 3–5 (p. 31) which clarify the location of bottles left by the French in 1772 and 1774.
13. As a philatelist I find it remarkable that postage stamps issued in the twentieth and twenty-first centuries by both South Georgia and the South Sandwich Islands as well as Kerguelen Island (*Terres australes et antarctique francaise*) parallel the observations made by Cook and natural scientists during their 1775 and 1776 visits.
14. Robin Stenhouse, 'Is the Poa Cookii Plant Named After Captain Cook?', *Cook's Log*, vol. 33, no. 3 (2010), pp. 26–8.
15. Seal Conservation Society, 'Antarctic Fur Seal', at www.pinnipeds.org/species/antfursl.htm.
16. Sources for the origin and volcanic activity on Kerguelen include www.volcanolive.com/kerguelen.html, the Smithsonian Museum of Natural History Global Vulcanism programme database at www.volcano.si.edu/world/list.cfm, and www.iomoon.com/kerguelen.html.

Chapter 14.   Natural Science and Cook's Journals

1. This article is based on the author's presentation to the 22 October 2011 annual meeting of the Captain Cook Society in Marton, Yorkshire. A version was published as 'Natural Scientist of High Southern Latitudes', in *Cook's Log*, vol. 35, no. 3 (2012), pp. 308; vol. 35, no. 4 (2012), pp. 4–8; and

vol. 36, no. 1 (2013), pp. 3–7. This chapter is a revised version of the presentation and the *Cook's Log* article.

2. For eighteenth-century science, see Porter, *The Cambridge History of Science*, vol. 4, *Eighteenth-Century Science*, Introduction, especially pp. 4–8, and chapter 26 by Rob Iliffe, 'Science and Voyages of Discovery', pp. 618–20.

3. Mary Fissel and Roger Carter, 'Exploring Natural Knowledge, Science and the Popular', in *Ibid.*, p. 130.

4. See Joseph Banks' entry in the *Dictionary of Australian Biography*, http://adb.anu.edu.au/biography/banks-sir-joseph-1737.

5. Larcum Kendall (1719–90), a London watchmaker. John Harrison (1693–1776) is credited with developing the first chronometer called a 'sea clock'. Examples can be seen at the Observatory Museum at Greenwich. Other examples are located at the Clockmaker's Museum formerly located at the Guildhall, London, and beginning in 2015, at the London Science Museum.

6. Cliff Thornton, 'Cook's Observations of the Aurora Australis', *Cook's Log*, vol. 34, no. 2 (2011), pp. 18–19.

7. Letter, Cook to the Navy Board, 10 March 1772, Cook, *Journal*, vol. II, p. 917.

8. Cook's Letter to the Admiralty, 1(?) August 1775; Cook, *Journal*, vol. II, calendar of documents, pp. 954–5.

9. N.A.M. Rodger, *The Command of the Ocean, A Naval History of Britain, 1649–1815* (W.W. Norton & Company, New York: 2005), pp. 308, 399–400, 484–6.

10. Brown, *Scurvy*. See also Tannahill, *Food in History*, pp. 271–3.

11. As to the hours of the 'watch', the working assumption is that, since the ship's day began at Noon, so did the watch. Therefore the first watch was 1200 Noon to 8pm, the second watch was 8pm to 4am, and the third watch was 4am to 1200 Noon the following day. Variations might occur due to weather or unusual circumstances. N.A.M. Rodger describes a seven-watch schedule for warships, with the First Watch beginning at 8pm. Rodger, *Wooden World*, pp. 39–40.

12. Cook, *Journal*, vol. II: Cook to Admiralty Secretary, 1(?) August 1775, pp. 954–5.

13. Rodger, *Command of the Ocean*, pp. 307–9.

14. Theriaca is an antidote to poisons (the word's first use noted in the *Oxford English Dictionary* as 1440), first developed by the ancient Greeks and Chinese, and associated to some extent with alchemy (cf., Alchemy references to medicine, *Encyclopedia Britannica*). In Cook's era theriaca was a universal curative, a concoction based on no single formula and containing multiple natural ingredients such as roots, bark, leaves, flowers or seeds, various oils and resins, animal parts and minerals. A plaster of theriaca might be similar to a 'mustard plaster', a homoeopathic treatment used to relieve aches and pains or promote healing.

15. G. Forster, *Voyage*, vol. I, p. 296; *see also* 291–7.

16. Sir James Watt, 'Medical Aspects and Consequences of Cook's Voyages', in Fisher & Johnston (eds), *Captain James Cook and His Times*, pp. 129–58, especially pp. 154–5. Watt was a retired Medical Director General of the Royal Navy and Dean of Naval Medicine at the Institute of Naval Medicine.

17. 'Milky Seas Detected from Space', located at http://news.bbc.co.uk/2/hi/science/nature/3760124.stm.

18. The South Georgia plants are identified in Cook's journal entry for 17 January 1775. The Kerguelen Island plants are identified in Cook's journal entry for 30 December 1775.

19. One dictionary definition of an 'Egg Bird' is a sea bird whose eggs can be used as food; the term is usually applied to the sooty tern.

20. Cook, *Journal*, vol. II, p. lxvi.

Chapter 16.   Antarctica and Sub-Antarctic Islands after Cook

1. Train is from the Dutch (*traan*) meaning teardrop, from the process of rendering blubber to oil.

2. Cf. references to 'whale oil' and 'whaling' in the *Encyclopedia Britannica*.

3. Bjørn Basberg and Robert K. Headland, 'The 19th Century Antarctic Sealing Industry: Sources, Data, and Economic Significance', 2008, located at http://ssrn/com/abstract=1553751.

4. Information about whaling is available at 'Whales and Whaling', New Bedford Whaling Museum, located at https://www.whalingmuseum.org/learn/research-topics/overview-of-north-american-whaling/whales-hunting; the Whitby Museum, located at www.whitbymuseum.org.uk; Robert McNamara, 'Brief History of Whaling', located at https://www.whales.org.au/history/19th_Century_Whaling.html. Information on whaling in South Georgia, as well as recent history, is found in Headland, *The Island of South Georgia*, and Gurney, *Below the Convergence*, pp. 59–60, 179–82.

5. Gurney, *Below the Convergence*, pp. 161–72; Bellingshausen's entry in the *Australian Dictionary of Biography*, located at http://adb.anu.edu.au/biography/bellingshausen-faddei-faddeevich-fabian-1767, and at http://www.south-pole.com/p0000073.htm.

6. https://www.falklandsbiographies.org/biographies/weddell_james; Gurney, *Below the Convergence*, pp. 186–9.

7. Gurney, *Below the Convergence*, pp. 214–15.

8. A brief timeline for James Clark Ross is located in his entry in *The Canadian Encyclopedia*, located at https://www.thecanadianencyclopedia.ca/en/article/sir-james-clark-ross/. See also his entry at South-Pole.com, located at http://www.south-pole.com/p0000081.htm.

9. Admiralty Instructions to James Clark Ross cited in Gurney, *Below the Convergence*, p. 211.

10. Maurice J. Ross, *Polar Pioneers: John Ross and James Clark Ross* (McGill-Queen's University Press, Montreal & Kingston: 1994), p. 217.

11. Logbook of C.F. Tucker, *Erebus* (ADM55, Log 48), entries for 5–15 May 1840.

12. A 1970 *Terres Australes et Antarctiques Francaises* air mail stamp depicts a sketch of *Erebus* and *Terror* sailing past the Arch of Kerguelen, marking the visit in 1840.

13. The Campbell Island Group comprises uninhabited sub-Antarctic islands administered today by New Zealand; it is also a UNESCO World Heritage Site.

14. Ross, *Polar Pioneers*, p. 226.

15. Log and meteorological record of the *Terror*, entries for 12–23 January 1841 (ADM55, Log 134); C.F. Tucker's *Erebus* logbook for 12–23 January 1841 (ADM55, Log 50).

16. C.F. Tucker, Log of *Erebus*, entry for 13 March 1842 (ADM55, Log 51).

17. Log and meteorological record of the *Terror*, entry for 13 March 1842 (ADM55, Log 135). Author not identified.

18. C.F. Tucker, *Erebus* logbook, entry for 16 January 1843 (ADM55, Log 52).

19. R.F. Scott, *Voyage of the Discovery*, introduction, cited in Ross, *Polar Pioneers*, p. 254.

20. Apsley Cherry-Garrard, *The Worst Journey in the World* (1922; reissued by Vintage Books, 2010), Introduction; *The Antarctic Exploration Anthology: Personal Accounts of the Great Antarctic Explorers*, Bybliotech Discovery Book 1, ASIN B00F08802S (2013).

21. The account of Douglas Mawson's 1912–1913 trek is based on the account in David Roberts, *Alone on the Ice: The Greatest Survival Story in the History of Exploration* (W.W. Norton, New York: 2013), pp. 208–55. See also general accounts in F.J. Jacka, *Australian Dictionary of Biography*, located at http://adb.anu.edu.au/biography/mawson-sir-douglas-7531.

22. A time-line for Roald Amundsen is the Fram Museum site, located at http://frammuseum.no/polar_history/expeditions/the_maud_expedition__1918-1925_/the_maud_expedition_1918-1925.

23. *Sasturgi* (or *Zasturgi*) is a German transliteration of Russian.

24. Roland Huntford, *The Last Place on Earth: Scott and Amundsen's Race to the South Pole* (Random House/Modern Library, New York: 1999), pp. 440–1.

25. *The Antarctic Exploration Anthology*, Amundsen diary entries 14–17 December 1911.

26. Huntford, *The Last Place on Earth*, pp. 465–70.

27. *Ibid.*, pp. 404–5.

28. *The Antarctic Exploration Anthology*, Scott's diary entries for February–March 1912.

29. *The Antarctic Exploration Anthology*, Scott's diary entries for 14–29 March 1912. Scott's final diary entry and letter to the public, dated 29 March 1912, is also located at https://www.history channel.com.au/this-day-in-history/robert-falcon-scotts-final-diary-entry/.

30. Huntford, *The Last Place on Earth*, chapters 31 and 33; see also *The Antarctic Exploration Anthology*.

31. Cherry-Garrard, *The Worst Journey in the World*; *The Antarctic Exploration Anthology*, Introduction.

32. See 'Scott's Last Expedition', which is this chapter's source for some information about Robert Falcon Scott, located at http://www.scottslastexpedition.org/expedition/robert-falcon-scott/.

33. Ernest Shackleton, *South, The Endurance Expedition* (1919; reissued by Penguin, New York: 2007).

34. *Ibid.*, p. 96.

35. Alfred Lansing, *Endurance: Shackleton's Incredible Voyage* (Basic Books, New York: 2007), p. 60.

36. Haakon IV was King of Norway, 1905–57.

37. The name 'Peggotty' is based on a family in Charles Dickens' *David Copperfield* who lived in a beached boat.

38. Shackleton, *South*, pp. 197, 201.

39. Frank A. Worsley, *Endurance: An Epic of Polar Adventure* (W.W. Norton, New York: 2000), p. 162.

40. Cited in Lansing, *Endurance*, p. 275.

41. Shackleton, *South*, p. 234.

42. Cited in Fergus Flemming, introduction to Shackleton, *South*, p. xiv. Video images of Shackleton's *Endurance* expedition are located in the bibliography.

43. In addition to his account, other Shackleton references for the Imperial Trans-Antarctic Expedition include his entry in the *Dictionary of Falklands Biography*, located at https://falklandsbiographies.org/biographies/shackleton_sir; Royal Geographic Society, 'Shackleton-Endurance Expedition Timeline,' located at https://www.rgs.org/CMSPages/GetFile.aspx?nodeguid=949d8f9d-ffee-474a-a0ad-bbdafcfdf738&lang=en-GB; a general biographical sketch is found in his and related entries in *Encyclopedia Britannica*.

44. See the James Caird Society, located at http://www.jamescairdsociety.com/ and http://www.jamescairdsociety.com/the-james-caird/how-to-visit/. This website contains information about Shackleton and the Trans-Antarctic Expedition. For the burial of Frank Wild's ashes at Grytviken, see *BBC News Magazine*, 29 December 2011, located at https://www.bbc.com/news/magazine-16165494.

45. A useful source for South Georgia today is Carr & Carr, *Antarctic Oasis*. See chapter 11, note 4.

46. Emma Maris, 'Large Island Declared Rat-Free in Biggest Removal Success', https://news.nationalgeographic.com/2018/05/south-georgia-island-rat-free-animals-spd/, May 2018. Information on the South Georgia reindeer eradication programme is located at http://www.gov.gs/environment/eradication-projects/eradication-projectsreindeer/.

47. https://www.researchgate.net/publication/268519947_History_of_whaling_sealing_fishery_and_aquaculture_trials_in_the_area_of_the_Kerguelen_Plateau.

48. A useful Kerguelen archipelago reference is Kaufmann, *The Arch of Kerguelen*. It includes a current topographical assessment of the island with accounts of Kerguelen's voyages and subsequent French and other European contact with the archipelago.

49. *See* 'Impossible Row' at https://www.discovery.com/shows/the-impossible-row.

50. For the 2018 crossing of Antarctica, see https://www.nationalgeographic.com/Adventure/2018/12/second-explorer-louis-rudd-crosses-antarctica/; for the 2019 search for *Endurance*, see https://www.telegraph.co.uk/news/2018/04/10/british-scientists-race-find-lost-shipwreck-ernest-shackletons/.

Appendix A.   Admiralty Instructions for Captain James Cook's Three Voyages

1. Perrin, 'Admiralty Instructions to Captain Cook', *Naval Miscellany*. Reproduced with permission of the Navy Records Society.

2. 'Westing' is defined by the *Oxford English Dictionary* as 'distance travelled or measured westward, especially at sea', the opposite of 'Easting'.

3. Edward Hawke, 1st Baron Hawke (1705–81), Admiral of the Fleet, First Lord of the Admiralty (1766–71).

4. Peircy Brett (1709–81), Admiral, Senior Naval Lord.

5. Lord Charles Spencer (1740–1820), Junior Lord of the Admiralty (1768–79).

6. Sir Philip Stephens, 1st Baronet (1723–1809), First Secretary to the Admiralty. Stephens, a long-time friend and supporter of James Cook, was a Fellow of the Royal Society and represented First Lord of the Admiralty Sandwich's interests in the House of Commons, of which he was a member from 1759 to 1806.

7. Footnote in the Perrin edition of Admiralty Instructions: 'Bouvet Island, now known to lie in lat. 54° 26′ South, Long. 3° 24′ East. The given position is so far out that Cook could not find it.'

8. Jean-Baptiste le Charles Bouvet de Lozier (1705–86), a French navigator for the French East India Company, discovered Bouvet Island in the Southern Ocean on 1 January 1739. He was unable to land on the island. Cook searched for it during the second voyage; references for the search appear in chapters 5–11.

9. John Montagu, 4th Earl of Sandwich (1718–92), First Lord of the Admiralty (1748–51, 1763, 1771–82).

10. Wilmont Vaughn, 1st Earl of Lisburne (1728–1800), Lord of the Admiralty (1770–82).

11. Augustus John Hervey, 3rd Earl of Bristol (1724–79), Admiral, First Naval Lord (1771–5).

12. Thomas Bradshaw (1733–74), Member of Parliament (1767–74), held civil service appointments, Lord of the Admiralty (1772–4).

13. Hugh Palliser, 1st Baronet (1723–96), Admiral, Governor of Newfoundland (where he came into contact with James Cook when he surveyed its coastline after the Seven Years' War, and later served as a long-time Cook mentor), later Comptroller of the Navy, and First Naval Lord (1775–9).

14. At the time the instructions were prepared, Captain Charles Clerke was acting as surety for his brother's debts and was confined to King's Bench Debtors Prison in London. During his confinement Clerke contracted consumption (tuberculosis) from which he died on 22 August 1779 (see chapter 1). Clerke was freed from prison and subsequently left England, with *Discovery* joining *Resolution* at the Cape of Good Hope on 10 November 1776.

Appendix B.   Journals and Log Books

1. O'Sullivan, *In Search of Captain Cook*, p. 11.

2. Beaglehole, *A Life of J.C. Beaglehole*, chapters 11–12.

3. An essay on the use of log books by a historian is located in James C. Hamilton, 'Interpreting Log Books – Cook's Second Voyage', *Cook's Log*, vol. 38, no. 2 (2015), pp. 16–22.

4. Derek Morris, 'Magnetic Observations on Cook's first voyage', *Cook's Log*, vol. 41, no. 3 (2018), pp. 30–3.

5. For general information on log books, see C. Wilkinson, *British Logbooks in UK Archives, 17th–19th centuries – a survey of the range, selection and suitability of British logbooks and related documents for climatic research* (2006, revised 2009, published as CRU RP12 in 2012, located at http://www.cru.uea.ac.uk/documents/421974/1301877/CRU_RP12.pdf/0eb44edd-b085-4617-a5dd-5a32e44b1e9a. A second source by C. Wilkinson (and others) is located at http://cdn.knmi.nl/system/data_center_publications/files/000/044/827/original/garciaherrera_koek_etal_2004_cc_preprint.pdf?1432895541.

Bibliography

Primary Sources – Journals and Maps

Banks, Joseph, *The Endeavour Journal of Joseph Banks, 25 August 1768–12 July, 1771*, Volumes 1–2 (Mitchell Library, State Library of New South Wales, Sydney, Australia: 1962).

Beaglehole, J.C. (John Cawte), Editor, *The Journals of Captain James Cook*, Volume I, *The Voyage of the Endeavour, 1768–1771*, Cambridge University Press for the Hakluyt Society (Cambridge: 1968).

Beaglehole, J.C. Editor, *The Journals of Captain James Cook*, Volume II, *The Voyage of the Resolution and Adventure, 1772–1775*, Cambridge University Press for the Hakluyt Society (Cambridge: 1961).

Beaglehole, J.C., Editor, *The Journals of Captain James Cook*, Volume III, Parts 1 and 2, *The Voyage of the Resolution and Discovery*, Cambridge University Press for the Hakluyt Society (Cambridge: 1967).

Edwards, Philip, Editor, *James Cook, The Journals*, Prepared from the original manuscripts by J.C. Beaglehole for the Hakluyt Society, 1955–1971 (Penguin Books, New York: 2003).

Forster, George, *A Voyage Round the World*, Edited by Thomas, Nicholas and Berghof, Oliver Volumes I–II (University of Hawai'i Press, Honolulu: 2000).

Forster, Johann Reinhold, *Observations Made During A Voyage Round the World*, Edited by Thomas, Nicholas, Guest, Harriet and Dettelbach Michael (University of Hawai'i Press, Honolulu: 1996).

Grenfell Price, A., *The Explorations of Captain James Cook in the Pacific, As Told by Selections of his Own Journals, 1768–1779* (Dover Publications, New York: 1971).

Hoare, Michael E., Editor, *The Resolution Journal of Johann Reinhold Forster*, Volumes I–IV (Cambridge University Press for the Hakluyt Society: 1982).

Holmes, Christine, editor, *Captain Cook's Second Voyage: The Journals of Lieutenants Elliott and Pickersgill* (Caliban Books, Dover, NH: 1984). Pickersgill's journal ends in early October 1773.

Hooper Beverley, Editor, *With Captain James Cook in the Antarctic and Pacific: The Private Journal of James Burney, Second Lieutenant* (National Library of Australia, Canberra: 1975).

Lavery, Brian, editor, *Shipboard Life and Organisation, 1731–1815*, The Naval Records Society (Ashgate, Derbyshire: 1998).

Perrin, W.G., *The Naval Miscellany: Admiralty Instructions to Captain Cook for His Three Voyages* (The Navy Records Society, London: 1928).

Rumsey, David, Historical Antarctica Maps, located at https://www.davidrumsey.com/luna/servlet/view/all/where/Antarctica/.

Sleleton, R.A., Editor, *The Journals of Captain James Cook on His Voyages of Discovery, Charts & Views Drawn by Cook and His Officers and Reproduced from the Original Manuscripts* (Cambridge University Press for the Hakluyt Society: 1955).

Primary Sources – Log Books

The log books accessed through the Colonial Registers and Royal Navy Logbooks (CORRAL), are located at the National Archives Image Library (http://www.archive.ceda/ac.uk/corral). Logs are numbered according to the catalogue at the National Archives. The numbers for logs accessed through CORRAL usually vary and are identified as (CORRAL *xxx*).

ADM55/Log 1 (CORRAL 1), *Log of Captain Tobias Furneaux*, 1772–1775 (*Adventure*).

ADM55/Log 21 (CORRAL 21),*Log of Master Thomas Edgar*, 1776–1780 (*Discovery*).

ADM55/Log 39 (CORRAL 39), *Master's Log*, 1768–1771 (*Endeavour*).

ADM55/Log 48–53 (CORRAL 49–54), *Log of C.F. Tucker*, 1839–1841 (*Erebus*).

ADM55/Log 110 (CORRAL 20), *Log of Master William Harvey*, 1776–1778 (*Resolution*).
ADM55/Log 103 (CORRAL130), Log of Lieutenant Charles Clerke, 1772–1775 (*Resolution*).
ADM55/Log 104 & 109 (CORRAL 131, 136), *Log of Lieutenant Robert Cooper*, 1771–1774, 1774–1775 (*Resolution*).
ADM55/Log 105 (CORRAL 132), *Log of Master's Mate Isaac Smith*, 1772–1775 (*Resolution*).
ADM55/Log 106 (CORRAL 133), *Log of Master's Mate John Davall Burr*, 1772–1775 (*Resolution*).
ADM55/Log 107 (CORRAL 134), *Log of Master Joseph Gilbert*, 1772–1775 (*Resolution*).
ADM55/Log 108 (CORRAL 135), *Handwritten Journal of Captain James Cook*, 1772–1775 (*Resolution*).
ADM55/Log 110 (CORRAL 137), *Log of Master's Mate William Harvey*, 1776–1777 (*Resolution*).
ADM55/Log 116 (CORRAL 106), *Log of Lieutenant James King*, 1776–1778 (*Resolution*).
ADM55/Log 120 (CORRAL 120), *Log of Lieutenant John Gore*, 1776–1778 (*Resolution*).
ADM55/Log 135 (CORRAL 171), *Log & Meteorological Record of Terror January to December 1842.*

Papers of the Board of Longitude, Log Books (accessed via https://cudl.lib.cam.ac.uk/)
RGO 14/58, William Wales, *Log Book of HMS 'Resolution'*, 1772–1775.
RGO 14/57, William Bayly, *Observations on HMS 'Adventure'*, 1772–1774.

Secondary Sources – Books and Articles

Ambrose, Stephen E., *Undaunted Courage: Meriwether Lewis, Thomas Jefferson, and the Opening of the American West* (Touchstone/Simon and Schuster, New York: 1996).
Amundsen, Roald, Scott, Robert Falcon, Shackleton, Ernest, Mawson, Douglas, Cherry-Garrad, Apsley, *The Antarctic Exploration Anthology, Personal Accounts of the Great Antarctic Explorers*, A Bybliotech Discovery Book 1, ASIN B00F088026 (2013).
Arlidge, Allan, *Captain Cook's Discipline* (privately published, New Zealand: 2013).
Aughton, Peter, *Resolution, Captain Cook's Second Voyage of Discovery* (Weidenfeld & Nicolson, London: 2004).
Baines, Stephen, *Captain Cook's Merchant Ships: Free Love, Three Brothers, Mary, Friendship, Endeavour, Adventure, Resolution, and Discovery* (History Press, Stroud, Gloucestershire: 2015).
Baines, Stephen, 'Where Did Captain Cook Stay When in Whitby?', *Cook's Log*, Vol. 39, No. 3 (2016), pp. 21–23.
Barnett, James K., and Nicandri, David, *Arctic Ambitions: Captain Cook and the Northwest Passage* (University of Washington Press, Seattle: 2015).
Beaglehole, J.C., *The Life of Captain James Cook* (Cambridge University Press for the Hakluyt Society: 1974. Also published in the US by Stanford University Press, 1974).
Beaglehole, J.C., *The Exploration of the Pacific*, Third Edition (Stanford University Press, Stanford, CA: 1966).
Beaglehole, Tim, A *Life of J.C. Beaglehole, New Zealand Scholar* (Victoria University Press, Wellington: 2006).
Boorstin, Daniel J., *The Discoverers* (Random House, New York: 1983).
Boreham, Ian, 'John Reinhold Forster,' *Cook's Log*, Vol. 8, No. 3, 1985, p. 368.
Boulaire, Alain, *Kerguelen: le phenix des mers australes* (France-Empire, Paris: 1977).
Brotton, Jerry, *Great Maps*, in association with the Smithsonian Institution (Dorling Kindersley Ltd., New York: 2014).
Brown, Stephen R., *Scurvy, How a Surgeon, A Mariner, and a Gentleman Solved the Greatest Medical Mystery in the Age of Sail* (Thomas Dunne Books/St. Martin's, New York: 2003).
Cameron, Ian, *Lodestone & Evening Star: The Epic Voyages of Discovery from 1493 B.C. to 1896 A.D.* (E.P. Dutton & Co., New York: 1966).
Carr, Tim and Pauline, *Antarctic Oasis: Under the Spell of South Georgia* (W.W. Norton, New York: 1998).
Collingridge, Vanessa, *Captain Cook: The Life, Death and Legacy of History's Greatest Explorer* (Ebuy Press/Random House, London: 2002). Published in the United States with the title, *Captain Cook, A Legacy Under Fire* (Lyons Press, Guilford, CT: 2002).

Coote, Jeremy, Editor, *Cook-Voyage Collections of 'Artificial Curiosities' in Britain and Ireland, 1771–2015* (Museum Ethnographers Institute, Oxford: 2015).

Druett, Joan, *Tupaia, Captain Cook's Polynesian Navigator* (Praeger, Santa Barbara, CA: 2011).

Dugard, Martin, *Further Than Any Man, The Rise and Fall of Captain James Cook* (Washington Square Press, New York: 2001).

Dunmore, John, *Storms and Dreams, The Life of Louis De Bougainville* (University of Alaska Press, Fairbanks, AK: 2007).

Dunmore, John, *Where Fate Beacons, The Life of Jean-Francois de la Pérouse* (University of Alaska Press, Fairbanks, AK: 2007).

Finnis, Bill, *Captain James Cook, Seaman and Scientist* (Chaucer Press, London: 2003).

Fisher, Robin, and Johnston, Hugh, Editors, *Captain James Cook and His Times* (University of Washington Press, Seattle: 1979).

Ford, Arthur B., For a brief reference to Polynesian navigators in or near Antarctica, see 'Antarctica, History', in *Encyclopedia Britannica* (Chicago: 1987), Vol. 13, p. 858.

Forgan, Sophie, 'Where did Cook Stay When in Whitby?', *Cook's Log*, Vol. 39, No. 3 (2016), p. 21.

Gascogine, John, *Captain Cook, Voyager Between Worlds* (Hambeldon Continuum, London: 2008).

Furneaux, Rupert, *Tobias Furneaux, Circumnavigator* (Cassell, London: 1960).

Gurney, Alan, *Below the Convergence: Voyages Toward Antarctica, 1699–1839* (W.W. Norton, New York: 2007).

Hamilton, James C., "Kerguelen: Captain Cook's 'Island of Desolation'", *Cook's Log*, Vol. 32, No. 1, January 2009, pp. 13–24.

Hamilton, James C., 'Captain Cook's Hawaiian Connections: Cook Pines and Feral Goats?', *Cook's Log*, Vol. 32, No. 3 (July 2009), pp. 28–30.

Hamilton, James C., 'Philatelic Images for Captain James Cook's Journals', *American Philatelist*, Vol. 124, Number 3, March 2010, pp. 222–231.

Hamilton, James C., 'The Second Voyage Publication Controversy', in *Cook's Log*, Vol. 33, No. 4 (October, 2010), pp. 34–39.

Hamilton, James C., 'Wild Rocks, Thick Fogs, and Everlasting Snow', Part I in *Cook's Log*, Vol. 34, No. 1 (January 2011), pp. 3–9; Part II in Number 2 (April 2011), pp. 3–9. Translated into French and published as '*Rocs inhospitaliers brouillards épais neiges éternelles*', for *Terres Polaires, Bulletin Trimestriel, Union Francaise de Philatelie Polaire – SATA*, No. 168 (*Septembre* 2012), No. 169 (*Decembre* 2012), et No. 172 (*Septembre* 2013).

Hamilton, James C., 'An Atlas of Vatican City Cartophilately – Part I', *Vatican Notes* journal of the Vatican Philatelic Society, Vol. 59, No. 348, 2nd Quarter, 2011, pp. 11–18, for Nicholas Germanicus, 'Map of the Known World at That time' (ca.1480).

Hamilton, James C., 'Captain James Cook CartoPhilately', *The New CartoPhilatelist*, Part I, No. 37 (April 2012), pp. 1–3, Part II, No. 38 (July 2012), pp. 5–7 and 11; Part III No. 39 (October 2012), pp. 3–6, Part IV, No. 40 (January 2013), pp. 4–8.

Hamilton, James C., 'Natural Scientist of High Southern Latitudes', Part I, *Cook's Log*, Vol. 35, No. 3 (July 2012), pp. 3–8; Part II, Vol. 35, No. 4 (October 2012), pp. 4–9, Part III, Vol. 36, No. 1 (January 2013), pp. 3–7.

Hamilton, James C., '*Endeavour*'s Future Home in California', *Cook's Log*, Vol. 35, No. 3 (July 2012), pp. 45–46 and Vol. 35, No. 4 (October 2012), p. 37.

Hamilton, James C., 'Exploring the Possible Remains of *Endeavour*,' *Cook's Log*, Vol. 36, No. 1 (January 2013), pp. 15–18; 'Exploring the Possible Remains of *Endeavour*,' two separate articles by James Hamilton and Phil Parent, *Cook's Log*, Vol. 39, No. 3 (October 2016), pp. 6–7; 'Exploring the Possible Remains of *Endeavour*', *Cook's Log*, Vol. 41, No. 4 (October 2018), p. 39.

Hamilton, James C., 'St. Pierre and Miquelon', Parts 1–4, *The New Carto-Philatelist*, No. 48 (January 2015), pp. 4–6, No. 49 (April 2015), pp. 5–6, No. 50 (July 2015), pp. 3–4, and No. 52 (January 2016), pp. 3–4.

Hamilton, James C., 'Interpreting Log Books – Cook's Second Voyage', *Cook's Log*, Vol. 38, No. 2 (April 2015), pp. 16–22.

Hamilton, James C., 'Cook's Crossing of the Antarctic Circle – Part I', *Cook's Log*, Vol. 38, No. 3 (July 2015), pp. 3–8, Part II, Vol. 38, No. 4 (October 2015), pp. 4–9; Part III, Vol. 39, No. 1 (January 2016), pp. 10–14.

Hamilton, James C., 'Separated in an Antarctic Fog, 8–11 February 1773', Part I, *Cook's Log*, Vol. 39, No. 2 (April 2016), pp. 17–21; Part II, 'Separated in an Antarctic Fog – Varying Accounts and Interpretations', Vol. 39, No. 3 (July 2016), pp. 28–32.

Hamilton, James C., 'An Agitated and Tempestuous Sea', Part I, *Cook's Log*, Vol. 40, No. 1 (January 2017), pp. 18–23; Part II, *Cook's Log*, Vol. 40, No. 2 (April 2017), pp. 18–22.

Hamilton, James C., 'My Favourite Captain James Cook, CartoPhilatelic Stamp', *The New Carto-Philatelist*, No. 57 (April 2017), p. 8. The article features the 1979 Canada stamp issued to mark the 200th anniversary of Cook's voyages and features the Nathaniel Dance portrait of Captain Cook and John Webber's painting of Nootka Sound.

Hamilton, James C., 'Georg Forster and His Antarctic Research Station', *Cook's Log*, Vol. 40, No. 4 (2017), pp 10–11.

Hamilton, James C., 'Search for the Southern Continent, January 1769', *Cook's Log*, Vol. 42, No. 1 (2019), pp. 7–13.

Harris, Jocelyn, *Satire and Celebrity and Politics in Jane Austen* (Bucknell University Press, Lanham, MD: 2017), Chapter 2 regarding satire about Lieutenant Molesworth Philips and Captain Cook's death in 1779.

Headland, Robert, *The Island of South Georgia* (Cambridge University Press: 1984).

Hoare, Michael E., *The Tactless Philosopher: Johann Reinhold Forster* (The Hawthorn Press, Melbourne: 1976).

Horwitz, Tony, *Blue Latitudes, Boldly Going Where Captain Cook Has Gone Before* (Picador/Henry Holt & Company, New York: 2002).

Hough, Richard, *Captain James Cook, A Biography* (W.W. Norton, New York: 1995).

Hughes, Robert, *The Fatal Shore: the Epic of Australia's Founding* (Alfred A. Knopf, New York: 1987).

Huntford, Roland, *The Last Place on Earth, Scott and Amundsen's Race to the South Pole* (Modern Library, New York: 1999).

Joppien, Rüdiger and Smith Bernard, Editors, *The Art of Captain Cook's Voyages, Vol. 2, The Voyage of the Resolution & Adventure* (Yale University Press, New Haven: 1985).

Kauffmann, Jean-Paul, *The Arch of Kerguelen, Voyage to the Islands of Desolation*, translated by Patricia Clancy (Four Walls Eight Windows, New York: 1993).

Lansing, Alfred, *Endurance: Shackleton's Incredible Voyage* (Basic Books, New York: 2007).

Lavery, Brian, *The Conquest of the Ocean, An Illustrated History of Seafaring* (Dorling Kindersley Publishing, New York: 2013).

Lee, Michael, '*Endeavour* and St Jean Baptiste', *Cook's Log*, Vol. 41, No. 4 (2018), pp. 48–53.

Lubenow, William C., '*Only Connect*' *Learned Societies in Nineteenth Century Britain* (The Boydell Press, Woodbridge, Suffolk: 2015), for information on the Royal Society and similar organizations.

Marquardt, Karl Heinz, *Anatomy of the Ship: Captain Cook's Endeavour*, Revised Edition (Conway Anova Books Ltd., London: 2010).

MacLean, Alistair, *Captain Cook* (Doubleday & Company, Garden City, NY: 1972).

McLynn, Frank, *Captain Cook: Master of the Seas* (Yale University Press, New Haven, CT: 2011).

Namier, Sir Lewis, *The Structure of Politics at the Accession of George III*, Second edition (Macmillan & Company: London: 1961).

O'Sullivan, Dan, *In Search of Captain Cook, Exploring the Man Through His Own Words* (I.B. Tarus & Company, London: 2008).

Parker, Kathleen, 'Pepys Island as a Pacific Stepping Stone: The Struggle to Capture Islands on Early Modern Maps', *British Journal of the History of Science*, Vol. 51, No. 4 (December 2018), pp. 659–677.

Parry, J.H., *The Age of Reconnaissance* (New American Library, New York: 1963).

Porter, Roy, Editor, *The Cambridge History of Science, Vol. 4, Eighteenth Century Science* (Cambridge University Press: 2003).

Quinn, Frederick, *The French Overseas Empire* (Praeger Publishers, Westport, CT: 2002).

Roberts, David, *Alone on the Ice: The Greatest Survival Story in the History of Exploration* (W.W. Norton, New York: 2013).

Robson, John. *Captain Cook's World: Maps of the Life and Voyages of James Cook R.N.* (Random House, Auckland, NZ: 2000).

Robson, John, *Captain Cook's War & Peace, The Royal Navy Years, 1755–1763* (Naval Institute Press, Annapolis, MD: 2009).

Robson, John, Editor and Contributor, *The Captain Cook Encyclopaedia* (Chatham Publications, London: 2004).

Rodger, N. A. M., *The Command of the Ocean: A Naval History of Britain, 1649–1815* (W.W. Norton & Company, New York: 2005).

Rodger, N. A. M., *The Wooden World: An Anatomy of the Georgian Navy* (W.W. Norton & Company, New York: 1996).

Ross, Maurice, J., *Polar Pioneers, John Ross and James Clark Ross* (McGill-Queen's University Press, Montreal & Kingston: 1994).

Russell, Peter, *Prince Henry 'The Navigator'; A Life* (Yale University Press, New Haven: 2001).

Salmond, Anne, Bligh, *William Bligh in the South Seas* (University of California Press, Berkeley: 2011).

Savours, Ann, Forgan, Sophie, and Williams, Glyn, *Northward Ho! A voyage Towards the North Pole 1773* (Catalogue to the Exhibition at the Captain Cook Memorial Museum, Whitby: 2010), reference to Captain Constantine Phipps.

Schaefer, Gerrit, 'George Forster: Scientist, Democrat, Revolutionary,' *Cook's Log*, Vol. 31, No. 4, 2008, p. 5.

Schlereth, Thomas J., *The Cosmopolitan Ideal in Enlightenment Thought, Its Form and Function in the Ideas of Franklin, Hume, and Voltaire, 1694–1790* (University of Notre Dame Press, South Bend, IN: 1977).

Seymour, David, 'Vancouver Day, Western Australia', in *Cook's Log*, Vol. 4, No. 2 (1981), regarding Midshipman Vancouver's 'furthest south', January 1774.

Shackleton, Ernest, *South, The Endurance Expedition* (Penguin Books, New York: 2004).

Sobel, Dava, *Longitude: The True Story of a Lone Genius Who Solved the Greatest Scientific Problem of His Time* (Walker Publishing Co., New York: 1999).

Stenhouse, Robin, 'Is the *Poa Cookii* Plant Named After Captain Cook?', *Cook's Log*, Vol. 33, No. 3 (2010), pp. 26–28.

Tannahill, Reay, *Food in History* (Stein and Day, New York, 1973).

Thomas, Nicholas, *Cook: The Extraordinary Voyages of Captain James Cook* (Walker & Company, New York: 2003).

Thornton, Cliff, 'Cook's Observations of the Aurora Australis', *Cook's Log*, Vol. 34, No. 2 (2011), pp. 18–19.

Thornton, Cliff, 'Stockton's Endeavour Replica Moves to Whitby, *Cook's Log*, Vol. 41, No. 3 (2018), pp. 24–25; 'Whitby's Endeavour Replica, *Cook's Log*, Vol. 41, No. 4 (2018), p. 37.

Villiers, *Captain James Cook* (Charles Scribner's Sons, New York: 1967).

Wales, Wendy, *Captain Cook's Computer, The Life of William Wales, F.R.S. (1734–1798)* (Hame House, Yorkshire: 2015).

Watt, James, 'Medical Aspects and Consequences of Cook's Voyages', in Fisher, Robin and Johnston, Hugh, editors, *Captain James Cook and His Times* (Seattle, WA, University of Washington Press: 1979), pp. 129–157.

Williams, Glyn, *The Death of Captain Cook: A Hero Made and Unmade* (Harvard University Press, Cambridge, MA: 2008).

Williams, Glyndwr, Quilley, Geoff, Arutiunov, Sergey, and Forgan, Sophie, *Smoking Coasts and Ice-Bound Seas: Cook's Voyage to the Arctic* (Catalogue to the Exhibition at the Captain Cook Memorial Museum, Whitby: 2008).

Woodburn, Susan, 'John George Bartholomew and the Naming of Antarctica', *CAIRT*, Newsletter of the Scottish Maps Forum (The National Library of Scotland, No. 13, July 2008).

Worsley, F.A., *Endurance: An Epic of Polar Adventure* (W.W. Norton, New York, 2000).

Wulf, Andrea, *Chasing Venus, The Race to Measure the Heavens* (Windmill Books/Random House, London: 2012).

Online Sources (alphabetized by individual or topic)

Antarctica, 'Fifty Amazing Facts about Antarctica':
https://www.livescience.com/43881-amazing-antarctica-facts.html
Banks, Joseph, entry in the *Dictionary of Australian Biography*:
http://adb.anu.edu.au/biography/banks-sir-joseph-1737
Bouvet-Lozier, 24 June 1739 letter to the French East India Company:
http://www.south-pole.com/p0000067.htm
Calculation of the Distance from Earth to the Sun:
http://curious.astro.cornell.edu/about-us/41-our-solar-system/the-earth/orbit/87-how-do-you-measure-the-distance-between-earth-and-the-sun-intermediate
Captain Cook Memorial Museum (Whitby, Yorkshire):
http://www.cookmuseumwhitby.co.uk/
Captain Cook Society (The):
www.captaincooksociety.com
Clerke, Charles, entry in the *Dictionary of Canadian Biography*:
www.biographi.ca/en/bio/clerke_charles_4E.html
Cook Strait entry, *Encyclopedia of New Zealand*:
http://www.teara.govt.nz/en/1966/cook-strait
Cutter, Donald, 'The Spanish in Hawaii: Gaytan to Marin', a paper presented at the Pacific Coast Branch of the American Historical Association in August 1979:
https://core.ac.uk/download/pdf/5014742.pdf (Fathom Expeditions Inc.)
Fram Museum (Roald Amundsen):
http://frammuseum.no/polar_history/expeditions/the_maud_expedition__1918–1925_/
the_maud_expedition__1918–1925_
Halley, Edmund, Complete Dictionary of Scientific Biography:
https://www.encyclopedia.com/people/science-and-technology/astronomy-biographies/edmond-halley#2830901830
Heard Island, 1997 Expedition to Heard Island:
www.cordell.org/HI/
Dalrymple, Alexander, *Historical Collection of the Several Voyages and Discoveries in the South Pacific Ocean* (J. Nourse, T. Payne, P. Elmsly, London: 1770–1771) (e-book):
https://archive.org/details/cihm_35631/page/n5 (pp. XXIV–XXX)
Dalrymple, Alexander, in *Australian Dictionary of Biography*, Vol. 1:
http://adb.anu.edu.au/biography/dalrymple-alexander-1949
Endeavour Replica, the Australian National Maritime Museum:
http://www.anmm.gov.au/whats-on/vessels/hmb-Endeavour
James Caird, James Caird Society:
http://www.jamescairdsociety.com/ and http://www.jamescairdsociety.com/the-james-caird/how-to-visit/
Kerguelen Island and Archipelago:
https://earthobservatory.nasa.gov/images/89328/kerguelen-islands
Kerguelen Island Minerals, A modern-day catalogue of Kerguelen Island minerals:
www.mindat.org/loc-30703.html
Mawson, Douglas, Jacka, F.J., *Australian Dictionary of Biography*:
http://adb.anu.edu.au/biography/mawson-sir-douglas-7531
Milky Seas (Mystery of), 'Milky Seas Detected From Space':
http://news.bbc.co.uk/2/hi/science/nature/3760124.stm
Orbiter Vehicle/Space Shuttle Endeavour, at the California Science Centre:
https://californiasciencecenter.org/exhibits/air-space/space-shuttle-Endeavour

Penguins, *Penguin World*:
 www.penguinworld.com/types/king.html.
Rhode Island Marine Archaeology Project (RIMAP), the search for *Endeavour*, at Newport, RI
 Harbour: www.rimap.org
Ross, James Clark, entry in *The Canadian Encyclopedia*:
 https://www.thecanadianencyclopedia.ca/en/article/sir-james-clark-ross/
Ross, James Clark:
 http://www.south-pole.com/p0000081.htm
Royal Society (London), History of the Royal Society:
 https://royalsociety.org/about-us/history/
Scott, Robert Falcon, letter to the public, 29 March 1912:
 https://www.historychannel.com.au/this-day-in-history/robert-falcon-scotts-final-diary-entry/
Scott, Robert Falcon, 'Scott's Last Expedition', located at http://www.scottslastexpedition.org/
 expedition/robert-falcon-scott/
Sealing Industry in the 19th century, Basberg, Bjørn and Headland, Robert K., 'The 19th Century
 Antarctic Sealing Industry: Sources, Data, and Economic Significance, 2008:
 http://ssrn/com/abstract=1553751
Seals:
 www.pinnipeds.org/
Seals (Antarctic Fur Seals), Seal Conservation Society, 'Antarctic Fur Seal':
 www.pinnipeds.org/species/antfursl.htm
Shackleton, Ernest, Royal Geographic Society, 'Shackleton-Endurance Expedition Timeline':
 https://www.rgs.org/CMSPages/GetFile.aspx?nodeguid=949d8f9d-ffee-474a-a0ad-
 bbdafcfdf738&lang=en-GB
Shackleton, Ernest, Falklands Biographies:
 https://falklandsbiographies.org/biographies/shackleton_sir
Smith, S. Percy, 'The Polynesians as Navigators', in *Hawaiki: The Original Home of the Maori, with a
 Sketch of Polynesian History* (Whitcombe & Tombs Ltd, Christchurch: 1904), p. 129:
 http://nzetc.victoria.ac.nz/tm/scholarly/tei-SmiHawa-t1-body-d7-d8.html
South Georgia and South Sandwich Islands (official website, 24/7 images at Grytviken):
 www.gov.gs
South Georgia, Rat Eradication Program, Maris, Emma, 'Large Island Declared Rat-Free in
 Biggest Removal Success':
 https://news.nationalgeographic.com/2018/05/south-georgia-island-rat-free-animals-spd/
South Georgia Reindeer Eradication Program, South Georgia reindeer eradication program:
 http://www.gov.gs/environment/eradication-projects/eradication-projectsreindeer/.
Volcanoes, The Smithsonian Institution's Global Volcanism Program (updated information about
 volcanic eruptions, e.g., South Sandwich Islands):
 www.volcano.si.edu/world/find_erruptions.cfm
Volcanoes, Kerguelen archipelago:
 www.volcanolive.com/kerguelen.html and www.iomoon.com/kerguelen.html
Weddell, James:
 https://www.falklandsbiographies.org/biographies/weddell_james
Whales and Whaling, Kerguelen archipelago:
 https://www.researchgate.net/publication/268519947_History_of_whaling_sealing_fishery_and_
 aquaculture_trials_in_the_area_of_the_Kerguelen_Plateau
Whales and Whaling', New Bedford Whaling Museum:
 https://www.whalingmuseum.org/learn/research-topics/overview-of-north-american-whaling/
 whales-hunting
Whales and Whaling, Whitby Museum:
 www.whitbymuseum.org.uk

Whales and Whaling, Robert McNamara, 'Brief History of Whaling':
  https://www.whales.org.au/history/19th_Century_Whaling.html
Wild, Frank, Frank Wild's ashes, burial at Grytviken, see *BBC News Magazine*, 29 December 2011:
  https://www.bbc.com/news/magazine-16165494
Wildlife at and surrounding the South Sandwich Islands:
  http://ngm.nationalgeographic.com/2006/12/south-sandwich/holland-text/2
Wilkinson, C., *British Logbooks in UK Archives, 17th–19th Centuries – a survey of the range, selection and suitability of British logbooks and related documents for climatic research* (2006, revised 2009, published as CRU RP12 in 2012):
  http://www.cru.uea.ac.uk/documents/421974/1301877/CRU_RP12.pdf/0eb44edd-b085–4617-a5dd-5a32e44b1e9a;
Wilkinson, C., and others, *Description and general background to ships' logbooks as a source of climatic data* (2004):
  http://cdn.knmi.nl/system/data_center_publications/files/000/044/827/original/garciaherrera_koek_etal_2004_cc_preprint.pdf?1432895541.

Novels and Video Productions

Lay, Graeme, *The Secret Life of James Cook, A Novel; James Cook's New World, A Novel; James Cook's Lost World, A Novel* (Fourth Estate/Harper Collins, Auckland: 2013–2015).

James Cook

Collingridge, Vanessa, narrator, *Captain Cook – Obsession and Discovery*, DVD 31165-D (BFS entertainment and Multimedia Ltd., Richmond Hill, Ontario: 2011), ASIN: B00D09AZ6M.
Dashwood, Robin (Producer and Director), *Voyages of Discovery*, Part 2, *The Making of Captain Cook*, narrated by Paul Rose, BBC-Four, DVD (2006). Focused on the voyage of *Endeavour*.
Scholes, Norman, *A History of Captain James Cook, The Yorkshire Years*, Video production by James Hutton, DVD, Bay Video Productions, United Kingdom, Year of Production not identified.
The Captain Cook Memorial Museum, DVD, Exhibits and related Museum features, Artfix DVD Production (2011).

Ernest Shackleton

Sturridge, Charles (Director), *Shackleton: The Greatest Survival Story of All Time*, 3- DVD set including additional Antarctica-related material (A&E Network: 2002), AISN B000063TON.
Butler, George (Director & Producer), *The Endurance – Shackleton's Legendary Antarctic Expedition* (Sony Home Entertainment: 2003), ASIN B0000A7W16.

Index